ALL GATES OPEN

Irmin Schmidt, pupil of the likes of Stockhausen and Ligeti, decided in the late sixties – after an extensive classical education as a pianist, conductor and composer – to combine classic 'New Music' with rock and jazz, and founded the band Can. After Can, Irmin returned to his work as a solo artist. The result is a vast oeuvre which includes a series of solo albums, an opera (*Gormenghast*, based on the Mervyn Peake trilogy) a ballet and over one hundred film scores. In 2015, he was made a Chevalier de l'Order des Arts et des Lettres. He lives in southern France.

Rob Young writes on music and culture and is a former editor of *The Wire* magazine. He is the author of the acclaimed *Electric Eden*, and the editor of *Undercurrents: The Hidden Wiring of Modern Music* and *The Wire Primers: A Guide to Modern Music*. He has contributed to publications including *Uncut*, the *Guardian*, *Sight & Sound*, *Frieze* and *Art Review*. He lives in Oslo with his family.

Max Dax is a journalist and art curator, and was editor-in-chief of *Electronic Beats Magazine* and *Spex*. Robert Defcon is an author, artist and musician. In 2005 they released *No Beauty Without Danger*, an oral history of the band Einstürzende Neubauten. Both live in Berlin. Book Two of *All Gates Open*, 'Can Kiosk', was edited by Dax and Defcon and draws on interviews made by Irmin Schmidt and Max Dax.

Further praise for *All Gates Open*:

'This two-part book is a portrait of a fiercely intellectual, but hugely sensuous, band who improvised and jammed, but sneered at those terms, preferring "intuitive music" and "collage" to describe the spacy, evolving compositions the collective co-authored in a kind of mutual trance-state. They were virtuosos who hated virtuosity, or anything that smacked overtly of American forms . . . *All Gates Open* is a cerebral book about a cerebral band.' Kitty Empire, *Observer*

'An in-depth, intimate and culturally roving biography . . . [Young] is capable of capturing the essence of the music in a single potent line, nailing "Can's signature monotony, in which everything appears to be changing over an unchanging same." . . . A work of deep access and impressive reach. Blending the granular detail of Can's intimate life with a sweeping purview of the culture that created and fostered them, *All Gates Open* is an invaluable illumination of why the music of Can matters, and continues to resonate.' Graeme Thompson, *Uncut*

'Superb . . . recounts how their unique entity sparked, grew, peaked and dissolved, with copious interviews with members and intimates, fascinating new insights, and as sure a grasp of Can's music, whether on film or live, as this reviewer has read.' Ian Harrison, *Mojo*

'The book this most inspiring of groups has long deserved . . . A study of not only a group but of a hugely important time in European history and a recovering Germany where the young were forced to create something new for themselves thanks to the mistakes of many of their elders. *All Gates Open: The Story of Can* will sit comfortably on either the syllabus of a degree course or on the armchair of a music fan, and it is in that balancing act where Young and Schmidt truly give respect and due honour to the subject matter, making this not only one of the essential books of this year but one for many years to come.' Simon Tucker, *Louder Than War*

'[A] seriously fucking amazing book . . . The tone's light and quick, and in the turning of stones there's obviously been a judicious amount of thinking about making a suitable testament to an astonishing band. A labour of love but not a fetish of rockism.' *Freq*

'*All Gates Open* does an excellent job of covering the 50-year journey from the band's unlikely beginnings . . . to Can's profile being higher than ever in the present day.' *Loud and Quiet*

'*All Gates Open* is as close as we're ever likely to get to rationalising Can's inspirations, motivations and emanations, applying a finely calibrated Enigma machine to the thankless task of decoding their abstract enigma.' *Record Collector*

ALL GATES OPEN

The Story of

ROB YOUNG
& IRMIN SCHMIDT

FABER & FABER

First published in the UK in 2018
by Faber & Faber Ltd, Bloomsbury House,
74–77 Great Russell Street, London WC1B 3DA
First published in the USA in 2018

This paperback edition first published in 2019

Typeset by Ian Bahrami
Printed in the UK by CPI Group (UK) Ltd, Croydon CR0 4YY

A CIP record for this book
is available from the British Library

ISBN 978-0-571-31152-1

FSC
www.fsc.org
MIX
Paper | Supporting
responsible forestry
FSC® C171272

6 8 10 9 7 5

Contents

Book One: All Gates Open
by Rob Young

Book Two: Can Kiosk

by Irmin Schmidt

All Gates Open

1

Dreams Seen by a Man-Made Machine
(PROLOGUE)

Can Studio, Weilerswist, February 1997

It's the mattresses that strike you first. There must be scores of them, fixed to these walls, floor to ceiling. And the ceiling is a good eight metres above our heads.

The entrance to the space I'm standing in – a former cinema with its seats ripped out – still retains its ancient ticket booth, with paper-stub dispensers and empty glass display cases where once snacks and memorabilia were on show. The price list, in Deutschmarks rather than euros, still hangs on the wall. Built during the forties, half a century ago the cinema would have seen the small population of the village of Weilerswist gathering for the weekly newsreel compilation of Nazi propaganda. But no longer. A quarter-century after the surrender of German forces, with the art of cinema having transformed itself from wartime black and white into colour, Technicolor, Cinemascope, business finally dried up thanks to the encroachment of the television as the prime source of family entertainment.

In the autumn of 1971 a very different invasion occurred in this quiet village, a half-hour's drive south-west of Cologne. A group of five musicians collectively known as Can were planning to build themselves a new musical laboratory and recording studio under the roof of the abandoned Kino. In fact, the group were at that moment about to hit the national spotlight themselves, precisely because of television. The very first recording they made in this studio, which

1

they named Inner Space, was a track called 'Spoon', and it was a response to a commission from the WDR television company to provide a theme tune for *Das Messer*, a popular TV detective series in West Germany at the time. Boosted by the success of the show, the track was released as a single and reached the West German Top Five in late 1971.

One of Can's first acts in the new space was to sound-insulate the walls with mattresses auctioned off by the local German army base. The drummer's girlfriend covered them with a layer of painted and embroidered sheets. Decades later, it all hangs there still. I can feel something uncannily different about the air in this space. There is an incredible, viscous silence hovering like some etheric putty waiting to be squidged and stretched by sonic vibrations. The ceiling is high, the floor is original wooden parquet and the mixing desk is down at one end, not separated off in a soundproofed chamber as in most conventional studios. It's built into a massive wooden frame, like the bridge of some colossal steamboat. A door at one side leads to a small garden that backs onto some incongruous allotments. It's a weird mixture of time capsule and functional, state-of-the-art music workshop.

It's 23 February 1997, twenty-six years after the group first moved in, and I have penetrated this Inner Space, trying to pick up echoes of its former life, like some NASA monitor scanning the deep galaxy for extraterrestrial ghosts. And there is indeed a palpable presence here. Can's instruments are still arranged in the space: amps, guitars, drums, a collection of vintage analogue synths, modern digital keyboards and a grand piano.

As they pose for photographs in front of four amplifiers the size of a person, the remaining core members of Can are wearing shades and are clad in black – save, that is, for the most visibly eccentric of the quartet, bassist and sound engineer Holger Czukay. This moustachioed fifty-nine-year-old is wearing a baggy black and white houndstooth suit and patent leather shoes, topped off with a black baseball cap. Holger also wears an almost permanent sardonic grin, a Cheshire cat who looks on the world as his creative playground. With his dark stubble and intelligent eyes, Irmin Schmidt is statesmanlike, solidly grounded. Jaki Liebezeit, one of the most tack-sharp drummers on the planet, is friendly but reserved in conversation, with minimal recall. The bags under his eyes speak of countless long nights, but the eyes themselves are wide and fully alert. Guitarist Michael Karoli, by ten years the youngest, with grey hair trimmed to a buzzcut that's starting to grow out, charms me during a forty-five-minute interview with his quiet, reverent intensity, speaking in a wistful near-whisper of how he still loves to dance. The soft, raptured tones of his voice convey a lightness of being borne with confident grace.

Naturally, as members of a group that broke apart in 1978, but who have remained bound together through its legacy ever since, they all speak of things that are happening right now. Jaki seems least interested in revisiting the past. He's more keen to discuss his new method of drumming, from which he has removed all cymbals and kick drums, focusing only on a series of tuned tom-toms, played according to a system he claims is mathematical and based on the earliest rhythmic forms used by primitive man. Michael is rhapsodic about his former group, though he discusses it in terms that are more abstract than specific. Irmin has a clear agenda of topics he wishes to get across, most notably Can's phoenix-like rise from the rubble of a broken post-war Germany, and the fights and struggles that gave birth to the group's music. Holger roams over both the history of Can and his current enthusiasm for – and collaborations with – Cologne's electronica/techno scene. He clearly believes Can had miraculous properties and leaves you in no doubt that some of his most significant musical experiences were had during its time.

At the time, I was writing the story for *The Wire* magazine. A couple of years later, I was invited by Hildegard Schmidt – Irmin's wife, and Can's manager since the early seventies – to contribute to a book she was putting together on Can. My brief was simply to write a short piece of text on each album in the band's back catalogue, and she was keen to stress that I was not expected to like them all. I should feel free to criticise wherever I felt it necessary. I quickly realised that Can was its own best (or worst) critic: the group's official line was broadly in agreement with the general opinion out there – that its best years were the first five or six, with a fairly rapid decline in reliability and quality from 1975 onwards.

I continued to write about Can over the following years: a *Guardian* or *Uncut* article here, an interview with an ex-member there; reviews of remastered and reissued recordings elsewhere. One memorable evening I found myself with Irmin, Hildegard, their daughter Sandra and her partner, the British musician Jono Podmore (who would later take in hand the business of remastering and un-archiving Can's back catalogue), in the private dining room of London's Groucho Club, with Irmin's increasingly gravelly baritone sinking deeper into a discussion of Germany's existential fate. At an adjoining table, U2's Bono, of all people, was holding court with friends and family, bursting into song.

In the course of writing this first extensive narrative biography of Can, I have reconnected with all the remaining founder members and other musicians and vocalists who passed through Can down the years, and have tracked down various of their friends and music-industry associates, both in the UK and mainland Europe. I have gone back to original sources in the music media at the time Can was active, including the music press in Germany and France, where the group was particularly well received (I take the credit or blame for all translations). In this way, retrospective interviews are complemented by quotes from the group in the midst of its lifespan. Most important of all, I have revisited Can's entire musical legacy, willingly immersing myself in the official canon of albums, the compilations of unreleased material that have appeared piecemeal over the years, and the relatively extensive array of bootleg recordings and video clips that have surfaced in various unofficial channels. I also took pains to watch as many as I could find of the films and television programmes for which Can made soundtracks. This process was Can's main source of income in its early years, and an important influence on the group's approach to editing tape, though the films – mostly German productions – have rarely been discussed in articles on Can and have almost never been screened outside Germany. This book contains the most extensive discussion of Can's film work to date; in certain respects, the process of shooting and editing film is a useful tool for understanding how Can's music got made.

Radio waves ripple from their source out into the universe until the end of time. With the right tools tuned to the correct frequency, their vibrations can be detected. Writing a biography about events half a century ago involves a similar process of scanning the echoes reverberating in the historical flux. You trawl for as many bits of information as you can pick up, and assemble them as best you can to create the most coherent picture.

Into the musical galaxy of the late sixties, Can appeared like a comet or unknown planet, sighted once in a blue moon. We did not have long to catch a glimpse or make sense of it while it was in its active phase. Can never toured America, Scandinavia, Japan or Australia. Its activities were confined over a ten-year stretch within the relatively close environs of western Europe: West Germany, France, the United Kingdom, and limited or one-off appearances in Switzerland, Austria, Belgium, Spain and Portugal. After the break-up in 1978, the gates have remained open. Can's status has risen dramatically in the years since its human components stopped making music together. Its music and vibrations roam out across the world. While the group had its fans among critics, the majority of responses in the music press were sceptical bordering on misapprehensive, with a dash of anti-Germanic feeling thrown in. At home in West Germany they were at best respected in the press, but there is little valuable or insightful analysis in the cuttings that remain. The French, particularly, loved them, with rock writers such as Paul Alessandrini and Pascal Bussy championing them and writing of their music in evocative Gallic tones. But these responses, of course, never penetrated the English-speaking world.

Since its earliest days, when experiments could be tried and permitted to fail, Can has risen to the position of unassailable genius. It exists among a small pantheon of groups routinely cited by aspiring younger artists as influential, but also, critically, it is up there with the great innovators of post-war music, such as Karlheinz Stockhausen, Miles Davis, the Velvet Underground and Lee 'Scratch' Perry.

Can's own music, which ceased to be produced with any regularity in 1978, has travelled forward into music's future, inspiriting it and informing it, transforming it and leaving it different. In summer 2016, coasting along the autoroutes of southern France on the way to Irmin Schmidt's residence to conduct a round of interviews for this book, my car radio starts pumping out Daft Punk's 'One More Time', from 2000. It sounds delirious and exhilarating in a speeding vehicle, its ambient breakdowns building to triumphant reappearances of a thumping beat overlaid with a vocal line of enormous positivity: 'Music's got me feeling so free . . .' As well as its title recalling Can's 'One More Night', there is something of the relentlessness of Can's most driving grooves, such as 'Mother Sky', 'Halleluwah' or their own disco hit 'I Want More', which has given permission for this type of European dance music to exist, urging the body forward, combining the sense of the feet connecting magnetically to the ground with a vital sense of lift-off, a transformative trip that characterises the very best dance music. It sounds sophisticated in its digital, twenty-first-century urban garb, but the primal pulse underpinning it has energised humans' ritual and celebratory musics for millennia. Being inside the music is supremely liberating, and there's no way to escape it. That's the feeling Can's best music gives me. And I willingly submit to its paradoxical pleasures.

In the beginning, members were sucked into Can from disparate backgrounds in avant-garde composition, free jazz and rock 'n' roll, all of them dissatisfied with what those genres could offer them at the end of the sixties. Can provided an opportunity to synthesize something new, building on the collective mindset learned in these different disciplines. Gates were kicked open whose previous existence was unknown. Jaki Liebezeit put it this way: 'All the Can material I have done, I think you can see it's never the same thing. On each tune I find some other rhythmical idea. I think it's like astronomy: the further you get into it, the more stars you can see. If I lived a hundred years, I would never come to an end. I always discover new stuff.'

Can is sometimes lumped into the catch-all 'progressive music' pigeonhole. Its attitude could be described as progressive in a general sense, but it refused to indulge in the kind of speculative fictional scenarios that characterised the heavy concept albums of the era. Instead, the music itself was the concept. Text became texture, submerged into the whole, not a message tossed to the world on the crest of a sound wave. The vocalist was the most tenuous, problematic position in Can. As well as Malcolm Mooney and Damo Suzuki, several others held tenure on the microphone, but none survived very long. For the critic used to applying lit-crit techniques to an artist's collected lyrics, Can's spontaneous vocal eruptions and nonsense didn't provide much to chew on. 'Whenever you use words for music, you start labelling it,' Irmin says. 'I always find myself using words like "poetic", and then I have to say, "Yes, but . . ." But it is some kind of poetry going on, because poetry is just what it is for itself, without anything that you can take away and say, "It means that." A good poem doesn't mean anything except what it is – it's an object. And our music . . . doesn't mean anything else than what it is as an object. Which makes it endure, because it's hammered so long until it's firm.'

Can made a mercurial, adaptable music that has aged remarkably well. It pushed instruments and machines beyond acceptable limits. It took full advantage of the impressionability and plasticity of concrete recorded sound. Can itself dictated the conditions under which this music was made – it lived comfortably apart from the music-business hurly-burly. Its economy was stable, if not extravagant – enough for the group to set its own pace. Hildegard Schmidt, Can's formidable manager since 1971, has played a crucial role here, channelling the music into the commercial sector, live arena and public consciousness. As the world went by, Can inflated its own bubble of creativity in its private studio spaces, giving it a power and control over its own output that was a luxury by the standards of the day.

A biography is usually a life recounted from birth to death, with all facts and anecdotes relevant to the development of that life told in between. In writing a biography of Can as a group, my aim is not to supply the complete life stories of the various individuals who have passed through it – the permanent residents and the fleeting tenants. Instead, in the pages that follow, the life of Can itself is being inscribed. A group is conceived, born, grows, matures, wanes and, one way or another, dies off, even if the individual members remain.

In one of our conversations, Holger expressed something that has been the key to my thinking about Can. 'I thought it was like a living organism, Can: it had a beginning, it had a youth, it had a time getting old and a time to die. And out of it came all the members of Can who are still creative and never changed profession and became watch repairers or something like that. The strongest parts of Can were when they didn't actually play – that means, when they *got* played, by a sort of secret machine behind it, *ja*? Then Can was really good. And that is when Can became an *in*human.'

Michael expressed the same thing to me in different terms. 'Can has its own soul. It's like a man-made deity in a funny way. I saw myself as a sort of . . . maybe computer, a sort of interface between my ears, between incoming sound and outgoing sound. Music was for us not a means of expressing anything; it was just applied mathematics.' The individual members who passed through the body of Can provided the raw materials, their personal and artistic struggles supplying the necessary heat-friction. Can was an anthill mob, a communal process, perpetually rebuilding and reshaping the space and conditions of its own existence.

This creature's soul continues to haunt others after its physical manifestation has gone. This can be through memories, the magical inscription of audio recording, and the influence and fascination it continues to exert in the afterlife. Several times Can has been laid to rest and resurrected. Its life begins in confidence; it enjoys a full ten years of existence, with a core of four members supplemented by sundry others coming and going; it is laid aside; it briefly reforms around ten years after that; it once more ceases to be; and though no longer a functioning entity by the late nineties, it spreads itself like a spore-cloud through a collaborative remix project back into consciousness.

Since then Can's status as a major pillar of influence has remained firm. Its genes have been transplanted into the larger musical body via subsequent solo works, collaborations with musicians from equivalent or younger generations, and via its self-managed recorded legacy, which has been refreshed, remastered and repackaged several times over the intervening years. Can's early efforts were mainly funded by making music for film and television, and to this day its music continues to pop up on the soundtracks of movies. The group's survivors have remained in contact, friendly or cordial, but have never elected to take the re-formation route so many other veterans have chosen. All involved agree that Can is not about nostalgia or attempting to reboot the wondrous, telepathic music-making that took place at a particular place and time. All have adapted and moved on, defying audience expectations for the past to be reincarnated.

Back in 1997, at the close of a day of interviews, I asked Michael Karoli whether he thought ideas have a life of their own, and that humans are mere carriers of information. 'That *is* what I think,' he replied, as if in a trance, his eyes directing themselves towards the airy space above us, among the mattresses and the memories. 'I think the personality of the musician is very much overestimated by our culture. The better he is, the less of an ego he has, definitely. Can is such a thing, Can is such an idea, and Can worked through us. Although we sort of created Can, Can created us, and Can created the music.'

2

Pandemonium Manifestos

Dortmund to Halle an der Saale, April 1957

Irmin Schmidt, aged nineteen, settles into his seat, opens his book and tries to block out the excited babble of fellow music students in the carriage as it hurtles over the border from one Germany to another. Just before stepping onto the train at Dortmund station, he impulse-bought this anthology of modern poetry, *Flügel der Zeit* (Wings of Time), to kill the hours on the overnight journey to an East German music festival. Irmin's colleagues in the student orchestra of the Dortmund Conservatory are a boisterous lot, extra-excited because they have been crammed into a single carriage along with a youth orchestra from Witten consisting of a thrilling proportion of girls, whom the students try to impress all night with sprightly renditions of Gypsy folk tunes. Irmin – who has been studying piano and music theory, but plays French horn in this orchestra – stays aloof from the badinage, playing cards with friends and, when they drop off to sleep, reading his book.

Gradually, he becomes aware of another pair of eyes upon the lines of verse. He looks up to see the girl he had briefly noted as the most beautiful in the carriage peering over his shoulder. She asks what he is reading, and he replies, a little arrogantly, Oh, it's modern poetry, you probably wouldn't be interested. Suddenly, she's sitting next to him, peering at the open page. My name's Hildegard, she says. What's yours?

During the concerts at the music festival, Irmin watches this seventeen-year-old girl plucking away at her Spanish guitar, her lips

11

pressed tight in concentration. A few nights later, at the closing ball for all the participating musicians, he and Hildegard fall heavily for each other. They spend the whole of the twelve-hour return journey talking and making out; a few days later, Irmin turns up at her home, not knowing if she will treat it as a disposable fling. She runs down the stairs and into his arms. It is the start of a relationship that will define the rest of their lives, personally, professionally and artistically.

Hildegard Reittenberger and Irmin Schmidt were legally wed six years later in 1963, but prior to that they had to all intents and purposes been living as a married couple. Hildegard worked in the finance and property industries but her abiding interest was music and the arts. The leader of her orchestra was a violinist in the Dortmund Symphony Orchestra, and he and his wife used to regularly take Hildegard and her twin sister to concert halls and operas, nurturing her interest in a wide variety of music.

It was clear Irmin was going places. Straight out of the gate from his studies, he enrolled at the Folkwang Academy in Essen, where over the next few years he would receive a comprehensive education in conducting under Heinz Dressel, take a piano masterclass with Detlef Kraus and study composition under the Hungarian avant-gardist György Ligeti. He discovered a particular affinity for the art of conducting, working with a number of local orchestras and ensembles, including the Bochum Symphony Orchestra and later his own Dortmund Ensemble for New Music, which he formed in 1962.

On one occasion Irmin conducted the West German premiere of John Cage's *Atlas Eclipticalis* for orchestra and performed Cage's piano piece *Winter Music*. With Irmin acting as soloist and conducting the Bochum Symphony Orchestra from the piano, it was a night memorable for the confusion and conflict it caused. 'There was the first clarinettist, who was a fan of any kind of avant-garde, and the second clarinettist, who was thinking, "It's really shit." These two clarinettists turned the whole performance into a war against each other. They played softly and they made their pauses. But when the first one made a tone, the second one tried to make a disharmony to it. And they created such attention that the whole orchestra listened to them and got into this mood of extreme attention, awareness . . . When I told Cage that, he loved it.'

Irmin Schmidt was born in Berlin on 29 May 1937, the son of Kurt and Margot Schmidt. His father was an architect and engineer who specialised in bridges and harbourside buildings; his mother ran the house. His earliest memories are of the noise and eruptions of war – specifically the Allied bombing raids on the city. 'We had a nice little house,' he recalls, 'and we were in our bombproof cellar, and came out, and there were all these red anti-aircraft flashes, like stars flashing, which were planes. And I remember an uncle of mine saying, "Oh yeah, they got him now, they got him!" And suddenly I realised that they were talking about somebody they were wanting to kill. It was like a revelation. A flash of illumination.'

The 'catastrophe' of war, Irmin insists, is the black heart of the music he would later make in Can, a refusal of the blank optimism of the immediate post-war period. Irmin's generation grew up in the ruins of Germany, cut off from their own cultural past, where the spectre of Nazism, despite outward appearances, had simply slunk away into the administrative structure of the nation. Irmin was expelled from one school for exposing some of his teachers as former Nazis in the school newspaper. His memories of his own parents, who openly supported the Nazi regime, remain double-edged. When the family's Jewish neighbours were sent to Auschwitz, his own parents made no attempt to oppose it. After the war, when they retrenched to Dortmund, they were much poorer, but still invested a great deal in Irmin's musical education. Nevertheless, he found himself getting drawn into ideological arguments with his father as he was growing up.

Having said all that, his remarkable ear for the musicality of concrete sound appears to have developed at a very early age. Both his parents played piano regularly at home – Margot had had ambitions to sing opera – and listened to classical music on the radio. Irmin has talked of his youthful sensitivity to sounds, when, aged four or five, he would sit alone in a forest for hours and soak up the bio-acoustic environment, or listen to cars pulling up on his neighbour's gravel: 'the sound of arrogance'.[1]

By the early years of the sixties Irmin was on a path to becoming an important and respected figure in the world of West German art music. He received a grounding in classical repertoire and technique, and attended the prestigious Mozarteum in Salzburg, Austria, to expand his conducting skills under the baton of maestro István Kertész. Prizes were starting to rack up: the Leistungs Prize at the Folkwang, first prize in conducting at the Mozarteum, and a national young artist's award in 1965.

At the same time he was helping out at the Bochum Theatre whenever a musical accompaniment was needed. Local musician Dieter Schönbach was the theatre's resident composer, and Irmin answered his call for an orchestral conductor for the theatre's productions of Brecht plays, featuring the music of Kurt Weill. Irmin found himself coaching the actors in singing parts for productions such as Brecht's *Mother Courage*. Schönbach, who also occasionally earned his bread and butter by composing incidental music for industrial and public-service films, introduced Irmin to his contacts in the film industry. This became a useful source of extra income, helping Irmin to fund his studies. 'At that time in German cinemas there was always what they called "Kulturfilm" – a short film about silly themes, like some hundred-and-fifty-year-old water tower in Essen, celebrating or explaining, or about a certain landscape, or the animals in the waters of an industrial creek. Dieter didn't want to do them all, so I started doing short film musics for this purpose.' Irmin and Hildegard would often find themselves sitting up late, spooling through a short animated film reel with a stopwatch, trying to figure out the right lengths for each film cue. It was a painstaking craft that would stand Irmin in good stead in the years to come.

Irmin also had his toes in the art world of the time. The schoolboy who had loved the expressionist paintings of Ernst Ludwig Kirchner, Die Brücke group and Max Beckmann now had a circle of friends including young painters such as Karl-Horst Hödicke, Bernd Damke, Markus Lüpertz, Peter Sorge and others, and even curated several group exhibitions in Dortmund and other nearby towns. He wrote the first article on Hödicke to appear in a West German national newspaper, and contributed quite a number of reviews and essays on art and artists to various papers and journals around this time. A big influence on his thinking back then was the veteran art collector and critic Albert Schulze-Vellinghausen, who also exhibited his own private collection in a barn on his family's ancestral farmstead near Dortmund. Irmin was occasionally asked to give talks or perform avant-garde music at openings at Schulze-Vellinghausen's gallery space, and afterwards frequently invited local artists, directors and critics to his home to take part in discussions. Schulze-Vellinghausen hired a young interior designer, Hans Mayer,[2] to curate his collection, and was so impressed with Mayer's work that he encouraged him to open his own private gallery. Mayer went on to become one of Germany's leading gallerists and would later play an important role in the foundational phase of the Can story.

Mayer set up his own gallery near Stuttgart, where Irmin was often called on to perform at openings. At one of these he debuted a performance piece called *Ob-scene*, involving a scantily clad actress playing a double bass. Schulze-Vellinghausen was outraged and paid for Irmin and Hildegard to travel to Amsterdam to see some 'proper' cutting-edge dance theatre. Crucially for Irmin, Schulze-Vellinghausen also introduced him to the writings of the French dramatist Antonin Artaud and his concept of the 'theatre of cruelty'. 'It's one of the roots of my idea to form a group,' Irmin states.

*

Irmin remained invested in contemporary music, and a key moment was enrolling in the legendary International Summer Course for New Music in Darmstadt in 1962 and '63. Held annually since 1946, these had become a rallying point for many European and international composition students. The summer school placed this German town on the world map of modern music, and the roll call of attendees includes many of the most respected names in twentieth-century music. Here alumni came into direct contact with Pierre Boulez, Karlheinz Stockhausen, György Ligeti, Bruno Maderna, Henri Pousseur, Luciano Berio and Stefan Wolpe, and heard cutting-edge compositions played by legendary performers of the avant-garde repertoire, such as Aloys Kontarsky, Siegfried Palm, the LaSalle Quartet, Severino Gazzelloni, Christoph Caskel and Cathy Berberian. Darmstadt became a workshop, ideological battleground and important meeting point for the next generation of composers. For the young Germans, one lecturer in particular made the strongest impression.

Karlheinz Stockhausen, who attended his first course as a student in 1951, participated as a lecturer two years later, and by the early sixties was one of the course's biggest draws as a teacher. The pedagogy was opinionated and lively, and at one 1965 session Stockhausen actually composed an entire work, *Stop*, during the course of a single lecture. The sessions were renowned for their frankness, with lectures affording students an opportunity for stern criticism of their masters. Stockhausen himself encouraged scepticism, and once accused the forbidding Frankfurt School critic Theodor Adorno of 'looking for a chicken in an abstract painting'.[3]

Irmin attended the Darmstadt courses during a period in which, as he recalls it, Stockhausen was in a phase of 'absolute dogmatism'. During a session analysing the maestro's work for three orchestras, *Momente*, he fought back. 'He was really like a father figure . . . I went there because I was totally fascinated and, I mean, I loved his early work – when I heard *Gesang der Jünglinge* for the first time, that was actually some kind of revelation, an epiphany. But I had really hard discussions with him. I could accept much more than he could. And I remember one time when he rhetorically slapped me away during an analysis of *Momente*. I could hardly follow it because it was so complicated. And at the end he said, "Tomorrow we will dedicate the last three hours only to questions." And then he said, "But I only accept intelligent questions." And he said it in a tone warning you . . . I mean, it was so discouraging: "You don't ask God stupid questions." And you went home and thought, "I cannot ask anything, it will be really stupid." And so next day I went. There had already been ten or fifteen questions already, and they were all totally uninteresting – "I don't understand this little detail, and did I understand you right when you mean . . ." And I said, "Do you think you will get really intelligent questions posed about the work if you act so that everybody thinks, 'I won't ask him, it's not intelligent enough'?" First there was a long silence . . . And I could see those faces . . . And he got so furious, and then there was [Helmut] Lachenmann, his favourite student, who then created this totally unapproachable world [*laughs*] – a real intellectual, even more dogmatic than Stockhausen. And Lachenmann and Stockhausen just stuck me into the ground with this for being the most stupid question.'

By the time Stockhausen announced he would be teaching a new-music course at the Rheinische Musikschule in Cologne, alongside Berio, Pousseur and Earle Brown, his charismatic approach had attracted a cultish following. Irmin signed up for the courses in 1964 and '65 and found himself gaining new friends. Among the American attendees, who distributed tabs of LSD among the more open-minded students, were David Johnson, an American flautist interested in electronics and sound-recording techniques, and an American trumpet player named Jon Hassell, who was in Germany with his wife, Marge Hassell, later known as the jazz musician

Katrina Krimsky. There was Serge Tcherepnin, the Paris-based scion of a Russian dynasty of composers, who would later become known for his pioneering work with modular synthesizers in the early seventies, and Portuguese new-music composer Emmanuel Nunes. (Another slightly later attendee was Conrad 'Conny' Plank from Düsseldorf, whose name became associated with some of the classic productions of German rock and pop.) And there was the eccentric, square-jawed young German who asked Irmin to assist him with a piece he had written for percussion.

Irmin remembers Holger Schüring inviting him to his home in Duisburg, asking him to help him premiere one of his compositions. 'He was still living at home at his mother's. He had no father, his father was dead. It was [the same background] we all came from: petit bourgeois, middle class. His father was like my father: a functionary. He was a *Staatsanwalt*, I think, which was a prosecutor. And his mother was extremely straight, even a little bit severe. I didn't feel very comfortable with her.

'His piece was for percussion only,' Irmin recalls, 'and he asked me if I could play it. I'm not a percussionist, but that was not the point. Actually, I was playing percussion in several symphony orchestras in Bochum, Dortmund, Essen and Cologne, and they had these complicated rhythms. They asked me because I was playing and conducting in new music, so they knew I was a specialist in complicated nine against thirteen or something. Holger had written this piece and wanted to rehearse it with me. It was so funny – it was so complicated that it was just maths. It had no music . . . and it was even more complicated than any Stockhausen piece.

'Holger has this tendency to "*überbieten*" [outdo himself]. And he always told this story to me: when he started in the music academy, on this composition course, he was supposed to start with counterpoint for two voices, and for the first lesson he had written five voices. And the teacher says, "No, we start with two." That was the minimum for Holger – five voices! We had quite a laugh. But that was actually how I met Holger, trying to play this piece. It was unplayable. And afterwards he was laughing about it too.'[4]

Holger Czukay was born in a contested zone destined to be erased by history. Situated on the Baltic coast, Danzig is now Gdańsk in modern-day Poland, but in 1938 it was still a semi-autonomous city state sandwiched between two outcrops of the old German Empire. Its precarious wartime ambience was immortalised in Günter Grass's *Danzig Trilogy*.

On the question of his nationality, Holger once said: 'That I am German is a falsification. That I am Polish is a falsification. That means that my whole person is a falsification. This happened because my grandfather told the Nazis that we must be Aryan. And he made a kind of family tree. And his family tree was just born from fantasy, with no basis behind it. It looked nice . . .

'This is how I lost my name Czukay. My father changed it. To Schüring, a Dutch name. When I changed it back, it was with Can, in 1968. When I asked my parents what happened here, nobody wanted to tell me the truth. I was playing for money in a band with two Polish girls who were singing. I said, "Before, my name was Czukay. Do you know what that name means?" And they told me: "Search." Search equals Czukay. And I thought, when we opened up Can, "This is a very good name for me."'[5]

Danzig was incorporated into the Reich at the outbreak of war, but the city's German loyalists were expelled by the Poles, and the Schürings fled the city in 1945. 'I was about five [*sic*] years old when I left. So I was a pretty small child then. But I remember everything, especially the house I was living in. I remember the birthday when I became four years old. On that birthday I went with my younger brother to see the trams coming by. I wanted to get it off the rails. I was very successful. It was a very triumphant day.'[6] His family had even booked tickets for a passage on the evacuee ship *Wilhelm Gustloff*, which was due to depart on 13 January 1945, but at the last minute his grandmother changed her mind and took them to the railway station, where they boarded a train carrying wounded soldiers to Berlin. The ship was hit by a Soviet torpedo en route, with the loss of nearly ten thousand passengers, the largest maritime disaster in history.

Peering out of the carriage window as they pulled into Berlin, Holger saw nothing but heaps of rubble. Eventually, the family – now with the Germanised surname Schüring – resettled in Limburg an der Lahn, near Frankfurt. The young Holger discovered music and film at a very early age – he recalled playing with reels of film he had found and his sister taking him to the biopic of Robert and Clara Schumann, *Träumerei*. 'I knew from some very beginning of my childhood, say two years old. It was clear that I will ever always become a musician.'[7]

As a teenager, in Duisburg, he attended the Gerhard Mercator Scientific School, and excelled especially in physics and maths. While at school, he worked in a radio and TV repair shop, where he became fascinated by the 'three-dimensional sound' of old-fashioned valve radios, which were built with one speaker in front and two at the side.

'Electricity was such a fascinating thing – it was something,' he said. 'And then I became the boy in a shop who carries the radios to repair them and carries them back again. That was so-called three-dimensional radio, before stereo. There was one front speaker in the radio and at the side, there were two treble speakers which gave an image of spatial depth. I must say these radios sounded fantastic.'[8]

During childhood, Holger had been exposed to much music in churches and had fallen in love with the sound of the organ, and the music of Bach. At the same time, in the late fifties, he was also playing double bass in local jazz bands, including his own Holger Czukay Quintet. In February 1962 these interests led to him moving to Berlin, newly riven by the building of the Wall, and enrolling at the Berlin Music Academy. Holger lived in the Soviet zone and found it a gloomy climate both in terms of its geopolitics and its musical innovation. 'I remember when I was studying, I was very young,' he told me. 'It was the middle of the fifties, and I had a very able and great pianist and composer who was teaching me. And he told me at the time, "What can we do that's new?" Everything was done. Twelve-tone music, all the other music. "There is nothing more that we can do." And I felt a depression in what he said.' He took lessons in double bass from a Herr Zepperitz, a member of the Berlin Philharmonic Orchestra, and met important figures in the music world, from American radicals John Cage and David Tudor to the celebrated conductor Herbert von Karajan. 'Karajan was one of those people who really evoked this desire of, if I make pop music there must be something which is so genuine that it can stand [next to] the classical music.'[9] Holger was expelled from the Berlin Music Academy, one of many times he was rejected from an institution, but he kept his musical studies going. When he heard about Stockhausen's new-music course in Cologne, he immediately applied.

Holger introduced himself to the master as someone who had been rejected by every other music school in town. 'At that time when I studied with him,' Holger once said of Stockhausen, 'he was the church in the village. Everything, all the houses were built around this church.'[10] Answering a question, decades later, about what he had learned from Stockhausen, Holger replied, 'Maybe humour. I remember how in a conference someone said to him, "Mr Stockhausen, you just want to shock us, and make a lot of money that way." He said, "Nope, I'm doing it for purely musical reasons and I don't need money, I married a rich woman instead . . ." He was a man who made me incredibly curious. And he taught me that as a creative person you will always eventually run up against a wall. Always. And that you can jump over this wall. "Czukay, you think too much," Stockhausen said to me, and that's it. You have to think less.'[11]

On another occasion Holger said 'the spiritual idea behind [Stockhausen's music], that is for me not so necessary. I am not an unspiritual person, not at all, but I don't want to feel so strange about it . . . For me, advanced as he is, he is actually a very traditional composer, probably the last traditional genius in our age.' He made another telling comment: 'Written music belongs to the past. It means: there is a creator, and there is a performer. They are different people. And performers are organised in unions . . . Stockhausen is a traditional composer – innovative, but a composer nonetheless.'[12]

Distinguished by the massive black towers of its Roman Catholic cathedral casting shadows over the Rhine, the city of Cologne abounds in multiple layers of sedimented history. Its name derives from the one given to it by its first-century Roman founders – Colonia (literally 'colony') Claudia Ara Agrippinensium. Retaining its sovereignty within the Holy Roman Empire, it developed a long-standing tradition of liberalism and enjoyed 'free city' status throughout the Middle Ages, hanging on to a strong Catholic tradition through the Reformation until the French invaded in the nineteenth century. After Allied bombing raids caused massive losses to its buildings and population during World War II, the city was extensively rebuilt and expanded to become the nation's fourth-largest city. It has a high density of cultural institutions and artistic events compared with the average German city: more than thirty official museums and many more private galleries; the headquarters of broadcasting and TV production companies; several resident orchestras; and a vibrant underground club scene.

Hindemithweg lies in a rhomboid enclave of modernist apartment blocks on the north-western outskirts of Cologne, in an area called Bocklemünd. The one-hundred-square-metre flat at number three is where Irmin and Hildegard Schmidt made a home, purchased via the property firm where she held down a day job as financial manager. The area of Cologne they selected to live in had been substantially rebuilt after the war with modern blocks, and the neighbouring street names are redolent of an era in which Austro-German contemporary music was being celebrated and lifted away from its Nazi-era 'degenerate' classification: Schönbergweg, Alban-Berg-Weg, Kurt-Weill-Weg and Bertolt-Brecht-Strasse (there's also a Max Ernst Gesamtschule near by). Hindemithweg lies at the centre of this cartography of great Germanic modernism. This is the spot, appropriately, where Can was incarnated towards the end of 1967.

Irmin intended to keep on with the new-music courses at the academy and was also taking an ethnology course at Cologne University, focusing on a study of Japanese gagaku court music. His main source of income was as a professional pianist and conductor, continuing his engagement with the Bochum Symphony Orchestra, and also waving his baton in front of the Norddeutscher Rundfunk Orchestra and even the formidable Vienna Symphony Orchestra. By 1966 he had taken up the post of Kapellmeister at the Stadttheater in Aachen, Cologne's neighbouring town, and was teaching vocal technique at the Schauspielschule (drama academy) in Bochum. He and Hildegard occasionally provided sanctuary and free lodging to some of their friends. The first guests to join them in this large two-bedroomed apartment, with a huge terrace outside the living room, were Jon Hassell and his wife Katrina Krimsky, herself a musician, who had been evicted from their own lodgings because their landlord was annoyed by their noisy dog.

Jon Hassell would go on to carve out an idiosyncratic course through contemporary music, working as a trumpeter in exotic and electric jazz, then collaborating with Brian Eno and making his own richly spiced 'Fourth World' ambient music, and even experimenting with sample-based electronics. Back in the mid-sixties these possibilities were still wide open. He had brought some LSD with him from the States. Irmin and his friends, such as Serge Tcherepnin, tried the drug on several occasions in the mid-sixties, paying attention to the advice to make sure it was taken in a trusting and safe, 'very disciplined' environment. 'My experience was only fantastic, wonderful,'

Irmin says. One trip he particularly remembers occurred when 'Hildegard was sober, and she was in the living room. There was this moment where I was lying on the bed and imagining Hildegard – she was ironing – so clearly that all of a sudden I had the feeling that I am in this room. I started to think, "Shit!" This can make you mix up reality totally, and I realised why people jump out of the window and think they can fly. So I got a little bit frightened, and Hildegard confirmed that now I am with her in the room. And then I put on Mahler's Fourth Symphony, the second movement with the solo violin. And I listened to it, I think, five times, only that movement, and at the time I had the feeling that I totally understood it, the structure and everything.'

A question hangs over whether Stockhausen himself took acid in the mid-sixties, but it is clear that many in his immediate circle – David Johnson, for instance, who moved into the Schmidts' apartment in late 1966 – were using it. As with so many pop stars at the time, something certainly happened to Stockhausen's music and appearance around 1966–7: he began growing his hair long and wearing flowing white outfits; his music stretched out into the long-form experimental electronic sounds of *Telemusik*, *Hymnen* and *Klangwelle*; and his pronouncements took on an increasingly universalist, cosmic dimension. 'Even if he had done it, which I think he did, he wouldn't talk about it,' says Irmin. 'He wouldn't talk with students. He invited us to his house and we had parties, we went to his sauna and everything, he was very social. But he wouldn't talk about previous experiences very much.'

In the freezing winter of January 1966 Irmin flew to New York to compete in the Dimitri Mitropoulos Conducting Competition. On his first trip to America he took time out to delve into the city's flourishing underground arts scene, where concept art, film, experimental sound and music were fusing in unprecedented new ways. He saw Andy Warhol's movies, met and hung out with some of the

24

young progenitors of conceptual and minimalist music – La Monte Young, Dick Higgins, Steve Reich and Terry Riley – and discovered the newly fledged pop art and Fluxus movement at first hand. In his own words, he 'got corrupted'. 'Right at the start, I met Terry Riley,' he says. 'He had this strange little grotto in the Bowery. We sat there night after night, and he made me play "de dah de dah de dah de" . . . Me on the piano and him on the sax. At first I thought this was totally stupid.' Stupid or not, Riley was at the forefront of a new compositional methodology, partly influenced by non-Western music, involving long-form sax improvisations over endlessly repeating tape loops, drones and feedback between pairs of tape recorders – a system he called the 'time-lag accumulator'. Dense and sometimes chaotic, but as intense and focused as a ritual chant, Riley's music of this period demonstrated that the idea of a 'composer' in the late sixties was shifting beyond the traditional notion of the genius in the garret inscribing notes on lined paper. His most famous composition, *In C* (1964), was an open-ended piece for an indefinite number of performers playing variations of short musical phrases over the throbbing pulse of a C major chord. It could be played by anyone, and every group of people would shape the piece in any number of different ways. For the conservatory-trained conductor of central European orchestras, this was a thunderbolt.

Steve Reich was also experimenting at the time with tape loops and fragments of found speech moving in and out of phase. Advances in media technology were creating entirely new roles for the modern-day composer. La Monte Young, meanwhile, was involved in the extraordinary, Indian music-influenced drones of the Theater of Eternal Music, a group that was effectively a brief moment of possibility which seeded a great deal of significant musical developments in the years immediately following. Members included Young's wife Marian Zazeela; John Cale, who would shortly form the Velvet Underground with Lou Reed under Warhol's guidance (a seminal group in the early months of Can's existence); violinist Tony Conrad, a musician, theorist and experimental film-maker who would end up collaborating with Faust, one of Can's counterpart German groups in the early seventies; percussionist and occultist Angus MacLise; and occasionally Terry Riley.

Entranced by the strange and hypnotic music he heard from this crowd, Irmin forgot about the competition he was supposed to be entering and missed out on several crucial rehearsals. He had squinted through an aperture and spied a galaxy of new attitudes and possibilities.

After returning to Cologne, Irmin started talking more urgently with David Johnson about instigating some kind of new music group. By now Johnson had become an important member of Stockhausen's entourage. He was becoming more involved in tape and electronic music, and is credited with operating sine-wave generators on the Deutsche Grammophon recording of *Mixtur*, recorded in Cologne in August 1967.

While it had not made much of a mark in the international pop world, since the war West Germany had produced some of the most advanced thinkers in contemporary composition. Many of them worked in the colossal tower-block headquarters of the Westdeutscher Rundfunk, known as WDR, one of the pillars of West German state broadcasting and home to one of the world's most advanced electronic music studios. Founded in 1950, the West German national broadcasting umbrella consisted of six regional broadcasters, including the Nordwestdeutscher Rundfunk (NWDR). On the first day of 1956 this again split into two, becoming NDR, operating out of Hamburg, and WDR in Cologne. The latter was already famous – or notorious – in musical circles as being the site of one of the world's most progressive electronic music studios, whose considerable resources were used by Karlheinz Stockhausen and his circle. The Studio für Elektronisches Musik des Westdeutschen Runkfunks was officially inaugurated in 1951 by a cadre of composers – Herbert Eimert, Werner Meyer-Eppler, Robert Beyer and Fritz Enkel – under the directorship of station chief Hanns Hartmann.

This was a cabal of musical and acoustic visionaries who were picking up threads first followed before the war. Robert Beyer wrote an essay in 1928 entitled 'Das Problem der "kommenden Musik"' ('The Problem of the "Music to Come"'). His argument focused on a new and unexplored notion of spatial sound for music, a textural and conceptual form of sonic thought that far outstripped new music's rate of change at the time. Believing that atonalism and serialism were merely the first tentative steps towards a long-awaited paradigmatic shift in music, Beyer rejected the conventional idea of 'tone space' – spaces between notes and voices on the tempered scale – and instead envisaged a new mode of conceiving sound in terms of 'new techniques based on the ability to separate the sound from its point of origin, from its original temporal flow, and from the physical limits of the human performer – in other words, the techniques of recording and playback; even more significantly, [Beyer] refers to the magnetic recording system on which film was based as a starting point . . . He anticipates that this will come about via collaborations of engineers and musicians; the results would be a wholesale reorganisation of sound material, in which traditional linear form would be replaced by a music which is in every sense spatialised . . .'[13]

Beyer wrote: 'Music is tending towards spatialisation, towards the exclusion of sequential presentation, towards objectification and reification, and it brings elements from the world of the eye into that of the ear. The atonalisation of music is one step in this development, even if it has advanced music merely to a freedom of gesture which remains carved as if in stone, to its total and final mobility on the twelve-tone space, to its centre in the human; the process of development strives however towards a regular, general and strictly numerical foundation of music . . . At the end of this development stands the sound, sounding in, filling and moving in space, resonating around a central point, in the changing light of a timbral world of cosmic proportions: a sound almost visible.'[14]

A timbral world of cosmic proportions. It's a heady phrase, but justified in the light of the WDR's achievements. One of Beyer's and Eimert's first collaborations at WDR was called *Musik im unbegrenzten Raum* (Music in Unlimited Space). Applying serial techniques to all aspects of a sound – including its timbre, duration and volume – gave these composers an unprecedented degree of control over sounds and their position in space–time; never before had a composer been able to break a musical idea down into its component parts and manipulate them at an atomic level. These composers were feeling their way towards a musical future, not by inventing daft instruments that would be outdated within ten years, but by rethinking the organisational possibilities of musical structure itself, taking off from the idea of a serialism extending outward from the musical stave into three dimensions.

But even serialism, by the early sixties, was ceding to more progressive forces that seemed to be melting its cool core. Stockhausen's technique of intermodulation, refined during the composition of his pieces *Telemusik* (1966) and *Hymnen* (1967), used the characteristics of one sound to transform another. For Stockhausen this was a way to advance found sounds, sonic *objets trouvés* (gathered around the world), from being merely tape collage to something more flowing and integrated, creating, as he did so, a powerful metaphor for transnational relationships. 'New sounds, which I produced in the electronic studio,' he wrote in the sleeve notes to the Deutsche Grammophon LP of *Telemusik*, 'are combined into a higher unity: a universality of past, present and future, of distant places and spaces . . .' *Telemusik*, as well as the gigantic work that arose out of it, *Hymnen*, was assembled from intermodulated chunks of field recordings and radio snippets collated by Stockhausen during his travels in Japan, North Africa, Europe and beyond. Existing in differing versions for pure electronics and an orchestra with soloists, *Hymnen*'s vast scale and unconventional organising principles called for a new musical language, and Stockhausen referred to its different sections not as 'movements' but with the more geographical term 'regions'. His belief in the power of this piece only increased over the years, and by the time it came to be performed at New York's Lincoln Center in 1971 he was referring to it as nothing less than a 'project for the integration of all races, all religions, all nations'. 'What more can a composer do', he added, 'than create musical worlds which do not merely mirror the human world as it is today but which offer visions, intimations of better worlds, in which projects in the realms of sound, of fragments, of objets trouvés become mutually compatible and grow together to realize the divine mission of ONE united world?'[15]

Hymnen's world premiere took place on 30 November 1967 in the auditorium of the Apostel Secondary School in Cologne-Lindenthal, as part of WDR's concert series *Musik der Zeit* (Music of Our Time). A significant role in its realisation was played by David Johnson, the American composer and flautist, who had already assisted Stockhausen for several years in both a technical and a performative capacity. For Johnson, as for the rest of his circle of followers, Stockhausen was a quasi-spiritual leader, a figure Schmidt and Johnson's generation either worshipped or castigated. English composer Cornelius Cardew – a man who also fought to shake off the shackles of instilled technique through improvisation and songwriting – would later deliver a scathing critique of Stockhausen in a notorious 1974 pamphlet entitled *Stockhausen Serves Imperialism.*[16]

In Britain, Cardew was in the late sixties making new alliances with AMM, a politicised group of ex-jazz musicians espousing a radical form of total improvisation. It was one of a number of international groups in which principles of free music and the contemporary avant-garde coalesced and initiated fresh dialogues. In the autumn of 1967 another such unit, Musica Elettronica Viva (MEV), played concerts in Cologne and Berlin. The group featured Rome-based Americans Frederic Rzewski, Alvin Curran and Richard Teitelbaum, plus Allan Bryant, who had constructed a DIY synthesizer, Carol Plantamura on free-form vocals and Ivan Vandor on saxophone. Using a variety of contact-miked objects and surfaces, a thumb piano mounted on an oil can and a modular Moog synth, these composers abandoned their learned craft and embraced freedom, noise and critical listening. More than post-serialism's glacial experiments with form and harmonic theory, the viscerality of these groups facilitated an engagement with the urgency of the times and drew audiences from different sectors of society, outside the conservatoire.

In 1967 Irmin managed to get a few of his own Fluxus-style diagrammatic scores performed, and published them as a set of thirteen sheets of manuscript, to be stacked in any order by any number of musicians, under the collected title *Album für Mogli*. (Mogli was Irmin's pet name for Hildegard.) One of these, 'Hexapussy', was premiered in Frankfurt using an array of metallic sound sculptures by the Baschet Brothers from France. Other titles included 'Oiml(g): Nightmares', 'Gagaku', 'Für Jackson MacLow', 'Erinnerung', 'Dieter's Lullaby', 'Nada', 'Prinzipien', etc. Only 'Hexapussy' appears to have survived in any recorded form.[17]

Via Johnson, Irmin and Holger had an excuse to make guerrilla raids on the WDR's facilities. 'Through David,' says Irmin, 'we could, with the permission of Stockhausen, at night go into the electronic studio and do, first of all, some work with tapes, and secondly, steal some tapes! They were expensive and we had no money. And Holger especially, he was quite good at stealing tapes. David too, but Holger did that very efficiently. I never did that – I have no criminal energy.' This covert activity continued into 1968, when Stockhausen was completing *Kurzwellen*, a piece for radio sets transformed by real-time sound processing. Much later in Can's life, the radio as a source of spontaneous sound would become a central element, and it connected back to Holger's childhood fascination with crystal wireless sets.

Since the early sixties a small revolution had been eating up the German art world. Georg Baselitz literally turned the world upside down in his paintings showing figures and landscapes flipped on their heads. Previously, his *Pandemonium Manifestos*, co-written with artist Eugen Schönebeck, had upset the art establishment, after a 1961 exhibition in a dilapidated house in West Berlin. A later writer describes the *Pandemonium Manifestos* as 'an angry declaration of support for an art of recollection, mysticism, ecstasy, and fantasy. Comprised of absurd and grandiose phrases conjuring up loathsome images, the manifesto employs a language of apocalyptic proportions.'[18] Raging against what they viewed as a widespread refusal to acknowledge and atone for the sins of World War II, in a West German society steaming towards rebirth, prosperity and respectability, the artists presented a vision of abjection and chaos, concluding in their second manifesto that, in modern West Germany, 'here surviving is now the most painful ordeal of all'.[19]

Since the end of the war, when the Nobel prize-winning author Thomas Mann, keenly attuned to the sensibilities of his own people while in exile in the US, wrote that 'Behind every sentence that we construct in our language stands a broken, a spiritually burnt out people . . . a people that can never show its face again,'[20] the fabric of the old Germany had been unzipped and turned inside out. Historically a fragmented nation of feudal states and perpetually shifting borders, now the North/South Germany of old – divided along Protestant/Catholic fault lines – had been twisted around by the occupying Allied forces into a horizontally separated East and West. The entire geographic psyche of Germany had been bent permanently out of alignment. Not only that, but the capital had been transferred to the lightweight and previously lowly city of Bonn, while the former heart of the country, Berlin, was riven down its centre by the building of the Wall by Soviet authorities in 1961.

As at Berkeley in 1964, students in Germany were concerned at the suppression of radical voices within universities, as the educational authorities sought to ban dissent. Student leader Daniel Cohn-Bendit wrote: 'In Germany, the call for university reform became a rallying cry for students and a strong one, in the absence of an effective opposition to West German capitalism. As a result, the German student movement became the standard bearer of resistance to both the state and also to American atrocities in Vietnam.'[21] Major unrest began as early as December 1966, when Berlin Free University students clashed with police during a Vietnam demo. The American operation in Vietnam was a significant pillar of radical opposition among German students, with opposition given credence in the writings of politicised playwright Peter Weiss, whose *Viet Nam Discourse* – a savage indictment of the US position, accusing America of a form of debased Nazism in its South-East Asian adventure – was premiered in 1968.[22] A faction within a faction known as Kommune 1, which formed in 1967 around the principle of total hedonism and shattering the family unit, brought a measure of absurdist provocation to the movement (they called themselves *Spass-Guerillas*, 'fun-guerrillas', and promoted *Witz als Waffe*, 'jokes as weapons') and became reviled by the hard-line left-wing Socialist German Student Association (SDS), even as it gained counter-cultural credentials via associations with Uschi Obermaier, an actress, glamour model and member of Munich avant-rock commune Amon Düül. 'We want a subversive university while you want the sacred rites of an academic empire,' runs a Kommune 1 communiqué sent as part of a somewhat misdirected funding application to the 'Academic Senate' in June 1967. 'We want things you aren't interested in but which are important to us. We want real communication and understanding among ourselves, we want to make love, to be tender, to have fun, to understand each other, we don't want to work.'[23] After two years of notoriety, the group broke up after burning down a Frankfurt department store; a splinter group was at the core of the formation of the Baader-Meinhof Gang/Red Army Faction.

For many years after the war, former Nazis were regularly unmasked in public life, having kept official offices or risen once more through governmental or administrative ranks: a case of 'Meet the new boss, same as the old boss', with potentially catastrophic consequences. Irmin Schmidt experienced this tendency first hand. 'After the war it did go on in school: there were all these teachers that were Nazis . . . and I fought them. Our teacher in modern history was *Schulungsleiter* [teacher of ideology] in the *Reichsarbeitsdienst*, and he was teaching history in the fifties. So I wrote all that down in our school newspaper, and finally was thrown out.' Such revelations about murky pasts continued into 1968, the task taken up by an increasingly radicalised student body. In that year students at Bonn University scrawled the words 'Concentration camp builder' next to the name of Heinrich Lübke, the West German president, who stood accused of personally approving barracks designs, including concentration camp blocks, while working as a building engineer under Albert Speer during the war. Such public outings crystallised a more domestic concern among the youth of West Germany at the time: What had their parents done in the war?

'That's extremely complicated for me to deal with,' says Irmin. 'Having parents who had neighbours who were Jewish and were sent into Auschwitz, and they didn't do anything – this is my history. I grew up in a country which was in ruins, culturally. And I don't think we recovered from this so easily. It's only one and a half generations, so we didn't recover from it. "Recover" is a strange word, the wrong word. It means a lot of things, and one of the things it means is what we did – putting something into the world which is genuinely reflecting this experience in the art you make. We are musicians, so we reflected this: the strangeness, the brutality, the harshness of what our parents' generation did . . .'

Lübke's party was the Christian Democratic Union, an appellation that served as a constant reminder of how large a role the church played in German public life. In 1968 church services were frequently used as platforms to air public concerns and grievances, and on 13 January the church of St Michaelis in Hamburg filled up with disgruntled students distributing pamphlets with a rewritten Lord's Prayer that attacked capitalism ('Our Capital, which art in the West . . .') and denouncing the sermon of the church's long-standing pastor, Helmuth Thielicke. Fifty soldiers of the Bundeswehr, in civilian clothes, were called to the church to protect him. Thielicke had not even been a Nazi; he had actually been on the Gestapo's wanted list and had loose ties to an anti-Hitler revolutionary movement during the war, but by the late sixties his smug preaching, harking back to a fictitious golden age of the Goldmark currency and Germany's days as an invincible imperial sea power, was infuriating members of the SDS who perceived a lack of freedom in the universities and a collusion between Establishment figures. They refused to remove their hats inside the church, recited their radicalised version of the prayer, kept a rumble of activity on the stairwells and had sex in dark corners. Reported in the current-affairs magazine *Der Spiegel* shortly afterwards, the story was accompanied by a satirical cartoon showing a student in the office of a radical organisation, surrounded by placards with the words '*Nieder Mit . . .*' ('Down with . . .') and a blank space to be filled in. '*Protestieren?*' he is telling the caller. '*Wann? Wo? Wogegen?*' ('Protest? When? Where? What against?')[24]

This was no fantasy. Two of those who could easily have been targets of that protest-happy caricature were Rudi Dutschke, also known as Rudi the Red, and Daniel Cohn-Bendit, both associated with the SDS, both outspoken critics of mainstream German politics. In early 1968 Dutschke was among rebellious theology students demanding the right to use church services to promote a dialogue against the immorality of the Vietnam war and other state-sanctioned atrocities; in February he was instrumental in a huge anti-Vietnam war protest in Berlin, as well as directing the gathering antipathy against Axel Springer, head of a colossal media group, 'that mini-Fascist publishing empire whose newspapers were pulling the wool over the eyes of the German workers', as Cohn-Bendit described it – an empire that included the right-wing tabloid *Bild*. Dutschke himself was shot in mysterious circumstances in early April 1968, an incident that led to violent demonstrations – with students throwing rocks and flaming torches – that were broken up by police with water cannon. Right after Easter five days of street battles erupted in major German cities including Hamburg, Hannover and Essen. Shortly afterwards, French television viewers were treated to footage of the German unrest, spun in such a way as to suggest that local troubles in towns such as Nanterre were insignificant. In fact, the scenes from Germany contributed to a polarisation of solidarity within France, leading directly to the *événements* which kicked off in Paris on 6 May. These were likewise driven by the desire to puncture society's bourgeois veneer. For many onlookers, the future members of Can included, it felt as though the institutions of civilised Europe were crumbling daily.

But ahead of these ructions, in the autumn of 1967 Irmin wrote to Holger, inviting him to a meeting in Cologne to discuss forming some kind of group. It would reflect the ongoing tumult, while rejecting any overt political affiliations. 'We were not involved in the '68 movement, physically or even theoretically,' cautions Irmin. 'In forming a group at that time we were not starting a commune; it was professional musicians who gave up part of their career, and gave up, above all, the idea of authorship. We were a collective, and inventing collectively.

'Any kind of contemporary music, especially German, should reflect our history, what we have grown up with: destroyed cities, people who experienced firestorms, but also which extinguished millions of people. It's such a strange history I grew up with: on one side having all this destruction, and on the other side I was a child, having parents who you accused when you grew up, "Who let all this happen?" That's a very complicated background, one that influenced me deeply.'

3

Mutter(ing)s of Invention

One day in the autumn of 1967 – the precise date is not recalled by anyone concerned – the doorbell rings at the apartment at Hindemithweg 3.

It's Holger Czukay, mustachioed and mischievous-eyed under a shock of wavy hair, with a younger, long-haired man in tow. Irmin and Holger had stayed in touch, even after Holger travelled to Switzerland in May 1966 to take up a lecturing post in music at the Institut auf dem Rosenberg, an elite boarding school for girls founded in 1889 in the historic town of St Gallen. He was, of course, taking Stockhausen literally at his word and trying to find a rich wife so that his outlandish compositional ideas could be funded.

One of his pupils was to have a profound influence on the course of his life. 'I went to the "sister" school – the boys' school, where the Mountbattens and the Prince of Prussia were pupils – and they made me teach a lesson. The principal asked the boys, "What do you think about him? Should we employ him?" and there was this one talented boy in the class – Michael Karoli – and he said [puts on a child's voice] "I want to have him as my teacher!" [laughs] And I was engaged immediately! Later – when he had left school – Michael came and lived with me and we founded Can.'[1]

Michael Karoli was an eighteen-year-old student when this classroom encounter took place. The only Can founder born after the end of World War II, he emerged into the world in the Bavarian town of Straubing on 29 April 1948. In that year his father, Hermann, had just been freed after testifying in the Nuremberg Trials. He had been a member of the Waffen-SS during the war, fighting on the

Eastern Front against Russian partisans. After receiving a bullet in the lung, he was moved back to Berlin, where he headed the audit department in the SS's Berlin administrative centre until Germany's surrender. In the year of Michael's birth he set up an accounting company with his brother that went on to become one of the most successful of its kind in Germany, based in Essen, an industrial Ruhr city between Düsseldorf and Dortmund. As a respected and wealthy financial consultant, Hermann Karoli rose to become the chairman of BMW's supervisory board, among others. Michael's mother Susanne had worked as a film editor before her marriage, so Michael and his sister Constanze grew up in an affluent, cultured household, surrounded by an art collection that included original German expressionist canvases.

Michael's earliest musical experiences involved a tin drum when he was an infant, and the Gypsy violin he inherited at the age of seven from his grandfather, who died in Romania. As his musical talents developed, he was presented with a banjo one Christmas, and before his teens he played it in a school Dixieland jazz band, the Steamboat Jazz Pirates. 'We had a trumpeter by the name of Frank Sonnenschein,' he told an interviewer in the late nineties. 'That was love at first note. He'd stand twenty centimetres away and blow straight into my face. That's probably when the ear damage first started. I played the banjo directly into his face as well. The banjo also is very loud. The rest of the band just gave us room. This relationship between two players inside a bigger formation helped to form my later style: hearing several instruments as one. I can't imagine music any other way. Musicians in a group should resonate in the same way that strings on an instrument do.'[2] When he was fifteen he bought himself an electric guitar, and an uncle gave him an amplifier. While he had already familiarised himself with a huge range of music, from classical and Roma folk to swing-era jazz, blues and boogie-woogie, he now started to play modern jazz with another clutch of more progressive school friends, and by the mid-sixties – by which time he was at school in St Gallen – had began to tune in to the rock, pop and soul sounds coming out of Britain and the US. By the time he teamed up with Holger Czukay, he had begun playing more avant-garde forms of jazz and would sit in with visiting musicians and groups.

The young Michael and his unconventional teacher, ten years his senior, became friends, offering each other access to hitherto unexplored musical domains. 'Holger was very modern in his thinking,' Michael told me, 'and he had been a fantastic jazz guitar player, and that's how I got close to him, because I wanted him to teach me guitar. He showed me a lot of tricks. But what he did was jazz guitar; he didn't have any idea about rock or anything, and he thought that jazz was too old-fashioned, and he thought that rock was totally, absolutely old-fashioned, until we listened to some Beatles stuff, where I told him: "You see what you can do in rock?"'

Holger: 'Michael Karoli was the only one who could play guitar and knowing something about this music at the time, but I didn't know anything! So Michael was the teacher.'[3]

Michael's musically adventurous mind was a fertile greenhouse ready to be seeded by Holger's classical and atonal music, while Holger in turn had never properly accepted the idea that pop music could be taken seriously as an art form. 1966 into '67 was the moment pop started to make serious progress. It was the time of the Beatles' *Revolver*, of Dylan's *Blonde on Blonde*, of the Jimi Hendrix Experience's *Are You Experienced?*, of British psychedelic classics like the Pretty Things' *S.F. Sorrow* and of acid garage outfits like the Seeds, the 13th Floor Elevators, the Doors, etc. 'I Am the Walrus', the Beatles' most psychedelic track to date, was a particular favourite and the one that converted Holger to the avant-garde pranks that could be perpetrated in a pop/rock context. It featured multilayered and distorted voices, backwards tapes and a density of production unprecedented in modern pop. Furthermore, Stockhausen himself peeped out from the *Sgt. Pepper's Lonely Hearts Club Band* cover.

It confirmed that important connections were to be made beyond the realms of teenbeat pop.

In St Gallen, which saw its share of brass band activity (and which, coincidentally, was the birthplace of electronic musician Dieter Möbius, future founder of Kluster, Cluster and Harmonia), Holger also taught the tuba. He later remembered one particularly influential occasion, when he perceived the strong effects this 'public' music could exert on a social space. 'I was marching in a brass band through a town,' he said. 'And just the loud swells of sound reflected off the houses gave an effect very similar to rock music. And for the first time I could understand why the Third Reich, with its marching bands, had such a big effect on people.'[4] Increasingly enamoured of these very audible and visible effects, Holger and Michael made tentative steps towards forming a group at the school. 'We played a session with [pianist] Tony Ashton. He was a member of Remo Four [a Liverpool band who were contemporaries of the Beatles] . . . so we recorded in a farm-house – me, Michael, Tony Ashton and some members of Remo Four. And it wasn't bad. So I said to Tony: "Let's form an experimental band!" Tony was very drunk and he said, "Yes! Well, of course . . . what else!" [laughs] Tony was a very entertaining guy, but he didn't really understand what I meant by experimental, so he eventually drifted away.'[5]

As Michael was finishing school, Holger was fired – 'for being too . . . er . . . intriguing!' he later claimed.[6] Holger returned to Cologne, while Michael began studying for a law degree in Lausanne. Where next? The answer came in the letter that arrived around this time from Irmin Schmidt, inviting Holger to form a group in Cologne. He brought Michael with him.

During Michael's early months in Cologne, an influential figure was Michael von Biel, another composer associated with the WDR studios. As well as being a regular poker partner at Irmin's flat, von Biel had developed his own unique style of playing the cello. He once interrupted a concert of conventionally atonal music with an uproarious 'proto-punk' attack on his instrument. Through von Biel, Michael discovered that 'You can portray an entire universe on a single instrument. Von Biel's cello playing had everything, although by "normal" standards he couldn't play the cello correctly at all. To me, the visionary part of music meant diving into the microcosmos of sound. Later, I called that microphonic music. By that, I rather meant microscopic music. The microphone is placed very close to the source of sound, and the instrument played very quietly, so that its full spectrum can be heard. A single note can be experienced as an entire universe. That was the musical vision I had at the time. That was something new for rock 'n' roll itself: you could amplify very quiet sounds so that even the smallest sound from a string could sound as loud as the explosion of a bomb. It fascinated me. I sat up all night in bed playing tambourine as quietly as possible, tapping on different spots on the rim . . . I borrowed von Biel's cello for a half-year: that was total ecstasy for me. I sat cross-legged on the bed and made noises with the cello.'[7]

Decades later, Holger described von Biel to me as 'a real punker'. Since the early sixties von Biel had been pushing musical material, within a compositional framework, to the limits of noise, using extended techniques including excessive pressure on bowed instruments, playing behind the bridge to create overtones, etc. *Fassung*, his first electronic work, was commissioned on the recommendation of Stockhausen himself, and realised over six months of working six days a week at WDR, during which time he frequently broke the mixing board faders with excessive use of force. His *Quartet with Accompaniment* (1965) called for a drone to be held on a cello using a vibrator. At the time he was influencing Michael Karoli, he was reaching a self-imposed limit. *Jagdstück* (Hunting Piece), premiered in February 1968, involved a screeching, electronically amplified barbecue grill, plus electric guitar and double bass, threaded among the more conventional sonorities of a brass ensemble playing hunting tunes. Following the premiere von Biel

41

turned away from music to study drawing with Joseph Beuys at the Düsseldorf Academy of Art. The experience helped Michael, at this formative stage, to consider the electric guitar as more than just an instrument of rock 'n' roll.

Back to Hindemithweg 3. Michael Karoli, as the youngest in this company, is the least affected by the cultural weight and expectations of the past, and has had no dealings with the professional music industry. But he is suffering under the weight of expectation from his family, who trust that the costly education they are providing will ensure that their son will take up a respectable, well-paid position in a law firm. However, enticed by the seductions of intelligent popular music and the liberated ideas seeping out of the British and American counter-culture, Michael is rapidly sensing a different door opening, and it is impossible to resist the temptation to step through and explore the extreme possibilities that lie so tantalisingly close on the other side.

'I had wanted to form a group for a long time,' said Michael, 'but a different kind of group, and [Holger] wanted to join in somehow. It would not have been a real pop group, though, because I was very much into free jazz. I was working with either an organist or bass player and I played in dance bars. I was studying law at the same time. And then I think Holger got a letter from Irmin saying that he wanted to form a group, so I came along as just the guitar player. That's how I got involved with Can. When I joined there was one film soundtrack to do. We made modern classical music. I had given up law school by then, I wasn't very successful in law. Before [Can] I [hardly] played electric guitar, only acoustic, finger-picking guitar. I got more into electric guitar, which means I got into feedback; an electric guitar makes more sounds by itself, if you just leave it with the sound turned up loud it will make something by itself.'

◦

The next visitor must, Irmin thinks, be the candidate for the drum stool. The day before, he had asked an acquaintance, Jaki Liebezeit, drummer in Germany's most famous free jazz outfit, the Manfred Schoof Quintet, to recommend a good jazz drummer in the style of Max Roach or Art Blakey. Liebezeit replied, 'Yeah, I know somebody . . . He'll be round tomorrow.'[8] Irmin can't hide his surprise when Jaki himself walks into his flat, announcing he's giving up free jazz.

'I have survived everything,' Can's drummer once said.[9] Born in the sleepy village of Ostrau, near Dresden, on 26 May 1938, Hans 'Jaki' Liebezeit remained enigmatic about his early years. There are still several Liebezeits in the Dresden telephone book, although Jaki never appeared terribly sentimental about his origins and rarely discussed them. 'My father was the village teacher,' he told me. 'In a primary school. My mother was from Lower Saxony.' His father died during the war in mysterious circumstances – not as a soldier, but a civilian. 'Nobody knows what happened,' Jaki said. 'I cannot say anything about what happened to him.' He could only speculate: 'He also made music – keyboards and violin. But they told me that they forbade him to make music. After that, he disappeared. Probably played some jazz-like music, or dance music. He didn't play the right music, anyway. A lot of music was forbidden at the time.'

His mother took him to live with his grandmother in Hannoversch Münden, another village near Kassel, at the head of the River Weser. At school he took up the trumpet and played in his school band and orchestra. 'I took up the trumpet because there were only three fingers – easy,' he would joke.

In those childhood marching bands – and listening to his first hero, Louis Armstrong – he would have been exposed to the martial beating of drums, and the young Liebezeit's ears were hard-wired for rhythm and bone-hard metre at that young age. 'For trumpet you have to learn rhythmical things because most of the time the trumpets only play rhythm. You have to move, then you can do simple rhythms.' When he changed to a different school in Kassel, in his late teens, the chapel band had enough trumpeters but needed a drummer, and Jaki, thinking it would be easy, bashed his way to the drum stool. 'There was a private pupils' band there making American dance music. That was the beginning of rock 'n' roll. They had no drummer, and so I became a drummer. It was easy. I didn't know so much; I could march, keep the rhythm. And play simple things. I didn't know anything about drums, but it was enough for the band, and that's why I started drumming.' Soon he discovered jazz and bebop, the sound of modernity in the fifties, epitomised by the likes of Max Roach and Art Blakey. His principal jazz ally at this time – they met at Kassel high school in 1956 – was trumpeter Manfred Schoof, one of Germany's most forward-looking jazz players in the sixties and seventies.

In 1958 Schoof moved to Cologne and enrolled at the Musik-hochschule, where he met many of its students, including the pianist Alexander von Schlippenbach. He encouraged Jaki to join him, and Jaki soon left his village home, sharing a flat with Schoof for three years. 'We were playing together from that time on,' says Schoof. 'Modern jazz style, and we went to jam sessions and played all over Germany, and in the wildest time developed a kind of group together.' Their circle included the likes of Gunter Hampel, Olaf Kübler (who would later manage the Krautrock group Amon Düül II and guest on Can's *Landed* LP) and Lothar Meid (future bassist with Amon Düül II), in a loose collective known as the Jazz Cookers. By the early sixties Jaki's listening was broadening out into Indian and Arabic musics, and between 1961 and 1965 he lived in Barcelona, Spain, where he studied the intoxicating rhythms of flamenco. Playing in local bands, including that of local pianist Tete Montoliu,[10] brought him into contact with musicians passing through the city, and he accompanied Chet Baker, among others. By the time he returned to Germany again, his friends had moved further out into free jazz. 'They said, "You and your old-fashioned rhythm, it doesn't exist any more, repetition and all that doesn't fly any more today." I couldn't argue. Anybody who said anything against it could talk until he turned blue . . .'

Schoof put together a challenging quintet in 1965, featuring saxophonist Gerd Dudek, pianist Alexander von Schlippenbach, Buschi Niebergall on bass and Jaki on drums. These were jazz heavyweights whose bible was the freedom storm of Ornette Coleman, Albert Ayler and John Coltrane, whose music systematically kicked away from stable harmony, scale and metre, pushing into instrumental extremes and fervent expressionism. But the sound of the quintet took an additional cool, hard edge from the current, mid-sixties Miles Davis Quintet. 'We were the first free jazz group in Germany,' claims Schoof.

It was certainly the one that made the biggest impact, both domestically and abroad. The band played prestigious festivals at Antibes and Lugano, and travelled to Prague and Warsaw. A record deal with CBS led to the great album *Voices* (1966), a whirling, testy yet exuberant set of tunes that included the five-movement mini-suite 'Mines'. A typical Schoof gig around 1966–7 would have featured Can's future drummer respectably sporting a pin-sharp flannel suit, white shirt and tie. He can be heard on scattered surviving recordings, including with the Globe Unity Orchestra in 1966, early Quintet tapes with Swedish drummer Sven-Åke Johansson, and with the Schoof Quintet on a CD of brittle studio recordings in Munich that emerged in 2013.

Via Schoof, around this time Jaki's orbit would have intersected with that of Irmin Schmidt. Schoof had connections outside the immediate jazz milieu, and in 1966 Schmidt roped his group into a soundtrack project he was involved in: a low-budget effort directed by Karl Hamrun entitled *Zwei wie wir – und die Eltern wissen von nichts* (We Two – And the Parents Don't Know). 'I asked Manfred if he thought that Jaki, who I only knew from playing free, would play a regular rhythm. And it turned out that not only could he play a regular rhythm, he could play a *very* regular rhythm!'

'He did real explorations for how to form rhythms,' adds Schoof. 'He was thinking of the musicians, the melody instruments, how to combine his rhythm with them and leave them space to realise their ideas. I think he was thinking, "How can I give them space to play?"'

The Schoof band also took part in a recording of a contemporary music work by composer Bernd Alois Zimmermann called *The Numbered* (*Die Befristeten*), which came out on a Wergo label LP in 1967. The piece was written to accompany a radio production of a play by Elias Canetti, and was described as an 'Ode to Freedom in the Form of a Dance of Death'. The play's second act included a 'Jazz Episode', and featured Jaki's solo timbral explorations on the orchestra's percussion section, with beaters, cymbal resonances and so on interspersed with 'straight' free bop passages. For the composer, the attraction of incorporating jazz performers was that they offered 'A completely spontaneous way of playing certain instruments, which is not necessarily to be learned at school, but which somehow functions like doors or gates through which something wishes to exit.'

In a statement that anticipates Jaki's future direction as a drummer, Zimmermann went on: 'It's not an exaggeration to say that jazz musicians have a special feeling for rhythm, and therefore possess a special feeling for time as a whole. A composition that sets out to move within time, which, till now, has only been considered as a utopian reality (time, for instance, on the floor of the ocean), has to accept the following premises: there are other time proportions under water than on earth. Time there has other durations; the lengths become longer – the brevities briefer. The drummer is the connecting link between instrumental phases, like the variations of a passacaglia which link together.'[11]

But even as he was extracting odd, subaquatic sonorities from his percussion, Jaki was looking beyond the bubble he currently existed in. The fire at the heart of the most extreme free jazz had burnt itself out by the end of the sixties. 'I was fed up, and I was afraid there was no real freedom in it, because it was so limited. Things like pulse were forbidden in jazz, so I was frustrated with free jazz, and I felt as a drummer you have to play some pulse and rhythm, and not always play around the rhythm like they did. Don't play the direct rhythm, but just feel it and play around – I think that's nonsense. So I came back to a kind of monotony in the beginning of Can.'

'He was a very straight person,' replies Schoof, when I ask him what kind of a man Jaki was when he first got to know him. 'He liked perfect timekeeping, and the whole free stuff was not really his thing. He liked to play a full, straight and expressful music, not making noise . . . That's why he liked Ornette Coleman's music: [Coleman] was also writing melodies, which was for us interesting.' Schoof also experienced a foretaste of the perfectionist attitude Jaki would strike in Can: 'He was very critical in discussions about rhythm-making. He was really straight, and liked to discuss his own way of playing certain musical expressions, musical parts or pieces. Of course, he could really criticise the performances and opinions of people about rhythm, and when it was not fitting. Some of the musicians were afraid of him because he was so critical. Sometimes he defended his opinion about a straight rhythm and continuing "*genau*" [exact], a perfect rhythm. He had his own performance and we would argue about it. But we were never enemies while these discussions happened . . . In every group it's normal to make a constructive result, and Jaki's opinion was very strong in this way.'

Jaki was looking for a new direction, and when Irmin Schmidt called him up in 1967, asking if he could recommend a drummer for a new contemporary music group he was assembling, Jaki surely heard the sound of a new gate opening. After all, as Zimmermann had said: 'If there has ever been an auspicious time for the meeting between jazz and art music as it has been understood till now, that time is now.'

'I thought the group should have a jazz side and it should be somebody like Max Roach – this kind of polyrhythm,' says Irmin on why he chose to involve Jaki. 'I saw him every time I could get hold of him. He played sometimes in Germany in jazz festivals in Essen, where I saw him for the first time. I would get so fascinated by these rhythms he was playing, and with the elegance of Elvin Jones [*laughs*]. So that was my idea. And I had only heard Jaki playing free jazz, which I wasn't very much into. For the same reason as Jaki – seeing him a little bit helpless with a bow on the cymbal, and making all this kind of . . . I felt he was not really convinced about what he was doing. So when I asked him if he knows a really good jazz drummer in Germany who would join an experiment like this, I hadn't thought about Jaki. Not at all. And when he appeared, in the first moment, I thought, "Oh shit, I didn't want him! I don't want free jazz!"'

Jaki quickly reassured him that his time as a free jazz player was over – he was looking for a fresh start. 'I was listening to a lot of ethno music, Indian music, Arab music, all kinds of non-European music. I never was a real fan of some rock groups. I used to be a fan of some jazz heroes like Miles Davis and John Coltrane. And, of course, the drummers – though I don't play like them at all! Elvin Jones I admire still. You cannot copy him.

'I said goodbye to jazz in '68! I was fed up. It's like it's a similar situation like I have today. I think a kind of revolution is coming. Like in the late sixties, the revolution came in the form of all kinds of beat and pop music and pop art. And so I said goodbye to jazz in that time, to do something completely new, which I did with Can.'

The eyes of this curious crew were drawn towards a cluster of extraordinary objects currently inhabiting Irmin's flat. At the time, he had taken on loan a handful of sonic sculptures fabricated by the Baschet Brothers, François and Bernard – a connection facilitated by the gallerist Hans Mayer. These exquisite sonic 'cristals' were constructed from petal-shaped sheet metal and vibrating rods

that could be struck, bowed, plucked and vibrated, creating percussive or unearthly marimba-like sounds. They have been used
on the soundtracks to, among others, Jean Cocteau's *Testament
d'Orphée* and Steven Soderbergh's 2002 adaptation of Stanisław
Lem's *Solaris*. Irmin had borrowed some for a concert of new music
in Frankfurt, where he premiered his composition 'Hexapussy', and
they were waiting to be returned to Paris when the group held their
first meeting. So it was that some of the first vibrations the group
emitted stemmed from the otherworldly Baschet sculptures. Like
Can itself, sound sculpture was an anomaly within the field of contemporary music, and loosely tied together the separate disciplines
of instrument-building, avant-garde composition and improvisation.

Irmin recalls that 'Everybody got very excited and we made a
lot of noise on these instruments, and had a lot of fun. Everybody
was excited about the idea of this kind of group which doesn't know
what it will become. Jaki didn't like them very much, he found them
too limited. In a way he found them a bit stupid, and from his point
of view he was totally right. He gave a shit about the aesthetics.

'We fooled around, all were very fascinated by these objects.
But we couldn't say, "Tomorrow we start," because Holger and
Michael were in St Gallen, Jaki was still in the [Manfred Schoof]
group. And none of us had money to put into it.' Plus, they needed
a space to meet. They parted from that meeting having agreed to
dedicate themselves to this group. Over the next few months, they
would make the necessary practical arrangements – severing former
employment ties, converging on Cologne – to make it a reality.

They arranged a time and place to meet again for their first
rehearsal. 'What we do here', Holger told the others, 'will become
one day our life insurance that we give our children, and you don't
need to make insurance contracts with insurers. Just this music
will do.'[12]

4

A Castle with Better Equipment

Early in 1968 Irmin received a commission to provide music for a new film by director Peter F. Schneider. The connection was the film's producer, Hans Wewerka, the music publisher who had issued Irmin's *Album für Mogli* score, and who was a close friend of the director. Around May Irmin had made a few tentative beginnings on it, aided by David Johnson, but now, rather than approaching the work as a solo composer, he decided to unleash his new group on the project. It made sense: *Agilok & Blubbo* was set firmly in the contemporary milieu of young idealism, free love and violent revolutionary politics. The tale of two angry young men (Agilok and Blubbo themselves) plotting terror actions from a forest shack captured the ferment of Munich's Schwabing district, then a hotbed of bohemian progressivism, while the arrival of Michaela to distract them injected a titillating note of erotic interest. That role was played by Schneider's girlfriend, Rosy Rosy (real name Rosemarie Heinikel), already well known by then as an actress, singer and soft porn model who had occasionally sat in with Guru Guru and had publicly romanced the likes of Frank Zappa and Donovan.

The black-and-white film has become a lost cult item, but its soundtrack, credited to the Inner Space, turned up on CD in 2009, providing a rare glimpse of the group's earliest sounds. 'I don't consider the music we made to this film a Can work,' says Irmin. 'This is sort of – we didn't know yet really, we hadn't found . . . we were not yet Can. It was trying . . . to find a style for this film.' The group sounds remarkably tight and focused, considering it has only been a working unit for a few weeks. The second cue, 'Es zieht herauf', begins with some improvised small sounds, finger cymbals, tootling flutes, a Jew's harp, then comes a motif that recurs through several of the pieces involving a steady chuntering rhythm with a one-note bassline and a breezy melody on guitar. Michael makes effective use of a wah-wah pedal to create a serpentine guitar line notable for its clarity. On the more atmospheric 'Dialog zwischen Birken' we hear a group still rooted in the avant-garde. Cymbals are bowed until they rattle, a steady migraine whine of feedback and flute is carefully manipulated; it's a saucepan kept on the simmer, watched so that it doesn't boil over. A two-chord riff recurs through several of the other tracks, picked out hesitantly by Michael. 'Revolutionslied' reprises the see-sawing melody, with a camply overacted vocal part sung by the two protagonists.

Agilok & Blubbo was no cinematic masterpiece. As an attempt to satirise the modern German revolutionary spirit, it fell as flat as its jokes about 'reactionary love-making', and it suggested that all the utopian aspirations of a generation could be forgotten as soon as the promise of liberated, no-strings sex was on offer. But the film's reels did distribute the first public airing of the newly recorded group, even if, at the time, they were still calling themselves the Inner Space. The much later CD release of the music, however – licensed from Hans Wewerka's archives – included extra cuts from the same time that did not form part of the film soundtrack. 'Memographie' is a version of the film track 'Es zieht herauf' that opens with several minutes of sparse, almost tentative noises. There's lovely interplay between Johnson's high-overtone flute and Michael's bottled-wasp guitar lines in the background.

The shape of things to come was most clearly audible over the closing credits. In a track later titled 'Apokalypse', the Inner Space tore apart their earlier leitmotif, Michael abrasively soloing, Holger obsessively strumming one droning bass note, Jaki bashing away a quick-stepping rock beat. This is the first recorded manifestation of

Can's signature monotony, in which everything appears to be changing over an unchanging same.

Irmin approached Hans Mayer, the young friend of his from the art world. Considered a prodigy among gallerists for his taste in pop, op and kinetic art, Mayer had recently opened spaces in Esslingen (launched to the sound of a John Cage piece) and Krefeld, near Düsseldorf (the first curator to show work by Andy Warhol in Germany), and was accustomed to taking his morning shower under a Jean Tingüely water sculpture installed in his garden. In search of a base for the new group, Irmin had put the word out among his art world friends. When Mayer heard about Irmin's plans, he immediately thought of an art collector they were both acquainted with, Christoph Vohwinkel, who had just leased a historic mansion, Schloss Nörvenich, on the outskirts of Cologne and planned to turn it into an artistic commune.

Early in 1968 the still unnamed group were invited to make use of a room at Schloss Nörvenich. A castle has been standing on the site since at least the year 1400, although the visible part was extensively restored and augmented in the eighteenth century. Its cylindrical towers and witch's-hat turrets are quintessentially Germanic, a Teutonic fortress. By 1967 the castle was being rented by Vohwinkel, whose fortune came from the coal industry. 'He had the plan to restore the whole thing,' says Irmin, 'and make a kind of art centre. We became friends long before Can, before we really settled.'

Vohwinkel offered them a residence in one of Schloss Nörvenich's currently unoccupied chambers, rent-free for a year. They quickly moved in and set up in such a way that they had a twenty-four-hour salon that doubled as a workshop space and primitive recording studio. Or, as a German article on the group romantically portrayed it, 'living quarters, a studio, a centre for discussions, protection against the injustices of today's world, a special room with a neutral auditorium for electronic experiments, and a private refuge'.[1]

Irmin: 'Christoph – I never called him Christoph, it was always Herr Vohwinkel – was very helpful and even invested money into the thing. Then we had to figure out how we move into there and how Holger can come back, and how [Michael's] parents accept he does not start his studies in Münster, where he was already expected to start law. But he wasn't interested in law at all. So we had to figure out all this stuff.'

The rooms in the castle were large, rectangular spaces with high ceilings, still with their stucco mouldings dating back to the eighteenth-century rococo period. The entrance hall featured several ornate doors leading off to different parts of the interior, with whitewashed walls and pale marble slabs on the floor. 'It was a quite extensive mansion and it was not all restored,' Irmin remembers. 'It had a huge entrance hall, a staircase and an upper hallway which actually was our reverb. It had an exceptional, beautiful reverb, so we were always putting loudspeakers into the hallway and using it as a reverb chamber.'[2] They began to refer to this room as the Inner Space.

Inner Space: could any phrase be more appropriate, more suggestive of Can's destination and destiny? The opposite direction from outer space, in contrast to the tendency towards 'kosmische', or cosmic, rock perpetrated by many German acts such as Tangerine Dream, Cluster and Ash Ra Tempel several years later. It suggested a retreat to a psychological state, a self-examination, a hermetic environment, a laboratory of the mind. It is possible that, while in New York, Irmin heard about or even saw Andy Warhol's film *Outer and Inner Space* – premiered in January 1966 – and the phrase lodged in his mind. The film featured thirty-three minutes of Edie Sedgwick in conversation with herself, using innovative techniques with videotape (in fact, the first documented use of videotape by an artist). There were resonances with contemporary music too: US composer Aaron Copland's 1967 orchestral piece *Inscape* was a fantastically moody sound cloud. In turn, it took its title from Victorian poet Gerard Manley Hopkins, who coined the word, according to Copland's own take, to suggest 'a quasi-mystical illumination, a sudden perception of that deeper pattern, order, and unity which gives meaning to external forms'.[3] Can would themselves remain highly sensitised to their own perceptions of deeper patterns, while never losing the illuminative quality of vision. In a year of ramped-up space travel, with the first manned flight to the moon exactly a year away, the focus on space travel in popular culture was intensified. There was, of course, David Bowie's hit 'Space Oddity', describing Major Tom's nightmarishly uncanny voyage into the uncharted galaxy of his own mind. And yet this track was still earthed in folksy strummage and neo-romantic strings, while Can genuinely floated in a most peculiar way. Coincidentally, the following year an American artist, Doug Hall, unveiled his *Inner Space Simulation Module*. This was a networked pod in which the artist resided for a stretch of time, connected to the outside world by a spaghetti of live video, audio, film and other inputs. Spectators could contact and communicate with him via these electronic gateways; at the same time, the artist was cast as a virtual prisoner in a cell fed only by electronic media.

Nörvenich placed Inner Space Productions, as they began to refer to themselves, squarely at the centre of wider artistic activity. One of their co-tenants was sculptor Ulrich Rückriem, who went on to become a celebrated artist in Germany and abroad, making a number of public artworks in monumental stone structures. In 1968 he occupied a unit upstairs in the castle, along with his family, and according to Irmin, his materials almost took their place within Can's oeuvre too. 'He wanted to have a recording of the sounds that were made while chiselling stones. We hung out with a microphone and recorded the noise while he worked. He wanted to sell the recording for rather a lot of money . . . If we'd made a record with this recording, it would probably today be quite expensive . . . Rückriem's work sounds were on our tapes. But I think we cut them out.'[4]

The Baschet sound sculptures accompanied them to Nörvenich too. 'We started to change them,' says Irmin, 'build them differently, and then forgot how the originals were – lost a screw – and started fooling around. They are on *Delay 1968* – like on "Empress and the Ukraine King", I'm playing one of these instruments. And sometimes Jaki played his percussive things, dubbing things. And one day the Baschets had a truck in Cologne, because there was something going on, and they asked if they could take them to Paris again. And they came to this studio, and of course I had to admit that they were in quite a state, and they were so unhappy . . .'

The group quickly discovered that the medieval castle walls had not been designed with modern amplification in mind, and ingeniously soundproofed their unit with a mixture of egg boxes and mattresses. Surviving photos from this period show a group hiding out in padded, bunker-like surroundings, as if frantically cranking out humanity's final musical bulletins while awaiting some imminent nuclear attack. 'Studio' would possibly be an ambitious name for what they had here. Irmin played it down in a 1976 interview: 'It was just a room with two microphones, and an old Revox [*sic* – it was actually two], and a couple of loudspeakers and two amplifiers.'[5] But they used it as a conceptual artist might use his or her studio: held the space open for inspiration to breeze through. Distributed around Inner Space, the group acted as sonic dreamcatchers. 'What we did was not improvisation in the classical jazz sense,' Holger said, 'but instant composition. Like a football team. You know the goal, but you don't know at any moment where the ball is going. Permanent surprise. Editing, on the other hand, is an act of destroying. And you should not destroy something if you don't have a vision to establish it afterwards. If you have that vision you can go ahead and do that. Can was a band. The editing had to handled carefully, because it could destroy the character of the band.'[6] Another time he expressed the personal epiphany of this period: 'The most important thing was the fact that you didn't have to think beforehand. The power of the spontaneity. The result on the media. And the way of listening, and making conclusions and decisions. This was really something that was completely new to me after having studied for a long time.'[7]

Nineteen sixty-eight brought an increased urgency in the air. Irmin's artist friends were directing shock attacks on public spaces. 'I was very often in Berlin,' he says, 'visiting my painter friends, and there we had this game: you went on the Kurfürstendamm and you started a discussion with somebody – it was all fake – and you started screaming at each other, and then beating each other. And of course you had lots of spectators around you, a circle looking at these crazy students discussing totally un-understandable bullshit. Then you heard the police coming, and then you disappeared in the crowd. The police came, people got confused and were standing around, the police were beating . . . That was a good game because people got conscious about the police and the current situation. We did that only in Berlin. Only a few times was I one of the agitators.'

Irmin and Holger had trained with some of the masters of absolute music, and they weren't about to give that up lightly. 'We hadn't been politically involved,' said Holger, 'because at the time it was a very strong political base. In Can we were not participating in that so much. We understood that music is something absolute, not something like a medium that transports a message. This is something we didn't have, which was a big fight of Karlheinz Stockhausen and other composers, and he insisted on the fact that music is indivisible.'

'It affected the music because it affected us,' Michael Karoli told me. 'But we didn't think of it while we were making the music. We were not trying to express any philosophical or political ideas in our music. Of course, Can was also a child of the '68 thing, but it's not like we went into the studio and said, "It's '68 now, we're going to make this kind of music." It just came together; we were products of our time. And so was Can.'

'We got the spirit in '68,' added Jaki. 'In Germany it was the year of revolution. Students, new ideas came. Traditional things were finished at that time, and there was a completely new feeling.' David Johnson took a microphone onto the streets of Paris in May 1968, an undercover audio-documentarist getting right in among the rioting. Some of these tapes ended up spooled into Can's early performances.

By mid-1968 the magnanimous Herr Vohwinkel felt emboldened to invite them to play some music at an art opening. 'It was the first step,' Holger said. 'It was the first time that I had played live with electric amplification and loudspeakers! I was on bass and I was in charge of the tapes, as well as David who played flute, Micky was on guitar, Irmin on piano and organ, and Jaki on drums, percussion and flute.'[8]

A tape of Can's magical opening night was made, and extracts were released in 1984 as a cassette, *Prehistoric Future*.[9] By any standard, for a band in its first months of existence the session is remarkable, and sounds like nothing else of its time. A snapshot of the pop landscape in mid-1968 shows releases such as the Beach Boys' *Friends*, Johnny Cash's *At Folsom Prison*, Sly and the Family Stone's *Dance to the Music*, as well as more psychedelically inclined albums such as the Small Faces' *Ogdens' Nut Gone Flake*, Pink Floyd's *A Saucerful of Secrets*, the Zombies' *Odessey and Oracle* and the debut of NYC synth group the Silver Apples. The rest of the summer would see LPs by the Band (*Music from Big Pink*), the Doors (*Waiting for the Sun*), the Grateful Dead (*Anthem of the Sun*), Family (*Music in a Doll's House*), Buffalo Springfield (*Last Time Around*), Cream (*Wheels of Fire*), the Byrds (*Sweetheart of the Rodeo*) and Blue Cheer (*Outsideinside*). All significant way stations on the trail of the new rock, but compared to all these the noise spilling out of the Can sounded like emissions from a distant galaxy. Or, at least, lost space travellers creating a new primitive society after fetching up on a far-flung planet.

The set generally veers between passages of rhythmic rock and moments of liquid meltdown. Joined on this occasion by Manni Löhe – a local hippy artist located at the fringes of performance, actionism and avant-garde music who played flute and percussion and made the odd vocal interjection – the group are disembodied, out of sync with one another in the opening minutes. Then Holger drops in a snatch of talk radio, from which Löhe picks up a phrase, which cues the band in to a galvanised four-square motorik groove. Flute and a smashed Baschet sculpture compete for dominance. Holger's bass shadows Jaki's pulse; Michael's guitar strays over the top like an elk in search of its young.

Towards the end of the first half, Jaki clicks into free jazz mode, as Johnson and Löhe surround him with curlicues of flute. Johnson's tapes of crowds demonstrating during the previous month's riots in Paris are spun into the mix, manipulated by Holger to create unsteady pitch-shifting effects. A few minutes earlier, it was the incongruous polyphonic religious music of Franco-Flemish Renaissance composer Pierre de la Rue; now, the sound of monastic contemplation has been replaced by a chorus of dissent, broadcast direct from the streets of Paris. Tapes of early music were frequently used by the Inner Space group at this time. 'I think that David had found a book of [Adam] de la Halle compositions at my house,' recalls Irmin, 'and brought it with him to the studio. Before Can, I'd been occupied with the music of the fourteenth and fifteenth centuries: Vitry, Machaut, Adam de la Halle. I still like this music very much . . . I've imagined that this music used to be played with a totally different kind of power. In those days, when you went to church, you had a different sort of ardour, a belief that you might find today, if at all, in certain gospel things. I believe that a lot of this music . . . often had an unbelievable rhythm; the people sang hard, so that they yelled it out. You'll find a lot of these musical ideas in early Can tracks.'

These 'samples' of early music add depth and texture to the picture. But Can's own spontaneous compositions can also be heard taking shape, as when, around five minutes into the second half, Michael's guitar tolls out the hymn-like refrain from the theme tune to *Agilok & Blubbo*.

Later memories of this event emphasise the violence on show, which became more than implicit as, carried away with the moment, Irmin obliterated an old piano standing in the space. 'I had the open piano in front of me, and I was playing a Remington electric shaver on the strings, and one night I went into it and it made a horrible sound when the strings came off, so I destroyed it in one of these evenings. It's on this tape, *Prehistoric Future* – "Get the Can" was the name, and later I didn't like it at all. As a performance we were in a kind of *"Wahn"* – obsession – but later I didn't like it. Holger likes it, but it describes the beginning, freeing ourselves . . . at least, Holger and me are the most destructive ones. And later on that tape you hear Holger screaming in a hysterical voice, and me making horrible noises destructing the piano. And people got amazed, they thought, "This is really modern . . ."'

In spite of Manni Löhe's negligible vocal interjections on this one occasion, at this point the group was essentially an instrumental quintet. In the surviving tape of the night, the group are clearly trying to exorcise musical ghosts, decontaminating themselves from all the outside influences and musics that have preceded and shaped them, inching their way from the uniformed towards the unformed. Once they had reached this limit, their task was to curb and reshape such outright brutality. In this the special chemistry of the individuals played a crucial part.

Irmin: 'Our performances in the beginning were really chaotic noise, and had nothing very much to do with music. Jaki was sitting there, drumming, drumming drumming drumming, really heavy. And Holger and me just making wild noises, and Micky being . . . quite helpless, he didn't like this aggression. He was not an aggressive person at all. I am much more aggressive, and all three of us, Holger, Jaki and me, can be very aggressive. But Michael was sort of unable to be aggressive. He didn't like it very much. He tried to convince us of the uselessness of only aggression.'

In July Irmin's film industry connections delivered the group's first commission. German public broadcaster ARD needed music for *Das Millionenspiel* (The Game of Millions), an adaptation of American writer Robert Sheckley's short story 'The Prize of Peril'. *Das Millionenspiel* expressed a new self-consciousness about the medium of television and a willingness to satirise and critique both its methods and the inflated desires it created among its viewers. The film, made for television and directed by Tom Toelle, is a nightmare near-future speculation in which Germany's most popular TV show involves members of the public being manhunted for days on end while striving to evade capture and grab a prize of one million marks. When it was aired in October 1970, many viewers were fooled by the film's 'documentary' segments into believing the action and the game were real, bombarding the station with phone calls and letters of complaint (plus the odd application to take part in a future contest). The music, as heard in the opening track of *The Lost Tapes* collection issued in 2012, is full of tension and release, with a dystopian electronic tremoloed amp hum and hesitant tapped beat. The 'chase music' is a headlong '*Batman* Theme'-type thrash with surf guitar and garish atonal chords on Irmin's organ. Jaki's strange double-tracked hi-hat effect was later used on 'Yoo Doo Right'. Gerd Dudek from the Manfred Schoof jazz group supplies a marauding saxophone solo. The film's opening scene features the television studio's choreographed dance troupe, clad in multicoloured body-hugging suits, throwing synchronised moves to the Inner Space's groovy beat.

'We would often spend hours, sometimes days, transforming the studio, the space, into a sound installation,' said Irmin in the sleeve notes to *The Lost Tapes*. 'A microphone, a speaker and maybe a bit of delay would be enough to make the room resonate. Every little noise, every sound became meaningful: steps, a chair, a few words, an accidental sound created by touching an instrument . . . When we were lucky a magical sound-atmosphere would appear.'[10] And so it does on 'Evening All Day', a collage of fragments from such improvisations released as part of *The Lost Tapes*. Irmin performs gilded sweeps of the inside of a piano, an effect reminiscent of Alice Coltrane's harps on 'Journey in Satchidananda' of that year. Holger's bass wanders through the mix searching for a key, while Michael's hammered-on guitar strings add to the layers of glimmering. Later, a wholly other passage emerges, more hushed and hunched, where glockenspiel and acoustic guitar are the delicate foils to ticking-over percussion, snide comments from the organ and a perky Jew's harp.

'Oh, we played on anything,' confirmed Michael. 'A lot of the sounds we made come from bottles and saucepans and stamping on the floor, and it's also a very important concept which I have also developed afterwards, is where to exactly place a microphone so that anything you hit or rub or blow into makes music. There is one point, if you bring the microphone there and find the point, you can play a whole symphony on a radiator.'

Neither totally free nor ever quite coalescing into any unified rhythmic direction, pieces like this placed the group utterly between the rock and experimental categories in the sixties. But if they genuinely wished to appeal more to the rock audience than to the classical aficionado, they still needed a focal point.

5

The Last Kick Towards Rock

Rewind to 27 April 1968, and a young American art student, Malcolm Mooney, is embarking on an Icelandair plane with his friend, Joshua Zim, as they begin the journey of a lifetime. They fly from New York via Reykjavik to Luxembourg, then hitch a ride to Paris, arriving just as the student riots are kicking off. The friends are hoping to kill two birds with one stone. They can use Europe as a base to travel the already well-trodden hippy trail around the Mediterranean, Middle East and India; and in doing so, they'll be uncontactable when their Vietnam draft papers land on their doormats back home in New York.

Malcolm has been studying on the arts programme at Boston University, and he has ambitions to become a painter and sculptor. Born in 1948 (he has never revealed his precise birth date), he spent his early life in Westchester County, and later moved in with his sister in the Mission Hill district of Boston. His father was a jazz piano player who had once been taught in North Carolina by a former teacher of Nina Simone. Malcolm once recalled being taken backstage at the Village Gate to meet the great jazz diva. His sister also took up the piano, while Malcolm tried first the accordion, then the clarinet. One time his dad interrupted his listening to the soft doo-wop of Frankie Lymon's 'Why Do Fools Fall in Love?' and put on Ornette Coleman's *Change of the Century*, one of the great free jazz LPs of the early sixties, which turned the young Mooney's head. Shortly afterwards, he tried to inject an Ornette-style clarinet solo into a concert by his school band, to horrified looks from his musical director and his mother in the audience. In his teens he also joined his local church choir, as well as a doo-wop group called the Six

Fifths. He was drawn more and more towards jazz – he was given a saxophone as a gift – and occasionally played with a friend of his, Chuck Davis, a sax player who had lived in Europe for twelve years. But his career was tending more towards the visual arts: he had an aptitude for drawing and painting, and he was admitted to the arts faculty of Boston University.

Come 1967, and the nineteen-year-old Malcolm – like thousands of fellow young Americans – feared the draft letter arriving in his mailbox. He had been working a handful of brief jobs – a chef and assisting at his father's silkscreen printing press ('My first job was to answer the phone and say he's not here,' he once said). Opposition to the Vietnam war was rising swiftly, in direct proportion to the spread of the counter-culture and hippy movement, and in this media war the horrors were plain to see on news bulletins and newspaper front pages. Although there was a military history in Malcolm's family – his father had been in the navy, and he had an uncle in the Tuskegee Airmen – they reacted sympathetically when he said he would prefer not to fight. 'I went down to the draft [office], and talked to a major, and at that time I decided I just can't do it. I wanted to be a conscientious objector.'[1] The army gave Mooney a nine-month window to process his request. This is when he formed the plan to vanish into the big world, carrying nothing but his sax and a change of clothes in a duffel bag. His friend Zim had a particular desire to meet the spiritual leader Meher Baba in India. Assuming the alias Desse Barama (the title of a tune by the Egyptian composer and oud player Hamza El Din, meaning 'peace'), Malcolm joined the pilgrimage.

In Paris, Zim, a Harvard student, looked up a young composer he had been put in touch with by some of his university friends. Serge Tcherepnin was a twenty-six-year-old of Russian-Chinese descent, born and raised in Paris, later educated in the US. Tcherepnin's father and grandfather were both celebrated Russian composers, and Serge himself had trained in France under Nadia Boulanger, before doing the familiar apprenticeship on music courses at Darmstadt and, later, Cologne between 1966 and 1968. While there, he remembers 'confiding to a friend that I had just seen a blonde Monica Vitti, but better'. It was Hildegard Schmidt, who swiftly introduced him to her husband Irmin. They became firm friends, and Irmin ended up playing the saxophone part at the premiere of Tcherepnin's *Morning After Piece* in 1966. Malcolm's circle of friends in Boston included Serge's brother Ivan and his wife, and via this loose network Tcherepnin invited Malcolm to use his apartment in Paris as a base while he was in the country. Also staying there at the time was the Portuguese composer Emmanuel Nunes, whose current work in progress was a vocal composition to be sung by eight hundred million Chinese singers. Malcolm was struck by Nunes's and Tcherepnin's expansive conceptions and intrigued by the world of sound they represented. 'I remember [Malcolm] telling me about a project of his for a large musical sculpture he wanted to build on a hill overlooking the Pacific,' Tcherepnin says. 'It would emit tones generated by large wind pipes catching the wind and surf. But I didn't think him a musician – a painter is what he said he was.'

Soon, though, Mooney and Zim lit out for deeper territory, making extra cash by busking. Sticking out their thumbs on the motorway, they hiked southwards through France, reaching Avignon and Lyon, where a helpful fellow named Joe Palucca heard them on the street and invited them to perform in a bar, Malcolm on sax, Joshua on piano. With a little extra money in their pockets, intending to continue their eastward journey by camel across north Africa, they headed for the southern coast of Spain to get a passage to Morocco. But the crossing was being shut down at the time and they were blocked at the port of Algeciras. Instead, they spent three weeks in the Balearic island of Formentera, the site of a lively – or, rather, permanently stoned – hippy artists' colony. 'We stayed in Formentera for three weeks,' said Malcolm, 'and we had this idea about designing plates. I go to the hardware store and I buy a bag of cement. I go down to the ocean, the Mediterranean, and I carve out in the sand the idea for these plates. And the plates were supposed to be lima bean shape, and I cast them in the sand and they were cement. I didn't think about the weight of these plates, but I packed them in my duffel bag, which I carried all over the world.'[2]

Lugging his cargo of monumental crockery, he and Zim passed through Salzburg in Austria, before embarking on a train to Turkey. Fetching up in Istanbul, Malcolm received another signal about the entrancing power of music. 'Behind the Topkapi Palace is a huge field,' he recalled, 'and I don't know if you've seen cartoons where there's a scent of food and somebody floating – well, there was this music coming from the bottom of this hill. And I was like, where is this music coming from? We went to this field, and there were these wrestlers dressed in black leather pants, hand-sewn, and the guy was the oil can. And there were these musicians in the corner of the field, oud, a shehnai player, harmonium player and the drummer. And they're playing while these guys do a wrestle-off. So it's like wrestle-mania. And they are playing music while they are doing this. I watched this and then there was this big uproar, and this guy comes walking down a pathway, and I say, what's all this noise about? And they said, he's the world champ.

'We're in Turkey, they're saying this guy is their champ. And that made me think about baseball at home – they call it the World Series. And I'm thinking: where's the rest of the world in the World Series? This is 1968 . . . It was an awakening.'[3]

Mooney and Zim hitched onwards, scoring a ride into pre-revolutionary Persia with the Iranian owner of a brand-new Ford Mustang. 'We found him at the University there, and he was going home. He had just had his car shipped from the States, and . . . he said no one in Tehran had a Mustang. I remember Ankara because it's north and the best rice I've ever had in my whole life. At one point in the mountains they were making yogurt, in a ceramic bowl with a piece of lemon on the top . . . You could see things, you could smell things, it was an opening up of my thoughts about how life was in other places. In Tehran everybody drove a Mercedes, and we had a great time. We got a bus east to the desert, and we did Kandahar and Lahore . . . and we hid in Karachi, and from there we got a boat to Mumbai/Bombay, we stayed in a minus-seven star hotel in Bombay. I bought a shehnai and . . . three flutes.

'We're in India now, with my plates and my saxophone and my shehnai. And in the streets of India, it was musical . . . People were making music continually. We stayed for a while then turned around and went back, headed home. To the Khyber Pass, and back to Germany. It's all overland, we hitch-hiked from Tehran . . . We get a ride with a guy in a very small car, with a lot of rugs, and we're heading back to Europe, and we get to the Bulgarian border and the Bulgarians say you have to get out of the country within twenty-four hours. We get to the border and this guy who was driving says, I gotta go. He owns the car. So I said "where?", and he leaves us with the car. We really can't go anywhere, we don't have the papers for the car. I know this is crazy . . . The first night we sat in this pumpkin field, and we woke up and there's a guy there with a rifle. And then two days later [the driver] shows up again.'

At their next stop, Munich, reality started to catch up with them again when they made contact with the American Embassy. 'The American council had told us to go back home, leave Germany. And I was on the verge of being terrified about the war, not about death so much, but about killing somebody. I couldn't understand because my thought was, everybody talks about the Bible, Christianity, "thou shalt not kill", but in terms of necessity. Kill for country and government.'[4] Malcolm Mooney's summer vacation was almost over.

Arriving back at Serge Tcherepnin's Paris residence around late August or early September, Malcolm found the apartment crammed with sound sculptures. He also met Hildegard Schmidt, who was borrowing the Paris flat while visiting the Folies Bergère.

On discovering he was an artist, she invited Malcolm to come to Cologne and make connections with the German art world. Zim was upset that his girlfriend back home had just married his best friend, and he proposed a Napoleon-style exile on the island of Elba. For Malcolm, the prospect of having an artist's studio in which to paint and sculpt was more tempting: 'I said, "I'm not going to be isolated on Elba, I'll go to Cologne." Serge encouraged me . . .' He scraped together the last of his cash, and a few days later boarded an early-morning train. 'I knew Malcolm would be a big hit in the Schmidt household showing up in Cologne,' says Tcherepnin.[5]

'There was a communication mix-up,' says Malcolm. 'Hildegard was talking about a recording studio. I didn't have any money, about enough for a train fare. So one night I left. So off to Cologne. Hildegard had given me their home address and telephone number. Arrived there and called the house. No one answered. I said, "What am I doing here?" So I got on the Strassenbahn. Went out and found their house. I was walking around a big complex. And I met this woman walking this dog, and I asked where this address is. She said, "Oh yes, I'm staying there also." I said, "Do you know Irmin Schmidt?" She said, "Yes, Irmin's my brother." So I got to Irmin's house, and there were three people there: Irmin, Michael and Holger. They were all sitting round a table, and I walk in. Apparently, they were notified I was coming. I don't know how. We talked for a minute about I don't know what. And I told them that I came about a studio. And at that point it was money versus a place to stay – circumstances. I told Irmin that I met his wife and blah blah, and he said, "Can you sing?" He said, "We're trying to organise a group, and would you be interested in singing in a group?" I told him the only singing I had done was with a church, back when I was a kid.

'So that's how it started. That day or that afternoon or the next day we went to the castle for, I guess, a try-out.'

Irmin and Hildegard promised to help Desse ('I didn't use Malcolm at all,' he says) make some useful connections with their artistic friends, such as Hans Mayer and Christoph Vohwinkel. Meanwhile, he became casually drawn into the life of the group. 'I didn't understand what I was doing there. I had the feeling, looking back on it, that too much drugs might be a problem for me. I'm talking about alcohol, smoke, marijuana . . . That whole thing was new for me . . . I'd say, half a year prior to that I think I smoked my first joint. For me that was a problem. Anyway, I was trying to get myself to a point where I was getting away from the whole thing.'[6]

On his first visit to Schloss Nörvenich, they play him a tape of one recent instrumental track: a sweepingly rhythmic piece, with a cicada warble on the organ, a deviously deep bassline and a frenetic drum line. Holger rewinds and hits the red button. Malcolm, moved to join in, steps up to a microphone, takes a breath, and words shower down over the tape like a monsoon. 'Look at the face of mine behind the kerb, through the layers found in urban drift, indeed that is you / And with you, mother screams, "I am mother", woman screams, "I am fertile," and the father cannot yell . . .'

The lyrics are not easy to decipher, but it's not fanciful to imagine them tangentially inspired by the sensory overload of Malcolm's recent travels in the developing world, with lines such as: 'You may drift there if you want to, luggage fits inside your pocket like a bill'; 'Mother who in pain creating, woman who just lies there waiting'; 'All has been forgotten and the plastic turns to rotten rays and smells'. Malcolm cycles around this rosary of vivid images that summon up impressions of the abject streets of a city like Bombay, and falls back on breathy abstraction ('Heh-*huh*-uh-huh-*euh*') in the middle, a vocal tic that would become a signature.

Malcolm: 'It was based on some kind of theory I had, which was based on a writing I had done between Istanbul and Bombay. It was about India, about a banyan tree. And it was actually a story about Zim, the guy I was travelling with, and his girlfriend, and I guess my girlfriend. It all took place in a tree, a banyan tree, which was supposed to be one of the largish trees of India. And I remember there was one they were talking about which happened to be one hundred and fifty to two hundred feet wide, loads of branches, which made it like a city street.'[7]

'Father Cannot Yell' was entirely unplanned, but this very take would end up as the first track on the Can's debut album, *Monster Movie*. It represented a massive evolutionary leap for the group, and even in 1976 one of their press releases was referring to the track as a 'Ski-Run into the New Neurology'.[8] 'Can wasn't sure yet which way musically to go till Malcolm jumped one day to the microphone and pushed us into A RHYTHM,' Holger admitted.[9] British rock critic Ian MacDonald called this moment 'one of the most urgent, explosive, and majestic ad-libs a rock group has ever laid down'.[10]

The Can had selected as its latest component one more renegade artist, who seemed instinctively to feel and deliver what was lacking. For Irmin, Malcolm arriving gave the group 'the last kick toward rock'.[11] Malcolm's vocal acted as a 'kind of handle for the listener, or some kind of anchor where you can sort of jump on and all of a sudden it's the opening, the mouth . . . it's the mouth of the group. In every sense, it sucks the listener in.'

'I remember when "Father Cannot Yell" was done,' says Irmin. 'I could listen to that piece twenty times and still not find anything wrong on it. And that was the first time, on the first piece, that I got really in total sync with what we had done and what we were doing. I took it on tape and played it to everybody who wanted and not wanted to listen to it, and got a very strong response to it because it was so different to anything anybody had heard before, and it sounded so different. That was actually the first moment with Can, when "Father Cannot Yell" was on tape. It was not the moment playing it, it was the moment when we really all said, "That's the piece." That was a sort of total acceptance of my existence with this group, and of course that happened while working. I remember working on "Aumgn" [three years later], specially together with Holger, when we edited the pieces together and collaged and dubbed one tape with another tape – which was really what we actually came from – that was also a moment where I felt that's what I wanted to do, listening to how this piece was growing. And doing it together in a group was very fulfilling.'

As they continued to work together over the following days and weeks, Malcolm's methods gelled even tighter with the group's own attitude. He took phrases out of the air, grabbed offhand snippets he had heard in conversation, or observational miniatures, and shoehorned them into the music, strange syntax and all. The flat he was sharing with Jaki was close to Cologne railway station, with its elevated tracks: this became 'I can hear the train whistle outside my door'. '"Four or five colours will make the ears blind" – Jaki said that'; 'Correction: the coat hanger should be upside down' – Malcolm's 'inhuman genius'[12] processed mundane sights and objects and made them profoundly uneasy and strange. He adapted some of his imagery from a vivid diary he had kept while travelling in the East. 'I started writing about the trip, kept notes about different people we met, images I saw,' says Malcolm, adding, 'Most of the book was burnt in the fireplace at Jaki's house for warmth – we had a charcoal stove.'

An early example of this channelling took place at one of the group's first appearances in front of an audience, at Schloss Nörvenich. The exact date is hard to determine, but Malcolm recalls it took place during the second Kölner Kunstmarkt, an annual art event in the city, which in 1968 happened between 15 and 20 October. Heard on the track 'Waiting for the Streetcar', on *The Lost Tapes*, the group was in hustling, garage-punk mode, repeating the same riff over and over for half an hour or more, as if daring each other to ring any changes. Malcolm's antenna has picked up one of the audience mentioning they are ready to go home, and are holding on for their mode of transport to arrive. Malcolm repeats the phrase 'Waiting for the streetcar / Are you waiting for the streetcar?', the words accumulating in intensity and menace, as if he's spitting them back in the speaker's face. 'In a way this is pop art,' Irmin has observed. 'These lyrics are like Warhol putting Brillo cartons on top of one another. Suddenly the banality of the Brillo carton becomes art and the banality of this sentence repeated in this context of music becomes something more than just a sentence.'[13] The surviving track fades in and out, so it's clear the group went on far longer than the ten minutes preserved here. 'I don't know about the rest of them,' Malcolm said of the show, 'but I was not ready to perform in front of anybody. But I drank a bit and I went up there and I started singing. [There was] no planned performance at that time. And we played from seven o'clock to two o'clock in the morning . . . At that point I had no songs that I had invented, we were just sort of getting to know each other really, the group. So we played, played and played and played. And it's a funny thing to look out – some of the time I had my eyes closed – but people seemed to be . . . carrying on conversations, in fact it reminded me of . . . [Charles] Mingus when he was playing at the Five Spot and he said, OK, don't touch the cash register, don't clink any glasses, be quiet. Demand some respect from the audience. In my case I wish I could have been on the same level as Mingus, but somehow I looked on myself then as being not really worthy of drawing that much attention to myself, and also I was quite egotistical in that situation. I like perfection.'[14]

'Deadly Doris', also on *The Lost Tapes*, is another example of Malcolm's infernally moronic monotone and his particular understanding of Jaki's rhythmic urgency.

Holger: 'When Malcolm dropped in, he was sort of a driving locomotive. Rhythmically, he was the pusher. So he had to push us, in a way. We had to follow him; we couldn't stand behind him. That was the reason we got into this rock direction, more or less. And when he left, we had some sort of rhythm experience. And that was the right time, when we met Damo [Suzuki], because he didn't have this attitude. He needed a group which was pushing him. So the timing for these two singers was perfect.'

'To Jaki,' remembered Michael, 'he was probably the most important point of reference in the band. I've never heard anything like that elsewhere. How those two fed each other with sounds! I had a strong personal, almost a love relationship with Malcolm. He, on the other hand, was in love with my sister. But that's got nothing to do with anything. He was something completely wonderful to me, because he forced this band – which was already an organism – to become an adult organism. He brought a sort of sexual maturity into the band.'[15]

Holger: 'He actually fitted perfectly into Can's "working methods" as he was inexperienced, as were we all. There simply were no methods; there was just a strong will by everyone to succeed in getting something on tape. Our methods consisted mainly of daily rituals. They were actually our motor to get on through the day. One of these rituals was our fights and quarrels. It was the turn of each of us being on duty to start arguing in order to keep that Can engine running. Most of the time Malcolm kept out of them. That might be because we could easily fall back into the German language when fighting.' Here, in its infancy, the group was finally developing a language, and fighting to define itself.

So in the autumn of 1968 Malcolm is in Cologne, his funds dried up. He cannot return to the States for fear of the draft. The 'studio' is not quite what he had been led to expect, but he seems to have fallen in with a pretty intriguing gang who are offering accommodation, comradeship and who knows what else. One brief loose end to clear up: he needs to nip over to Denmark to collect his duffel bag, saxophone and cement plates, which he had left with the Iranian driver. He makes the trip, and by the time he comes back he seems to have joined a band, one that holds out the promise of 'a landscape, a really large place to be'.[16]

The group had another engagement: to finish off music Irmin had composed for a soft porn film directed by Kobi Jaeger, *Kamasutra*

– *Vollendung der Liebe* (translated as *Kama Sutra – Consummation of Love*). Jaeger had founded Stern TV in Germany in 1963, and had produced and directed a series of travelogues and documentaries around the world. *Kamasutra* was a pet project that contrasts the sexual lives of two Western couples with some counterparts in India, where couples practising the art of Kama Sutra achieve erotic fulfilment in dreamy, idyllic surroundings. The Europeans are hassled, tired of their marriages or selfish in their attempts to achieve their desire. The Indian characters serve as an instruction manual, pointing up the supposed failure of European lovers to coax each other towards new, ever-changing varieties of sexual bliss.

Parts of this soundtrack were as conventional as the Inner Space ever sounded. David Johnson's flute found a natural habitat in 'I'm Hiding My Nightingale', sung by Margarete Juvan. A fair amount of the incidental music recalls the work of contemporaries Popol Vuh, who famously soundtracked Werner Herzog's *Aguirre, the Wrath of God* in 1972. The Inner Space pick up on the Indian/oriental elements and generate their own strain of Indo–jazz fusion, in a manner they would later pursue in their 'Ethnological Forgery Series' ('EFS'). On a cue titled 'In Kalkutta I', Jaki keeps up a spate of beats on a pair of tablas, while tendrils of guitar and flute creep around the edges.

'Im Tempel' inventively spins off the imagined sound of an Indian zither – probably Irmin strumming the inside of the piano with broad strokes. A track named 'There Was a Man' is Malcolm performing 'Man Named Joe', an inferior mix of a track included on *Delay 1968*. 'Mundharmonika Beat' is as straight a blues as the group ever recorded, with the lead line taken by a harmonica and Jaki coralling the rhythm into the Germanic groove that would soon be taken up by Klaus Dinger in the propulsive Neu!.

Artistically and financially, films like this and *Agilok & Blubbo* were baby steps. Irmin doesn't recall getting paid much for *Agilok & Blubbo*, although 'there was more money for *Kamasutra*. And then

Malcolm appeared and they still hadn't paid. And then one day in Munich, we were sitting in a café, because we were already involved in some new film, and then all of a sudden this producer came in who still owed us quite a lot of money. Malcolm took him, like in a gangster film, up against the wall with one hand, and slapped him left and right, and said, "This is only a warning! We are leaving Munich in two or three days, by then the money is here. Remember, it's only a warning." He slapped him quite heavily! And we got the money – all of a sudden it was there. So sometimes this kind of trick works.'

The *Kamasutra* soundtrack was still credited to the Inner Space, the blanket alias they were giving to all activities stemming from their workshop – as well as being the name of the studio itself. Apart from one song, by the end of 1968 none of the Inner Space's officially completed projects so far – the three soundtracks – featured Malcolm. The group was still in a loose, informal, unfinished state (and perhaps always would be). There is the sense that Malcolm is participating, but his status in the group has not been fully resolved – possibly the source of some tension between David Johnson and the rest. Over the autumn of 1968 Malcolm has been coming to the studio but, when not needed, assisting in Ulrich Rückriem's sculpture workshop. 'He hired me,' says Malcolm. 'And I really wanted to, [it was] my dream. At that time I didn't have my degree, I was still at Boston University when I left [the US]. There were a couple of projects – I'm just the guy that goes along with him and helps him install. He did a piece for a cemetery, a rebar cross, and also we installed what looks like horseshoes, or a U-shaped rebar, like a snake motion on the ground. I remember it was winter, because we went out there and hammered these things into the earth.'

But when Malcolm takes the mic, it's like he hits the group over the head with a hammer. It seems to accelerate away at a different tangent to Johnson's preference, one that catapults them into the new world of primitivist experimental rock – the Velvet Underground, Frank Zappa (both of whom had their tentacles in the contemporary music and free jazz worlds). 'Unity is not to be attained simply by calling yourselves unified,' says Johnson in hindsight. 'Desse was a wonderful person, even if he did have an over-proportional influence – singers often do. Trying to strengthen an ensemble by expansion usually has the opposite effect, tearing itself apart more than unifying or expanding.'

As the year wore on, the great leap forward from post-Darmstadt ensemble to garage band was too much to handle. Johnson was still hearing the group's music with ears attuned to the idiom of avant-garde post-war composition at its most rarefied.

Abstract, refusing to take prisoners and developing organically and slowly over long durations, the type of music David Johnson wanted the Inner Space to commit to was also a kind of music that involved procedures and techniques that Irmin and Holger had been exposed to for years already; the kind of sounds they associated with the high-minded, controlling Stockhausen. Unlike rock 'n' roll, it often fell on deaf ears and inert bodies.

'As far as I was concerned,' says Johnson, 'most of the sound material which got used in Can's music depended on too much constantly high-speed and flat, loud dynamics.' As well as alluding to nightly drives to a 'secret temple' near Nörvenich – memories that are 'mixed with suffering breakdowns after too much hashish' – Johnson attributes his departure to fundamental musical differences. 'We all felt the tension of having to make choices and going different ways. Remaining in the group would have demanded too much unstrained dedication, which cannot be mustered up artificially.'

'I thought there was tension,' says Malcolm, 'but I have nothing against David, he's a good musician. It might have been based on different directions. My direction with the band is not something where I say, "We gotta do it this way." I just started doing what I wanted to do. And I think everybody said, "Let's go in that direction."'

'When it became more rock, then [David] didn't like it,' says Irmin. 'And he couldn't deal with Malcolm, with his craziness and spontaneity and totally unforeseen sudden outbursts . . . it was basically not the music he wanted to do. He became quite unhappy, actually. He accepted more this Cardew or Rzewski kind of direction. I think he was also sad because he had expected something else, and it didn't happen. And he became . . . he had a sad love story, and it came all together. He was in love with somebody who didn't want him, but then he found a good wife. Then life went quite well for him afterwards.'

Johnson founded the Feedback Studio for electronic music with Rolf Gehlhaar in 1970. In the same year he accompanied Stockhausen to the Osaka World's Fair, where his music was played in a Buckminster Fuller geodesic dome. Two years later, Johnson had a daughter with Mary Bauermeister, who had been married to Stockhausen since 1967. He continued making and teaching contemporary music, and was finally appointed as the director of the electronic studio at the Music Academy in Basel, Switzerland. In the mid-eighties he returned to play flute on one of Irmin's television soundtracks.

Now, everybody had to decide whether this was going to be a commitment or not. For Holger, it meant abandoning the world of Stockhausen and academic tape composition. Jaki cast off from his lucrative, if predictable, jazz drummer's stool. For Michael, it meant giving up a career in law and disappointing his ambitious parents. 'Michael had to fight with his family,' says Irmin. 'I had to go, and Holger did too, to talk to his father and say that it's really something serious. He reluctantly gave in. When the first record came out, at least he liked "Father Cannot Yell". He was very convinced that we had a marvellous group. And it was Wagner[ian], heavy, symphonic, which of course comes from this place I come from. Holger's bass is very symphonic on it. He heard that piece, which we had before anything else we had on tape, and it was the first piece we played to others. And then he was sort of impressed. He said music should have power, should have some depth and power, and he was very much into Romantic [music].'

Irmin: 'My parents were first quite disappointed that I gave up the promising conductor's career – for which they had given everything, without any reluctance, had been supporting me with everything they could. After the war we had lost everything, had very little money, but they did everything so that I could study music. My father would have loved it if I could have been like him, become an architect, because I was quite gifted at that.'

As David left, Malcolm's position in the group was firmed up. The big event kicking off 1969 in Cologne was the appearance of Jimi Hendrix at the Sporthalle on 13 January. Attending was some kind of bonding exercise, Malcolm recalled, and also reinforced their conviction about moving in a more rock direction. 'From that day on,' he said, 'we were doing some brainstorming on what the name was going to be.'[7]

They didn't quite feel comfortable with Inner Space Productions as a band name, and with bookings for gigs, festivals, soundtracks and a possible album deal starting to emerge, they needed to take a decision. 'We didn't want to get mixed up with these hippies . . . and Inner Space sounded very hippy-esque,' says Irmin. 'It was nice for a production, because it was a studio . . . But we didn't like it as a group name, and we were always discussing group names.' Irmin credits Malcolm and Jaki for suggesting the word 'Can'. 'And since it's very short, very . . . we liked it. Said, "Yeah, why not?" Malcolm said, in New York slang, it means also "ass", so we were totally *d'accord*. And "Can" was neutral – it was the time Warhol had made his [Campbell's soup] can [screenprints], and so cans were something . . . That made sense for me, and for everybody. So we said, "Can, yeah." First we were *the* Can, then we got rid of the "the". We thought the Can was one word too much! And all the groups were "the . . .". Then it was a bit difficult to get rid of the "the" in the media, but as time went by we were Can. And I still think it was a good decision. It's a good name, because you remember it easily.'

'Can' is:
To be able, to have sufficient power
To know, to have skill
A portable metal container for food or film reels
Positivity (can do)
Life, soul (Turkish)
Cannabis (Japanese slang)
Toilet (US slang)
Cancan, popular dance by Jacques Offenbach (born in Cologne)
Communism, Anarchism, Nihilism (rumour spread by band members)

6

Thieves of Fire

Shortly after watching the Jimi Hendrix Experience, the group recorded the tenth in their occasional 'Ethnological Forgery Series', or 'EFS'. Almost none of Can's 'EFS' tracks appeared on any of their official albums, but these miniatures, or fragments, have turned up on rarities compilations, such as *Unlimited Edition* and *The Lost Tapes*. 'EFS' was how Can dubbed their occasional dabblings in which they indulged their fascination with non-Western instruments, scales and rhythms. Surviving footage and photos of their studio spaces show glimpses of an expanded instrumentarium of pan pipes, bouzoukis, finger cymbals, gongs, exotic shakers, etc. Two brief tracks from late 1968 and early '69, later titled 'E.F.S. No. 7' and 'E.F.S. No. 8', eventually surfaced on the compilation *Unlimited Edition* in 1976.

'Can's version of Indian, African, Greek, avant-garde and other musics, of jazz, even of sailors' hornpipes and Scottish reels, are so patently bogus as authentic ethnic manifestations that they become second cultural realities in their own right,' said the sleeve notes of *Unlimited Edition*'s original release. 'The suggestion is that all art is forgery, which in a sense it is: which begs the question – when is rock music "real", when is it not? Can has frequently been described as "not rock" (always negatively put, though not always intended as adverse criticism). Yet in retrospect it seems as if rock music, as it "moves on", through vogues for this style and that, often arrives at one of the frontiers already crossed in the recordings on this album.'

On 'E.F.S. No. 7', something that sounds like a Balkan oboe, but which is actually a clarinet reed stuffed into a broken flute, wends its way around a thudding ethnic drum and meandering xylophone. On 'E.F.S. No. 8', recorded in November, the marimba reappears, played four-handed in a piece that makes you think of West African percussion musics. These miniatures were thought experiments rendered in sound, a quirky exercise the band periodically indulged in. Usually taking some aspect of ethnic music or exotic instruments as their starting point, they evolved over the next few years as an adjunct to the group's 'official' canon. The *Tago Mago* sessions produced plenty too, including 'E.F.S. No. 27', a free-form drum/vocal chant. It's clearly made up on the spot, with Jaki tracking Damo Suzuki's mumbling with foaming flurries on his hi-hat.

'We couldn't play,' Holger admitted. 'Now, if a band can't play, if we had played rock 'n' roll, it would have been ridiculous, so what can we do? We can do as if we were primitive native people from somewhere else, who are not able to play, but somehow being musical. And that was it. It was combined with a lot of humour during the recording. Jaki, for example, took a clarinet. He mixed the mouthpiece of a clarinet together with a flute. He combined this together and played. Fantastic!

'How is it possible to take someone from Iran, a singer from Iran, who doesn't fit at all into our harmonic tone system . . . how is it possible that it becomes so fascinating suddenly? And the wonderful thing behind this is, I don't know who he is, I don't care if he has washed his cups, yes or no, and if he has flushed the toilet . . . I don't know him, and somehow there is a very strong connection, spiritual-wise. That is interesting; here electronic media make a lot of sense.'

In this, Can were not entirely alone. A few years later, Mauricio Kagel, an Argentinian composer based in Germany, known for his playfully subversive works, was executing a commission to be premiered at the 1972 Olympic Games in Munich. *Exotica* was a subversive work for six classically trained performers on an array of two hundred non-Western instruments. The idea was to put so-called instrumental virtuosi in the difficult situation of singing at the limits of their voices and getting sound out of utterly foreign tools, questioning the dominance of Western music values and returning to a more primitive, practical musicking.

Similarly, the last thing Can wanted was to appear as musical tourists, cherry-picking from the world's sonic exotica. 'We tried to avoid that with all our might,' Irmin said. 'Of course these elements influenced our music; we just didn't bring them back as souvenirs from Istanbul. Instead we kept a certain distance; we acknowledged the ever-remaining inability to understand. ['EFS'] were tracks in which we very clearly assimilated something non-European: nothing imitated, simply a forgery. But "forgery" also means "forging" and has a lot to do with alchemy. It is . . . a melting of these things.'[1]

Tentatively, Can began locking down their songs onto tape. Holger took charge in this department, often combining his bass playing with wrangling the tape machines. The core of the set-up was two Revox quarter-inch-reel machines, and the tape stock was often private home-recording reels dating back to the fifties that Holger had salvaged from garbage piles and the WDR studio – who knows what experiments, test tones, banal conversations, family get-togethers and other sonic detritus were first imprinted upon them? Listen closely to the very early, garage-punkish number 'Nineteen Century Man', on *Delay 1968*, and at 2:10 you can hear a momentary dip where the tape has been edited.

Over the coming months Holger would teach himself to cover these cracks far more smoothly. 'When we started, that was for me a big, big adventure,' he told me. 'I wasn't sure if I was really able to lead the technical process of being a mixer and a musician at the same time, and being the responsibility for the overall sound which goes straight on the record. Therefore, I was very happy that we had another member in the group who came from the Stockhausen crew [David Johnson].'

'The singer stood in front of two microphones from the left and on the side,' Holger explained in a nineties interview.[2] 'He was accompanied by two speakers [monitors], from guitar and organ. The bass was going directly in and the drums – they were separately recorded.' Effectively, they were simply jamming onto a two-track tape, then sifting the tape for the best segments and splicing those together. If they wanted to add extra layers, they would play while dubbing the first tape onto a second tape recorder, and bounce down again and again if they wished, until the quality degenerated.

Irmin: 'When we were remastering [the tracks on] *Delay 1968*, Holger was there, and at one point we were listening to something with Malcolm singing and he started chuckling to himself. We were getting really into the detail of, like, a tiny little bit of lower-mid here, and he said, "If only you'd seen the recording process. We recorded the bass and the drums and then we did the guitar, the organ and the vocals as an overdub. We put the guitar cabinet facing the organ cabinet, with a gap in the middle of about a metre. Then we taped together the two microphones and Malcolm sang into the microphones and we just turned up the other two instruments loud enough to get the balance." That's how basic it was sometimes.'[3]

At the same time, the limits of two-track recording meant they had to learn how to get the best out of the physical space they were in, using both the natural acoustics of a room and the optimal microphone placements relative to their instruments. They favoured Schloss Nörvenich's high-ceilinged entrance hall, an architectural reverb chamber. Holger: 'We recorded . . . without a mixing board. Because we only had a few microphones, we all stood around the microphones and balanced our amplifiers. If anyone had moved, it would've destroyed the recording: there was no extra engineer.'[4]

Malcolm described the daily routine: 'We worked every day. I would say thirteen hours a day at the studio. I don't know what possessed me but I was the first one up . . . Jaki and Michael would come over to Irmin's house and we'd go up to Schloss Nörvenich.

To record. It was kind of strange, because I had no concept of rock music, except for maybe Hendrix.

'Every day we played, every day. Starting at least at eleven o'clock. Coming out maybe at one or two o'clock to have some lunch, or bringing some lunch in, and then playing straight through until eleven o'clock that evening, driving home. Get home, we'd review the tapes we had made, take notes on what we had done. At least Irmin and Michael always used to take notes. I listened to the tracks, and I'd plan a change of lyric, or tell Irmin. Because Irmin for me was a tutor in this music. Irmin basically was a coach: he would try to help me get through certain tracks . . .'[5]

Working from winter into the spring of 1969, their group-mind as players improved in equal proportion to their studio technique. Irmin: 'Everybody wanted that. Nobody of us wanted to impose, be a bandleader, be the composer. We really wanted to create a collective, to prove that this is possible. And everybody put this energy into it, that it becomes one thing, and everybody had ideas – that's why the music has so many styles, so many different aspects, got so rich, because everybody contributed everything he knew.'

Hendrix and the Velvet Underground seemed to be guiding lights at this time. Malcolm's lyrics found an alternative mode from the impromptu observations of mundane reality: he also exercised a quirky storytelling ability that was part indebted to 'The Gift', a track from the VU's second LP, *White Light/White Heat*. There, John Cale deadpans a short story about a man mailing himself to his girlfriend, with fatal consequences, over a backing of crunching art rock. Several of Malcolm's songs in 1969 have a similar 'written', almost literary quality. 'Empress and the Ukraine King', taped in January, 'True Story' and 'Mother Upduff' (Malcolm's sax prominent) are tales read off a handwritten sheet of prose. 'Düsseldorf 1969: Mr and Mrs Upduff and Grandmother Upduff decided they were going on a vacation. Mother Upduff had been now in Düsseldorf eighty years. They packed in their car their tent and equipment and started driving off to Italy . . .' This was apparently based on a true occurrence reported in the local paper, in which a whole family, including Grandmother, went touring in Italy, only for the old lady to perish en route. They returned to Germany with the corpse on the roof rack, rolled up in a tent, but the car was stolen before they made it home. It's not clear whether the detail about the octopus attack in a fish market finishing her off was a fictive addition by Malcolm or not.

A sixteen-minute out-take, 'Upduff's Birth', was bootlegged, revealing the original, much slower jam, engendered around a nervy tennis rally between the sax and guitars on one side and the drums on the other. Malcolm barely deviates from one or two notes throughout the whole take: he too has been infected by Can's swing towards monotony. The version on *Unlimited Edition* is cranked up much higher, the music sweeping the narrative along with it in a herky-jerky torrent, towards the black humour of its conclusion. A piercing whistle zaps the sound stage where you might expect a guitar solo, momentarily drowning everything else out, and you can almost hear Holger leaping to the faders to rebalance the mix.

The lumbering rock of 'Little Star of Bethlehem' and 'Nineteen Century Man', taped in this period, takes you right into their sweaty, smoky quarters in the castle. Tracks like these strive for the heaviness of Hendrix's 'Spanish Castle Magic' or 'Voodoo Chile (Slight Return)', although being Can, the sense of protean flash is subordinate to a consolidated group meld. They were pushing their own limitations in the search for new forms. Holger: 'With Can on our first recordings, first of all I tried conventional bass, but then Jaki said, Holger don't play where I play. Never try to double a foot drum, a foot drum has to stand alone, you play somewhere, something else.'[6]

Malcolm described those early days in these terms: 'We sat around the camp fire, beating on the ground, or beating sticks together, mumbling and possibly whistling, creating sounds with our mouths, creating, soon to be become an understandable reaction to the sound, "the action hears the sound" and vice versa.'[7]

Rückriem the sculptor occasionally grumbled about the noise from below. But in return, the clangs, chippings and thumps in making his monumental granite sculptures filtered out of his art space into Can's own consciousness. Certainly, the heaviness of tracks like 'Soul Desert', 'Thief' and 'Little Star of Bethlehem' suggest the attack of mallet and chisel on stone. There was more than one type of rock in the castle: avant and igneous.

The newly christened Can's efforts in the first half of 1969 were increasingly motivated towards assembling enough finished tracks to constitute a first album, with a working title of *Prepared to Meet Thy Pnoom*. Most of the previously mentioned songs were part of this first batch, but would not see the light of day until the early eighties, years after the group had disbanded, on the posthumously released *Delay 1968*. One vestige is the twenty-six-second instrumental shard 'Pnoom', a lithe, rhythmic shimmy peppered with a staccato squabble between Malcolm's sax and Michael or Irmin puffing one of the group's Middle Eastern horns. Midway through the year, they thought they had achieved their goal, but – possibly because of the relatively low fidelity of the recordings – they decided to come at their first release from a different angle. 'One thing shouldn't be forgotten,' said Holger, 'when our first album entitled *Prepared to Meet Thy Pnoom* was finished no record company wanted to get hold of that kind of music. So we decided to go on recording and try it again.'[8]

At this point Karlheinz 'Kalle' Freynik enters the picture. Freynik had led a varied career in the entertainment industry since the early sixties, with one album of folk/protest/comic songs to his credit, *Ich bin ein Deutscher!* (1966), an effort to be a light-hearted German Bob Dylan. By the late sixties he was living in Munich, where he hung out on the anarchistic fringes of Amon Düül's circle, although

'I never really got into it', he admits now. 'They never really turned me on like Can turned me on.' At the same time, he was beginning to carve out a career as a film producer and scriptwriter, and worked on the German adaptation of the hippy musical *Hair*. He knew a film editor called Peter Przygodda, who would play a decisive role in many of Can's forthcoming film projects. Przygodda was a friend of Irmin and had already shot some footage of Can in their studio in early 1969.

'He told me about a strange band from Cologne,' Freynik says. As soon as he viewed some of Przygodda's rushes from Schloss Nörvenich, Freynik knew he had to meet up with these characters. 'I met the band and went with them to the studio in their castle, and it was an amazing place. We all were, of course, in our high days of drugs and rock 'n' roll, so it was really some kind of very peculiar trip to be there, and to hear them improvise. They were getting in, grabbing their instruments, starting to play, and about eight to ten hours later they put them out of their hands. And this was about what their concerts were like too.

'It was all very anarchic. And they were fiddling around with scissors and this kind of stuff. I had the impression everything they did was very handmade. This didn't interest me too much because, of course, I knew all the big studios in Europe, and compared to those Schloss Nörvenich was not even the garage. When the five of them started playing, it was like five people turning away from the others, and diving into their subconscious, and playing their things. Sometimes it started as a horrible mess, cacophonia, and slowly, after a while, they gathered and their minds kind of connected to each other. And they started the main part of the improvisation. But they were so within themselves . . . each one kind of made an inner migration, they migrated into themselves. There was hardly any communication in the studio 'cause everybody was introverted – everyone was concentrating on his own.

'I talked to each of them, except Jaki Liebezeit, because he was a man of drumsticks and he wasn't a man of words. And when I said, "How do you do what you are doing?" he answered, "Loud." But the others all tried to communicate in a more positive way and tried to explain what made the secret of Can, the secret of their music. And there was one thing common to all of them, when they said: "Our communication is not intellectual. Our communication is a spiritual communication that happens while we play, and we don't hear what the other plays. We listen to ourselves and to what we are doing. And if we are good, if it works, everything melts together and we'll make a good performance." I saw many, many concerts where this *didn't* happen. And they were, of course, extremely bad.'

When Freynik, described by Irmin as 'a quite clever guy, and crazy too', came to hear the Can out at Schloss Nörvenich, he was already informally setting up an independent record label – the first of its kind in Germany – with the nose-thumbing name of Scheisshaus Records (Shithouse Records). He aimed to release material the majors considered too way out, while developing artists to the point where he could make some money licensing them to majors further down the line. His ideal music at the time was the hard-nosed psychedelia of British freaks Hapshash and the Coloured Coat (featuring the Human Host and the Heavy Metal Kids), whose 1967 self-titled LP has a similar fry-up of granite-hewn monotony, harmonica and cosmic overtones (they even had a chanted drone called 'Aoum'). What Freynik heard on the Can's tapes impressed him so much, he wanted it to be the first release on Scheisshaus.

'To be honest,' says Freynik, 'I never quite understood what was going on in the studio, because when they interrupted to discuss changes and trying to repeat stuff, I never had an idea what it was all about, because *everything* sounded good, sounded reasonable, and it came from the musicians' heart. Usually, Holger took the tapes and went home with them, and tried to fiddle around, and add things in and take things out . . . Puzzling around with the tapes. If I remember right, this was the major disagreement. They said,

"We're here to play improvised music and we're not here to puzzle parts like somebody who doesn't know what he's doing, and then putting something together that wasn't there before." So they were kind of mad about Holger doing this, and he said, "Well, what we've done is good, but what I have in mind is better.'"

This perseverance led to Can's first masterpiece. Holger strove to fine-tune the recording quality at Inner Space, and on 25 July 1969 the group spent around twelve hours returning to one colossal, grinding riff, subjected to endless variation and intensification. Jaki beats the skins with Stone Age clubs; Holger see-saws bass notes across an octave. 'I'm in love with a girl and she's away,' moans Malcolm. 'Man, you got to move on, man, you got to move on, man . . . Once I was blind, but now I see / You made a believer out of me.' Irmin recalls one of Malcolm's girlfriends, an American with links to the Amish community who was in Cologne for a while but then left. They continued to exchange letters, and one of those formed the basis of the lyrics Malcolm extemporised on that day.

'Yoo Doo Right' is a drum and bass riff that begins like a squadron of mechanical deities manoeuvring through a ravine, and then over twenty minutes gets extruded and fractalised into an ever-shifting array of byways, blind alleys and wide-open roads of rhythm. Even the vocal is eventually shredded and spat out by this crushing, remorseless music, pulped as it gets dragged into the machinery. Finally, using self-imposed restrictions, Can had cracked the problem of integrating minimalism with cutting-edge rock.

Malcolm: 'The early gigs and recordings were sheer excitement. I never knew what I was going to do. Nothing at first was planned. Then I became self-critical of my approach and tried to eliminate the unpredictable. The reasoning, as I mentioned before, was rigorous, I must have weighed a hundred and forty pounds at the time and I could lose ten to fifteen pounds at sessions.'[9] It's on 'Yoo Doo Right' that you can hear Holger crawling inside the beat in a new way. 'Jaki . . . always told me I would never get rhythm, but I thought, what does he know? He's just a stupid drummer!' Holger said in a later interview. 'But he was right and Jaki is one person whose criticism I take to heart. Jaki always demands a drummer to play as simple as possible, that he should invest all his musicianship into the *infrasound*, that essential in the music which is beyond the note itself.

'Today we have so many good, functional drummers, guitar players, all of them interchangeable, all sounding the same. For they do not possess that indefinable quality. Jaki has that. He made me understand rhythm is the greatest concentration of music, that one single drum beat can contain all the music in the world.'[10]

The session lasted roughly between eleven in the morning and eleven at night, during which time they laid down successive takes on the same riff. 'It was quite a session,' Malcolm remembered. 'I left the studio at one time for lunch, when I returned the band was still playing the tune and I resumed where I had left off.'[11] It's possible to hear the incredible interplay of vocal and drum between Malcolm and Jaki, who occasionally even performed as a duo in 1969. 'Him and Jaki were just a drum unit,' says Irmin. 'Jaki adored him, because there was a partner who everything he did was rhythm . . . He could sing one riff and one sentence, and Jaki played his monotonous pattern for ages, and they could go on like this for ever. They were ideal for each other, actually. And with a clear mind, a not too troubled mind, that would have been great if [Malcolm] would have stayed. It could have driven us to really crazy things, even in a sense which got for me a little bit lost. We talked about Artaud. I was always thinking about performances which got more violent, strange, theatrical performances, but then we ended up doing just concerts.'

Financially, the Can was living hand to mouth, and to a large extent was financed by Irmin, Hildegard and Holger. Like hundreds of thousands of West German citizens, in the first half of the sixties both Holger and Irmin had taken advantage of a large public flotation of shares in Volkswagen and the energy company VEBA. Holger now liquidated his shares and used some of his savings to purchase equipment and a small van for transport. Michael was still getting support from his wealthy family. Jaki was the least well off, as he refused to take any work other than drumming for Can, and he was no longer on his retainer from the Manfred Schoof group. Through much of 1969 it was Irmin who was most gainfully employed, still taking conducting engagements and composing and directing music for theatrical productions. Theatres were a rich source of income at the time, and Irmin describes his situation as 'immensely well paid'. He could earn eight thousand marks for an afternoon's arranging work, five thousand for taking singing rehearsals. Then, in addition to his standard performance fees, he could pocket his hotel allowances while actually staying with his parents. On top of all this, he was still giving vocal lessons at the dramatic academy in Bochum, taking amphetamines – slimming pills called 'Ein-und-Eins' – to help him keep on top of it all. 'Sometimes I took about six to ten, because I had no sleep. I slept only a few hours, worked all night with Can, then had two hours' sleep, jumped to the airport and slept another hour in the plane, then had a rehearsal in Munich, and another in the afternoon and again in the morning, and in the afternoon flew back and gave lessons in Bochum, and then came back to the studio.' One time when the band's finances hit a particularly low point, the group also received a generous donation from Hans Mayer.

'We were totally convinced that it would be absolutely impossible to get a record company. Kalle came to the studio, and he was a friend, and he said, "We have to make a record out of your material,"' remembers Irmin. 'We had lots of pieces – all the music which is on *Delay* was already there, plus the ones which are on *Monster Movie* – and then we all together, even with Kalle, we chose and said, "We won't shorten 'Yoo Doo Right', it's a whole long piece of twenty minutes.'"

Freynik remembers it slightly differently: '"Yoo Doo Right" took about a week to record, if I remember right. This was one of those examples of when they went into the studio and I said, "What are you gonna do today?" They said, '"Yoo Doo Right".' I said, "You already have it, it's great, isn't it?" "No, no, it's very imperfect and we are very unhappy with it." I couldn't understand why. So they did another version of it and new tracks and everything. In a way, it changed, but every change to me sounded absolutely perfect. And next day again they said, "No."' It's an early illustration of the group's collective quality control. They would rarely allow themselves to be rushed into releasing any material they weren't all totally satisfied with.

With 'Yoo Doo Right' sprawling across the whole of side two, the first side of Can's first album, *Monster Movie*, comprised just three tracks, opening with Malcolm's debut, 'Father Cannot Yell'. 'Then [we chose] "Mary, Mary, So Contrary",' says Irmin, 'which was a kind of slow piece, and then a wild one, "Outside My Door", a rock 'n' roll piece, at the end. That made a side of twenty minutes, which made sense to us. It has even some kind of classical structure, because there is the first movement, the big one, then comes the slow movement, and then comes the scherzo! So it has this structure, a faint memory of the structure of the symphony.'

Monster Movie's original sleeve, designed by commercial artist Helge Bauch, was white, with a large orange circle in the centre containing a reproduced fragment of an engraving. 'We said, "We want something mystical from Greek myths that fits to the music,"' says Freynik. Its style is hard to place – Albrecht Dürer meets Alan Moore – and shows a naked old man peering into what looks like the flaming portal of hell. He is surrounded by demons and a goat-headed man gnawing on a limb. As well as the band's name and the album title, the cover displays the phrase 'Made In A Castle

With Better Equipment', placed there at Malcolm's suggestion. 'I don't know what the equipment was like when Damo was there,' he said, 'but when I was there, the equipment was primitive. But that's why I put on *Monster Movie*, "made with better equipment". It was actually a joke.'[12]

This lack of connection with the aesthetics of rock worked to the Can's advantage at this stage, giving them an odd aura out of kilter with the times. The back cover featured a group photo taken in Irmin's living room, and Malcolm came up with a musical credits list that self-mythologised the group as a platoon of high-tech sonic scientists, guiding a futuristic sonic weapons system:

Irmin Schmidt – adminaspace co-ordinator & organ laser
Jaki Liebezeit – propulsion engineer & mystic space chart reader
Holger Czukay – hot from Vietnam; technical laboratory chief & red
    armed bass
Michael Karoli – sonar & radared guitar pilot
Malcolm Mooney – linguistic space communicator

Monster Movie came out initially in late August 1969 on Music Factory, 'a division of Scheisshaus Records'. (Liberty Records/ United Artists had agreed to help Kalle Freynik out with distribution, but they needed a more salubrious name for the label.) Freynik: 'It was a gentlemen's agreement, and I regarded myself as a fan of Can, putting out the record because nobody else wanted to. The deal was, "Let's promote the product as good as we can, and when there's any reaction we try to get it on a major label." This was the plan from the start.' The initial pressing was five hundred copies. Freynik placed these in carefully selected 'head shops and underground shops' to boost the band's reputation by word of mouth, and the first pressing quickly sold out. As well as his informal arrangement with Liberty/United Artists, Freynik also had a promising connection with an executive at EMI Switzerland, who liked what he was doing and guaranteed to buy two thousand copies of each Scheisshaus release for cash in hand.

Freynik set in motion Can's eventual signing to Liberty/United Artists, under the auspices of its boss, Siegfried 'Siggi' Loch. By the time Liberty's issue of *Monster Movie* stomped out in May 1970, it looked very different. Painted in acrylics or spray paint, the torso of a robotic colossus emerges from clouds above a purple mountainscape. The group's name and album title appear carved into a low grey stone wall in the foreground. On this can also be seen the painter's signature, 'Wandrey'. This was Peter Wandrey, a graphic artist who frequently made illustrations for record covers, posters and magazines at the time, and went on to become a celebrated artist specialising in futuristic and dystopian imagery, influenced by cybernetics, surrealism and digital graphics. The robot in the image bears a close resemblance to Galactus, a giant robot who first appeared in Marvel Comics' *Fantastic Four* series, where he is a cyborg deity sucking energy from inhabited planets for sustenance. Subliminally, this could describe the Can's relationship to various musical spheres: draining as much nutrition as possible from contemporary classical, jazz, world, rock and experimental music, synthesizing the extracts into something mighty and new. For someone like Malcolm, living in fear of the American authorities even as his position in the group strengthened, Galactus acted as an avatar of strength and determination. He said: 'I was trying to make myself aware of the world – all its good – by trying to rid myself of the negatives. In so doing there were truths revealed. *Monster Movie* sort of crystallizes those times emotionally.'[13]

Monster Movie took its time to filter through to the media's attention, but was eventually picked up by Richard Williams, whose brief review appeared in the *NME* in May 1970. He quickly identified the Velvet Underground influence on the shorter tracks, but allowed that 'they have a lot of themselves to offer, mainly in the field of electronics, which they use with sparing brilliance, and the interplay between the Morse-code organ and the machine-gun drums on "You Do Right" [*sic*] is extremely startling'. A few lines later, Williams stated how Malcolm's 'wailing and screaming fits perfectly where a less reticent singer would obtrude. In fact they use another of the Velvets' favourite tricks, putting the voice beneath the instruments so that it tantalises the listener unbearably. Nobody in Britain', the review concluded, 'is playing this kind of music, which is well worth hearing.'[14]

Monster Movie was mastered at WDR's Studio für Elektronische Musik in Cologne, under the nose of Stockhausen and his entourage. Especially via Holger, and the fact that they were using 'borrowed' tapes from there, the group's links with the studio were strong. 'A few months after the foundation of Can',[15] Holger and an acquaintance, Rolf Dammers, had recorded *Canaxis 5* at the WDR studio. Before the actual recording took place, the pair had tried out a method of combining sounds at home, using three tape machines and a five-track mixer. Holger had met Dammers, a painter and writer, in Switzerland at the boarding school in St Gallen. Dammers had gone there first to explore employment possibilities, and once installed at the school, encouraged his friend to follow. 'It was our goal to meet a millionairess in Switzerland and to marry her so we were financially secure and could exclusively take care of our music,' Holger admitted in the sleeve notes of *Canaxis*. Of Dammers's musical aspirations at the time, Holger said, 'For him, it was more interesting how one could bring together exotic music and the harmony of Western civilisation.' Irmin's memory is less favourable: 'I didn't like him. I always thought he was taking advantage of Holger and Michael. Not really contributing something essential to Holger's work, but being always a partner. He was also with Michael von Biel, and I know von Biel didn't want to do anything with him. I didn't – I just avoided him, and so did Hildegard.'

'I met him three or four times,' recalls Kalle Freynik, 'but I can't remember very much about him. He was a little bit like Holger . . . Of course, nobody was like Holger, because Holger was a really weird guy . . . he wasn't really a part of society, he was something totally special. His lifestyle was different to all the others, his imagination . . . even his interpretation of reality was kind of somewhere between Friedrich Nietzsche and Frank Zappa. And Rolf was a bit like that – he was a loner too, and they agreed on a lot of things *not* to do. So when they agreed on things like *Canaxis*, it was always a huge fight, and they could never reproduce anything live on stage. I think Rolf was afraid of showing up and going on stage. He didn't want to be a performer, he was a philosopher. Well, this they had in common: Holger also regarded himself as a philosopher, not a musician. The worst thing you could do was to ask a simple question, like, "Holger, why did you play it that way?" And he could tell you for hours why he played it that way, and why he didn't do it the other way.'

Canaxis stands now as one of the great crossover works of the sixties, an electroacoustic tape piece created in do-it-yourself circumstances. Occasionally credited as the origin of sampling in music, an assertion that's not strictly true, it nevertheless adeptly dovetails the parallel disciplines of loop-based minimalism, superimposition and cultural appropriation, a picking from the 'exotic' Far East that is firmly rooted in the horrors of Western war being waged there. It is, therefore, a non-academic piece of concrete tape music that plays directly to counter-cultural geopolitical concerns. Much was made, on the original Music Factory sleeve, of its connections with present-day Vietnam as war zone. Its goofy sleeve notes play with the notion that this is a prankster cavorting under the aegis of the academy, playfully generate a myth around the elements of the piece, and situate it in the moonwalk summer of 1969:

CANAXIS 5 was written in the light year 77, sometimes called the year of Galactical Score Expedition. Time elapsed between the first founding of the lunar calendar with the man's first cough on the moon cow settlement. Leaving behind a flag that waved in a strong moon storm! Plastic man turned himself around on the planet of the moon, trying to reach CANAXIS 5. Which is the galaxy of the sound expedition?

It was lightning's stroke procedure onto a 45 track recorder, engineered by the robots Ho and Ro. Their laboratory was a stationary space with an orbit outside of the planet KO —— , produced with a better equipment which was connected electronically with the Inner Space Production's Sound Space Team in a little village in Vietnam.

There you can find a secret computer center of all greater kinds of coloured lightnings.

On the front cover is a photo of an elderly female hand, ringed and braceleted like a queen in a fifties period movie, proffering a joint between outstretched finger and thumb. The reverse was slathered in a wacky hand-drawn cartoon by Malcolm on school graph paper, like some distracted but overstimulated child. It's partly a series of advertisements for itself: 'The Can . . . Coming your way' and 'Our Next Can', shout fat capital letters; and, smaller, 'remember "Monster Movie"'. A sheet of paper headed 'Yoo Doo Right' lies next to a tin labelled 'Can', while on the left is scrawled 'Hildegard How is Canabit?' Arrows indicate where 'pictures of the two composers' should be placed. Full of in-jokes and references to Can's activities, it is clearly in the first flush of excitement at being 'in a band', or having found a gang. Yet a few references to Vietnam are visible too: the artists are credited as 'Ho Szukay (as great as the late Ho Chin Minh)' and 'Ro Dammers'; South-East Asian ceremonial dragons square off in the centre; and a rocket stands ready on a launch pad. Another slogan, punning on Holger's surname, reads: 'Shook-Eye's Ammunition and Ho Mai Nhi'.

This last was a direct reference to the secret weapon that lay embedded in the music itself. 'Ho Mai Nhi' is the title of a track on *Music of Viet Nam: Tribal Music of the Highland People*, an album of field recordings originally released by the American Folkways label in 1966, and it translates as 'Boat-Women Song'. Recorded by Pham Duy and compiled by Folkways' Stephen Addiss and Bill Crofut, this album surveyed the region's rural and ancient music forms, from the pre-Vietnam era to the music of the Cham people, 'Ancient Imperial Music' and 'Ancient Folk Music'. Appearing in the midst of the US military campaign in the country, and on an American label, there was more than just ethnographic interest behind its release. The 'Boat-Women Song' itself was sandwiched between other work songs, including a 'Rice Pounding Song' and a 'Paddy Carrying Song'. Although Addiss's sleeve notes don't make explicit reference to the war, they mention that Pham Duy had been making recordings around the country for the past two decades and was a composer in his own right: one of his pieces, included, is called 'The Wounded Soldier'. He also observes that through listening to these folk songs, 'One can . . . find the soul of the Vietnamese nation: peace-loving, sensitive to the beauty of things, generous, serene, not at all mystical, realistic but still with a sense of poetry . . .' He concludes by stating that the more recently composed folk music 'will bring to future generations the images of a past made up of battles, grandeur and the misery of the Vietnamese people'.

To use a word like 'alchemy' would sound a little strong, and would deny the practical aspects of preparing a piece like 'Ho Mai Nhi', but Czukay and Dammers take this river-borne hymn – already, in its brief original form, an astonishing, melismatic feat of the human voice – and, by superimposing it with a tape-loop sample of a troubadour lament by Adam de la Halle and electronic tones, downshifted in pitch, express the dignity of an indigenous people under the threat of genocide in the midst of an ideological war.

Canaxis – the 'axis' dimension also hints at the militaristic imagery employed collectively by Can at this juncture – is a melange of ethnic samples and electronic textures spun in from tape loops. Originally released in an edition of five hundred, with a similar arrangement between Scheisshaus Records and Music Factory, it was credited to the Technical Space Composer's [*sic*] Crew and issued in a black-and-white sleeve. 'It was a big surprise to me that it worked,' Holger recalled. 'Because it was really a sort of experiment with a tape recorder, all these big loops were running around beer bottles, and everything was done on the floor. The whole floor: everything was a network of tapes which were running, actually. Then going at night into Stockhausen's studio, because I knew someone who had a key, and he left the studio, and everything was prepared, because I couldn't do it myself – I couldn't for example slow down a choir, or a machine, make the machine run slower or faster. This was impossible at that time. But the studio had the possibility to do that. So the next day, *Canaxis* was done in four hours! In four hours. It was prepared for a long time, everything, but the finished product was done in four hours.'

In August 1969 the doors of Schloss Nörvenich were thrown open to the public for an exhibition in some of the artist spaces. Can were invited to display their sonic wares too, and they set up equipment in the entrance hall. It seems there was a tense atmosphere within the group that night. 'It is very rare that Jaki will change a once-started rhythm,' said Holger, 'he did it once after criticising Michael's guitar playing, who consequently ran to his guitar in anger and began to push Jaki into one of Can's best ever live recorded pieces, "Uphill".'[16] As the instrumentalists hit their stride, and Malcolm spat the lyrics of a track that was also sometimes called 'Moving Slowly Going Uphill', he became distracted, hypnotised even, by the constant flow of visitors up and down the central staircase. According to Can legend, he began to recite the phrase 'Upstairs . . . downstairs . . . upstairs . . . downstairs . . .' over and over, repeating it obsessively until he became locked into a mania of repetition. This continued even while the group took a break and into the second half of the performance. 'It was really true,' confirms Irmin. 'He could get himself into this kind of strange obsessive trance, repeating "Upstairs . . . downstairs . . . upstairs . . . downstairs . . .", because all these people went upstairs, downstairs – upstairs were some sculptures of Rückriem, downstairs was the champagne. And Malcolm spent two hours screaming. We went and had a drink, and he was standing there, foaming. And still going on. Which was in itself an amazing performance, the energy he put into this thing, and I mean, later it would have been a famous performance in galleries if he would have done that again. It's like Marina Abramović, it had the same kind of frightening energy. And also this kind of self-torturing . . . doing something until you just wipe yourself out.

'All this stuff became, in the Cologne intellectual and arts scene, quite famous locally. We weren't considered as a rock group in the beginning; considered as a crazy bunch of artists who make the most amazing, strange and violent performances, and slowly out of this developed music.'

Kalle Freynik remembers his own experience with Malcolm: 'I didn't know much about psychology – I only knew that this guy was very unhappy. No idea why, and people, especially Hildegard and the women around the Can, started talking about him and told me stories about him, but I couldn't understand it. I always thought maybe it's because he wanted to be a real singer. Like Tom Jones! But he didn't. Of course not. But on the other hand, he was very insecure about everything he was doing. So he always depended on how he felt and on the reaction from the others, and as far as I remember everybody was very helpful to Malcolm, because they all had the feeling that he was the one who was balancing on a tightrope all the time.'

These were faint indications that Malcolm's state of mind was getting increasingly precarious. Can veered all over the place in the unsteady, experimental year of 1969. An outdoor event in which the whole band beat on giant blue plastic oil drums with sticks, filmed for a promotional advert for the industrial manufacturer Mauser. A night-time garden party at a villa belonging to the owner of Herta, one of Germany's biggest meat producers. Driving for hours into the countryside to appear at a hippy rave-up in a windswept barn for twenty minutes, before abandoning the stage and joining the party.

And then there was the notorious Düsseldorf art gallery incident. In July 1969 Irmin, Hildegard and Malcolm attended the Städtische Kunsthalle for the opening of an exhibition by Arman, a celebrated French artist who at the time was married to the electronic composer Éliane Radigue. He was exhibiting *Accumulations Renault*, a series of sculptures of multiple stacked car parts. All the great and good from the Cologne and Düsseldorf art worlds had turned out to see this show consisting of public sculptures and an edition of smaller pieces – scrap metal and objects embedded in cubes and oblongs of transparent Plexiglas – for sale to private buyers. Irmin: 'In the middle of one of the halls was a huge table with about a hundred multiples by Arman, and these multiples each cost a thousand marks or whatever. And all of a sudden, we saw most of the people concentrated around this table. And we went there, Hildegard and me, because we had lost Malcolm somewhere.'

Malcolm: '[I was] fooling around inside a couple of steel sculptures. And the usual routine with any museum in the world, even with new sculpture, is "please do not touch". Now I have laughed at that for a long time, when a piece weighs close to a ton . . . in order to remove them or destroy them you'd have to have a bulldozer. And the guards tell you to stay away . . . And all of a sudden an idea came to me . . .'[17]

When Irmin and Hildegard caught up with Malcolm, they were horrified to discover him selling off these valuable artworks for chump change. 'Malcolm was standing on top of this [table], doing an auction,' recalls Irmin. 'Holding them and saying, "How much do you offer? Twenty marks? There it is!" And got the money. And then [there was a] big scandal, and he had his pockets full of money – he had sold twenty – and people went out with this thing in their arms as quick as they could! Arman was crying . . .'

Malcolm: 'For a joke I said to somebody, "Ma'am, how would you like to buy this piece?" . . . She said, "Oh yes." I said, "Write a cheque." I went through this whole thing. There's a photograph of me at this museum, white sheepskin coat on, which was a friend of mine's coat. And all of a sudden, it seemed like it was getting out of hand. I don't know if it was me, or the crowd, or both."[18] Hildegard grabbed Malcolm, who by now had accumulated several hundred marks, and pulled him as fast as she could towards the exit. The museum guards had already been told not to let anybody leave until they had found the perpetrator, but somehow she managed to persuade them that the miscreant was still inside, and they were let out. Irmin: 'We were outside and it was cold and we didn't dare go anywhere. We said, "Now you give me the money you collected." And he . . . found a way to give back all the money, and we went back to Cologne and made sure that the guy got the money, and he collected the pieces again. Everybody in Düsseldorf knows everybody in the art scene, so some of the people had doubts . . . They got them all back. But this event was even worth a note in *Spiegel*. So they wrote about it: "The singer of Can". Some papers said "an unknown black man", but some knew that he was with us. But he was so new with us. But that was so typical: he got this idea, and between having an idea and doing it was a split second. He was just doing it immediately.'

Before it could bring any further havoc to West German art establishments, Can was offered a residency of several months in Switzerland. The invitation came from stage director Max Ammann, who had just taken up a new position at the Zurich Schauspielhaus. (Irmin had arranged the music for Ammann's production of a Brecht play in Munich the previous year, and Ammann had been bowled over by the tape of 'Father Cannot Yell'.) In the summer of 1969 Ammann invited Irmin to bring his group to Zurich, to provide the music for the premiere of Heiner Müller's adaptation of Aeschylus' Greek tragedy *Prometheus Bound*. Müller, from East Berlin, was one of Germany's most feted playwrights of the late sixties, an inheritor of the legacy of Brecht, known for radical politics often expressed in myth. *Prometheus Bound* rewrote the myth of the legendary Titan who stole fire from the sun and was condemned to an eternity of captivity while an eagle feasted daily on his liver, recasting the central character as 'a failed revolutionary and class struggler in a coded puzzle about political relationships, greed, betrayal, lies and terror',[19] as one review put it. The central character, played by Norbert Kappen, was confined in unnatural postures by cords and foam-rubber pads, while clouds hung over the stage like giant potato chunks.

The residency, including rehearsal time, lasted from around late August to October, with Can staying in an apartment rented by the theatre. It resulted in almost thirty performances, and proved a valuable testing ground and workshop for Can as a live act, as well as giving them the opportunity to record several key songs.

Holger was frisked for drugs by the Swiss border guards. 'The man who did the job I felt a bit sorry for him, I had to ask him, "Have you ever seen hashish?" "No." "I feel so sorry for you, I have here a little piece of it, ask your wife to make a tea of it." He thanked me!'[20] At the theatre, the engagement got off on the wrong foot. Before they left for Switzerland, Can were under the impression that they were allowed to be on stage and improvise openly to the action. When they arrived for rehearsals, however, they were placed out of sight in the orchestra pit and instructed when to play and when to keep schtum. 'We were very furious,' recalls Irmin, 'and the most furious was Malcolm. When the performance started, he didn't come like us from downstairs, he made a detour and went down the aisle, and was screaming, "You know, people? This house is *scheisse*! This *Haus ist scheisse*! This *Schauspielhaus* is a *Scheisshaus*!"'

Can deliberately cranked up the volume, creating a deafening overture that drowned out the first half of the opening monologue, spoken by Kappen, who opened the play in an uncomfortable hanging position and was naturally keen to get his speech over with. A review in *Die Zeit* cursorily mentioned the audience's confusion thanks to a 'superfluous beat band'.[21] That beat band reacted *ad absurdum* to the controls placed on them in the orchestra pit, using music stands and insisting that a light should go on when they were required to play. When the light was turned off, they cut the music instantly and returned to their books and newspapers until the next cue. If they were to be treated as a theatrical orchestra, they were damn sure going to behave like one.

At least the work was well paid, and after their own fashion, Can took control of the situation and turned it to their advantage. The play lasted only seventy-five minutes, and Irmin had made sure their contract included the right to extend the evenings with free Can concerts on the theatrical set. 'Sometimes it was fuller after the people went out, and then the young people were staying.'

The contract also allowed Can to host one special extended event of their own, lasting from around six o'clock until midnight. A poster was placed next to the stage, encouraging the audience to participate in a full-blown happening. Irmin: 'We didn't have any money to invest in a stage set, so what I did was first of all the crew, the workers, officially had a day off. So there was only a kind of urgent scene kind of stuff. And I asked, if any of you would like to help us and be with us? And surprisingly enough, a lot of these stage workers loved to be involved.' Malcolm befriended some of the stagehands and persuaded them to construct a giant tin can made of wood to use during the band's show. Irmin: 'Inside was a ladder you could climb up, and a little platform where you could stand. And we had one hippy who got totally naked, he went up there and was making a very holy speech . . .'

This one-off live action included freaky dancing with the band on stage (borrowing an instrument if necessary), rearranging the scenery and raiding the props table, or slapping paint over the transparent backcloths. 'It was a wonderful, very, very peaceful evening,' remembers Irmin. 'We tuned up and played, and at eight it was more than full. And all the Zurich papers expected that the Schauspielhaus would burn down because they were so against us. "The Schauspielhaus will burn down and will totally be destroyed." And it was the most peaceful . . . sometimes one or the other lit a joint or cigarette, but immediately somebody came and said, "Oh, excuse me," and they put it away . . .

'And next day the papers wrote: "Well, obviously they are not so exciting – nothing happened." They were so disappointed!' Describing them as 'Die Best-Band', *Der Spiegel*'s critic noted that 'Can strove, with droning interlude music, to shake up the house – the only time it happened during the evening, because the audience seemed quite unmoved by the drama alone.'[22]

The solemn and funereal 'Thief' was one song Can recorded – 'in a cellar room with awful acoustics', according to Irmin – while still in Zurich. One of Malcolm's most abject vocal performances, and featuring Can at their most gravitas-laden, the subject matter is clearly riffing directly off the scenography of *Prometheus Bound*, with its references to 'the hanging man', 'the Jesus man . . . cursed to the holy ground' and 'trying to fly'. Irmin: 'The hanging man is this actor hanging there, because he *was* really hanging . . . There was [some scenery] symbolising the rock, and he was in this very strange thing where he was hanging in it. Great actor! And a great piece, wonderful . . . Very unusual language.' The song was used in the comedy thriller *Kuckucksei im Gangsternest*, directed by Franz-Josef Spieker and starring Hanna Schygulla and Herbert Fux, released at the end of the year.

Other tracks taped in Zurich included 'Fall of Another Year', which turned up on *Unlimited Edition* (1976). 'The wheels that are ever turning the world / Are moving ever faster / You have to erase so much in your head / Taught by the master,' sings Malcolm. There are traces here of the paranoia that would engulf him in the next few months, although in this period he was also capable of singing on some of the most simply romantic music Can ever made, in 'She Brings the Rain'. The first version of this, taped in a Zurich cellar in November 1969, would go on to become one of the group's best loved and most accessible songs, and ushered in a new phase of involvement in the world of film.

7

Truth at 33 rpm

One of the many resonances of Can's name is the canister housing reels of celluloid film, a precious container protecting that most flammable and crumply of media, long before the age of digital retrieval. Film crews, as well as music producers, use the cliché 'It's in the can' on wrapping a scene. But Can's relationship with film extends further than semantics. Their entire modus operandi in terms of constructing music was closer to film editing – patching together the most effective takes or sections of longer takes; occasionally utilising the long uninterrupted take. You can hear the grain of Can's sound as a kind of overexposed film stock. As in a film, with its multiple options and wealth of surplus material honed, pruned and recombined by the editor and director, there is no definitive mix or master for Can's recordings. The peculiar crossfades and splices used to construct tracks such as 'Yoo Doo Right', or the epically widescreen 'Bel Air', are filmic from the root of their conception. Chief tape cutter Holger Czukay's personal interest in the cinema emerged explicitly in the titles of his later solo albums *Movies* and *Moving Pictures*, while Irmin's post-Can career was largely bankrolled by regular work creating music for television and film.

Can's beginnings coincided with an interesting moment in West German cinema, and Irmin was able to capitalise on his already blossoming connections in the theatrical and cinematic worlds to secure several film soundtrack commissions for his new group. These were collected on the 1970 release *Soundtracks*, a record that sounded markedly more consistent than *Monster Movie*, as well as documenting the handover of Can's vocal slot from Malcolm Mooney to Damo Suzuki.

To watch the films worked on by Can between 1969 and 1971, you'd think the chief issues of the day occupying the minds of contemporary West Germans included wiretapping, swinging sex, domestic terrorism, rape and hedonism, with a dash of moral philosophy and nihilism thrown into the mix. The passage of time, and the lack of distribution for most of those films outside of central Europe, has meant that the tracks have largely detached themselves from the films (and have more listeners than these films ever had viewers), most of which are rarely viewed today (a couple of them are almost impossible to find, even in the web's darkest corners). Additionally, the music on the *Soundtracks* album is not the sum total of all the music Can made for these films. While they're not all cinematic masterworks, there are some fascinating period pieces, the odd exploitation flick and voyeuristic rape movie aside. Together they form a snapshot of a German counter-culture shot through with undercurrents of disconnection, disaffection and violence.

The first of *Soundtracks*' seven tracks to be recorded, in November 1969, was 'She Brings the Rain'. The album sleeve assigned the track to a film called *Bottom*, directed by Thomas Schamoni, which is a red herring, as the film in question was actually released as *Ein grosser graublauer Vogel* (A Big Grey-Blue Bird). Of all of these movies, that one film embodies Can's particular essence. Schamoni had previously produced Fassbinder's *Love Is Colder Than Death*, and *Ein grosser graublauer Vogel* was his first cinema feature as director. Its running theme is electronic eavesdropping, surveillance and the relationship of electronic media to perceptions of space and time. The premise is that a group of scientists who have cracked some kind of secret regarding the space–time continuum have been held hostage in a mystery location, and at least two sets of people – a bunch of sophisticated gangsters and a hedonistic yet urbane hippy documentary film crew – are trying to track them down. Many scenes in the film are packed with racks full of cool vintage electronic devices, reel-to-reel tapes and flickering TV monitors.

The cutting style is very much in keeping with Can's own methodology, thanks to its editor, Peter Przygodda, a German film editor – later the self-styled 'Schnittmeister' – and good friend of Irmin's who would remain a close collaborator with the group, practically their resident documentarist. Przygodda went on to work on many of Wim Wenders's and Volker Schlöndorff's films, but here he is given free rein with the material, and immersed the viewer in a hallucinatory, cross-cut fiesta of captured sounds, replayed video and films-within-films. 'I went to Przygodda,' says Irmin. 'What we played would be edited to the film's structure, and so the structure of that music, with sound and music going in and out, was actually made by what the film asked for.' The activity of filming appears many times in shot, as the documentarists are filmed documenting. It's a landscape of filmic mirrors and self-referentiality, strung around a plot that almost certainly wouldn't stand up to any sustained narrative analysis. 'The film was about these strange hippies. Nobody can explain exactly what they did!' laughs Irmin. 'And on the other side there were these gangsters with this very fancy equipment where they listened and watched, surveyed these guys, and they had these screens and earphones, and all this created sounds. So I recorded a lot of shortwave radio on handmade loops, and went to the studio and we played to the shortwave sound. Sometimes the shortwave is actually my keyboard, it's my sound.'

On another occasion Irmin said: 'We painstakingly made a soundtrack out of the shortwave signals, in which the sound world of the film and music itself blended and flowed into each other. Someone sat in front of a set of speakers, out of which the shortwave noise came; they became music in a mysterious way. Then, for instance, there would be an edit: people sitting in an aeroplane, and the noise of the propellers and the shortwave signals resonated together. A guitar bored its way in, like a hallucination, as if you could hear a noise and something singing inside the noise.'[1] Fifteen minutes of this type of music – taped at various times between January and April 1970 – was montaged and released on *The Lost Tapes*, under the generic name 'Graublau'. Can's music here is harsh, a relentless lashing force restating the film's general frenetic pace and atmosphere of steadily accumulating paranoia and threat. Lifting off from the same launchpad as 'Mother Sky', Holger's familiar bassline, see-sawing between two notes an octave apart, pokes its head above the froth as the group occasionally chime together in a sequence of triumphant tonal chords. Can jam out one of their heavier Stone Age grooves, while the sound of a propeller plane from the soundtrack turns into the noise of shortwave radio, and then is folded into the groove itself.

'She Brings the Rain', which is reprised several times during the film, was not made specifically as a soundtrack piece. Irmin: 'That was a song made totally independent from the film. When we got the commission for the music for *Graublauer Vogel*, we had this song made, for the next record. Malcolm had already left, and then we got the commission for that film and we made the music, and this song fitted as if it was made for the film. It fitted so perfectly as the title song, and it reappears in the film several times. It was not made for the film.' It is one of the most 'mainstream' songs Can ever made – a jazz-inflected, gentle number that allowed Mooney to release his inner crooner – and a rare Can song where only a few members perform: the trio of Holger, Michael and Malcolm. The accompaniment is a simple, walking bassline and Michael's comping on and around three lugubrious minor chords (a distant cousin to Disney's 'Everybody Wants to Be a Cat'). Halfway through, as Malcolm's voice splits in two, Michael overdubs vapour trails of electric guitar that begin emulating a cello solo and end up surfing thermal updraughts. The crystal-clear instrumental duet, implying an absent set of 'round midnight brushed drums and tinkling jazz

keyboards, is a triumph of understatement. Of its sparse arrangement and reduced personnel, Jaki later said that his and Irmin's
contribution was to stay silent – an important philosophical statement on behalf of the Can collective.

If 'She Brings the Rain' sounded like Malcolm taking a breath of
clean air, it was a misleading impression. In December 1969, barely
a month after recording it, his already unstable mental condition
began plunging beyond any hope of rescue. In those bleak weeks
Malcolm recorded his last pieces with Can, until their short-lived
reunion twenty years later. The vocals he laid down confront his
inner turmoil head-on. 'How do you deal with something . . .?' he
yells, on the weightless *Lost Tapes* track 'When Darkness Comes',
going on to juggle words such as 'electric', 'liberty' and 'heart' in no
syntactical order. While working on a theme tune for *Mädchen . . .
nur mit Gewalt*, an insalubrious picture written and directed by
actor/director Roger Fritz, Can lapsed into a restrained, resigned
riff, as Malcolm, through a parched, cracked throat, began inton-
ing nothing but the words 'salt desert . . . it's a salt desert . . . it's
a salt desert . . .' Endless repetition turned the phrase to ashes in
Malcolm's mouth, wheezing out as 'soul desert'.

Fritz, the director, had trained under Pasolini and would go on
to act in such films as *Cross of Iron* and *Berlin Alexanderplatz*,
but since the late sixties he had been involved in a number of low-
budget soft porn flicks. *Mädchen . . . nur mit Gewalt* – whose international titles have included *The Brutes* and *Cry Rape* – attempts to
chronicle the despair of a young woman after a violent sexual attack
by two men in a bleak quarry, but can't avoid a sense of voyeuristic pleasure in its depictions of physical and psychological violation.
Can, at least, responded to the horror with several intense variations
on 'Soul Desert', including one with just Malcolm's unaccompanied
voice – the only instance of Can a cappella. '*Mädchen . . . nur mit
Gewalt* was quite a desperate film about violence, rape,' explains

Irmin, 'so the music to that film was a little bit too much. It was kind of too brutal for the film, I think. This minimal, incredible rhythm is one of Jaki's masterpieces. It's so frightening – and it should be. We worked on creating this kind of emptiness in the pattern. But then the way Malcolm sang, he was already in a really desperate state.

'It wasn't such a masterpiece, the film,' admits Irmin. 'But it was an interesting film and the music made it really harsh. It didn't take away any of its brutality and sadness, it even enforced it, and made it a bit stronger, a little bit stronger than I would do it today. That was the most brutal music to a film we ever did. Holger plays one tone, I play one tone and the guitar plays one tone. And the drums are the most skeletal . . .' The monotony the group often claimed to be trying to achieve plumbed previously unknown depths. By the time they recorded the song's final version, 'Soul Desert' had become an insistent throb of psychic pain. The group sound like penal colony inmates, swinging doomed sledgehammers against solid rock. The vultures are circling. Wordflakes rasp from a desiccated throat. Although – *because* – it ended literally with a whimper, Malcolm's final Can appearance would also be his most memorably intense. 'You might think you know somethin',' he snarls in a last moment of coherence, before 'desert' crumbles away in his mouth and his larynx gives out. He delivers the whole song in a desperately constricted death rattle. It's the sound of a man, eyes pecked out, stumbling towards the end of his rope.

After his dry spell in the soul desert, the depression overpowered Malcolm and he couldn't find his way back. The problem stemmed from a combination of elements, including drinking – he would consume a bottle of wine on stage most nights – and hash smoking, fatigue, inability to cope with sudden fame/infamy and the ever-looming threat of the US authorities catching up with him. He himself intimated that the beginning of the end was already in the wind during the Zurich residency. 'I got tired, physically tired. I was getting dissatisfied with performances. I had never worked in theatre before, and to repeat the same lines over and over again is a new thing.'[2]

On another occasion he added: 'I remember going to the theatre . . . for a rehearsal one afternoon, and I was listening to the band play. It was supposed to be a rehearsal, and I was just in the back of the theatre listening and I said, "Wow, why do I need to be in the band? I like what I hear."'[3]

Soon that feeling of obsolescence merged with wider realisations about his personal displacement. 'It got worse with him and his paranoia, which is so understandable,' says Irmin. 'He was afraid of being drafted into the army. He was terribly afraid of having to go to Vietnam. He was afraid that he would be prosecuted for desertion. And that was the main thing. Besides this, he was in this group and didn't really know where that would go, and of course we could all speak English and did speak English most of the time, but we'd talk to each other sometimes in German. And then you feel excluded, and if you are already paranoid, you always think they're talking about you. He was like a manic depressive because he could just fall into this kind of soul desert, and next day he could be the most jolly, gay, funny and spontaneous and crazy person. And on top of that, he had these complicated and sad and not very successful stories with girls, although he could be very successful – he was a really charming man, with a lot of charisma.'

With Christmas approaching, his behaviour became increasingly erratic. 'I remember going to Irmin's house pretty upset,' said Malcolm, 'and then . . . the next day I went downtown – I was going to walk, which is about eight miles or so. I went out and started walking. It was freezing . . . Got to where this Strassenbahn used to come out . . . it was the end of the line, and I started wandering down there. Two or three miles . . . and there were some workers, ditch-diggers, fixing the road. I believe the road was cobblestoned. So I asked if I could help put this road together. Something I had never done before – I would try anything. So I started working with these construction workers, I must have continued for about an hour and a half. Then I continued downtown. I had left early and I got downtown late in the day . . . and I remember calling back to Irmin, and they said, "We'll come and get you." I said, "I'll get the train back out there." Got back to the house, got back to my new place, and I had a black light in my house. A black light, white sheet, makes a great look.'[4] He sat at his desk and picked up some textbooks he had been using to try to improve his German. 'I was studying, and next door I could swear I was hearing sounds, television or something, so I couldn't stand that . . .

'Somewhere in there I remember I just couldn't find everything. And I started saying to myself, this is really planned. I had the feeling that I was really an experiment. And I said, wow, I mean the situation was that, the technology was right. Holger had talked about it once: how to increase the oxygen. Wiring the floor – this might be all B.S. in terms of science – but he said you can wire a floor and the ceiling. And turn the current on in the floor and the ceiling and create more oxygen. And being that Holger is from that school of electronic wizardry, I figured anything was possible.'[5]

Irmin's parents had come from Munich to stay in a flat on the twelfth floor of a nearby apartment building, to help Irmin and Hildegard, who was five months pregnant. Malcolm started spending more and more time in their presence, hiding away in a cupboard or standing on an outdoor ledge, which made the family nervous. 'Up there, from the balcony,' Irmin recalls, 'we had to look out that he didn't jump down. My parents liked him a lot, especially my mother. She was also this kind of very spontaneous and inventive person. We went [up] there, often. And then we couldn't, because we were afraid he would jump down in the moment when we weren't watching out. And then we all agreed that he had to go back to New York . . .'

With Malcolm acknowledging, when he surfaced for brief moments of insight, that he needed to get out of this environment, Irmin and Hildegard checked him into a local psychiatric clinic, where he stayed for a few days. 'They calmed him down a bit,' Irmin recalls. 'He was sort of clear enough to agree. He knew he needed help, and he knew we weren't any more able to help him. And neither his friends in Cologne. And the German psychiatrists neither.' He speculates that Malcolm may have considered the possibility that, arriving back in the US as a sick man, he would be ineligible to be either drafted or jailed for desertion.

Irmin: 'Then came his friend, Zim, and he stayed too, and we brought him to the psychiatrist, and he spent three days there. Meanwhile, we got the flight and everything ready. Zim was with a black wife or girlfriend, she was very militant, Black Power. She was a friend of the famous Angela Davis. They both had quite a distance to Can, and to us. Because they thought we were a bit guilty of making him crazy. I don't think so, but maybe. In a certain way it might have forced this whole environment to drive him over the edge. Nevertheless, I drove him to the hospital, and they had given him tranquillisers and stuff. I don't remember exactly the last day. Maybe because I didn't want to. I was crying . . .

'He was in the clinic for quite a while in America – twice, I think. And, of course, he has amazingly funny stories to tell about it, like he was imprisoned in a single room for a while, because he had fucked a girl on the loo. Because everybody tried to fuck, of course! I mean, they gave you this medicine which makes you [impotent], and he knew that was the medicine and he didn't take it or something, and then, of course, the need was there. And the same with the woman. So it was a big drama that they got him and her.'

Irmin insists, though, that it's a mistake to reduce Malcolm's breakdown to an outbreak of madness. 'It was not insanity – there is already the kind of genuine insanity, social insanity you are born into. If you were black in the sixties, born in America, that's already the first state of insanity.'

In the event, Malcolm's fears were not entirely justified. After he arrived in the US, he discovered that he was classified as '1Y', meaning that he would only be called up to the army in the case of a national emergency – 'So my fears at that point were completely nullified.'[6] Decades later, Malcolm published a chronology of his life online, in which he stated that during the years 1970–3, he worked as an art instructor on the Hudson River Museum's 'Art Cart' programme and as a ceramics and painting instructor at Leake & Watts Children's Home, both in Yonkers, NYC, and as an art teacher at Wilkwyck School for Boys in Yorktown. So his stay in psychiatric institutions back in the US appears to have been brief. Since then he has made and exhibited paintings, sculptures and installations involving light and shadow at many different institutions and galleries, and has also worked as a stage designer and graphic artist. In 2005 he was appointed Professor of Basic Drawing and Colour Theory at the Wentworth Institute of Technology in Boston. Although he continued to correspond with various Can members, he wouldn't see them again until 1986, when they re-formed to record *Rite Time*. On that album, he was finally able to exorcise the Furies that drove him away from the group in the first place.

Nineteen seventy began with a big freeze, and Can flailed around without a mouthpiece. 'Apparently they're having some trouble replacing [Malcolm],' wrote *Melody Maker*'s Richard Williams, in a short article surveying the new 'Euro-rock' detected on the continent, 'which doesn't surprise me since his voice is used in a highly unorthodox instrumental way, particularly since all of their music is improvised – nothing written at all. Amazing!'[7]

That winter the remaining members of Can made an appearance in *Mein schönes kurzes Leben*, a television drama for WDR directed by Klaus Lemke. The black-and-white film was transmitted in July 1970 but shot at the beginning of that year, in the slushy streets of Cologne. It's another period piece exploring that popular West German theme, juvenile delinquency and anti-authoritarianism, and features Michael Schwankhart (who looks not unlike Michael Karoli) as Mischa, a long-haired, incompetent but sympathetic petty criminal whose contacts are on the fringes of the underground scene. About a third of the way through the film, in a Cologne espresso bar at night, where Mischa is offered bootleg copies of contemporary rock LPs, Holger, Irmin, Jaki and Michael appear as vaguely threatening patrons, clad in knee-length leather greatcoats. Overhearing a dodgy promoter discussing payments on the café's public payphone, Irmin asks him, 'What about our money?' and the group rough-house him to the ground (in an echo of the real-life event that took place with Malcolm the year before). The film then cuts to Can on stage, roaring through a garagey punk tune, with Janet, played by actress/model Claudia Littmann – an aspiring professional singer in the film – taking the mic. When she auditions a vocal in a commercial studio later, it's Can's backing track she's using on the playback.[8]

In real life, the Can with Littmann on vocals might have been an interesting proposition, but it was not to be. They made attempts to find a substitute for Malcolm, placing wanted ads in the local papers and mentioning the vacancy whenever they were interviewed. 'People even said, "Could I sing with you?"' says Irmin. 'And we never said no, we invited them: "Come to the studio . . ." We had several once.' For a brief period it seemed another black African American, Lee Gates – a cousin of blues singer Albert Collins – might be in the running to replace Malcolm. 'He was knitting all the time,' recalls Irmin. 'No, he wasn't really knitting – with his hands he made these kind of hats – and he was very mild. Much too nice for us [*laughs*]. He had a very beautiful voice, but even his singing was too nice for us, it would have been drowned . . . There is always quite an edge to Can, and . . . so that was him. He never performed live with us, I don't think.'[9]

Behind the scenes in the autumn of 1969, while Can were in Switzerland, Kalle Freynik had been trawling the cities of West Germany and Switzerland selling the Music Factory pressing of

Monster Movie from the trunk of his Mercedes, generating an underground buzz. In early 1970 Siggi Loch became excited about signing Can to Liberty/United Artists. Loch, a record producer and manager, was handed the job of managing the company in 1966, with the intention of running it as a jazz label. 'I spoke to him,' says Freynik, 'and he listened to our record, and he said, "It's great," and so we started to talk about a deal and to make a contract, which took a bit of time.'

Just after whetting Loch's appetite, Freynik, infatuated with a new girlfriend, took off to Greece for a few weeks. 'We planned an instant honeymoon,' he admits. 'We stayed for three months. And a week after we left, the contract with Liberty was ready to be signed. But I wasn't there. So I asked my then very close friend, Abi Ofarim, to sign the contract in my name. He said, "Of course, we are friends, I'll do it for you." And when I came back after three months, I found out that everything went along as planned, with one little exception – he didn't sign it in my name, but in his name. Everybody was crazy with me, especially Can, because they said, "We were just about to sign the contract and you were gone – nobody knew where you were." So everything was done more or less behind my back, and this led to this horrible legal thing between Can, Ofarim and me, and United Artists, which lasted six or seven years.'

Abi Ofarim was an Israeli born in Palestine in 1937 and based in Germany since the mid-sixties. Born Abraham Reichstadt, he had been involved in music and dance since his early teens, until in 1959 he partnered up with Syrian Jewish singer and actress Esther Zaied. After coming second in the Eurovision Song Contest in 1963 – representing Switzerland – and reaching the top of the German charts in 1966, her career soared in Europe, with new husband Abi in tow. As Esther and Abi Ofarim they had a Bee Gees-penned hit, 'Morning of My Life', in Germany in 1967 and a novelty smash, 'Cinderella Rockefella', an irritating marriage of old-time saloon-bar swing and yodelling that spent three weeks as Britain's number one in early 1968 and was reputedly the last record played on pirate station Radio Caroline before the rogue ship was tugged back to shore.

As a producer for Philips Records, Siggi Loch sometimes produced tracks for the Ofarims – a few of them even written by Kalle Freynik, who was touting himself as a Dylan-style folk protest singer. After a few years the stardust wafted away. The duo broke up in 1969 and divorced in 1970. Even as their relationship was coming apart, Abi was making moves to turn his hand to artist management. In late 1969 he moved to Munich, where Freynik was living, and set up a publishing/production company called PROM (the name is printed on Can's original vinyl pressings from this period), with a roster of songwriters and artists. 'I was one of them,' says Freynik. 'I wrote a lot of stuff for those people, and I should have wondered why nobody is paid. But we were too stoned to find out, because everything was very friendly and very hip, you know? Buddies. We even went on holiday together. We spent almost every day doing something, playing music, smoking, whatever. And I regarded him as a really close friend. But obviously he wasn't.'

In a newspaper interview in autumn 1971 Ofarim claimed he just wanted to help boost the German music scene, but he didn't sound altogether convinced by Can. 'I think I am a real fan of theirs,' he said, 'as Can indulge in rambling improvisations.'[10]

For a group that was routinely spending eight hundred marks to play a gig that paid a thousand, his promises of high-level connections and international stardom must have seemed alluring. He also claimed that it was he who had persuaded Siggi Loch at United Artists to sign up Can in the first place. But from the beginning the partnership seems to have been as treacherous as the shores of Tagomago. 'He was also in his high days of drugs,' says Freynik. 'I think he didn't breathe [air] at all, he only smoked pot, day and night.' Ofarim proved inadequate to the tasks of organising and steering an artistic career.

Freynik: 'I was mad, because I could have made some money with Can, if everything went the way it was planned, and they were mad [with] me, because they had the impression that I just let things go at this very important moment, where they're about to sign the first contract and decide which way to go. A lot of decisions had to be done. Which was, of course, true in a way, so I could understand them.'

8

In at the Deep End

To be a hippy and let your freak flag fly in the West Germany of 1970 was not the benign act of passive resistance it was in San Francisco or Canterbury. Even the British *Guardian* newspaper picked up on the disturbing results of a poll in which 56 per cent of West Germans thought the solution to the hippy 'problem' was some form of compulsory work programme. A report from that year, headlined 'Long Hair a German Badge of Courage', concluded: 'In a conversation about work-shy youth the other day, I heard a man who had previously impressed with his tolerance say: "Hitler was evil – there's no doubt about that, but you know these labour camps he set up were not a bad idea. There were no long-haired louts about in those days."

'This atmosphere of intolerance reached its peak in Constance. For several months, in the words of mayor Dr Bruno Helmle, there has been confrontation between the citizens and long-haired youth. At a pop festival last month, some young people were attacked by members of the public. A local councillor, Walter Eyermann, of the extreme Right-wing National Democratic party, offered to organise a band of 40 respectable citizens to settle the hippy problem once and for all.'[1]

With this in mind, it's possible to gauge the effect on the notoriously respectable burghers of Munich of the rock musical *Hair*, when it took up residence there in 1970. Arriving straight from the liberal off-Broadway of Manhattan, *Hair* – while featuring relatively innocuous music – caused infamy on account of its espousal of so-called hippy values and featured scenes of nudity.

Anyone watching the Munich production of 1970,[2] which featured future stars Donna Summer and Boney M's Liz Mitchell among the cast, might have also caught a glimpse of a tiny Japanese figure – an outgrown moptop on a short stick – bent over a guitar in the musical pit. This was a nineteen-year-old itinerant from Japan named Kenji Suzuki, who had travelled from his home in Atsugi-city in Japan's Kanagawa Prefecture two years earlier. He was generally known as 'Damo', a nickname (based on a misfortune-prone anime character) he had picked up while staying on a farm in Wexford, Ireland.

Little is known about Damo's early life in Japan. He has previously been quoted as saying that 'Expression comes quite often from the experience, which begins in childhood. I had a strong mother, and I have so much DNA from her, so this is inspiration too.'[3] Music was drip-fed to him from an early age: his sister, who worked in a bank, gave him a new instrument on every birthday. 'When I was eight or nine years old I got my first instrument, a flute I think, then a clarinet and a saxophone . . . I also had a guitar and an organ. She wanted me to play music.'[4]

In his teens, Damo gradually became dissatisfied with aspects of Japanese society and felt some kinship with the country's various protest movements, which began as early as the anti-American demonstrations of 1960 and flared up again in 1968. He would carry the spirit of that era with him through to late in life. 'I'm an anarchist,' he told an interviewer in 2004. 'I don't believe in any kind of politician and I'm not so interested in economic things and materialism, so it's my dream to continue this so that people get a feeling that brings them much more together. But I don't like to be a leader – you must believe this – and if someone tries to be a leader there is no anarchy.'[5]

He would end up making his home in Europe, specifically West Germany, and harboured a critical attitude to his homeland even as he got older. 'Japanese society is like a pyramid,' he told an interviewer in 2013. 'Each stone is exactly the same, and it's built up into a pyramid. Each of them is able to function, but all together it's not very flexible to react to something. So they must be part of this society, but out of the society they cannot do anything.'[6] Damo made it his life's work to do something – anything – outside these constraints, in a perpetual pattern of self-(re)invention. 'If you're a creative person,' he told the same interviewer, 'it's important to break rules. If you're in the middle of the system, you can't create much. But if you're on the outside, you can just avoid it, start from zero and make your own stuff with no influence at all.'[7]

On 29 November 1967 a tiny listing appeared in the 'penpals wanted' section of the Swedish newspaper *Expressen*, under the headline 'Wants to study Swedish traditions'. 'I am a Japanese boy who is interested in Swedish customs and traditions, says KENZI [*sic*] SUZUKI, 2-1-3 Midorigaoka, Atsugi-city, Kanagawa, Japan. He is planning to come here to look closer at our customs and traditions and wonders if somebody wants to accept him as a guest for a month.'

Twenty-one people from all over Sweden replied to Kenji's request. Among them were Gösta and Helga Andersson from Gräsmark, a tiny rural hamlet in south-western Sweden, about thirty kilometres from the border with Norway. Of all the places in the world he could have travelled to, Kenji lighted on Sweden because he was attracted by its functioning social democracy and generous welfare state. As he stepped off the Trans-Siberian Railway in February 1968, this village, barely registering on maps at the time, was to provide Damo – clean-shaven, with a John Lennon-style grown-out bowl haircut, and bearing his guitar, clarinet and sax – with his first experience not only of snow, but of life in western Europe.

The Andersson women, who lived in a typical detached, wooden-slatted fifties Swedish house, ran the local taxi service, commanding a fleet of two vehicles. They provided Damo with board and lodging and a weekly allowance of ten Swedish kroner, although Gräsmark had no village shop of any kind to spend anything on. On one occasion, desperate to buy cigarettes, Damo hitch-hiked out of the village and ended up taking a seven-day round trip via Switzerland.

A few weeks later, the numbers of Gräsmark's temporary Japanese community swelled from one to two, when Kenji was joined at the Andersson residence by a friend, Shuji Kawamukai. In such a tiny community, the presence of two foreigners could not escape the attention of the local press. The *Värmlands Folkblad*, on 19 March 1968, ran a profile of the two visitors: 'When they are not exercising, skiing, or having snowball fights . . . they are teaching the family . . . how to prepare Japanese culinary delicacies or spreading musical harmony . . . An interview with the Japanese youngsters was not possible: so far they are mostly communicating with head and arm gestures, but are very interested to learn the Swedish language and are starting to make small progress with our strange idiom . . .. And through a little English and a big interest in music they have made many new friends among the teenagers in Gräsmark. They are fantastically polite and nice, says their Swedish mother.'

The rest of the article shows how music was clearly the dominant element in their daily life at the time. Their landlady mentions that they play and sing almost all the time, and have introduced their own music to the local population. 'According to Mrs Andersson Värmlandish and Japanese pop has been mixed into a very harmonious unity. The teenage musicians of Gräsmark compete against each other in order to play together with Kenzi and Shuji. And it is easy to understand that for the listeners in Värmland it is something very special when the two Japanese boys start to sing in their own wild native tongue. Kenzi is also on his way to become a pop idol back home in Japan as well. He has made a record which has been pressed in thousands of copies. They have also introduced their beloved Japanese courtesy to Gräsmark. When they greet someone they put their hands together in front of their chests and bow, making their long black pop star hair touch the floor.' The piece goes on to mention that they are also hoping to extend their planned one-month stay in Sweden by looking for work in Karlstad, either as judo instructors or chefs. Clearly, they had been taking over in Gösta Andersson's kitchen. '"Delicious!" says Mrs Andersson. Shuji has made different kinds of rice, of course, chicken, soups and salads. But unfortunately he had to manage with our "Swedish" spices, because the shops of Gräsmark were not prepared for Japanese cooking. Kenzi and Shuji hope that the grocery stores of Karlstad have a bigger selection of spices.'

Birgitta Engman, known as Gittan, still runs a hairdressing salon next door to her childhood home in Gräsmark, where her sister now lives. As a sixteen-year-old girl in 1968, the daughter of the Anderssons' neighbours, she was befriended by Kenji Suzuki during his months there. On that first night Gittan recorded him on tape, and in the weeks that followed she introduced him to her circle of friends, all willing pupils as Kenji sat around with his guitar and tried to teach them Japanese pop songs, particularly Kyu Sakamoto's slushy hit 'Sukiyaki'. They also enjoyed shooting air pistols together. She still owns a clutch of intimate letters, sketches, self-caricatures and scribbled lyrics by Kenji, dating from between 1968 and 1972. His affection for her is clear from the tone of his letters, and from the handwritten lyric, 'For My Birgitta', written in 1968: 'I wanna spend with you for ever / More the time with you together / This is to much for me / the existing state of things . . . I wanna spend with you for ever / I must come back to my home / that distant about 5700 km / Still, you follow me, isn't it? / isn't it?, isn't it?' According to her reminiscences more than forty years later, he wanted to take her back with him to Japan and open a record shop together, but first he needed to carry on travelling around the world in order to finance the plane tickets required to attain that distant dream.

After barely a month Kenji and Shuji eventually moved on to Karlstad – their arrival was reported in *Värmlands Folkeblad* on 23 March. Damo himself later recalled staying 'in a commune in

Sweden in the countryside with fifty people just enjoying living and doing nothing, and being in nature . . . In the countryside you have much more communication with the people, so I stayed in Sweden with fifty people and I spoke with all of them. If you live in London maybe you speak with none of them.'[8]

Kenji's wanderings are hazy over the next year or so, but this Swedish commune apparently eased him fully into the kind of gentle anarchism and detachment from urban capitalism that attracted him to Europe in the first place. From now on he would live the life of an itinerant minstrel and street artist: after Sweden, he has said, 'I travelled around Europe busking and painting, in Germany, France, Switzerland, Finland. I was busking for about six months. Then I lived in Wexford in Ireland for six months, and also in Seven Sisters in London.'[9]

He had certainly reached Wexford by August 1969, as he sent Gittan a letter from there, including a self-portrait in biro, now with drooping moustache, shoulder-length hair and brooding scowl, and the announcement that he had been given the nickname Damo. To an Irish newspaper he later said, 'I was in County Wexford, New Ross, with Mary and Tom Murphy . . . My memory of Ireland from that time is of kindly, friendly people, folk dance and music, fields, cows, bees, flowers, Guinness, Murphys, etc. . . .'[10] He considered moving back to Japan to study, but during his brief sojourn in north London he sold enough paintings in Green Park and the Underground to afford a ticket to West Germany. While passing through Munich in early 1970, he was hired to play guitar in the local production of *Hair*. After months of living hand to mouth through busking and performing various arresting actions in public, the income from the production was too good to turn down. He stayed in the city, occasionally at the squat occupied by the anarcho-freaks of the Amon Düül collective, and it was there, in late May, that his path crossed with Can in a way that was either total coincidence or willed by some planetary alignment. 'After about three months,' he said, 'I was very frustrated because I was doing the same thing every day. I can't really remember what I was doing when I met Can, but every day I would go into the street and do a kind of street performance or just scream because I was frustrated. But they saw me and asked me to be their singer not because they liked my voice but because they wanted somebody who looked like an alien. Japanese or Chinese people in the early seventies were seen seldom, totally different to now . . . They wanted me for this, they didn't know how I sang.'[11]

So it was Damo's eccentric screams that caught the attention of Holger and Jaki as they sat outside a Munich bar in May 1970, round the corner from the Blow Up club, where they were beginning a four-night residency with a sold-out show. Holger remembered the moment: 'I was sitting with Jaki in a café and Damo came along and he was making an incantation to the sun or something strange like that. I said, "Jaki, this man will be our new singer." He said, "Come on, are you being serious? You haven't even heard him and you say that?" So I went to Damo and said, "What are your plans for tonight?" He said, "Nothing." So I said, "Do you want to be a singer in a band for a sold out concert?"'[12]

'I had no other appointment that night, fortunately,' Damo recalled drily.[13] He asked Holger if there would be any rehearsal, and after receiving a reply in the negative, he needed no further encouragement.

This utterly spontaneous manoeuvre by Holger would have a crucial impact on Can's most strongly defined years of music and stage presentation. Even though Damo joined the band on stage with no preparation and limited communication, their potent chemistry flared up from the very start. 'During the concert,' Holger recalled, 'he started very, very calm but then he developed into a samurai fighter and the people got so angry that they left the venue. There was only about thirty people left in a venue that holds fifteen hundred.'[14]

Several band members retain a blurred memory of the English actor David Niven being ushered backstage by Abi Ofarim before this show at the Blow Up. No one can remember what brought the suave thespian into Can's orbit, or what he was doing in Munich, but Niven can be placed in Italy in May 1970, shooting a film called *The Statue*, and might have been doing the deal that led to him appearing in an adaptation of Vladimir Nabokov's *King, Queen, Knave*, directed by *Deep End* director Jerzy Skolimowsky in Munich a year later. Whatever the reason, Can rewarded Ofarim's complacent desire to show off his 'protégés' to this famous actor by sabotaging their own show.

'On Saturday in this discotheque,' says Irmin, 'it's the people from outside town; the real insiders would never go to the Blow Up on Saturday evening. So we didn't have our public, and we had a terrible war with the owner, besides Ofarim. So when we went on stage, we bought a few cakes, these really German ones with cream, really juicy ones which you throw into other people's faces. We went on this stage, like a mezzanine or balcony, and when I came in from the artist entrance, there was a building site beside, and I took two bricks and put them on the organ keys and turned it to full . . . And then sat down with Michael, leaned his guitar against the speaker and didn't touch it the whole evening. And I didn't touch the organ. And the guitar was screaming, the organ was screaming, and Holger was lying on his back with his bass. And besides, all three of us, Holger, Michael and me, were eating cake, like really grabbing it and [shovelling it into their mouths] in the most disgusting way!

'Jaki was still the only "musician". He was never ever performing in those kind of protests. He was sitting there with a red face because he was trying to go against this incredible noise and was drumming like a madman. And our new singer was standing in front of this mezzanine and every now and then taking some cake, [munching it] and then screaming! Like getting tortured. So we succeeded [in making] most of the people leave. I think there was a bunch of

English-speaking tourists, twenty of them. They stood there, totally dumbstruck! Like, "This is Europe!" They were quite impressed. And down there was sitting Abi Ofarim with David Niven. They were drinking whisky and then left. But for some time they listened to our orgy, and Mr Ofarim didn't really know what he should think about it. And he knew it was against him.'

Niven was somewhat perplexed by what he had seen, according to Holger. 'I asked him, "Mr Niven, what did you think about this music?" And he said, "It was great, but I didn't know it was music."'

On the *Soundtracks* LP the thunderous tympani dying away at the end of *Deadlock*'s instrumental theme give way to the muted Latin cowbell of 'Don't Turn the Light On, Leave Me Alone', the product of Damo's first visit to the recording studio with his new colleagues, which Irmin remembers as quite a bad-tempered affair. 'Damo first had real difficulties to see himself in this group . . . he had doubts that he did the right thing. He was not really arguing, just in quite a bad mood. And we thought he is a moody person. He isn't that much – he was just really uncertain [if that] is the right thing to do. That's bloody understandable! Because with a bunch like us – and, of course, he is right – we were very disciplined workers. And he had never done discipline in his life! So it must have been pretty hard for him. We sometimes felt it, but we didn't care; we just thought he is good and it's nice to have him, but if he can't make it, he can't make it – *basta*.'

Notably, 'Don't Turn the Light On, Leave Me Alone' contains one of the first iterations of a signature modal sequence in the Can songbook: four descending chords that revolve in a cyclical pattern. Taped in June 1970, the tune – in a variety of alternative mixes and instrumental edits – edges its way among the bourgeois interiors and scurrilous encounters of *Cream – Schwabing-Report*, directed by Leonidas Capetanos and released in Germany in 1971. A few years later, it cropped up in certain sleaze-pit cinemas in the

English-speaking world, under various titles including *Secret Life of a Schoolgirl Wife*, *Schoolgirl Bride* and *The Servicer*. It's hardly worth elaborating the plot, as the movie is a typically titillating effort, soft-core by early-twenty-first-century standards, involving an Italian stud in Munich, a porno film producer and a bored young bride played by Barbara Scott (billed as Barbara Klingered), who had recently appeared as a topless pagan in an appalling X-rated Hansel and Gretel adaptation, *The Naked Wytche*. 'A reflection of erotica today', 'After she finished with the men . . . she started on the boys!' and 'Too much woman for one man . . .' were a few of *Cream's* poster taglines. Elsewhere in the film, as the young protagonists share a joint or indulge in snail's-pace love-making, you can hear some of Can's deep, slow, experimental pieces, creaking away with bowed bass, tinkling inside-piano strumming and Jew's harp. There's also a nightclub scene where the dancefloor heaves to the sound of an unreleased but highly funky Can track, with Malcolm on vocals.

'Don't Turn the Light On . . .' remains a fine piece of music, with Damo's vocal strangely dispassionate against the saucy goings-on. 'I can only compare [his singing] with Billie Holiday,' Michael stated, 'this strange, modal way of singing a very refined harmony, with some slight dissonances.'[15]

Deep End, directed by Jerzy Skolimowski, is probably the most critically acclaimed piece of cinema Can ever soundtracked, feted by David Lynch for its colour design and occasionally compared with works by the likes of Truffaut, Godard and Polanski. It narrates the infatuation of a fifteen-year-old boy, Mike (John Moulder-Brown), with the older Susan (Jane Asher), his co-worker at a London public swimming pool. Despite several exterior shots of Soho and a public baths in Leytonstone, east London, the bulk of the movie was filmed in Munich in the first half of 1970, with Can's contribution recorded in July. When Mike floats in the pool, half dreaming an erotic encounter, there's a soporific theme on organ and bass. Midway through the film comes a five-minute sequence in which Mike wanders through an array of sleazy Soho locations and the London Underground and encounters odd, violent or threatening characters. He refuses a free meal from a Chinese hot-dog seller (played by a youthful Burt Kwouk). In a changing booth at the pool, Diana Dors, in a grotesque caricature of her former glamour-puss days, hugs him to her bosom as she climaxes while fantasising about George Best. Then Mike is set adrift in the neon forest of Soho's notorious streets, in a disorientating montage of impressions and actuality shots.

Deploying Can's 'Mother Sky' for this extended sequence of wandering disorientation was a masterstroke. It appears in a fourteen-minute version on *Soundtracks* and was the most intense sustained piece since 'Yoo Doo Right'. From the instant the track cuts in, with the group already in overdrive, it's a heads-down, primeval, one-chord race to oblivion, with Jaki hammering down a straight backbeat and Holger playing two bass notes an octave apart. While the whole duration of the piece is held together under the same jackhammer beat, whose tempo does not falter, it is also a set of variations stitched together by subtle cuts between takes, each new one punctuated with a booming strike on a bass drum. In this way 'Mother Sky' resembles the splicing together of visual sequences in the film. In one fragment, Michael's guitar is the lead voice, ranting a hysterical perpetual solo. In a later section, Irmin's keyboard rasps a shrill, overdriven screech. Elsewhere it gears down to a chapel-like serenity, allowing Damo's tobacco-and-incense chant to come through. At the centre is an astonishing passage of overdubbed tom-toms, Jaki souping up his monotonous, four-square blueprint by rolling around his tuned toms with rattling bombinations.

To date, Can had never sounded so one-minded as they did on 'Mother Sky'. Minimalising the musical elements even more starkly than before, the group's individuated sensibilities finally crashed together in lockstep. Irmin recalls: 'That was a very special case. Skolimowsky had heard "Yoo Doo Right" and was totally blown away by it, he loved it. And he said he wants a long piece for this whole sequence of totally different scenes all kept together by this young guy going through town looking for this girl. But they are totally different scenes. I got the idea to keep it together by this one monotone rhythm that goes throughout the whole eighteen minutes, and then according to every scene, very abruptly, really with the cut, changing what's on top of it. So we played the basis of "Mother Sky", which means we played this rhythm, and some sounds and rhythm guitar, very little things on it, and then we played different characters and moods on it. Michael playing this wild, strange, wonderful solo for the scene with the Chinese, and then when they enter the disco. So we had this and dubbed different characters on it, and then edited it in time with the film. It was a very complicated work, so it's always the same – what we call the ground tape, and then we did different characters on it. And then we edited the different characters according to the needs of the film – the film dictated the cut.'

Resonant thuds detonate throughout the track, marking the changes of scene, and also delineating the visual edits. 'To make the cuts somehow musically logical', explains Irmin, 'we invented this thing that something ended abruptly, but then . . . it's always Jaki doing this overdub with these drum shots – all of a sudden he creates a strange silence, but it's not a silence, because the ground tape goes on. Those mark the cuts. That was very special.'

Sounding lean and hungry but also increasingly confident, 'Mother Sky' again demonstrates how fast Can was able to evolve and react to its latest mutation, absorbing and assimilating Damo into its organic matter.

'Mother Sky' was the best example so far of Can's music-making dovetailing seamlessly with the film-maker's methods. In practice, this was achieved each time after a good deal of shuttling back and forth by Irmin between the film's production base – normally Munich or Berlin – and the group's studio at Nörvenich. 'It was much too difficult to travel with five people, to sit with five people in front of the screen and have a discussion with the director and producer. That would complicate it. And it couldn't be brought into our studio and shown. Everybody in the group found that totally natural. They knew I had done this before, and the discussions with directors I had done for ten years before Can, so that was a normal thing for me. And they weren't that interested anyway.

'The normal thing is, I get the film, the post-production is not yet finished but the dialogue is sort of on it and the editing is nearly finished. So you have the reel. And then I look together with the director at the film, very carefully, and discuss it. And he says what he imagined, and normally I look before that and get ideas – not musical ideas, more dramaturgical or structural, architectural ideas. I'm discussing it with the director, and basically you make a cue list [for] where there should be music on each scene, and what it means to have it there. Because what I like very much is to make bridges from one scene to another later on, which is now going out of fashion, because the music itself doesn't tell anything any more – it's a neutral background mood and doesn't create structure.

'So then I went [back] to the studio with my cue list, knowing what is going on, and I told the others the film. Just told the story and the mood, like a storyteller. And said we should play this and this and make scenes that have this length and whatever. And then we started just playing. I started picking out moments where I thought, "Oh, that would be wonderful for this scene, let's go a bit deeper into this kind of mood."

'When we worked, we made music. We didn't discuss abstract things. We made music like any other music. I only had to take care that it went in a certain direction. Sometimes we made much more than was needed for the film, and other snippets became part of the next record or something. But there was then all of a sudden something which really fitted to the film, and then we jumped on it and made variations.'

Jaki confirmed this account: 'We'd never seen the film before, but Irmin had. He'd tell us what it was about, and things just went on from there. We could simply put ourselves in the right mood. The rest was completely normal studio work. We didn't bother with what went on in the film. We simply made the music and it always fit. Irmin structured it so that the timing was right. Naturally, we knew something about the atmosphere of the film and whether it was a lighter, or more tension-filled story.'[16]

An exception to this method came in August 1970, when Can were asked at short notice to make some music cues for *Deadlock*, a bleak German spaghetti western by director Roland Klick. The commission came about after Peter Przygodda, who was editing the reels, felt that Klick's initial idea for the soundtrack – himself improvising on guitar – was a self-indulgence too far. Irmin: 'Peter and others said, "Look, Roland, this has become such a wonderful film, it's a pity to mess it up with your banal music!" So Peter convinced him to come to us and ask us if we could make the music. But the thing was, the film was about to be mixed, and the date was already fixed, which means you can't cancel it, it costs you a fortune. So he had really to hurry up with the music. And he said, "We start mixing the film in two days, do you think . . .?" And we said, "Oh, we'll see what we can do."'

Deadlock features a small group of tormented individuals thrown together in a remote hellhole in the middle of some unspecified desert. The frames are saturated with sweat, blood and mutual distrust, as the balance of power constantly shifts between them by means of cunning or brute force. Kid, a young, hip gangster (played by Marquard Bohm, another actor who resembles Michael Karoli), arrives on the scene with a gunshot wound to the arm and a suitcase full of cash. At the mercy of Mr Dump, who discovers his inert body, he is forced to recuperate for several days in a tumbledown shack, surrounded by the strange denizens of this post-apocalyptic locale, including a sex-crazed older woman and an enigmatic, slightly backward teenage girl. Can's 'Tango Whiskyman' appears almost as a character in the film, as it appears on a seven-inch single that the Kid is also carrying in his suitcase and is spun repeatedly on a turntable. '. . . And that music – that's no coincidence . . . He plays it for a reason,' says one character, after hearing it for the umpteenth time. Its repetitive intro provides significant punctuation to the atmosphere of woozy threat that pervades throughout. Occasionally, the vinyl skips, and at the end the jumping record accompanies a psychotic episode. At one point Dump is force-fed whisky and made to dance as bullets explode around his feet – hence the track's title.

At another juncture, the Kid is compelled at gunpoint to play a harp/xylophone-type instrument, while his captor, Mr Sunshine, shoots at his fingers. The effect is reminiscent of Can's 'Ethnological Forgery Series', in which they coaxed strange sounds out of unfamiliar and exotic instruments.

'Roland came to the studio first and tried to tell us how the music should be made,' says Irmin. 'And after one hour I said, "Look, either you just leave the studio and leave us alone, and you'll get the music in time, or you had better do it yourself." Which created a certain type of tension of course! That was the only way to do it, because he was unbearable, talking all the time – you can't really come to the point. So then we just created the parts at night. In the morning at eight o'clock I flew to Berlin, put it to the film. I assisted with the mix, and in the afternoon I flew back to Cologne and made the next session with Can. That went on for about five or six days, me having at least twelve ounces of speed per day and sleeping for one hour on the way to Berlin and one hour on the way back to the studio.'

The desert locale and ever-present sense of threat gave Can permission to unleash a tribute to the funereal bombast of Ennio Morricone. Irmin's organ is especially prominent, generating a heat-haze shimmer at certain moments when the camera lens is tipped up and flooded with sunlight. 'It's so clear and obvious: a homage

Single A side: 'She Brings the Rain', from the soundtrack to *Ein Grosser Grau-Blauer Vogel* (*A Big Grey-Blue Bird*) by Thomas Schamoni

Single B side: 'Soul Desert', from the soundtrack to *Mädchen mit Gewalt* by Roger Fritz

Outside Schloss Nörvenich, 1969. From left to right: Michael Karoli, David Johnson, Jaki Liebezeit, Holger Czukay, Irmin Schmidt and Malcolm Mooney

At the Can studio in Schloss
Nörvenich, 1969

Malcolm Mooney, 1969

Damo Suzuki, 1971

Outside the Can Studio, Weilerswist, 1971. From left to right: Michael, Holger, Jaki, Damo, Uli Gerlach (Can's tour manager) and Irmin. Also present is Irmin and Hildegard's dog, Assi; a rescued lab dog, she became Can's mascot and often guarded the equipment van on tour.

Holger Czukay

Michael Karoli

Irmin Schmidt (in the background is Robbie Müller, cameraman for the Can film)

Jaki Liebezeit in the Can Studio, Weilerswist, 1972

Cologne, 1972 (Gesine Petter)

to Morricone in the beginning, which is my side, and there's a cool rock piece, "Tango Whiskyman", a totally different style, and they are all very balanced against each other. Certain themes in the end repeat the Morricone theme. It's very structured.'

On the instrumental title that closes the movie, Jaki's tom-toms resound like orchestral tympani and Irmin's Farfisa is as solemn as a mausoleum dirge. Irmin says: 'The film ends with this very melancholic song, very heartbreaking. There's a lot of organ in this film, it plays a very important role, and for this song I used a piece of Johann Sebastian Bach from the *Matthäus-Passion*, and I played the harmonies and we built the song on that. Which we rarely did – this kind of quotation stuff. But it helped to hit the mood, after [the two protagonists] had killed each other and all that. And Damo was fantastic in all of that; his melody is so touching. I remember it was a sunny morning, about six o'clock in the morning in summer. We just finished it in time, and I had to go with the tape to Berlin. Michael listened to the tape and stood there, and of course, after one week without sleep, we started crying like little girls, we were so touched by the music!

'So with tears in my eyes and the tape in my bag, I went to Berlin and did the last session, and at a certain moment my memory is gone, because we had a discussion about something in this end scene, with "Tango Whiskyman" – it's all very constructed, the music coming out of the music box, and it's all related and it should have the right loudness and effect – and suddenly I found myself lying on a bed and a nurse above me saying, "It's OK, everything is OK . . ." And Roland and Peter Przygodda and the whole crew told me I got angry, then I started crying, and then just fainted! Fell off the seat, after a week without sleep.

'It was fun to do,' he enthuses, 'because we really put a lot of energy and emotion into it, and you still feel it. There is not one second of music which is neutral or banal or trivial. Every moment tells a story. Also, it was a very good film. It plays with different genres. That's what we did then too. It actually became Can's most successful film music – this film is shown every few years on German television.'

Soundtracks – 'a selection of title songs and soundtracks from the last five movies for which THE CAN wrote the music', as the brief sleeve note put it – emerged on Liberty in the month after work on *Deadlock* finished. Its psychedelic purple sleeve, with a collage of film stock from the various movies bulging through a fisheye lens, included one of the alternative titles briefly suggested by Thomas Schamoni (*Bottom* instead of *Ein grosser graublauer Vogel*) and even misspelt Michael's name. But the back cover featured one of the most revealing shots of the group yet made public: a large black-and-white shot in the entrance hall of Nörvenich, bare except for a few of Ulrich Rückriem's blocky stone sculptures. Holger stares slightly manically into the lens, holding an amplified koto-like string instrument. Damo, in an odd, rustic, sugarloaf-shaped hat, perches on a bench of marble, growling into a mic. Irmin, his face lost in a cone of hair, sits astride a pile of stone blocks, tugging the strings of a ukulele. Jaki bends to tap a bass drum, and 'Michael Caroli' is playing an upright bass at the far end of the room. This uncanny mixture of art, architectural elegance and unconventional sound-making creates a seductive and enigmatic impression.

And this was a group already in transformation. With the microphonic baton now passed to a new vocalist, Can were ready to embrace a new phase in their brief lifespan. 'Album no. two will be released in the beginning of 1971,' bulletined the sleeve notes. Damo mailed a copy of *Soundtracks* to Gittan in Sweden, with a covering note dated 11 November 1970: 'We still are making another long playing record which will be released biging [*sic*] of next year. And next record will be a world-class record which is good as musicaly, and the music not pop music but the music which we like to play and really our original and personality. We are working for it from beginning of September. But, still working on it.'[17] That record – *Tago Mago* – was the one on which all the disparate ingredients that constituted Can would finally bed down and take root; and the first proper, major statement after two years of experimentation and research.

9

Witchy Surprisings

The island of Tagomago basks in the Mediterranean Sea, less than a kilometre off the north-eastern tip of Ibiza. Only a kilometre and a half long, it's hardly more than an outcrop of rock, the last vestige of an ancient volcanic rim. Even in the early twenty-first century, there is little more than a handful of luxury hotels scattered around its rocky acreage, connected by a single road; from the air it looks almost deserted, with rocky coastal crags, odd-shaped inlets and a light covering of greenery and parched scrubland. Nowadays Tagomago is owned by a Spanish entrepreneur and is hired out to politicians and celebrities for luxury holidays or business functions. But despite its exclusivity, there is still a wildness about it that no amount of infinity pools or minimalist villas will entirely wipe out. A brother of the Carthaginian commander Hannibal, Mago Barca, who lived in the second century BCE, is believed to have used the island as a bolthole during his many Mediterranean military campaigns. Its name literally means 'Mago rock'.

The members of Can considered *Tago Mago*, recorded in the closing months of 1970 and released early the following year, to be its second album. Unlike the previous two releases, which had been compiled from tracks assembled over a longer time frame, *Tago Mago* was a planned album from the start. From the giant head painted on the gatefold sleeve (which, at a stretch, resembles the outline of the real island), to its sprawl across four vinyl sides of a double LP, including two monumental tracks filling an entire side each, *Tago Mago* felt big. Taken as a whole, its seven cuts were confident yet exploratory, at times perilously close to collapse. The radical sound it proposed left the group standing as isolated from its peers as Tagomago itself. At last, after several months of bending to this sole task, Can's energies were focused and intensified, the magnifying glass tilted to just the right angle for the grass to smoke.

'If you study music from all over the world,' Irmin mused to an *NME* journalist in 1972, 'it seems that in lands surrounded by water the music is influenced more by water and air while the more you go into a continent, the more you get into a land mass, the melody of the music becomes less important in comparison with the rhythmic heaviness. It seems water has something to do with melody, while countries like Germany produce music more of earth and fire.'[1] At various times *Tago Mago* is wreathed in all of these elements, the roofless island and the horizonless interior.

Myths surround Can's *Tago Mago*, just as they swirl around the Balearic island itself. One repeated assertion is that the island – and by extension the album – has a connection with the occultist Aleister Crowley. While the group members often referred to magic and occult practices around the time it was made, there is no provable link between Crowley and Tagomago – it just seems to be one of those fanciful legends repeated unquestioningly in print and online. As we'll see, though, there is a Crowleyan link to one of the album's most significant cuts.

Several conflicting stories of Can members' visits to the island circulated at the time too. Even as late as 2014 Holger was spinning this blatantly nonsensical yarn to an American interviewer: '*Tago Mago* is a magical work. Before Jaki came to Can, he was trying to commit suicide. He was playing with Chet Baker in Barcelona, as a jazz drummer. Then he went to Ibiza. And south of this island is a rock called Tagomago. Mago means magic, and Tago was the name of a magic master who lived there. And Jaki was on that rock and tried to spring down because he thought his life didn't make any sense. I think he is the one who said we should call it *Tago Mago*.'[2]

But whether you choose to believe any or none of these unverifiable legends, one way to make sense of *Tago Mago*'s barrage of aural sensations is to consider the album itself as a magic isle of the mind, the remote site of initiation rites that take the listener – and the musicians themselves – on a hermetic journey from light to darkness and back again. In the course of its seventy-two minutes, it hits peaks of rapture and plunges into the void. In texts that spin forwards and backwards, it entertains visions of blood flow, disturbing drug experiences, gnomic chants, mass destruction, and winds up pleading to be cleansed. It's a garden of earthly delights teetering over a hellish, all-consuming abyss.

It was on this album that Can at last learned to harness its extra-sensory faculties. A few years later, Irmin described the events on the record as 'witchy surprisings'. Michael, in 1974, told Nick Kent: '*Tago Mago* was our real magic album. Irmin kept making these spells throughout the time it was being recorded, and I was warning him against it. It's something that you just understand and get into if you read a lot of books about it.'[3] Much later, he added: 'We were interested in everything . . . in the universe . . . in nature. Magic is a way to influence nature. That intrigued us. We never tried to commercialise magic. We were also interested in things like astrology . . . because it was an opportunity to explain certain things. Why are people born in the spring . . . different from those born in the autumn . . .? Your environment is your music, and thus we were a German group. If you live in the desert, you'll make a music that's different from if you lived in a rainforest. We lived near Cologne, an area with a lot of industrial sounds and beautiful scenery.'[4]

As Can embarked on the choppy voyage towards the edifice of *Tago Mago*, the group's make-up, and the powers at their disposal, had altered considerably. Their last appearance of 1970 was supporting Black Sabbath at Essen's Grugahalle on 16 December. As the new year broke, the West German *Sounds* magazine – the nation's equivalent of the *NME* – voted them second-best German group (after Amon Düül II) and *Soundtracks* the second-top German album of 1970 (after Düül's *Yeti*). Since the spring Can had not only scooped up a new vocalist, they were also supposed to be under the management wing of Abi Ofarim's PROM organisation. Until now their affairs, bookings and general arrangements had been casually handled collectively by the group; private artist management was not permitted under West German law at the time (all such dealings were supposed to be handled by a state bureau), but the rules were relaxing fast in the new music-business climate.

As for the new vocalist, his lines could be as meaningful – or meaningless – as the other instruments. Unlike Malcolm, whose enunciation was usually piercingly clear, Damo forced listeners to strain to hear what he was singing about. Today there are many websites devoted to reproducing lyrics, but Can's texts – especially those from the Damo era – are notably inconsistent, vainly transcribed by fans with cans, littered with apologetic question marks and disclaimers. Can songs are neither arguments, logical statements nor message-carriers; they're certainly not the expressions of sentiment modern ears have been trained to receive since the origins of opera and the birth of the Romantic song in the age of Schubert and Wolf.

'I like Jim Morrison, but I'm not a Jim Morrison so I don't have to sing like Jim Morrison,' Damo said. 'I'm not a protest singer, I'm not interested about politics really. I'm just not so much interested about anything. That's why I'm singing nothing – It's how myself is.'[5]

'I was captured when I realised that he was a loud whisperer,' recalled Michael. 'He yelled only occasionally; usually he simply whispered loudly. I thought that was ideal . . . Naturally, the sound of the band altered, from a group that had a screaming singer to one that had a whispering singer.'[6]

'He couldn't really speak English,' adds the writer Duncan Fallowell, who got to know the group around this time. 'He'd been busking on the streets and he'd invented this pseudo-language of sounds, which is very original – something Johnny Rotten later tried to do with PiL, but it didn't go very far – but Damo brought terrific range and invention into something that's actually gobbledegook. In order to register these songs [with a publisher], they had to have lyrics, because in fact Damo was using his voice like an instrument. The titles came later – I gave them some, they gave some. And there occasionally the odd phrase would appear. But in a lot of them, the so-called lyric you're hearing is actually just sound, it's not language. So I actually invented lyrics that approximated to the sound, to satisfy some legal requirement. I felt like Leonardo da Vinci, who was trying to put an enamelled surface of exactitude over a violent sketch underneath, just to satisfy the demands of the emperor!'

For a heart-stopping moment, they nearly lost Damo. Back in May 1969, before he met Can, he had been picked up by the police while busking in Hamburg, where it was found that he didn't have the required residence permit. A visiting Japanese citizen was not technically allowed to earn money in West Germany, even as a busker, without the proper paperwork. The case finally caught up with Damo in 1971 and he was re-arrested. A friend of Irmin's who worked in the police force happened to notice Damo in custody and reported back to Irmin that he was being threatened with immediate deportation. Can's damage limitation mechanisms went into overdrive: they obtained references from various distinguished individuals, including the writer Paul Schallück, Cologne's cultural councillor Dr Kurt Hackenberg, and Stockhausen himself, who wrote open letters in support of Damo in the national press.

Letter from Karl-Heinz Stockhausen to the Immigration department of the City of Cologne:

Dear Director,
My name is Karl-Heinz Stockhausen; I am the head of the WDR Studios for Electronic Music, composer, and a Cologner by birth.

My former student Holger Czukay, a member of the beat group the Can, has explained to me that their singer Kenyi Suzuki has been arrested by the police and will probably be expelled from the country, and that he was certain that the group could not function artistically without him (I hear that he had been playing guitar on the high street and accepted money). In case my opinion means anything to you, I would now like to urgently request that you do not lump such artists alongside criminals and parasites. Society dearly needs birds like these. Perhaps you do not care for beat music or pop music, but maybe your children do. This group is the finest in Germany at the moment.

'Where would we be . . .' you must be thinking.

Now, you must judge musicians like these differently and put aside your prejudices, and you should not allow these people to be deprived or simply chased away, even if they have broken a public law. Do not clean out the stables on account of any inbred German 'love of regulations', as if it was 30 years ago. And please do not destroy such a sensitive soul in custody, etc.

Please take heed of this.

Yours

Stockhausen[7]

At last Irmin thought of the well-connected current head of WDR, Werner Höfer, who was already favourably impressed with Can. (He liked Irmin's interview responses on the steps of Schloss Nörvenich, and invited the group to perform at a televised music awards ceremony. They delivered a monotonous pounding beat, dissonance and extreme volume, pressing on for several minutes after they were asked to turn off. Höfer loved this even more.) On the day that Damo was being driven to the airport to be deported, Irmin pulled out all the stops, begging for Höfer's help before putting on his smartest suit and, in a bid to try and hold up the plane, presenting himself at the foreign ministry, where he was treated somewhat snootily. Höfer telephoned a close friend – no less a personage than Walter Scheel, the German foreign minister at the time. Half an hour after the call was put through, Damo was granted permission to stay in the country. Irmin returned to the ministry in his scruffiest hippy attire, and relished being bowed and scraped to when the staff realised his request had been sanctioned by one of the highest-ranking politicians in West Germany.

A short piece, less than ninety seconds long, survives from October 1970, early on in the process. Constructed from the most minimal means – plodding bass, tetchy percussion, meandering synth, someone whistling through their teeth – 'Blue Bag (Inside Paper)' is the most impromptu doodle, perhaps the fag end of a nocturnal session as sleepless musicians surrender their grasp on inspiration for the night. Irmin once recalled Damo 'lying on a garbage bag filled with Styrofoam, fidgeting and giggling because the thing is somehow sexy and squeaks so beautifully'.[8] Damo's vocal has a muffled, claustrophobic timbre, as if he is indeed wrapped in the blue bag he's singing about, and we are there with him. The impression is of someone stuck in a fragile paper shell, in a ring of taunting instruments, Irmin's synth patrolling the borderlines, repeating 'blue, blue bag / cry for ever / inside paper' as a survival mantra. 'Blue Bag' now looks like a wobbly prelude to *Tago Mago*'s opening track, which is called 'Paperhouse'.

A paper house is one that can blow away in the wind, that can fly. It's a house of the imagination, whose walls can be inscribed with words, drawings and dreams. Decorated, then erased and drawn upon anew. In similar fashion, 'Paperhouse' transmutes imperceptibly around its metre, occupying three distinct 'rooms' that all nevertheless throb with the same pulse. Jaki's illusionistic riffs are a key element here: he introduces a signature technique on the hi-hat, the left foot pumping a steady libration, exerting an eccentric gravitational pull on what he does with his hands. The first shift – which sounds like a tape edit but was actually a change played in real time – converts the maudlin, dirge-like aspect of the

introduction into a purposeful race, with cowbells and twin trac-
eries of fuzz and guitar jockeying for pole position. A few minutes
later, all the elements of the drum kit reach an equilibrium, before
it pitches over and spins down into an explicitly jazz mode, an Elvin
Jones-type swing. A last cutaway to the threshing machine again,
and even as 'Paperhouse' is crumpling, a deep gong is sounded and
'Mushroom' sprouts into life, its snare off-beats so tightly wound
that they cease to sound like wood hitting skin, more as if the stick
is being absorbed by the skin.

Much of Damo's vocal performance on *Tago Mago* is extremely
hard to decipher, the text either slightly too low in the mix or too
garbled to hear with total clarity. On 'Mushroom', though, he chants
close up to the mic, competing against the uncannily stuffy, fluttering acoustic space of this recording, which sounds like it was made
in a nuclear silo. Damo had seldom cut to the existential quick more
than on 'Mushroom'. With its references to red skies and the mushroom shape of the title, it's impossible to suppress the overtones
of nuclear unease, and he ends up in a limbo, chanting 'I was born
and I was dead' in a barely audible whisper. Can's monotony is once
again to the fore, with harsh blocks of gagaku-influenced sound, and
an organ line that Irmin says includes small cells of musical quotation from Schönberg.

Back when Holger and Michael were jamming together in the
Swiss boarding school, they used to vamp over Bix Beiderbecke's
1927 tune 'In a Mist', which the jazzman originally recorded on
piano. Holger later claimed elements of the tune were germinal to
'Mushroom', and it's just possible to hear the phrasing of Damo's
vocal lines 'I was born / I was dead' in the many Bix cover versions that have been made since then – like the glimpsed ghost
of another song (Holger called it a 'premonition'[9]). The wintry
chords of the original also seem the faintest of echoes behind Can's
track, which shivers around the core beat with monotonous insistence. In extremely concentrated and minimal form, 'Mushroom'

compresses jazz, dodecaphonic composition and rock into an abject four minutes.

Along with the Velvet Underground, Can was one of the first rock groups to make a virtue of anti-virtuosity. Where the classical pretensions of prog rock were taking over in the UK, France and the US at the dawn of the seventies, Can chose the low road to the monotone. 'The point is, we don't think in terms of technical ability,' Irmin told an interviewer in 1972. 'That's a political term – an old value. The need to reach a certain technical standard is unnecessary. If somebody wants to express himself he doesn't need to study eight years to learn how to play quickly. To me, somebody who is the fastest on the guitar may well prove to be the most alienated to the guitar of all. His guitar doesn't have anything to do with his life. His aim is just to be a fast guitarist.'[10]

Discussing 'Mushroom' on another occasion, Irmin noted a technical anomaly: 'In the middle . . . there's one place where it goes pretty quiet and there was a lot of noise and little clicks which were quite disturbing. So we made them even louder and richer and added little bells and stuff. If you use your imagination, little bit of fantasy, any sound can become music.'[11] The explosions were, according to Michael, made by letting off firecrackers in the marble staircase of Schloss Nörvenich, and slowing them down to around one-sixteenth their normal speed.

'We took a very strong part in the editing and all these things,' Michael told me. 'In "Oh Yeah", we had made a rhythm tape, so we played the tape backwards and played on it, and Damo sang, and then we turned it back around, so the whole dub is going backwards. I think that was Jaki's idea. We did not make rock music in that sense; we rather made new music in the techniques of modern composers.'

Many times I have manually spun the vinyl of this album backwards, and I still can't understand a word of Damo's lyrics to 'Oh

Yeah'. The portions that are recorded backwards are almost as incomprehensible as the odd, desultory phrases like 'Nothing to do every day' that run in the right direction. The single Japanese stanza (preceded by the sound of a bomb) could be translated as something like: 'The crazy guy / Sitting alone over there / Pisses from the top of rainbows / We call him our pimp / We leave the LSD town / And fearing hungry ghosts / We take it as a lucky thing / That morning still won't come.'[12]

It's another reminder that Can lyrics shouldn't always be read as literature. But sonically it was one of the most sophisticated of the group's productions so far, cut together from segments of varying pressures and dynamics, with backwards cymbal, panned guitars and Irmin's gruesomely modulating organ insinuated like a viscous chemical cloud into the heart of the mix. Rather than speeding his fingers up and down the fretboard, Michael gets his guitar to emit a 'splinter-shriek', in Ian MacDonald's memorable term. He also called the bass ostinato 'a bleak harmonic irresolution – nothing complicated, yet rootless and unstable in a way mirroring the dislocated unease of post-war continental Europe'.[13] If you sped up 'Don't Turn the Light on, Leave Me Alone', you might end up with the rhythmic pattern to 'Oh Yeah', though like the rest of side one, it barrels forward with a ruthlessness that justifies Michael's description: 'cosmic coldness'.[14]

'Halleluwah' is a highlight of Can's recorded catalogue, and one of the triumphs of Jaki's career: eighteen minutes of music that surges and teems with the inimitable, illimitable force of life. It's actually a slowed-down, spacier version of 'Mushroom''s rhythmic cellular division, and it carries the seeds of its own continuing regeneration inside it: every rebound to the next rhythmic cell re-energises the flow. As the beat stretches ever further ahead, passages of time are allotted to each of the other instrumentalists for solos that rise out of the maelstrom.

Digital music, with its horizontal progress bars, has encouraged a generation to visualise the passage of music as a journey from left to right. 'Halleluwah' is best listened to without the time indicator of a digital or CD player in view, as with each listen something different rises out of the mix, and getting lost inside it is part of the point.

With the rigour of its drums/bass combination, the sheer surrender to the underlying pulse, the proximity to James Brown's funk cannot be denied. Damo punctuates the track's introductory drum motif with a softened version of one of the Godfather's 'Sex Machine' grunts. Michael's guitar slips into a little motif reminiscent of Hearlon 'Cheese' Martin's scratchback funk. Since 1967 Brown had been transforming his youthful emotive soul into sinuous funk grooves that theoretically could have continued vibrating for ever. On tracks such as 'Hot Pants', 'I Got to Move' and 'Funky Drummer' all the conventional logic of song structure (verse, chorus, refrain, solo) was subordinated to the beat, while lyrical texts did not dictate the song's shape but surrendered to it, just as Damo does on *Tago Mago*. Brown's voice is a disembodied spirit roaming endless rhythmic corridors. Together with the J.B.'s he would nurture the beat like an eternal flame, coaxing it into being and urging it to rise and fall at the behest of its funky high priest. In a similar fashion, Can acted as if the eternal groove must never be extinguished.

Bom bo-bo *bap*, ba-*bap*, ba-bo-bo-*bap*. Repeat ad infinitum. For the eighteen minutes that we are allowed into 'Halleluwah''s titanic presence, Jaki's ankles and wrists calibrate the beat accents with arithmetic precision, his left foot pumping the click cymbals. The kick drum and snare seem to snap back at each other as if they are connected by a hairspring. As on 'Mother Sky', he sculpts a parallel track of tuned tom-toms. It's a watchmaker's mechanisation – a human quantization – of the fluid funk backbeats of Clyde Stubblefield and John 'Jabo' Starks, both of whom worked as James Brown's drummers during the course of that year. In an era of virtuoso showing off in rock and pop, these rhythmatists held the beat close, subordinating personal traits to the demands of the flow, constantly, tantalisingly resisting the temptation to fill in after the fourth bar. 'Before,' Michael said of Jaki, 'I hadn't really understood him. During the recording of "Halleluwah", I suddenly understood Jaki's greatness, the direct effect that he has on the associative centres of the brain. All you hear is a drum kit. But celestial choirs line up behind it. That happened to me during the editing work on the rhythm tapes.'[15] That is a reminder that 'Halleluwah' is also an artificial construct, a cyborg, crudely bolted together from many different takes.

In the run-up to recording *Tago Mago*, Can might just have been able to hear iconic James Brown tracks such as 'Funky Drummer' (recorded late 1969, released March 1970) or 'Get Up I Feel Like Being a Sex Machine' (recorded April 1970, released in July). Furthermore, during precisely the same period as the album was sprung, the soul godfather was recording 'Get Up, Get Into It, Get Involved' (3 November 1970). A similar recipe can be detected on a lesser-known Brown track, taped in early 1970 but not released until much later, called 'Since You Been Gone', which features a metronomic hi-hat ticking over scurrying snare paradiddles, with an undertow of bubbling congas. But something telepathic was being communicated across the Atlantic: some of the Brown tracks that Can's rhythms most resemble did not get made until later in the first half of 1971, which means they could not have reached the Germans' ears in time. Brown's relentless controlled energy release had a powerful impact on much of the music of that moment, not least Miles Davis's rich stew of electric jazz rock, whose long, edited jams in collaboration with producer Teo Macero – this was the year *Bitches Brew* was released and *Jack Johnson* and *Live–Evil* were recorded – offered another correlative to Can's working practices.

In the course of his improvised verbal flow, Brown would often refer to the song itself, describing and commenting on the beat as it unfolded. Much later, this would become totally normalised, as everyone from Prince to a host of hip-hop vocalists would exhort their band or DJ to 'make it funky', 'turn the beat around' or 'take it to the bridge'. He would also directly address other band members, naming them on mic, revealing the workings of the music and the space in which it was being recorded even as he urged them towards trance, and transcendence. But here in 1970, to hear a song making reference to itself – becoming aware of its own sentience – was practically without precedent. Around eight minutes into 'Halleluwah', Damo likewise refers to the process itself: 'Songs they must appear where I am singing / "Mushroom Head", "Oh Yeah", "Paperhouse" / I went there before she could / It was a day like this.' He has already mentioned 'My recording station' at the start of the song, his voice flitting among the heavier textures like some bird of paradise glimpsed at the edge of a jungle. Even this, one of the most abandoned, ego-freeing examples of rock music ever created, contains an extra meta-textual dimension.

'Halleluwah''s predatory pace is extraordinary, a beast stalking its quarry. After a bludgeoning passage at 4:11, in which Michael's searing solo traces an ovoid ellipse between the speakers, Jaki piles on the pressure with a high-speed train rattle on the closed hi-hat. As the track temporarily breaks down at 4:43, that solid cymbal melts into the air and hisses quietly behind Damo, duetting with Michael and Irmin before a repeat of the opening tattoo ushers in a solo for scraped catgut and plucked kithara.

At 12:50 it accelerates fractionally again. At 16:40, after a stunning swirl of synth from Irmin, the drums audibly gear down, with an infinitesimal deceleration of beats per minute, and Damo returns for the final, devotional ululations that give the track its title. For at its close 'Halleluwah' does indeed have the quality of worship about it, or at least, it strives to attain a state of total physical and mental awareness ('Searching for my blood flow, yes I am'). And it is there that *Tago Mago*'s 'magic' lies, for magic comes of attaining complete mastery of the id, total control of the environment. 'We didn't intend to do that, to create magic things,' said Jaki, 'but we had experiences in playing, so that sometimes it seemed that you could not explain why things happen – you think it's magic. I think it comes from group playing: you get a result one person can never get. There are moments in it, they are so wonderful, you cannot understand it, so you think it's a kind of magic.'

The sorcery is not only contained there, but also in the other track that's so huge and potent it had to be quarantined on a whole side of its own. 'Aumgn' is the inverse of 'Halleluwah': a looming, amorphous, vaporific storm cloud that hangs in the atmosphere, threatening to burst. The entire studio is bewitched as its members tumble into the throat of the Beast.

During Can's time, there was an abandoned ballroom in Schloss Nörvenich awaiting renovation that the members sometimes liked to clamber around in. 'It was full of building rubble but in the evening light it filled with a ghostly atmosphere,' described Irmin in the sleeve notes to *The Lost Tapes*, which contains a track specifically recorded as an investigation of that space. Over eight and a half minutes, 'Blind Mirror Surf' is a throwback to the avant-garde musical milieu of Irmin and Holger. For nearly half its duration there's little except a flute and a violin gliding microtonally in and out of phase, punctured with bursts of fast-wound tape. An alien babble encroaches, along with deep throbs from an electric guitar and shoes tramping on broken brick and glass. The ghosts suggested by Irmin almost audibly float into view in this supremely eerie noise abstraction.

'The studio has a special spirit and atmosphere,' Holger once said. 'It depends who is in there. It is as you can see sometimes in houses. There are so-called houses with a spell on them, and you might want to rent that house and you come in, and you know something has happened. Maybe a murder . . . Inner Space was a place where every day we were together and did something together. It

was not our studio, it was our living place. It was a place of ceremony, of rituals. It was more a ritual place actually, and the recordings were at the side. They were not the important thing. That was
how we somehow found each other in the music and the recording
just happened.'[16]

Irmin: 'We had snippets of little crazy things like this "EFS"
stuff, which we had recorded, short, only thirty seconds of interesting stuff . . . And we dubbed it in. That's what makes the whole
beginning of "Aumgn" so interesting: there are these little appearances of something, there is this huge thing going on, and inside
sometimes it's like you project an image onto something. That was
actually Holger and me did that. And I remember we loved it; we
were there for nights. And all of a sudden it became this spooky . . .
this big strange space, and sometimes these things came and disappeared again. And that was the idea, and it worked, and it was such
nice work to do.'

Explorations like this set the tone for *Tago Mago*'s avant-garde
odyssey. When it was remastered in 2005, the full spatiality of
'Aumgn' was revealed by going back to the original tapes. The
seventeen-minute track is built up from incidents taking place in
real time over a two-day period in the live room of Inner Space, a
fluid montage of noises constructed retrospectively on tape by the
whole group. With the central chant of 'aumgn' as directional pull,
the track is a genuine electronic meditation, with polylinear mixing
suggesting access to multiple universes.

Holger: 'Can had a great sense for atmospheres. For example,
when a recording is finished, of course, you make a pause. Now, go
into a classic studio, that means a pause where people drop their
instruments, go into the monitor room and listen to what they have
done. I always said, "I have now something to prepare for the next
recording, and it takes some time," and people felt a little bored.
To get over the time, they started playing. And this was all secretly
recorded; it became actually the other side of Can. *Tago Mago* sides

three and four were these recordings . . . I always recorded even on the multitrack machines secretly, and mixed it immediately, without letting the others hear.'

'I could have killed Irmin during "Aumgn",' Michael said. 'It was incredibly complicated. Damo and I had discovered a super-soft, microscopic sound. We played "pling, pling, pling", very softly. Jaki played very softly. Holger recorded; every now and then he made a sound. We had already been in the studio for two hours and had recorded everything, when Irmin suddenly appeared.' It has been said that Irmin erupted into this meditative moment by smashing a chair. It's difficult to hear this actually occurring on the tape, but after three minutes his basso profundo chant begins to flood into the track.

'Aumgn"s antique origins can be traced from the Hindu mantra 'AUM' to the Egyptian god Amon to the Judaeo-Christian refrain 'Amen'. In Aleister Crowley's *Magick in Theory and Practice* (1929), he assimilated the word into his own magical religion of Thelema, declaring that physically uttering the word 'AUMGN' 'represents the complete course of sound'. 'Symbolically,' Crowley explained, 'this announces the course of Nature as proceeding from free and formless creation through controlled and formed preservation to the silence of destruction.' So, if the stories are true about a peaceful improvisation being broken up by a series of destructive actions in the studio, then 'Aumgn' would appear to have fulfilled its destiny. Crowley concluded that, with all its numerological and spiritual significations, the word added up to 'a mantra of terrific power by virtue whereof [the student] may apprehend the Universe, and control in himself its Karmic consequences'. Irmin was unaware of any of these connections at the time.

In 'Aumgn', Can's 'EFS' approach and their training in contemporary music join forces to create one of the all-time 'out there' pieces of music. In the opening minutes, discrete events can clearly be heard being chopped in and out of the master tape. Michael's intricate delay-guitar fades in, then around the 2:30 mark there is some 'EFS'-type Balkan mandolin work, as well as frenetic activity in the background that may be Irmin thrashing around with the chair. The guitar uses an infinite delay, reminiscent of the kinds of extruded noises Jamaican producers Lee Perry and King Tubby were squeezing out of their mixing desks in Kingston, Jamaica.

Four minutes in and Irmin's vocal cords are sonorously thrumming, alongside rasping bowed bass. Handclaps and tin whistles join the fray as the 'aumgn' intensifies with the force of a Tibetan Gyütö priest. At around nine to ten minutes, there is some play with vari-speed instruments, the bass pitched down to a crawl, guitar sped up to a tinkle. Around 12:35, there's an abstract bombardment on the drums, and the percussion perks up to a frenzied assault. There's a brutal cut at 13:30, the moment the band refer to as 'the appearance of the black dog', as Irmin's dog Assi, who used to accompany him on tours, begins barking excitedly. The track expends all its accumulated energies on the final few minutes, with Jaki beating a mindless tattoo around his hollow-log tom-toms, and the synthesizer gathering a head of steam ready for lift-off. The young daughter of Ulrich Rückriem, the sculptor upstairs in the castle, bursts in and her screams and whoops surface above the morass in the closing seconds.

While *Tago Mago* was being pieced together, Can were visited by a young English journalist, Duncan Fallowell. Fallowell had recently left Oxford University, where he had been part of a small coterie of acid heads tripping out to the sound of the psychedelic Beatles, the Velvet Underground and the Stooges. He picked up a copy of *Monster Movie* on impulse and was smitten instantly by its striking sound and its affinities with his other musical tastes. Fallowell was beginning to contribute to the music and underground press, and approached *The Spectator*, a relatively conservative journal, which at the time had no form of rock or pop coverage. He proposed writing a rock column for them, which they agreed to on the condition that it was headed 'Pop'. 'The idea behind that column was that I wanted to go and see Can in Cologne,' says Fallowell, who went on to be a published novelist and travel writer, and who remains one of the Can fraternity's oldest friends and occasional collaborators. 'I didn't have any money to fly around Europe on my own. And so it proved: in my second column I was writing about Can, in 1970. Then I got in with all the press officers, and they sent me to Cologne, and I was the first in the mainstream press to write about them. And got to know them.'

Although Can had been wary of the press so far, they hit it off instantly. 'When I met them it was as if I already knew them, through this music. I remember Holger picked me up at the airport in Cologne in a Volkswagen, and told me that he'd trained to be a bass player with an orchestral bass. And he then started going on and on about rhythms and things like that, and he was giving an incredible lecture about the function of the orchestral bass and what you could do with it, electronically as well.

'And this was totally me, because I also had an intellectual interest in all these things. And it felt marvellous. It just felt – if I were in a rock band, it would be this one. I love the way they went for it – they were shameless in their love of the wildness of rock music and also the intellectual ambition of the conservatoire tradition they had come from, which is at its most distinguished in German music.'

Holger drove Fallowell to Irmin and Hildegard's flat. 'It was there that I discovered this wonderful German mix of sensuality and practicality,' Fallowell remembers. 'Because one side of their sitting room was covered in fur, with bean bags piled up against the wall, in front of the television, and then loudspeakers behind. And this is where everybody lolled . . . everybody lounged in this space. And when you go to somebody's flat and are asked to lie on the floor and perhaps have a joint and a glass of wine, it is rather relaxing – you do feel at home quite quickly! So that started rather well.'

Fallowell was given access to Inner Space, and hunkered down quietly to observe the making of Can's masterpiece. 'I just sat there, hour after hour, rather contentedly drinking it in and making very little comment. Because they were working. And OK, one of them might drop out and sit with me and we'd have a few words, but the atmosphere was very subdued, with the work in progress. No screechy groupies, no silly drunken episodes, nobody flipping out – it's very subdued and almost zen-like. So you can go for hours without saying anything, because you're listening to a sequence of notes being repeated in various ways and then modified various ways . . .

'They wouldn't jump from track to track. They would be working on one piece, and the instructions for what was required were always discussed among the group, but I think Holger would make the final decision – "I would like to try this again, or that." Or they might just let rip. And he would say, "My God, that's enough, sounds great." But what he would never say is, "Oh, OK, we're getting a bit stale on that one, let's try another track." It wasn't like that.

'Days passed like this. After the third day Micky or Irmin, just after they'd done their stint and one of the others was in the tracking booth, sat down and said, "You've passed your test." I said, "What do you mean?" They said, "We feel perfectly comfortable with you sitting in on this, but we never knew if it would be." That's when I realised that I was inside their world and not outside. And I felt very happy about that.'

The two tracks on *Tago Mago*'s final side draw together Can's opposing attributes: the free-form sonic innovators and their increasing mastery of shaping song form. 'Peking O' – with Damo now returning to the vocal mic – opens in a fug of ponderous flutter-echoing guitar, as if someone is pulling back a bead curtain on a weird incense-filled chamber. Irmin's organ and Jaki's hissing cymbal roll rack up the gothic suspense. 'Driving my way back to yesterday,' Damo moans, lost in the dark, then as the reverb springs are twanged ever more violently, 'The night never sleeps . . .' He repeats these phrases, with Holger varying the echo and reverb on his voice as syllables break down into shrieks. A cheap bossa nova drum machine and jaunty mandolin enter after two and a half minutes and we're in a parallel universe, or the restaurant at the end of it. The synth chips in with squidgy space chords and molten-plastic timbres, edging into distortion. At 4:25 the rhythm box starts pummelling motions and we are thrown headlong through a portal: 'Let's just go / Through the window.'

At 5:15, in what may be the first recorded example of improvised drum machine, Jaki switches to manual and emits dental-drill bursts and random staccato pulses. Damo freaks out into a Dadaistic vocal scat. At 7:50 the noose tightens another notch: a high-pitched squeal from the synth, bowed and bashed cymbals and gongs, and plectrums scraped on guitar strings. A crisp packet is crumpled near the mic, and in the last minute the rhythm begins to organically open out into a typical Jaki and Holger lope. And so ends this series of contingent sound happenings, whimsically combined into something that sounds important and mind altering. Irmin: 'When we were recording these tracks there were times when we felt we couldn't do any more on that particular piece, so we just freaked out – went completely wild. These sections were played with no previous thought at all. We cut out the best of them and put them on the album.'[17]

After the meltdown of 'Peking O', *Tago Mago*'s last gasp, 'Bring Me Coffee or Tea', lowers the psychically bruised listener gingerly back to the realm of Earth. With its baroque church organ chorale, and bass plucked way up high, in a style that Holger would repeat on 'Sing Swan Song', it begins lullaby-like, with a rocking, soothing motion. Constantly upwards-bending notes on acoustic guitar suggest the arc of a cradle as it swings back and forth. Coming in the aftermath of *Tago Mago*'s visions of darkness and light, the Stygian descents and rapturous highs of what has gone before, the spiritual traveller has deserved well-earned refreshment at the end of the quest. But all is not quite settled. Here, at the album's conclusion, is Damo, materialising in a chimney, as dazed, dizzy and disorientated as the listener. 'Bring me coffee or tea / Call me Penelope': identity, even gender, has been suspended; normal service has turned topsy-turvy.

It speaks volumes about the prevailing turbulence of *Tago Mago* that this track, with its scurrying percussion, clashing cymbals and disorientations, actually offers some kind of a cushioning comedown, though it's less a calm after the storm, more of a comfortable numbness. 'Throw me out of my bed / And ask me, "Are you dead?"'

The music becomes more agitated for the last three minutes, and Damo seems to be wandering around the studio, off mic, repeating 'I'm here' and 'Inside my head' without total certainty. There is a vivid impression of Damo physically in motion around Inner Space itself, perhaps connecting with each instrumentalist in turn, before a tornado-twist of noise buffets the music into a last flurry. *Tago Mago* comes to rest with a flourishing crescendo, building in intensity around Jaki's whirling sticks, which collide with each other, rapidly fading out after the final crunch.

By February 1971 *Tago Mago* was done. As Irmin recalls, it was originally intended as a single album, leaving out the more experimental material on the second disc. 'We had three pieces on one side and "Halleluwah" nearly filling the second side. And then Hildegard came to the studio, and we played her the stuff which now is on the second record. And she said she liked it, and maybe in some years somebody will be interested. But we didn't consider that to be on the record. It was actually Hildegard who listened to it and said this had to be a double record, this is really representing this group. And she went to United Artists and Liberty and said, "No way – you don't get the first if you don't take the second!"'

Despite having given birth to a daughter, Sandra, in April 1970, Hildegard was having more and more influence over the group's affairs by now, in the absence of strong steerage from Abi Ofarim. 'Someone who drives a Rolls Royce and looks like Pancho Villa, with flowered shirts and ammunition belts, can't be expected to be taken seriously as a manager,' commented Michael.[18]

'He didn't really manage them,' believes Kalle Freynik. 'He liked the music, because to him it was trip music. But it wasn't his kind of thing, not really. He wasn't the one to say, "I want you and I'll buy you with all of my heart, with all I have, and I'll make you big stars because I love your music and you need me as sixth man," or something like that. This never happened. So he liked it, and then United Artists/Liberty were very successful with *Monster Movie*, and this came to him like an unknown child. He couldn't expect that.'

Can blamed PROM management for annoyances such as the poster for a Cologne gig that advertised a higher price than it should have been, thus ensuring a certain percentage of fans would stay away. Michael claimed Ofarim choreographed various cute girls to come and distract the other band members while he held a conference with Irmin alone: 'he knew how to keep anyone busy who was too curious'.[19] In spring 1971 Ofarim neglected to arrange transport for the group back home after a gig in Berlin,[20] leaving them stranded in the middle of the night. It was the last straw: they no longer had any confidence in Ofarim and tried to edge him out in favour of Hildegard. She said: 'Ofarim had given the band the idea that, with him as manager, they would go straight to the top. At that time I never dreamed of becoming Can's manager. That absolutely did not come under discussion. But afterwards the first euphoria wore off, and, despite Abi, we were left standing there with no money. However, the Can virus had taken hold of me; I couldn't resist my fighting spirit anymore and simply got going.'[21] In July 1971 Can sued PROM for DM 300,000, citing non-fulfilment of contract. Ofarim launched a retaliatory injunction against the release of *Tago Mago*, delaying it until the autumn. The case would drag on for several years and affect subsequent releases.

Irmin: 'Both superstar lawyers said we can only be as good if we are perfectly, precisely informed about every detail. And the more you understand why, the better. So I got really into it, and they taught me. They were wonderful, both of them, just really explaining to me why this kind of detail, because we thought, specially Hildegard, [Ofarim] is such an asshole, every judge would see what an asshole he is. But this is not how it works in court! It works so formal, and there are such formal details which you never thought of which are important. So I had to learn how important certain formal things were. When it was over I really didn't want to think any more about it. Buried it deeply!'

When it eventually did appear, Michael Watts, in *Melody Maker*, praised *Tago Mago*'s 'strange, alien quality', contrasting it favourably against the 'placidity and unadventurousness' of Pink Floyd's recent *Meddle*, while complaining that he didn't 'get the impression that there's any deep sense of the spirit of rock and roll in the music. It's music of the head, and not the heart.' Still, he concluded, the music of this 'weird bunch of geezers' was 'guaranteed to spook you'.[22] In the *NME*, James Johnson speculated that 'probably the only British band with anything in common with them are Hawkwind'.[23]

In *The Spectator* that November, Duncan Fallowell was smitten. 'It is yet a further reminder of how hugely inclusive the term "rock" has become. The Can's particular sub-category is rock in the field of advanced electronics, but for once, and at last, it is not just a case of appending cosmic twirls and swoops to a simplistic rock rhythm. Here the two features become indistinguishable, mutually fertile and bulging in a series of ectoplasmic spasms. Returning to the other records [in that week's review pile], in comparison, is rather like going back to school after a holiday on cloud nine.'[24] Decades have not dulled Fallowell's love of this music. 'The Can sound is symphonic, and they got a huge symphonic range into their music, without using synthesizers . . . Organs and electronic manipulation.

Monster Movie was done on four tracks, wasn't it? I would compare that to Phil Spector, who again had a fantastic symphonic range compressed into mono. And the Can symphonic Niagara of sound that comes out has more in common with the way Spector was producing records than, say, the Velvets.'

Music of the head. The sleeve told you that, literally: Ulli Eichberger's rough painting of a terracotta head seen in profile, speaking or spitting out a cloud of the same squiggly matter as in the massive brain that is also visible. The band themselves nicknamed it the '*Kotzkopf*' – puking head – but its primitivist inscrutability, like some ghostly apparition spray-painted on an ancient limestone wall, suited the spontaneous, instinctive contents.

A single was released on Liberty, 'Turtles Have Short Legs', in March 1971. With a stomped-up rhythm similar to 'Halleluwah' (which appeared in edited form on the B-side), plonking piano and singalong chorus, this three minutes of Germanic yob rock was a hormonal release after the intensity of the *Tago Mago* sessions, which had left many more sonic relics and out-takes, some of which would appear on future compilations. A promotional film accompanying the single showed glimpses of the band's residence at the castle: games of table football, and the cluttered workspace, with teetering speaker stacks and Irmin's Alpha 77 synth, where *Tago Mago* had just been birthed. Whenever the group are seen playing in their studio, a yellow lamp, similar to those used on building sites, is flashing behind Irmin's head.

Prefaced by a one-off late-April 'Freak Out' date at Munich's Blow Up, they spent most of May touring Germany.

Just after that, and before the main tour got going, Damo contacted his old friend Gittan in Sweden and travelled to meet her in Gräsmark, staying in a small cabin, fishing and catching frogs at the local lake. A calm rural interlude before the whirlwind of activity live and in the studio. Since joining Can he had posted sporadic letters, including one in July 1970 that proudly announced he had joined 'A Quit[e] famous group in here, Germany . . . now, I really happy Because I can make music which I like. To sing on the stage is sometimes complex like a big open air festival that kind of stuff. We played with very famous musicians like Deep Purple, Pretty Things, Fat Mattress, Pink Floyd . . . etc. I really like this job. And I really happy.'[25] Eight months later, on 6 March 1971, he writes to her again saying that he has received a German work permit: 'I can stay in Germany as long as I want to work.' He gives her a sketch track listing for *Tago Mago*, sides one and two only. '[Sides three and four] will be free music,' he explains, '(we make this one tomorrow). Price: 29 DM– from Liberty record.' Alongside a doodle of himself standing tall in winklepicker boots, with a headband and long hair in pigtails, he adds, 'I changed my hair style. But, I have long hair. I'm like this now. It looks like an American Indian . . . I hope this year will be the success year for us. We were voted the 2nd German group and our record "Can Soundtracks" was 2nd German Album . . . I think it was quite good for first year.'[26]

Can were increasingly visible on television too, which allowed snapshots of how they were developing as a live band. An entire eighty-four-minute set taped in November 1970 in Soest, near Cologne, was part of WDR's *Karussel für die Jugend* series, and the black-and-white footage gives a vivid impression of Can's collective tightness: Holger bouncing and rocking in motion, Damo finally showing self-confidence at the mic. The crowd, mostly students and teenagers, stand stock still or sit cross-legged for the most part, occasionally clapping and shaking heads in rhythm. A blonde woman seated at the back of the stage wigs out while reading a paperback comic book, then lights up a pipe. In a clearly stuffy marquee, at half-time Damo has stripped down to the waist, his long hair falling midway down his stomach. This was a short set by Can's standards: their shows in 1971–2 rarely lasted less than three hours, when they were given the chance. Familiar songs begin but stretch in unfamiliar directions, while there are at least two totally new numbers that seem to have spontaneously generated on this stage, never to reappear again. The 'Paperhouse' that ends the set winds up as a hard-rock swing and the rhythm is more laid-back than the LP version. Can songs were seeds with many possible outgrowths.

In January they broadcast 'Deadlock' and 'Mother Sky' live from WDR's television studio. 'TV Spot', recorded some months later, is another mysterious unused take from the studio's cutting room. Damo is at his most impromptu, giggling as he calls and responds to himself on several tracks of tape ('Somebody loves you / Nobody loves you . . .'). Just before the fade he affectionately namechecks Holger, Michael and Jaki – 'We all love you . . .' This was made for a TV documentary, in which Can are pictured sitting awkwardly on the hard steps of the Schloss. Irmin is the main interviewee, and he wrongfoots the interviewer's expectations that he should act as a spokesman for politically disaffected youth. Instead, he attempts a McLuhanite deconstruction of the Fourth Estate. 'TV is interested in the opinions of beat musicians in politics because it knows they have nothing to say, or a confused message,' he says. 'They are not interested in anything that has a clear socialist message, but they know they are not going to get it . . . Television knows that only a sound bite can be included. But this bit of the revolution that we want is included in the music. But you can destroy this sound bite when you manipulate the musicians in such a way that they are forced to interpret their music with words, and this cannot work. With that it takes off again, and television has achieved what it wanted.'

'It's cold on this stairwell,' adds Michael.

This awkward interview highlights Can's often sceptical attitude towards their youthful audience's political affiliations. Schooled in pure music, Irmin and Holger generally quashed any attempt to align the group with protest or revolutionary movements. Irmin remembers being invited to perform at an annual gathering of one of Germany's biggest communist parties, in a large concert hall in Stuttgart. Already incensed because nobody was on hand to help the group shift their equipment, bamboozled by the narrow, labyrinthine corridors of the concert venue, and irritated by endless dogmatic speeches and charmless folk songs, Can began their set in 'an aggressive mood', as Irmin recollects. 'I saw that and felt I fought my Nazi father long enough, so I got this shudder – it's the same fucking thing. And I got so angry, I saw all these believers with this stupid believing expression on their faces, so we went on stage and made the loudest we could do – which was a lot. Within ten minutes the hall was empty. It was just a chaotic, awful sound.' Without leaving his keyboards – so as not to break the contract – Irmin told the promoter they would stop upon payment of their agreed fee. The cash was immediately handed over on stage, and Can were left to clear away their equipment and quit the premises. 'Of course, nobody helped us out again!'

Towards the end of the year WDR's TV news magazine *Hier und Heute* put together a three-minute report intercutting studio footage at Nörvenich with band member portraits intercut at crazy angles. In subtitles that flash on screen introducing each player, Michael is described as 'influenced by East European and gypsy music', Holger 'studied with Pousseur and Stockhausen', Irmin 'loves the music of Bix Beiderbecke and John Cage', and Jaki 'prefers oriental rhythms'. The brief report contains possibly the only moving images of Can in 'EFS' mode – playing a faster variant of 'TV Spot' – unplugged outside the building: Irmin on bongos, Jaki playing wood flute, Holger sawing on a double bass, Damo holding a banjo, and so on. There's a plug for *Tago Mago*, and their tour beginning in Cologne that day is announced. And finally there's a preview of *Das Messer*, the TV film that would take Can's public exposure to a whole new level.

10

Concord of Sounds

By the end of 1971 the castle's limitations were becoming apparent. Other artist residents were being disturbed by Can's ceaseless, loud sound-making, especially as their favoured space for recording was the building's central stairwell. The very essence of Can's music relied on their being able to play through ideas for long periods, hours and hours on the same riff or chord, and to have a space available twenty-four hours a day. They needed even more isolation than Nörvenich could provide.

Researching available spaces, Hildegard found an ad in a local newspaper advertising a likely place for rent in Weilerswist, a village about half an hour's drive away, twenty kilometres west of Cologne. The village had its own secret history as a pagan cult centre: archaeologists in the thirties had discovered remains of a giant Roman temple complex, including a shrine to Diana and a monument dedicated to Jupiter. But there were more practical and economical reasons for the move. The village's old cinema had been shut down and was hard to re-let 'because the door was difficult to reach with a truck', Irmin said. 'There was no interest from enterprises which needed big space, because normally they need an entrance or something where they can get in with a truck, which was impossible.'[1]

The rent was cheap, and they signed the papers as soon as possible. In December Can left Nörvenich and headed out to Weilerswist, and immediately began to transform the old projection space into the new Inner Space. Here, Can would exist as a living entity until its dismemberment seven years later. The place was bigger than the room they had used at Schloss Nörvenich: essentially one big empty space – the shell of a cinema, with screen and all seating removed – with a wooden floor and high ceiling. Jaki: 'It was a completely empty room in the beginning, the old village cinema. The cinema had given up, because everybody had got a car to go into town, or a television. It was ten years empty, this room, so we got it and started with nearly nothing.'

In planning how they were going to put it to use, they immediately decided to keep the space as open and free as possible. 'We designed it in a way as a very open studio, without a control room, done like a bar,' recalled Holger. 'It meant the communication was very easy without intercoms. The Technik was not much, but it was somewhere in the centre, and around were the musicians and the atmosphere of the studio and the instruments, which were all collected. Instruments are most important. If you were short of an idea, you just look around you and you get it, because you see the right instruments.'[2]

This building, which included an upper floor with a small apartment consisting of a couple of rooms and a bathroom that was inhabited by Jaki and his girlfriend, would become the womb in which the remainder of Can's music would be conceived, and its operational hub. 'These were eight years spent in this room,' Irmin told me. 'Our normal life when we were here, we started working at two, three o'clock here, sometimes four o'clock, and then went away when other people went to work, at six o'clock in the morning. And we did that day after day, all year long, without any interruption, except to tour.'

The first issue was improving the building's acoustics. Hildegard struck a deal with an army barracks at Cologne-Ossendorf to purchase fifteen hundred used seagrass mattresses for around three hundred Deutschmarks. Can's newly recruited all-round helper, Uli Gerlach, collected them and transported them to the new premises (over the years Gerlach would become an invaluable member of the team, acting as tour manager, repair man and occasional babysitter). A local carpenter was hired to clad the interior walls with a frame to suspend them on. The locals, who had been betting that he would never be paid, were astonished when he was reimbursed the day after.

Michael later observed: 'All the time we were working here we were surrounded by wet dreams. There are one thousand five hundred mattresses: three per person, three make one bed. So five hundred people have been dreaming about sex on these mattresses for a long time. It must have inspired our music somehow.'

Duncan Fallowell, a frequent visitor, recalls the 'German combination of sensuality and practicality – the mattresses had been salvaged for soundproofing but they produced this wonderful visual effect'. Jaki's girlfriend, Christine, had painted colourful psychedelic paratroops, jet fighters, clouds, flags, polygons and magical symbols from Egypt and elsewhere on large hangings in front of them. 'So the whole thing was sumptuous as well as practically correct,' says Fallowell. 'In one of the elaborate editing booths Holger was in charge of the editing alone . . . there was a sitting-out area that was also part of it . . . It was a very large space, but people were allocated their subdivisions of these spaces, even though the spaces flowed into each other. The drummer was there, the singer was there, that kind of thing. There was a rather primitive kitchen inherited from the old cinema with a concrete floor, where mugs of coffee could be made, and a fridge with beer and vodka, and odd drugs floating around from time to time . . .'

With the work ongoing, and under the curious gaze of the local inhabitants, Can needed to crack on with their next commission. Irmin: 'When we came into this village, Weilerswist, of course we looked pretty wild – that was a very normal middle-class and working-class village. They were very bourgeois, and we looked so wild, people got very suspicious about us.'

The German detective serial nicknamed 'Durbridge' (based on the Tim Frazer novels by English thriller writer Francis Durbridge) was one of the most popular TV features in the sixties and early seventies. Can's success with *Das Millionenspiel* led to a commission for the latest instalment, to be directed by Rolf von Sydow and titled *Das Messer* (The Knife), starring Hardy Krüger as British secret service agent Jim Ellis. 'We accepted, of course,' says Irmin, 'and started working, and it was about the first thing we did in the new studio.'

'Spoon' – the track they came up with – is mostly the sound of Can playing as a real-time unit, live in the studio. A wayward Latin program on the rhythm box was the catalyst, but Jaki's scurrying, mechanical groove, Irmin's stabbing synths, Michael's searing guitar lines and Holger's bass depth charges add up to a vintage Can dish. In the film it explodes into the opening scene, as a young courting couple uncover a bloody corpse in the bushes of an idyllic park. The track plays out over the famous triangular New Scotland Yard sign and establishing shots of Detective Durbridge rushing to his office on the London Underground. Elsewhere in the three-part series other Can pieces are deployed as incidentals, usually in transitional scenes, such as when Krüger is driving his Morris Minor around the streets of Hereford. Jaki's teeth-grinding bowed cymbals are heard when one character displays a cruel-looking Chinese ceremonial knife – '*das Messer*' itself.

An eight-minute suite of this music was put together for *The Lost Tapes*, entitled 'Messer, Scissors, Fork and Light'. Every piece sounds like a mutation of the familiar single: Irmin's distinctive triplet of synth discords; elsewhere a whispery vocal from Damo. Something closer to the finished version is chiselled out after about three minutes, with a popping analogue drum machine. At one point Jaki's drum track is heard naked, sped up, phased and fed through a spring reverb. As television music it lent a wholly alien dimension to this small-town British murder mystery. Then again, this is a Britain in which everyone speaks German.

The theme tune was released as a single on Liberty/United Artists in early 1972 and spent two weeks at number six in the German chart

– a huge achievement at the time for an unconventional group such as Can, guaranteeing promotion and airplay. The single condensed all the work they had done into a claustrophobic three minutes, with a complex rhythm that overlaps a four-square beat – emphasised by Jaki's regularly pumping foot on the hi-hat – with powerful snare emphases on the third beat, as if the track is snagging on a spike. Picking up on the '*Messer*' theme, Damo improvised a lyric about cutlery that managed to sound comical and edgy by turns: 'Look out at the moon in the afternoon / Hide your spoon, she will be soon / With your fork, with your knife / Speaks a joke, she stops your life.' The song, according to Holger, was 'a companion to the knife [in the film], less aggressive'.

'Damo never made what you could call proper lyrics,' says Irmin, 'because it always was a kind of Dada mixture of totally meaning-less syllables and some words and phrases which came to his mind. And actually the whole thing in Can was more using the voice as an instrument, as one of the five instruments – it never had this kind of lead singer. And above all, the lyrics never had this sense of trans-porting any kind of message; it was just music.'

How many hit singles in those days started off with the sound of an electronic rhythm box? The drum machine was a strange out-cropping in the pop landscape of the early seventies, heard only on Sly and the Family Stone's 'Family Affair' and Hot Butter's novelty hit 'Popcorn'. 'That sound [on "Spoon"]', recalled Jaki, 'was one of the first rhythm boxes, a Farfisa rhythm box. It could play bossa nova, tango, jazz, waltz, all kinds of dance rhythms, and you could also press down all the buttons at the same time and get that mix-ture of everything. It was fun – we didn't take it too seriously.'

'It was actually more Michael's and my idea,' adds Irmin, 'and we three had to convince Jaki to use it, to play to it. At first he was a bit reluctant. And then it was more or less Michael who started with a guitar riff, which was using the box not in the sense it was programmed. So let's say it was foxtrot, beguine, whatever these old-fashioned boxes had, and he used it against its rhythm. So not starting on the "one" that's indicated, but on the "two" or whatever. And Michael and his guitar riff together became such an interesting thing that Jaki really joined in, and there it was – there was the groove. That was always the basis of everything we did: the groove had to be right, and all of a sudden the groove *was* right. Everything was building on it.'

Another important technical innovation in Can's sound involved Irmin's synth bank. Up to now he had stuck doggedly to his two electric Farfisa organs, processing and transforming them with the same kind of cumbersome kit he had encountered in Stockhausen's electronic music studio. He particularly enjoyed using the Farfisa's 'Sphaero-Sound' pre-amp, which was supposed to emulate the fluctuations of the legendary rotating Leslie speaker. Recently, though, he had taken delivery of a complex effects unit, dubbed the Alpha 77, which allowed far greater degrees of spontaneity in the way he handled his synthesizers. A huge, heavy unit incorporating multiple switches and tape loops, the Alpha 77 was one of a kind, Can's unique secret sonic weapon, built to order by Hermi Hogg, a maverick Swiss engineer whom Irmin had met in 1969.

'My Alpha 77 was actually conceived already in the very early days, and then slowly made in Zurich during our early stay. There was this engineer who later made a good living from inventing electronic machines for hospitals – cardiological devices. And he developed after my wishes the Alpha 77. I told him, "I want something I can spontaneously work with." All the electronics from the early seventies, the Moog and stuff, you had to listen to. That was [a lot of] work, and by the time you found an interesting sound, the groove was already somewhere else. So it was totally uninteresting to use live. I told him what I wanted: that with one Kippschalter switch I could have the organ or electric piano, and the oscillators going through. I could change the organ sound with one movement. The main thing came from my work in Stockhausen's studio: the ring modulator. So I could modulate the organ with the oscillator, or the piano with the organ. And that was what created the sound world, these three instruments. The Farfisa, these shitty amps and the Leslie played an important role by totally overloading and distorting them, especially when I freaked out on what we called the "Godzillas", these absolutely orgiastic noises.'

When he first heard Can's efforts at a theme for *Das Messer*, director Rolf von Sydow was not impressed. 'We did our best,' remembers Irmin, 'and then when I came with the music to the editing room, the director flipped out – he didn't like the music at all. He said, "I wanted commercial music, not some avant-garde music." He was totally against it. Big trouble – but the producers and head of department loved it and said, "No matter what the director says, this music should remain – it's fabulous." That was a few days of sleepless nights, because I thought we had done it all in vain.

'The film itself got very bad critiques, and a hundred different papers all over Germany, even the little provincial papers, all wrote, "It's a very mediocre Durbridge this time, but the music is extraordinary." And we went into the charts with it.'

The seven-inch was backed with a delicate little number called 'Shikaku Maru Ten' ('Square Circle Dot'), whose nimble rhythms, in an unequal seven-time, anticipated the polyrhythmic Can of two or three years in the future. For now, though, the group had significant amounts of money flowing in, allowing them to keep on keeping on at their own pace.

Irmin: 'It turned out to be commercial because we sold 350,000 singles, and that wasn't bad. Neither for this piece nor in the future did we think about being more commercial. We went on like we did before. We had more money, with which we bought a van, and we bought a PA and mixing desk. Before that we had extremely little equipment, and even if we got it at a good price, nevertheless we could buy equipment and the van.

'At that time it didn't change anything. It didn't change the relations between the members, or our insistence on doing what we were really after. We were just happy because we were not trying to be an extraordinary art group. We just wanted to be what we were: very arty in a way, but also reaching, doing both sides, things which were extremely strange but, let's say, understandable and palpable.

'The people of the village saw us working sixteen hours a day, and paying the carpenter immediately the money he asked for, and then all of a sudden being in the papers and television, getting a prize. So the whole village was all of a sudden proud of having us there. There was this moment when a journalist came and wanted to make a documentary story about Can, and was expecting that everybody in the village would say, "Oh, these are hippies . . ." and that they would forbid their girls to talk to us, and all that. So the opposite was the case: they all said, "Oh yeah, they are wonderful, they are really working hard and they have this wonderful song," and so he was really disappointed. All he heard from the people was [that] we were really accepted in the village.'

Early 1972 featured two significant Can concerts. They kicked off the year on 9 January in Berlin, at the Technical University (Technische Universität). Since the events of 1968, the Steinplatz Student Building, at Hardenbergstrasse 35 in the Charlottenburg district, had a reputation as a headquarters of student activism, and by playing there Can was reconnecting with its roots in the summer of that turbulent year. 1972 would prove to be another disquieting year for Germany, including shootings and arrests involving key or suspected members of the Baader-Meinhof group, and the massacre of Israeli athletes by Palestinian Black September militants at the Munich Olympics. The times were jumpy: Eveline Grunwald, Michael's girlfriend at the time, remembers frequently being stopped by police in Michael's BMW 1800 after being mistaken for

Andreas Baader and Ulrike Meinhof, who looked similar and drove the same type of car.

In a more benign fashion, the tensions between student radicals and the authorities were on display at Can's gig that freezing winter night. 'Berlin at that time was the capital of insurrection,' says Irmin. 'There the police were the most brutal and awful ones. Outside it was incredibly cold, at least minus ten at night, and the police were not allowed on campus – that was German law. So the police were outside. And this hall has on one side all windows, which wasn't very good for the acoustics, but since it was so full it didn't matter. And outside, just a few metres away, hundreds of police were standing out there just waiting for something to really happen inside.'

To the students' collective joy, Can announced that they planned to play a six-hour set, to test how long the police could remain standing still out in the cold. One of the audience members later recalled the scene with abandon: 'The old refectory of the Technical University was full to bursting – everywhere on the bare floor, in the window niches and on the stairs were long-haired youths, mostly in parkas. Smoked weed, got high, anything was possible. I can't remember the individual pieces so well, there were definitely "traces" of "Mother Sky", "Spoon" and "Yoo Doo Right" in there. After the first and second sets, the enthusiastic audience began to beg for encores. Then a surprise: after two hours of playing, Can are indeed exhausted, but also in a good mood . . . they offer a further encore, if they can get an extended break. In exchange for the longer breather, we got yet another encore, lasting an hour . . .'[3]

Irmin: 'And yeah, we won, because when we came out at three o'clock in the morning [the police] were nearly all gone. This is typical Berlin; the audience were wonderful. There were clouds of hashish smoke and herb in the air, and after every half-hour, we played, and people came onto the stage with spliffs, and then we smoked all together, and we talked, and students went to the window and showed the spliffs to the police and blew big clouds against the glass, but peaceful and unaggressive. And the police couldn't do anything.'

Such gentle, unthreatening provocation was very much in the spirit of Can. The German police were known to be infiltrating underground events in the hope of destabilising and discrediting subversive activity, and Irmin recalls journalist friends pointing out one or two recognised operatives in the crowd that night. He also tells a story of plain-clothes police provoking a riot at Berlin's Sportpalast in April 1970, during a set by pre-Mahavishnu Orchestra outfit the Flock, when their amplifiers blew two speakers lent to them by Can. The set was cut short 'and it started this horrible thing in the hall, I mean a real massacre. And I saw a man not in uniform – I saw it from upstairs in this cabin for projection – I saw this guy beating a girl between the legs, really strong . . . There were two journalists who could prove that it was police in plain clothes who actually provoked the whole thing, more or less.'

Ultimately, though, Can kept their distance from direct political involvement, although it was often assumed that they were more active in their radical sympathies. Irmin: 'One night I had all of a sudden six or seven [Baader-Meinhof fringe members] in front of my door [saying they needed] to stay here overnight because of something. Then I became even more the bourgeois, because I didn't let them in. The last time, I remember, there came two very charming people – they were not German, American, but they were involved in the scene. They were very nice, and they said that they wanted to assist one of the trials, which was, I think, in Düsseldorf. And we let them in, and in our living room it was easy because there was this landscape you could easily sleep on, with flokati and lots of cushions and all that. Next morning I went up and there were twenty people in the room. And that was definitely the end of my hospitality! Hildegard freaked out, and of course the fridge was empty, nothing to drink any more.'

✳

Even as the 9 January concert was taking place, bigger moves were afoot. Can was cementing its reputation among German music fans, as evinced by the readers' poll on German music in the homegrown *Sounds* magazine of February 1972. Can was voted second-best group, *Tago Mago* second-best album; Damo was second-best vocalist; Holger and Irmin took seventh and fifteenth places in the Musician of the Year category, with Holger also fourth-best instrumentalist. Fourth-best track of the year – after Kraftwerk's 'Ruckzuck', Tangerine Dream's 'Alpha Centauri' and Et Cetera's 'Raga' – was 'Halleluwah'.

Can planned to unleash themselves on the home Cologne crowd, to give them a taste of what they had already been brewing up in Weilerswist. Having made a decent amount of money from *Das Messer* and 'Spoon', they set up a free concert on 3 February at the city's Sporthalle, a giant indoor sports arena. Demolished in 1999, the venue was occasionally handed over to local rock promoters to host large concerts by artists including the Who, the Rolling Stones, the Beach Boys and Led Zeppelin. They planned to make this a special Can showcase, and Irmin asked Peter Przygodda, the film editor he had befriended on the *Grosser graublauer Vogel* project, to direct a concert movie of the event.

Irmin: 'We thought we might give it back to the people, something . . . And we'd do a big event in this big Sporthalle, which held about nine thousand people, really big. And they were there – it was full. To make it free it needed a huge amount of logistics and investment. Together with Manfred Schmidt – a guy who was into event managing later, at that time he was younger than us . . . he was into cultural managing and stuff – we both went to the head of culture for Cologne and got him to pay for the hall, because the hall belonged both to the town and it was a private enterprise. So the town paid for that. Can's music never got any support from the state. But there, all of a sudden we were famous, we were *the* group . . . so it helped. And this guy was quite a nice guy, the head of culture, and he was convinced it was a good idea to make a free concert. So the whole thing evolved and it turned out that the town paid.

'So we said, if it's such a big thing and we fill it, you have to entertain them more than playing three hours of music on an empty stage. But we didn't have any money to make a stage set. So I got a friend making lights, who made it because Pryz and me, we said if there is such an event, Hildegard said we should invest the money and make a film of it.'

Przygodda persuaded three great cameramen to work on the project: Robbie Müller and Martin Schäfer (eventual cinematographers on various films by Wim Wenders, who would soon have his own connections with Can), and Egon Mann, who'd filmed *Mädchen . . . nur mit Gewalt*. With thoughts of a future live album, David Johnson, who was still living in Cologne, was roped in to handle the technical aspects of the audio recording, which was controlled from a mobile recording studio outside the venue.

These men were working for free, and Can was paying for the lighting and equipment hire, so there needed to be a degree of make-do with the staging. 'We said we should invent something,' says Irmin, 'so I said, "Let's make something really poor – *arte povera* – something ridiculous."' The fifty-minute film shows the group from multiple angles and close-up on stage, and also the view from the back of the hall. They are in driving, explosive form, yet calm and stock-still even in the dense midst of the rhythmic maelstroms of 'Spoon', 'Halleluwah' and the closing, hard-rocking number recognisable as 'Full Moon on the Highway', which only resurfaced three years later as the opening track on *Landed*. Holger plays bass like a Buddha, silently communing with the undertones. Irmin hunches, meticulously picking out note clusters on the Farfisas. The film paints a disorientating picture of the event: the final chord is struck and the band take their leave halfway through; an elderly gentleman in a suit is on stage for most of the concert, juggling bottles, plates, apples, umbrellas and a pocket handkerchief; a troupe of acrobats create teetering human pyramids. This was all part of Can's ironic idea of 'putting on a show'.

Irmin: 'I had heard, at a very funny event in a village, that this guy with the singing saw had played. And I found him and got his address and asked if he would [do it] for very little money, and he found it so interesting . . . And somehow I found this juggler, who actually was cheap because he was not great! And he liked the idea and hadn't done anything for a while. I had also seen the Weilerswist firemen training. They had this pyramid, and they knew us, we knew them, and I asked them, "Would you do that in a concert, just for fun?" And they were excited about it. So I put that together. Totally insane . . . this guy juggling during this music, and then between two sets, the singing saw, and I thought, "That is so different and shows so definitely we don't try to make a super show; it's something absolutely simple, even a little bit idiotic. Circus-like on the lowest level!"'

There's another sense in which *Can Free Concert* is not a straight concert film. The stage scenes are frequently left behind, intercut with footage from Inner Space of the group and their friends and families playing, relaxing, posing for the camera or carrying out daily functions. There was a technical reason behind this structure. On the night, according to Irmin, 'We made an intermission and went to David and said, "How is the sound?" He had a four-track machine installed. And he said, "I'm sorry, the fucking machine gave up!" There's nothing on it except hum. There was only the camera tone . . . So the whole thing [from] which we expected to make a super-duper live film and record ended up with totally poor sound. The mic had picked up Holger and even the singing, and Jaki quite well, but Michael and me were sometimes not existing on the tape.

'And then we were thinking, "We can dub it in the studio." But our ideology wouldn't allow us to fake the dubbing and say it's a live album. So we said, "OK, we film the dubbing. We film that we overdub the live recordings." And Robbie came again to our studio during our dubbing. Przygodda said, "It's good, we'll jump from one to the other," and he made the wonderful film, which jumps from live to the studio, and the live [sound] is going on and you see us overdubbing it.

'Looking back at it, it made a more interesting film, the fact that it didn't work. Because we were forced to extend it and tell another story. And then, of course, crazy Peter Przygodda anyway made a crazy film out of it with crazy stories, because when Robbie was filming, my nephew, five years old, was sitting on the drums, and he filmed him, and the film starts with these guys. And it's so nice.'

Irmin claims he and Przygodda informally planned a more outré follow-up film to *Can Free Concert*, but they had to drop the idea as it would have taken away too much energy from the group's studio work. 'Jaki would be upset if you went to the theatre or a film or interrupted the daily work,' he says. 'Jaki made such a fuss: "Let the others do a film, that's none of your business. Anyway, what the hell do we have to do with film? We are musicians and we have to play every day." That was a moment when I got really cross with Jaki, being so dictatorial. He was a dictator anyway! But I can be one too. I mean, I'm a trained conductor.'

In the April edition of the West German *Sounds* magazine, it was reported that Can were currently hard at work in their studio on the music for a series of TV ads for Peter Stuyvesant cigarettes. With this, they were hoping to be able to fund the pension payments for their recently sacked manager, Abi Ofarim. Another news snippet on the same page announced that Can had had the honour of being asked to compose a new theme tune to accompany the ZDF hit parade – the equivalent of being asked for a title theme for the BBC's *Top of the Pops* – in order 'to further emphasise the unified character of the German pop scene'. Damo, it added, was going to be the TV show's new presenter. A brief glance at the top of the news page – '*zum 1. April*' – told you all you needed to know about the truth of these rumours. But it does indicate how Can's ongoing hassles were assumed to be common knowledge among the hip readership of Germany's music press in mid-1972.[4]

On 28 April Can appeared for the first time outside Germany, with the first of three dates in southern England. The big news in the UK that spring was the reinvention of David Bowie as Ziggy Stardust, whose 'Spiders from Mars' tour was chugging around the country at exactly the same moment. Nevertheless, Can's opening show at University College London garnered their first live review in a British music paper: 'In around three hours of experimental, heavily electronic music, the band proved their worth in no uncertain terms, with some sinister, sometimes chilling, pieces . . . it made for a spellbinding, slightly horrific effect,'[5] was how an *NME* critic, James Johnson, assessed it. He had already interviewed Irmin and Damo back in January, writing encouragingly about the new music from the continent: 'Judging from their newly released *Tago Mago* double album, they will finally kill the notion that European musicians are the poor country cousins of rock. In fact, Can are further ahead in many respects than most British bands. Their music is dark, mysterious, often frighteningly cold . . .' He asked Irmin why German bands were interested in 'the heavier side of music'. '"Basically I think it's because people on the Continent no longer think making music means imitating British or American groups," he replied. "People in Germany, for instance, were born, educated and brought up in a completely different environment, so if they express themselves in a true sense they are bound to have a different feeling to their music . . . but without having any nationalistic feeling, which is something I hate – and this is what's coming through."'[6]

Were the British ready for an influx of German music? Could they take seriously the sounds of a nation they had conquered in war only twenty-five years before? Readers of *Melody Maker* had already been softened up for a Euro-rock invasion by a June 1970 article by Richard Williams: 'Having come into contact, quite accidentally, with some of the products from Germany, France, Denmark, and other countries, I feel sure that they have something we don't have, and furthermore that something is exceptionally valid and interesting,' he mused. He praised Can's 'insane thrashing drums and the extraordinary guitar, so reminiscent of Lou Reed. If anything they're harder and even more unpleasant than the Velvets.'[7]

Can's UK sojourn was prefaced by another high-profile article extolling the newly discovered virtues of German left-field rock. Under the headline 'Deutsch Rock', *Melody Maker* surveyed many of the emerging, torch-bearing acts, such as Can, Amon Düül II, Embryo, Kraftwerk, Guru Guru and Tangerine Dream, and name-dropping dozens more. 'Germany's new music is possibly more interesting than any in Europe,' ran the subheading, indicating a willingness to excavate this new precious rock ore.

'Of all the continental countries trying to create their own rock situation,' wrote journalist Michael Watts, 'Germany is the one that seems most fertile and experimentally-inclined . . . What is natural reveals itself as a preoccupation with uncompromising rhythms, with drum patterns that are as rigid as piston strokes and just as inexorable; and, moreover, with sound per se.' He pointed out Can's connections to Stockhausen and stated that both Irmin and Holger 'are intellectuals and perhaps see the rock tag as a means of packaging music which is nearer to the avant-garde than to the Top Twenty'. Watts had actually witnessed the Sporthalle concert in Cologne: 'To hear them thundering away like a non-stop express is something of an experience, but the repetition of their open-minded act was finally a little too much for these English ears at first go. Their enthusiasm seems to work better in the edited context of an album.'[8]

On another occasion Watts noted it was 'no coincidence' Can were playing so many university dates while in Britain. 'It's among students that they will find their most receptive audiences, because a degree of patience and an open mind is needed in coming to terms with their music.'[9]

Can played Plymouth Guildhall, then the University of Essex, Colchester, on 8 May, during rag week, appearing right after a turn by comedy duo Cheech & Chong. 'The audience were expecting some sort of comic operetta revue act,' as one commentator put it. 'What they actually got was Can in full flight . . . The music rose in intensity and drove towards the first break after twelve minutes. There was a stunned silence, broken only by the cry of "play us some fucking music" from one of the less affected members of the audience.'[10] Although the gig started with a small crowd, word that something extraordinary was in progress apparently spread around the campus and the cellar venue was teeming for the second half. A murky recording of part of this show – the thirty-seven-minute 'Colchester Finale' – was officially released by Spoon on a collection of live cuts in 1997. Beginning with searing, grungy noise slugs, it's audibly instant-composed, with all the tension and occasional longueurs that implies. Damo doesn't find his way in until thirteen minutes have elapsed, and Jaki and Holger never really get airborne until they launch 'Halleluwah' ten minutes later. But it's a fascinating window on the risks the group were taking, leaving options totally open even in gigs that had the chance of making or breaking their reputation overseas.

They returned for a show on 22 July at the Rainbow Theatre in north London's Finsbury Park. There they hung out with members of Hawkwind, a group in the ascendant that was openly espousing 'space rituals' and trading in a kind of machined, minimalist variant on trance-rock boogie, with mind-warping light shows to boot. Hawkwind appealed to the hippy festival crowd and had test-flown their music around European festivals the previous month. Their current bassist, Dave Anderson, had previously done a stint playing with Amon Düül II, and Damo apparently befriended Ian 'Lemmy' Kilmister, future leader of Motörhead. Irmin mistily recalls mock fencing spats with Hawkwind members in various hotels.

*

Can were nominally touring to promote another single. In the first half of 1972 United Artists requested a follow-up 45 to capitalise on the success of 'Spoon', and Can released 'Vitamin C'/'I'm So Green', the latest tracks to be polished off in the newly refurbished Inner Space. Just as before, Holger kept the tapes rolling almost all the time, but after 'Spoon' they had exhausted the supply of vintage reel-to-reel tapes salvaged for their early experiments. From now on they would be purchasing brand-new tape stock.

One of the keys to Can's unique sound quality is the fact that they always kept a dedicated physical space for developing their music. The cinema's live room was much bigger than Nörvenich and each player carved out their own personal area within it. Vibrations from their instruments coalesced in the physical space between them and filtered into their new Neumann microphones, judiciously positioned. 'Evening All Day' (which emerged in 2012 on *The Lost Tapes*) is an instance of the group wiring up the acoustic space itself and the objects within it into a sound installation in which every movement would register as ambient sound, either more or less musical. 'A microphone, a speaker and maybe a bit of delay would be enough to make the room resonate,' Irmin wrote in the sleeve notes. 'Every little noise, every sound became meaningful: steps, a chair, a few words, an accidental sound created by touching an instrument . . . Highly concentrated and alert we would explore the space . . . more attentive listeners than players. When we were lucky a magical sound-atmosphere would appear, the room, everything around us, the ambience became music.'[11]

'Now Jaki didn't need to play heavy,' explained Holger. 'He could play softly, and then the condenser microphone was recording everything perfectly – that was a big change here. We could mic him up with the overheads, quite far away from the drums, and the room would allow us to do that. Previously, we had dynamic microphones, and the distance from the instrument to the mic was quite narrow. It was a difference suddenly: we were trying to become more sensitive.'

The difference can be heard on 'Vitamin C'. The instruments, marching around the core of Jaki's more tightly wound 'Halleluwah' riff, appear more separate and distinct from each other, as was literally the case. Over two melodramatic chords from Michael's guitar, Damo implores, 'You're losing, you're losing, you're losing, you're losing your vitamin C.' At the end, the organ, trilling like an elvish wood flute, fades up. In 1973 the track was incorporated in the soundtrack for 'Die tote Taube in der Beethovenstrasse' (Dead Pigeon on Beethoven Street), directed by Samuel Fuller, an episode of the long-running WDR police drama series *Tatort*. 'I'm So Green' is more throwaway, featuring a lithe James Brown-type backbeat and conventional rhythm-guitar chording.

With momentum building, Siggi Loch at United Artists was pressuring Can for a new album. Under a strict June deadline, they had only a piecemeal assemblage of tracks and out-takes in the bag. Two 'EFS'-type tracks recorded in March, 'I'm Too Leise' and 'LH 702 (Nairobi/München)', had been created specifically as incidental music in the *Can Free Concert* movie. The former sounded like eavesdropping on a warm-up; 'LH 702' was a brief 'EFS'-style instrumental, with oboes and violins wheeling over a bustling ride cymbal. The title refers to an incident involving Klaus Lemke, film director and lead actor in *Ein grosser graublauer Vogel*, and it could have been a happening from that movie. Expecting a large consignment of marijuana coming in on a plane from Kenya, Lemke convinced German airport police that he was shooting a film scene about a dealer getting arrested with a suitcase of drugs at customs. While the sniffer dogs went crazy over the fake prop luggage, a real dealer slipped through with enough narcotics to supply most of Cologne's underground scene – although a second dealer it was sold on to got caught by the police, and Lemke's home address was discovered on a scrap of paper in the suitcase.

Intra-band relationships were not at their smoothest. Can has always made a virtue of its argumentative nature, insisting that conflict was absolutely integral to its identity and output. Even in May 1972 Jaki was telling the local press: 'We argue over trivial stuff. For instance when we are in the studio and one of us is playing too loud for another, he yells at him or something. We actually love squabbling with each other now and then. Everyone with everyone else, although we don't take it so seriously either, because five minutes later the argument has been laid to rest again. It's part of us in a way. And also those arguments clear up any situation as well. It's not like we're hitting each other.'[12]

Michael concurred. 'Fighting between each other, very much. We only had fights about musical matters, never about money or anything like that. There was total trust on the personal level between the musicians, and very hard fighting about the music. Also on stage many of the violent parts were actually fights between the musicians, that were musically carried out.'

Irmin told me: 'It was a battleground! That's what it is. It's blood all over the fucking place, and I still see it!' But he was referring mostly to the struggle to let the music live. 'It was just a battle for the music. Everybody had the idea, and we were fighting like hell for it. And that's what makes the music so loaded, because even the happiest music, and the most ironic, was really the result very often of fights for how it should be . . . So that every music you play, if you improvise, comes out of something you want to say. And then you really go after what actually *is* what you want to say, and say it right, so that's why it stays, because the effort was to say it clearly, right and precisely. And that was a fucking battle!'

Inklings of that precision, where Can sounds fully in control of its material, can be heard on the music that ended up on *Tago Mago*'s follow-up, *Ege Bamyası*. The frenzy of Can's early days has vanished on tracks like 'One More Night', in which Jaki's mesmerising method reached its gyroscopic peak. There's plenty of breathing space around the instrumental parts, as well as a sense that they didn't have to fill out every available corner of the stereo image.

Inner Space began to live up to its name as they produced a liquid, glittering music: a repeating pattern of harmonics on guitar creates a luminous, flickering sensation; Irmin's synth is a goldfish glimpsed twitching through the weeds of a lagoon. The electronic trill that interrupts Damo's cackling interlude halfway through is often thought to be the studio telephone going off, a fortuitous noise accident that the group left in, but it's actually Irmin's perennially versatile organ.

After a few opening seconds of multitracked trickling water, 'Sing Swan Song' is a beautifully poised lullaby waltz, again spattered with delicate droplets of keyboards, splashy cymbals and long, arching guitar trails. Holger's bass is the cat's cradle in which everything rocks. Unable to hear his acoustic guitar against the drums, Michael recorded his part sitting outside in the garden. Where some Can tracks seemed to be chips from an infinitely large block, 'Sing Swan Song' showed they could also come up with a perfectly formed, crisply cut diamond if they wanted to.

One day before the deadline to turn in the album, only the three tracks that ended up on side one – 'Sing Swan Song', 'One More Night' and the cramped, edgy funk of 'Pinch' – were in any kind of finished state. Michael blamed that partly on the fact that Irmin and Damo were only interested in chess games, while he and Holger were trying to edit a record together. They hadn't originally meant to include the songs from their singles, but now the only option appeared to be, throw in 'Spoon', 'Vitamin C' and 'I'm So Green', and conjure up one last piece to fill side two. So that afternoon they took up position in the studio and abandoned themselves to a monstrous ten-minute improvisation which they vowed to include, whatever the outcome. Piercing flute sounds from the organ usher in a brief mumbling prelude, before Can bursts out of the trees in an explosion of mastodon funk. Halfway through, the group telepathically decide on a nose-dive, and Damo's voice is ground into the pestle of overloaded organ noise. 'Into the mine . . . into the ground . . .'

Language dissolves into gibberish. As the cauldron tips over and everyone backs away, he sing-shouts in an invented language, a fluent ur-tongue. It recalls the Dada text of artist Kurt Schwitters in his *Merz* poem 'Ursonate', or the sound poetry experiments of Bob Cobbing or Henri Chopin. This was a shortened form – one of few examples from the studio – of a mode Can would often click into on stage, in which the whole band would descend into meltdown. They referred to these moments as 'Godzillas', and it was a lightning conductor for the intensity of energy their rhythmic repetition could build up, discharging in crazed sonic debauches. 'Sometimes the pieces would end in a mad orgy of sound,' explained Irmin. 'A Godzilla could grow to considerable length and become almost a piece of its own.'[13] There are plenty of examples on the various existing live bootlegs, and on *The Lost Tapes* these are represented by 'Abra Cada Braxas', 'Networks of Foam' and a live 'Godzilla Fragment'. Heard in isolation, this garbled screeching and illegible chatter – the triumph of Dionysus over Can's Apollonian concentration – can come across as self-consciously oddball, a forced chaos; the price of trying to push music into the forbidden zone. As soon as the tapes stopped rolling, Irmin and Damo sat down to finish another chess match.

Onto this cacophonous medley they slapped the title 'Soup'. Over a year later, *Ege Bamyası* reached the ears of an American critic, who described it thus: 'Suzuki's voice . . . tear[s] through the entire sonic morass like a lobotomised Jagger just back from a week in an opium den; he has the power of any ten of your normal raunch and rollers put together . . .'[14]

'I make it with my own special language, not Japanese,' Damo told an interviewer the following year. 'I don't have any meaning because text is not really so important. If I hit you, you can find some word, "ow" or something like that . . . Some language from, like, a very long time ago, like Stone Age people speaking a strange kind of language. Just "ow, ow" or something like that.'[15]

'There are moments I'm just losing myself and reaching out to the other world,' he reflected in 2002. 'Sometimes I'm a shaman. During our shows I'm very concentrated, I have contact with somewhere. I even feel that the voices I use are not mine at all. I think I have some contact with the other side. Do you know about Emanuel Swedenborg? He travelled to the world after death, tripped to heaven, also to hell and wrote reports. He was there a couple of times. He was a very famous scientist. I think there is some connection between our life here and the beyond life. I make a live composing transmission, so every word I make is just an interpretation of the moment, this moment, I'm very concentrated like a shaman with his contact to death and after.'[16]

If *Tago Mago* sounded like a paranoid trip, *Ege Bamyası*, despite its chaotic, last-minute assembly, sounded in all respects healthier: like an invalid suddenly developing a ravenous, restoring appetite. It took its name from a can of okra found in a Cologne Turkish restaurant (the words are Turkish for Aegean okra; *Okraschoten* in German). Exhibited floating on an indeterminate black background, the tin can takes advantage of its Warholian fifteen minutes, proudly displaying its teeming green contents along with a rogue tomato. The Can logo was part of the found object's design: the brand name. Can wrote to the Turkish food company, asking if they could send a batch of fifty tins as promotional items, and pointing out that they were intending to use the image and it might be good for their profile. In return they received a letter from a lawyer forbidding them to use the name Can. The nutritious image coincided with the album's restorative titles – 'Vitamin C', 'Soup', 'I'm So Green', 'Spoon' – reflecting Can's move into lusher territory. *Ege Bamyası* is effervescent, chlorophyll-rich and aligned with the element of water.

Meanwhile, during the summer Inner Space Studios had been approached by Alex Wiska, a twenty-two-year-old German multi-instrumentalist who had previously played in local rock 'n' roll bands in the late sixties. He had also studied music formally at the Cologne Music Conservatory and had spent some time travelling the world, via New York and Ibiza. At the dawn of the seventies he ended up in Turkey, where he became a guitarist in Kardaşlar, the band then led by radical Anatolian rocker Muhtar Cem Karaca. 'They wanted to have an electric guitar,' recalled Jaki. 'He played for some years living in Turkey and learned a lot of Turkish . . . I met him here [Cologne] and I liked it.' Jaki would have appreciated the fact that Alex had applied himself to Turkish stringed instruments such as the saz, bağlama and the divan. 'I played quite a lot with him, small concerts, and made some records too.'

Back in his German home city, Alex was asked to be the support act at the Can Free Concert. Having secured a record deal with Ariola, he now wanted to record his debut solo album at Inner Space. With the group in late-summer limbo, Holger and Jaki took on the project during August and September and ended up credited as joint producers, as well as playing on the record.

In many ways this was the perfect Can side project: it played to Jaki's obsessions with Middle Eastern scales and rhythms; it was a chance for Holger to test whether Inner Space could accommodate any musical project other than just Can; and it was something they could take charge of without the infighting. Alex plays a range of stringed and percussion instruments, but the texture is dominated by his bağlama, a long-necked lute-like instrument closely related to the Persian saz. But Can's engine room is purring from the first seconds of opening track 'Patella Black': a complex time signature in a similar mode to a Can track like 'One More Night', coursing with Jaki's familiar rippling tom-tom rolls. Jaki and Holger's willingness to stick in the same key gives a satisfying flow to the heavy, surging folk rock of 'Derule' (released as a single), and even the most conventional rock song, 'Silent Farewell', has unmistakable Can-ness as part of its fabric. The final track, 'Tales of Purple Sally', slathered in Middle Eastern modes, is a sun-baked version of Can's 'EFS' dalliances. Released in early 1973 on Pan Records, the *Alex* LP has stood up well over the decades, though it was hardly noticed when it came out and remains a highly obscure curiosity. Wiska himself continued to make music until his death in 2011.

Meanwhile, Liberty Records were readying the release of *Ege Bamyası*. The paper inner sleeve featured the band credits on the white paper bag. Also included was a quote from Shakespeare's *Merchant of Venice*:

> The man that hath no music in himself,
> Nor is not moved with concord of sweet sounds,
> Is fit for treasons, stratagems, and spoils,
> The motions of his spirit are dull as night,
> And his affections dark as Erebus;
> Let no such man be trusted.
> Mark the music!

This fits with the group's growing self-identity as a non-expressive conduit for sound, merely channelling music from a distant, other-worldly source. The 'concord of sweet sounds' suggests the music of the spheres, believed in the Renaissance to be the sounds made by the revolutions of the planets, whose distances were directly equivalent to the intervals between the notes of the tempered scale. The speech, by the character Lorenzo, is intended to reassure his lover that the sadness she feels when she hears happy music is a positive thing, meaning that her soul is tuned in to the cosmic dimensions encoded deeper in the music.

Apart from Damo getting married on 21 November, an unfortunate gust of bad karma swirled around Can in the last quarter of 1972. After a long nocturnal session, in the early hours of 12 September Michael came back to Irmin's flat and collapsed onto the floor, groaning and writhing in pain. Irmin rushed him to the St Elisabeth-Krankenhaus in Cologne, where he was diagnosed with a perforated stomach ulcer. He was confined to bed on doctors' orders, with one medic suggesting he could easily be out of action for up to a year. Eventually, he and his girlfriend Eveline took off to his family's holiday home in Portugal to recuperate. 'I think that did him really good,' she says. 'He was never really a hectic person at all. He was quiet, but I think [he kept things bottled] all in here. This is why he had this stomach problem. He wouldn't see it. He would sometimes say, "I am nervous," but he never had any outbursts, aggression . . .'

With Michael in recovery, the rest of the group could have been excused for developing their own stress-related ulcers. A tour of Germany slated for September and October had to be scrapped entirely, losing them an estimated sixty to seventy thousand Deutschmarks in revenues. And the success of 'Spoon' alerted their old enemy Abi Ofarim, who popped up again at the scent of cash. Just as he had done with *Tago Mago*, Ofarim mounted a legal challenge.

Now the already protracted dispute was going public, and getting nasty. The first pressing of eight thousand copies of *Ege Bamyası* had officially shipped in November, but in a court order filed at the Munich District Court in the first week of December, Ofarim sought to hold up the sale of the album. A local Cologne newspaper[17] reported on the spat the next day, quoting Irmin, who accused Ofarim of non-compliance with the terms of the original management contract, which included obligations to promote Can internationally, increase their concert bookings and produce their records. Irmin ranted to the paper that Ofarim had done nothing for the group, being content to let them starve, and had never even looked into their studio.

In reply, the paper reported, Ofarim asserted that the group had to repay a loan of 38,000 DM, and that he had donated them a van – which Irmin claimed never to have seen. Irmin denounced Ofarim's business practices as extortionate ('*wucherisch*') and immoral ('*sittenwidrig*'), and pointed out that Ofarim's cut of LP sales was set at 26 per cent, while Can were 'merely fobbed off with eight per cent' ('*lediglich mit acht Prozent abspeiste*'). The skewed deal meant that Can would have to sell an unrealistic 50,000 copies just to cover costs. Lawyers acting for Liberty/United Artists formally accused Ofarim of 'fraudulent misrepresentation' in relation to his contract with Can.

Finally, a bittersweet note was hit by Can's appearance in another big survey of new German rock in the *NME*. In the second of a three-part series called 'Germany Calling', deputy editor Ian MacDonald wrote: 'A strange, unique band of intellectuals struggling to make people's music in a prevailing anti-cerebral climate, Can epitomize a central contradiction of German rock, play some good and some awful music, and look unusually happy for a bunch of incipient schizophrenics. At the very least they're honest and articulate and cannot be ignored. Try *Ege Bamyası* for yourself. I'm not a Can person, but it's possible that the world is full of them and they ought not to be denied.'[18]

It's a strangely offhand assessment, especially since MacDonald went on to become one of their biggest champions, both during the group's lifetime and retrospectively thirty years after. His mild disparagement was a minority view. Duncan Fallowell's review of *Ege Bamyası* in *The Spectator* praised a group 'who ought to become hugely successful in this country during the coming year. They have been making stunning noises for over three years now and a new record, *Ege Bamyası* (United Artists £2.25), draws from both the extreme rhythmic physicality of *Monster Movie* and the blood-curdling sophistication of *Tago Mago*. Their growing acclaim seems only to provoke a richer outflow of ideas. *Ege Bamyası* is Can's most approachable album so far, revealing a new lightness, assurance and originality in song-making which is quite exceptional for German musicians. Their inventiveness with sonorities seems endless, the production will undermine your walls, and if you consider yourself in any sense involved with modern music you cannot overlook them.'[19]

Here, at a crucial moment in Can's breakthrough year, there was still no critical consensus around their music or that of their compatriots. And the music was refusing to stand still.

11

Wanderers in the Fog

I can't begin to tell you of the glory of a night by full moon
when we strolled through the streets and squares to the endless
promenade of the Chiaia [in Naples], and then walked up and
down the seashore. I was quite overwhelmed by the feeling of
infinite space. To be able to dream like this is certainly worth the
trouble it took to get here.

> Johann Wolfgang von Goethe, *Italian Journey* (1816)

For centuries, Germany's borders have remained in flux. From
the barbarian hinterlands invaded by Rome and the expanded
Germanic states of the medieval Holy Roman Empire, to the revolutionary Germany of the late nineteenth century and the divided
Germanies of post-World War II, it is a nation that has constantly
been engaged in a process of reshaping. In the post-Napoleonic era,
German Romantic art began to explore the connections between
national identity and the landscape. Caspar David Friedrich's exquisite paintings evoked the mystery of forest and peak, and the lofty
aspirations of Enlightenment man. His friend Carl Gustav Carus
– landscape artist and natural scientist – painted a series of vistas
around the 1820s, looking out towards the border zones of the
German Empire. They were indistinct, longing; solid natural forms
and familiar ground dissolved into aerial perspective, cloud, fog.
The edge of this domain is not a single hard line. It is ambiguous,
unknown, potentially hazardous terrain. There would be some who
believed that everything outside these borders was rotten, decayed
and corrupt – in need of purging.

Some prominent Germans had already broken through to explore the world beyond Germany. Goethe, the forefather of German modernism, who like Carus straddled the fields of art, literature and science, undertook a two-year pilgrimage to Italy in the late 1780s and delighted in the warmth, light, ancient ruins and passionate character he discovered there. His colleague, the botanist and explorer Alexander von Humboldt, went much further, opening up the interior of Latin America and proposing that the continent might once have been joined to West Africa. These enlightened German geniuses perceived a world, and a geological timescale, vastly bigger than the national story.

For many artists the German Enlightenment involved a mental shift from murky woods and mountain-ringed inwardness to the sunny skies, expansive horizons and blazing heat of the Mediterranean. The sea – not the freezing Baltic of northern Germany but the balmy, translucent waters of the classical south – was the magnet that drew thinkers like Goethe and the Italianate 'Nazarene' painters downwards, as they immersed themselves in the ruins and crumbling traces of classical antiquity, Europa's foundations. One of the most famous lines in all German poetry – set to music by many of the country's composers – is from Goethe's 'Mignon's Song', expressing the wistful pull of the temperate climates several hundred kilometres to the south: *'Kennst du das Land, wo die Zitronen blüh'n?'* (Do you know the land where the lemons blossom?).

For the philosopher Schopenhauer, writing in 1818, music 'reveals the innermost essence of the world, expressing the profoundest wisdom in a language our reason is incapable of understanding, like a galvanized sleepwalker offering an insight into things of which, waking, reason has no conception'.[1] This was the world of Beethoven, Schubert and Wolf. German and Austrian Romantic music dominated the nineteenth century and, via the duodecaphonic systems

of Arnold Schönberg, left an equally heavy imprint on the twentieth, paving the way for the emergence of Stockhausen.

Imaginatively and literally, Can started to replicate the same
gravitational attraction to warmer climates and a pan-European
state of mind. 1973 was a year of convergence and unification in
Europe, principally around the formation of the Common Market
(EEC), which paved the way for the European Union. It was a
smaller Europe – the Eastern Bloc still concealed behind the Iron
Curtain – and Germany remained divided into communist East and
capitalist West, with Berlin literally cut in half by the Wall. But in
that year western Europe, despite an oil and energy crisis, was at
the zenith of a golden age of economic growth dating back to the
beginning of the fifties. The resorts and rivieras of southern France,
Spain and Italy – now open for mass tourism on an unprecedented
scale – were affordable, sun-drenched escapes from the gathering
clouds of austerity in central and northern Europe.

The mystery of the Mediterranean had already been evoked by
the title *Tago Mago*. Two years later, Can would make headway in
France and beyond and come up with the most glittering, airy and
warm music they would ever conceive. German culture in the seventies experienced a renaissance, as the post-war generation sought
enlightenment from beyond its Teutonic legacy. In music, a group
that Can had played with in 1970, the Organisation, had now recon-
figured itself as Kraftwerk, and in 1973 was a year away from releasing its defining album, *Autobahn*, which effortlessly evoked the long
unwinding highways criss-crossing Germany since the early thirties. Their love of efficient movement and fluid motion eventually
resulted in *Trans-Europe Express* and 'Tour de France': man and
machine in perfect harmony. In Cologne's neighbouring Düsseldorf,
a former associate of Kraftwerk's Ralf Hütter and Florian Schneider,
guitarist Michael Rother, formed Neu! in the same period, a group
whose motorik rock had 'no discernible goal except to get lost in
speed'.[2] In the seventies the future still seemed like a utopia on

the horizon, politics, the arts and society making progress towards a time of plenty, leisure, comfort, renewable energy and miracle technology. Can's technical upgrades, heightened musical telepathy and increasing stylistic refinement made them feel like an integral part of this futuristic zephyr.

Thankfully, Michael was able to leave hospital in the new year, and Can set about rebuilding their stupendous momentum, buoyed up by being declared winners of the *Sounds* readers' poll for Best Band of 1972.

At the beginning of 1973, Irmin had been working hard on his legal studies in the battle against Abi Ofarim. Hildegard had not been idle either: she had booked upwards of thirty live dates around the UK, Germany and France for the year ahead. First off, Can spent a month touring Britain, from the middle of February to the middle of March 1973. Their nineteen dates included a stint at the Paris Theatre (19 February), a London venue where BBC radio regularly recorded special performances in front of a live audience, broadcast on their *In Concert* series. A typical Can concert in 1973 consisted of about an hour before the interval, then another sixty to ninety minutes, and aimed to deliver what Michael called 'the shameless impact, the wickedness'.[3]

In an interview with Richard Williams in *Melody Maker*, Irmin sounded off about the progressive rock dogma that stigmatised pieces of music lasting under five minutes. 'We've made long pieces, because we like them, but sometimes it's nice to do shorter things. What I don't like is music that's said everything it has to say inside three minutes, but because of the dogma it's extended to 30 minutes. A long piece is a long piece. You shouldn't shorten "Pinch", but equally, to extend "Vitamin C" would be ridiculous.'[4]

At the Paris Theatre date they seized the collective consciousness in the first minutes with a heavy funk workout, not so far from the grooves Miles Davis was employing with his own electric groups at the time. Slow pre-hip-hop pulses allow double-time percussion to bubble to the surface as Damo slips between menacing rants and whispered pleas. Michael's overdriven guitar plays a key role, jutting askew over the beat, sometimes sounding as if he's trying to file his way through prison bars; Irmin shapes some of his jazziest chords; and Holger thrums his upper bass strings, fusing with the drum kit. In the last ten minutes the 'Pinch' riff appears, but Jaki's polyrhythmic dexterity hatches a skeletal framework for minimal interventions from all the other players. Despite one brief flurry of a 'Godzilla', Can comes across as controlled, effortlessly morphing through changes, with glimpses of music segments that come to life and become extinct before they have time to mature.

A day later, they attended the Langham Street studios to tape their first BBC session, transmitted on *Top Gear* on 13 March, hosted by the young DJ Anne Nightingale, a rare female voice on Radio 1. The nineteen-minute track was actually broadcast under the title 'Up the Bakerloo Line with Anne'. Eventually released – without the group's permission – on a *Peel Sessions* CD in the nineties, it's a brilliant sequence that overlaps with some of the previous night's feel, prefaced with some casual banter before ripping into a hard-driving, almost punkish battering ram. Damo's voice is cranked up hysterically high and the band appears to cellularly coalesce around the rhythmic core, sucking itself into its own vortex.

This tour took Can all over mainland UK, supported on many dates by Gunner Kade, a short-lived outfit formed by ex-Groundhog Ken Pustelnik. They roamed from Newcastle and Stirling (where they heard some Scottish traditional music and were struck by how much British rock had assimilated folk influences) to Plymouth and Penzance, from Chatham and Westcliff-on-Sea to Norwich, Birmingham and Hull. The Leicester crowd hauled them back for six encores. If the previous year's British tour had been attended by the curious, seeking exoticism, now they were turning out on the strength of Can's swiftly growing reputation and the quality of their LPs. 'For the English,' Irmin attested in an interview that year, 'pop music is an integral part of their lives. Their parents have been familiar with jazz and early rock. In Germany it's the opposite: we had to fight to defend this music. I myself was expelled from my college for having organised the first jazz concert in the town[5] . . . In England now, a pop musician has social status, he's recognised as a member of society.'[6]

Four days after their last British date, at Bristol Top Rank, they were off to make their first appearance in France.

Pop 2 was a prime television slot for live rock on France's national ORTF station. Can appeared there on 22 March, and the visual evidence that they were doing well is there in the footage – filmed as if by a roving handheld camera operated by a stage invader. Hair length is at its peak. Damo has squeezed himself into one of his favourite stage outfits: a red velvet leotard, body-hugging down to the flared bottoms. Jaki has acquired a gleaming electric-blue drum kit, Michael plays a bone-white Fender Stratocaster, and Irmin has his two Farfisa organs plus – a new addition – a horizontal steel-string guitar, whose sound was treated by the Alpha 77. Their staging is also unconventional compared to most rock of the day: Jaki's drums are centre front, with the other players ranged around him – Holger behind his right shoulder, Damo seated in front of Holger, Michael at Jaki's left, Irmin's synth bank even further left. This arrangement eliminated any sense of a 'frontman' and installed the rhythmic engine at the heart of the operation.

In a somewhat desultory, scrambled interview intercut with the performance, the group talk over each other to explain that this is not the conventional model of a singer accompanied by a group, there is no rhythm section . . . or alternatively, everybody is a part of the rhythm section. In describing their methods they dismiss all attempts to break down their music into distinct parts. It's all one flowing entity. In the countryside they are exposed to birds, air, lakes, mountains; in cities it's 'technical environments', says Irmin. It's been hard breaking through the dominance of English and American pop in Germany, adds Michael: being in Can is like taking a 'difficult holiday'.

In April there was a single West German date, in Esslingen; then, on 12 May, they were back in Paris for one of their most significant live shows. Shortly beforehand, West Germany's *Sounds* magazine expressed the hope that 'postwar made-in-Germany euphoria' could act as an ambassador for the nation's culture abroad: 'teaching an emotional appreciation abroad, an appreciation that, based on the music, should be able to draw a line under years of ignorance, and the incomprehension and the prejudiced attitude of Anglo-American agents, producers, managers, record executives, media etc against rock music made by German bands'.[7] The Olympia was a venerable concert hall in Paris's ninth arrondissement that had opened in 1888, and which had seen triumphant performances by the likes of Marlene Dietrich, Edith Piaf and Jacques Brel. It held around 1,700 people and the previous year had hosted a massive show by the Grateful Dead. With appetites whetted by the TV spot, Parisian counter-culture and the local press turned out in force. In that month's *Rock & Folk* magazine, Paul Alessandrini – who would remain France's biggest Can champion – previewed the concert with his own experience of seeing their 'slow, vertiginous ascent towards electroacoustic ecstasy' earlier at the Bataclan. He described their music as 'by turns savage, flamboyant, anguished, frenetic. An avant-garde music, since it uses absolutely all the possibilities of sound, but which constantly remembers to appeal to the body, to the dance. In other words: a premonition of what rock will increasingly come to be: the convergence of musics and sonic experiences, mixed with the achievements of an entire cultural background to be revisited, then forgotten or rejected.'[8]

The French audience wasn't disappointed. On the thirty-six-minute improv (titled 'Whole People Queuing Down' on subsequent

bootlegs – possibly spinning off the vision of the lines of tickethold-
ers outside the venue that night), Can coasted majestically on a
straight four–four tempo, blanketed in a Milky Way of synth tone,
with the guitar leaving buzzing comet trails all over the night sky. It
rocks, but in a svelte, liquid fashion, far from the jutting, thrusting
riffage of Led Zeppelin at the time. After around twelve minutes
the whole group seems to knit together briefly in a compressed
huddle, before the groove breaks out again, like a jetliner emerging
from a dense cloud bank into blue skies. A hyper, breathless 'One
More Night', followed by a tense build into an elongated 'Spoon',
has the crowd clapping in unison.

There was a further concert two days later at the Stadthalle in
Heidelberg, then it was time to face the future.

There was a new album to create, in order to capitalise on Can's
recent live appearances. But first it was time to take a break –
from music-making, from each other – and the members went
their separate ways for an extended holiday. Holger finally jour-
neyed to south-east Asia, the region that had so fascinated him
ever since he sampled Vietnamese music for his *Canaxis* project.
Visiting the ancient mountain city of Chiang Mai in Thailand, just
for fun Holger paid a trifling sum to have his fortune told by a
Chinese astrologer. Among other things, the man predicted great
financial success in three springs' time. In early 1976 Holger would
state that everything the man had told him had in fact taken place
exactly as predicted.[9]

Damo flew back to Japan for the first time in six years, using Can
expenses with the vague hope of scoring some connections for concerts and record deals over there. He stayed at his mother's house
for three weeks, and he returned with his wigwam of hair cropped to
just below the ears. On his return he spoke to an interviewer about
how he was due to be featured in, and to write for, a new Japanese
edition of *Rolling Stone*, and that he was doing a lot of painting and

drawing for a comic book. He also vented, 'I'm fucked off about [it] – horrible country. Outside it's raining, you cannot walk outside because radioactivity from China is coming in through the rain. I am living near Tokyo and so much factories, so much traffic, it's really busy, I find it much better to stay here because everything is going more slowly. It's much better for me.' The break with the land of his birth was total: 'I don't think I'm Japanese. I'm some kind of German who speak Japanese very well.'[10]

Irmin took his family to the south of France, a region he began visiting in 1971 which would eventually become his home. Michael took a vacation at his family's summer villa at Carvoiero on the Portuguese coast, soaking up the sun and sinking comfortably into a leisurely, mildly bohemian riviera lifestyle, with drinks at the Sobe e Desce bar, run by an Irish expat.

'It was a big place with a swimming pool,' recalls his girlfriend Eveline Grunwald. 'In those days there were just three odd English people living down there. Old people with a house, having been in India, typical English people from abroad who didn't want to go back to England when they retired. Tim Motion, who ran the bar, was married to a Portuguese and was a friend of Ronnie Scott's. He got us to get in contact with Bryan Ferry when he was there. We didn't like the jazz in his club, so Connie [Michael's sister] and I took down our records. We really managed to put records in the suitcase – "Play something decent now!"'

When they reconvened in July, Can settled to the task of making a new batch of recordings. 'We were in a very good mood,' remembers Irmin. 'First of all, that was a time we were pretty successful, so everything went well. It was summer, it was warm, sun was shining, studio door was open. And you hear it on the record. Definitely our mildest, the sunniest we ever did.' What was to become their most complex production would take around two and a half months to complete. In Britain and the rest of Europe progressive rock was at its zenith, a forward-looking form of art rock whose high ambitions (and pretensions) were still, miraculously, supported by a major-label infrastructure. In statements from that year, Can revealed their own hopes to make the group as big and popular as possible, through playing at ever larger venues and trusting that the power of the recordings would translate into healthy sales. Irmin had earlier told a French interviewer: 'We absolutely have to participate in this big-stage-public ['*grand-scène-publique*'] as the scene we existed in before was made up of an elite imagining it had bought the whole spirit and culture for itself . . . What was lacking in the [contemporary] music I was making before, was that it had no relation to the body . . . What I want now is to play music with my whole body.'[11] On the album that resulted from this period of studio isolation, *Future Days*, Can sounded like it was one body, not so much embracing the future as gently caressing it.

At the start of the sessions, the group convened a reunion party with a small invited audience at Weilerswist. In the course of more than half an hour's spontaneous music-making, Jaki set up a plodding beat like a donkey bumping along the mountain trails of Provence, as Damo vented his frustrations with his recent stay in his homeland. A two-minute extract, 'Doko E', showed up on *Unlimited Edition* (1976), but excerpts from the whole piece, newly transcribed and translated here, give a vivid sense of his disillusionment and rootlessness:

Factory pollution Tokyo . . . This has become a polluted, dirty city – let's escape. Where to? I don't want this . . . Dirty, stinking city . . . In this dirty country, dirty city, you can catch fish which are full of mercury / Let's stop and go back . . . Even Europe is better than this / Go back to Germany / It's a dirty country . . . The trees have withered away and there's nothing / Clean people, clean rice, clean homes, clean earth, no chance. Let's eat fresh vegetables, but stop eating the fish. / Countless rubbish bins . . . How far is this filthy air going to go? / I'm back . . .

going back to Germany / Here or there or over there or where? Or is it after that? Fly fly fly . . . / There's no one flying there either / There's nobody who understands there either / So fly fly fly / Let's be a fly guy . . . Someone told me I'm a seagull, but this is a seagull which doesn't seem able to fly any more. Dirty factories and the smell of smoke . . . I died from the smell of cigarette smoke from dirty humans. / I died . . . I am a seagull . . .

And then comes a rambling rant: 'Basically, it's completely ridiculous for humans to do anything by standing on top of other humans. I often wonder why the same humans stand on other humans. So what everyone can do about it is: it's not something like women's liberation, it's not [something about factory pollution, inaudible], but instead change your eyes [i.e. change your whole ethos] and wear them with your feet [i.e. act on your convictions] – do you understand? Fly fly fly . . .'[12]

Damo returns to Japan and finds it isn't home any longer – or that he no longer recognises himself in the mirror of his childhood surroundings. But neither has he entirely acclimatised to Europe, Germany or even his bandmates. Everything is foreign. '*Doko e*' means 'where to' in Japanese, and the desperation comes across like a trapped bird frantically flapping to get out of a cage. The dream of ascent is the imaginative way out of the double bind. 'I've climbed up . . . the air was delicious,' mumbled Damo at the close of 'Doko E'. 'Where are the green parks . . . Where the pretty butterflies are flying? And where are the green mountains? I can't see anything now.' The music Can created over the next few weeks was a collective attempt to visualise the eco-paradise Damo found wanting in Tokyo. *Future Days* proved to be Can's most weightless achievement, *perpetuum mobile*, solar-powered in an eternal peach sunset, skipping over the tips of green coastal sierras, gulping lungfuls of delicious air.

❁

Their next recording session of that hot summer led them in the direction of the piece that ended up occupying the whole of *Future Days*' side two. 'Bel Air' – also credited on the label of the UK vinyl pressing as 'Spare a Light' – lasts nearly twenty minutes and flows through in three 'movements' constructed from takes made on separate occasions. The sustained live work of the past months had helped Can to evolve into a smooth dreamliner of a group. As an example of their refined artistic magic, their telepathic integration as a unit and the total mastery of their still relatively primitive recording facilities, there is little to compare with the track.

It fades in on a scene of utmost tranquillity: the distant lap of surf against a sandy shore, an echo-laden guitar motif like ripples in a bay, a gentle sea breeze ruffling the surface. This was an explicit attempt to paint a picture of the Portuguese coast where Michael had stayed, with its concave inlets receding into the distance like the background detail of a Leonardo painting. 'I used to go down to the beaches and absorb the sound of the sea and waves,' recalled Michael, 'just using my head as a kind of tape recorder. There, the beaches are often shaped in half-circles, with cliffs and sand around, and if you stand on one you can see the headlands of the others receding, less distinct in the mist each time, into the distance.

'When I went back to the studio I found that the echo machine that I was using with my guitar got this feeling of the cliff's outlines perfectly, with a strong chord, then a softer one, and so on. Then Irmin got the exact sound of the wind which was blowing in the house where I was staying . . .'[13]

'The whole atmosphere at the beginning just came up one day,' Irmin explained in 1976. 'Everybody played very soft and we had headphones on, whoever was at the mixer didn't want to bring the sound up because we would have heard that and it would have disturbed the atmosphere so he didn't dare to move the controls. Thus it got a lot of tape noise. The piece starts off with pretty much just tape noise, but then afterwards we mixed in the sounds of the sea, waves and water.'[14]

You can imagine Damo as a seabird, wheeling far above this coastal paradise. The music picks up momentum and the drums coalesce into uprising thermals and downdraughts as Damo describes 'spinning down again' – his wings are caught in the aerial vortex. We might also think of Caspar David Friedrich's famous *Wanderer Above the Sea of Fog*: the visionary rover reaching a craggy summit, gazing out towards a misty azure sierra. The telling phrase of one art critic about Friedrich's paintings seems appropriate for Can's music of this period too: that they 'offer views into the distance that are also paths through life'.[15] After four and a half minutes, we are up there too, cresting the thin mist at the peak; the music drops away, leaving just Michael's wandering guitar scaling the final few paces . . . it hovers there a moment, teetering on the brink, and then a new edit kicks in with a more frenetic rhythm and we have no time to enjoy the view; the inevitable momentum is carrying us flying down the mountainside. The drumming is magnificently pitched for a moment, the gyrocopter is perfectly balanced. This is microlight musicianship at its most precarious, and you can hear Can's struggle to remain airborne. Strangely, the take seems to yaw a little around 7:15: the knot binding the players together slackens and the common key is fumbled. The group later reported that while they were recording this track, the studio's heating system sprung a gas leak, so perhaps the slip can be explained by the potentially dangerous levels of carbon monoxide in the mix. At any rate, Jaki's gyro wobbles temporarily, but then is tipped back on track. The last eight minutes are a delicate descent in a silver helicopter. Whirring chopper blades bring the whole contraption safely down to the horizon.

At 9:10, the instruments drop out entirely. We have been abandoned – or perhaps just woken up? – below the snow line, in a meadow. In the distance, a rare bird sings its distinctive song: two chirps and a long whistle. Honeybees hum around our head. We are in a different place now, a temperate Arcadia. The sound of Can fades in again, softer and more gently undulating, with soporific wah-wah effects applied to the guitar. Damo's vocal sounds calmer, centred, reassuring. Just before the twelve-minute mark, Can briefly reprise their signature four-chord downward progression (heard on 'Don't Turn the Light On, Leave Me Alone' and elsewhere). But we're not heading for home just yet. Slowly, with some effort, the music slips away from gravity again, yaws and begins to rise again, as if the pilot is tugging insistently on the joystick. Holger and Jaki combine their energies to make the blades whirr. 'The standard of creative interplay during this section is close to supernatural,' wrote Ian MacDonald about this mission's final minutes.[16] 'The most wonderful moments', recalls Irmin, 'were when I looked to my hands and had one thought: listen, and never interfere. I was just one big ear, looking stunned to my fingers. There are moments in "Bel Air" like this.' There is a sensation of struggling to ascend, and winning the battle against gravity. We pass cloud strata on our way up; the air thins out. By seventeen minutes we are floating in space. Glass clinks on metal; solid bonds come apart between objects, between musical atoms. Our umbilical cord to the planet is severed as one amniotic organ chord comes to dominate. We hang in the void, rotating in this galactic panopticon as we view the great round blue-grey home planet, cosmic wanderers above a foggy milky way.

The idea of a programmatic 'musical journey' is an old one, familiar from Romantic symphonies and tone poems, the song cycles of Schubert or the pianistic grand tours of Franz Liszt. Can always refused the notion of representation either in their music or lyrics. But by the same token Michael's mention of the landscape as the starting point cannot help but encourage a descriptive picture forming in the mind as this music plays out. And the inclusion of a proto-ambient fragment of field recording – the bird in the meadow, which Irmin took pains to locate in the WDR's sound library – adds a further picturesque element.

Like an opulent oil painting, 'Bel Air' was an edition of one. It was a luminous singularity: never played live in the same form again. 'From beginning to end it was totally unforeseen,' said Michael. 'It happened once and it was not repeated. We did it in one go and we never played it again.'[17]

A final notable fact about 'Bel Air' is its dedication, on the original LP sleeve, to Hedy Lamarr, the Vienna-born Hollywood actress who combined glamour with a secret parallel career as a designer of electronic communications systems. Known for her roles in films between the early thirties and fifties, including Cecil B. DeMille's *Samson and Delilah*, she fled from a marriage to an Austrian Nazi-sympathising arms dealer and emigrated to the US, where in collaboration with the expat composer George Antheil she designed a frequency-hopping system for the US navy's torpedoes, an invention subsequently claimed as the forerunner of Wi-Fi technology. The links between her status as a sex icon, an intellectual embedded in popular culture, a renegade from Nazism and her tangible achievements in electronic innovation feel somehow appropriate to Can's own history. Irmin professes his admiration to this day. 'She was working, a little bit like [Alan] Turing, on cracking German secret codes. I always had a big adoration for her, on every level. And Bel Air is in Hollywood, so all of a sudden I remembered her, and that's the reason that I dedicated the song to her . . . . It's not because she was such a beautiful Hollywood actress. That's one thing, but it's because of this other story.'

The feeling of expansiveness, weightlessness and spatial movement ran through the whole of *Future Days*, beginning with the title track. Again, according to Michael, it sprang from a concrete image. 'With the title song, I was always thinking, wouldn't it be great if one could make a film – because video didn't exist – one could have made at that time a clip of "Future Days", and I had very exact ideas. And it would be a space story, a spaceship. That's what I saw in my inner eye when I heard the music: like a sort of Jules Verne spaceship, a nineteenth century spaceship.'[18]

The track 'Future Days' opens with a minute's fragment of abstract electroacoustic sound sculpture that enfolds the listener like a magical mist. Cymbals froth up, something pops its head out of a primordial soup, and there's an undercurrent of electric alien hum. After seventy-five seconds a nomad-train shimmies out of the sandstorm. This Latin-tinged groove is where the song proper starts, an aerodynamic bossa nova at languid cruising speed, but which also scuds along a turbulent, undulating course. Its shimmering, scouring texture, reminiscent of buzzing cicadas, was created by overloading the organ through the Farfisa's rotating speaker, processed with the Alpha 77, with extra gating in the mix.

Irmin: 'The atmosphere came from Damo sitting on his big cushion, and if you moved it made this "sch-sch" sound. And that's actually how this piece started: he sat down and had his mic in his hand and he was already on speakers, and started and it made this sound. So he put the mic between his legs and started. It looked very funny and all of a sudden there was the noise in the air. So we took it up, and Jaki and me started having this space conversation . . . And that was a really good mood.'

The resulting track's metronomic mantra floats light as foam. It's endlessly, effortlessly inventive, a rainforest teeming with exotic flora and fauna. 'Future Days' is kissed with gentle percussion, while abrasive keyboards and glittering guitar sand the surface down. Booming congas act as pacemakers over sprinklings of fishbone harps from inside the piano. Holger's bass is activated at the low and top end, his extraordinary harmonics chiming with the percussion. He saves one more editing conjuring trick for the coda: like a germ self-replicating inside the song's nucleus, he feeds in a double-speed segment of the rhythm track. Accelerated, unheard frequencies and rhythmic dynamics are briefly, tantalisingly revealed, before the sirocco wafts away into thin air. Talking to me about his love of the electric guitar, Michael once said: 'I have the idea of the Silver Surfer, of this cartoon character. The electric guitar, when I play it, allows me to fly with some energy that comes from outside me, and I can just lift off on this energy.' That feeling was never better realised than on 'Future Days'.

Once more, it's difficult to decipher all Damo's words – they sound as if sung down a long-distance telephone line. But two refrains ring out clear as a bell: 'Saving money for a rainy day / For the sake of future days . . .' There is a note of melancholy here, more of the disillusionment heard on 'Doko E'. Is there a feeling that pleasures are being delayed, held at bay, safely shoring up the present against an uncertain future? 'You gonna have nothing from me / You cannot have nothing for me' is another line that leaps out. A picture is building up of a daily existence that feels empty of meaning, a life postponed. Perhaps this is reflected in the way the music seems less constructed around Damo's vocalising; his voice is more of a feathery addition, pulled along in the slipstream, searching for a way in. Can always made a virtue of its lack of a lead singer. But on *Future Days*, as one commentator put it, 'He's more often than not an evanescent sprite, poking his head in on select passages of each piece, as if to prod or enhance, only to dash away as the band takes off on their rigorous roamings into the unknown.'[19]

A curious fact about contemporary music's biggest breakthroughs is that they often invoke antiquity rather than a notional future. It's as if a new era of sound assumes the mantle of the dawn of time, year zero, provoking thoughts of origins and ur-texts. Stockhausen's *Gesang der Jünglinge* (1955–6) was a setting of an apocalyptic passage from the Old Testament Book of Daniel. Morton Subotnick's groundbreaking synthesizer composition *Silver Apples of the Moon* (1968) had a title inspired by W. B. Yeats's Celtic-flavoured poem 'Song of the Wandering Aengus', while his *The Wild Bull* (1970) invoked ancient Mesopotamian tablets. Iannis Xenakis composed scientific, complex works that still managed to reference Dionysian rituals and the philosophy, mathematics and dramatic traditions of ancient Greece and Persia. Even the progressive rock that was at its ripest around the time Can recorded *Future Days* could be regressive in its frames of reference. Its roots in British psychedelia were nostalgic: think of the Beatles' 'Strawberry Fields Forever' and 'Penny Lane'; the parochial Englishness of the Small Faces' *Ogdens' Nut Gone Flake*. By the early seventies King Crimson stretched out instrumentally to Pete Sinfield's medievalist texts, whose hippy neo-romanticism felt closer to the Gothic verse of Tennyson and Browning. The Mahavishnu Orchestra's jazz-rock odysseys sucked their inner strength from ancient Indian spiritualism and meditational practice. Genesis's *Selling England by the Pound* – recorded in the same month as *Future Days* – gently mourned the withering of English ways of life and folk culture.

There was no such sense of nostalgic longing in Can's friends, Hawkwind. With author Michael Moorcock in their retinue, they embraced the notion of science fiction through a highly rhetorical, dramatised 'space ritual' that formed the core of the live act. And 'act' was the key word here: their invocation of cosmic travel was explicitly performative, theatrical, histrionic – a spectacle of a kind purveyed by the likes of Sun Ra's Arkestra or the Parliament/Funkadelic axis. By contrast, Can used no such flummery in their own aerial voyages. 'I'm not progressive because I don't know what it means,' deadpanned Irmin in a 1973 interview.[20] The sense of travel towards the future remains potent for the way it rejects the illusion of futurism, refuses to imagine worlds that will never come to pass. The future we hear receding in Can's hazy blue cliffs is a melancholy one, familiar to all: the future that is always, tantalisingly, one step ahead. The future we continually put on hold.

'The pendulum is not to be disturbed,' Jaki Liebezeit once informed me, talking about the sometimes hair-trigger tightrope he walked when in the middle of drumming. 'Spray', the second track on *Future Days*, is a recklessly determined game of keepy-uppy with the beat. The instrumentalism, while masterfully juggling percussive cycles within cycles, doesn't sound showy or professionalised; it hurtles headlong with minimal loss of energy. Jaki pumps the hi-hat with his left foot; the snare taps, forever in motion, do not land squarely on a backbeat but relentlessly ricochet off the pulse in seething drifts. Accents on the kick drum resolve the whole pattern into a tidal figure, underwater sea grass surging and receding on every third beat. The concentration required to achieve this waveform effect is superhuman. Jaki brushes and strokes his drums as if they were a tuned instrument. The bass is a distant drone. Michael chops across the beat, whose pointillism is accentuated with tight-skinned bongos and blips from the organ and Alpha 77.

A track like 'Spray' fully justifies Can's comments about extra-sensory perception. The four instrumentalists move as one, finely calibrated after endless hours of playing. 'The whole thing is to avoid mistakes,' Jaki said. 'I know what I should not do. So I don't do it, otherwise I'll fall down . . . The movement has to be absolutely harmonic, in the sense of yin and yang . . . The brain should not interfere too much, the brain should not give too many orders to the player. The brain is only a control system: it controls me not to make mistakes, or controls me to keep the car in the lane.'

Holger later commented: 'If you play very precise together, for example, bass and bass drum, and you hit the bass wave on the same point, you get what Jaki called infra-sound. In other words many of our recordings sounded bad. Of course you look up from what is technically going wrong. Maybe the microphones are standing in the wrong position, the EQs are wrong or something like that. And always Jaki said about infra-sound, if you are so tight together and understanding each other so much you get to something beyond sound. You can say a shadow world of music which becomes soundwise incredibly good. It has something to do with two frequencies, they give overtones by addition and infra-sound by subtraction.'[21]

This is a music that can simultaneously host multiple types of life: it has a metabolic system that can freeze or fire up, as at 1:07, when it accelerates a few clicks, or the later passage from 5:45, ushering in the vocal, when the whole thing adjusts itself to a colder climate. Damo has to wait that long before he gets to sing: in Can, singers had to obey the law of form. As if to cement that point, his vocal is half submerged behind the twitching curtain of instruments, making interpretation almost impossible, though the word 'waking' seems to materialise several times. But even though he said the responsibilities were 'spread' at the time, here Jaki is firmly in the driving seat. 'Actually, with the drums, I think I was always pushing the band,' he said. 'I think that's what the drummer has to do: it's similar to the director of an orchestra. You have to keep the orchestra together, make the musicians come to that one point where the beat is. And play like the people come together and make a unit. I play like a machine, but on the other hand I'm not a machine in that way. A soft machine, maybe. I can make decisions, which a machine cannot do. I can decide, "Now I stop," have a break, or come louder, come lower, have more dynamic, and the machine cannot do that. The only thing the machine can produce is precision. I think I have learned from the machines to be nearly as precise as a machine. But in the end [*chuckling*] I can make my own decisions. And of course, I can listen, which a machine cannot.'

Nestling among these odysseys was a three-minute wonder. 'Moonshake' belongs in the Can catalogue of perfectly formed pop songs, like 'She Brings the Rain' or 'Sing Swan Song', though it's tougher than either. The song leaps into action as if hot-wired, with throbbing, gated bass aligning with dry drums and chopping guitar chords. 'We started with the idea of one of those motor boats on the Rhine: thoom-thoom-thoom-thoom-thoom-thoom-thoom-thoom . . .' explained Michael.[22] 'The idea was, let's play

212

a one-cylinder motor.'[23] An entire minute is given over to a synth solo that's strikingly similar to the robotic chirps and squeaks that would be heard, a few years later, emanating from R2-D2, the can-shaped droid of *Star Wars*. A melodica-type instrument croons in the distance, played by Jaki, who also punctuates the track with laser-guided drum fills. It's a classic instance of Can taking trace elements of rock convention and erasing any sense of cliché around them.

Future Days was completed in early September. 'Moonshake' broke away from the mother album as an escape-pod single, backed by, of all things, 'Future Days'. The seven-inch came to the attention of John Peel in a review for *Sounds*: 'Another record about which it is not easy to murmur a great quantity. This single from our German chums employs the same urgent, thrusting rhythm as much of the best music from their country. Some of you may think of it as "the Hawkwind beat". You are welcome to continue doing so . . . I know all of this looks less than promising but I think it's great, although I will concede that "Moonshake"'s chance of being a hit are roughly comparable to my chances of being asked to join Ivy Benson's All-Girl Orchestra on harp . . .'[24]

The pragmatic Peel need not have been so guarded in his praise. On its release that autumn, *Future Days* made a big impact critically, across Europe and especially in France. It looked and sounded like a very different beast from most of its peers. The prevailing wisdom in 'progressive' artwork was for multilayered, composite, quasi-surrealist paintings depicting fantasy landscapes (à la Roger Dean) or staged photographs of unsettling incidents (à la Hipgnosis). Can's fifth studio album (designed by Ingo Trauer and Richard J. Rudow) was a square of midnight blue embossed with a gilded art nouveau cartouche, the kind of decorative flourish you'd expect to find on Gaudí-era tiles in Barcelona. Below the letters spelling out the group's name is a serif version of psi, the twenty-third letter of the Greek alphabet. The character is shaped like a trident, and perhaps because of this traditionally represents the planet Neptune – which suits the album's thalassic, Mediterranean vibes. It also symbolises or denotes a number of other factors that relate to Can: parapsychology and ESP; the mathematical Fibonacci sequence; and wave functions in quantum physics.

Below the album's title, looking almost more like a record company logo, is inserted the six lines of the Cauldron (Ting), the fiftieth hexagram of the Chinese I Ching. It is a positive symbol, heralding nourishment, supreme good fortune and success. It is about harmonisation: a fire's ability to burn strongly depends on the nature of the wood underneath. Irmin: 'We didn't know what to call the album so one night I went home and threw the I Ching to find out. It came up with the Cauldron, which is the only one anywhere near a can. It's right for the record, too – the upper trigram means the wood, tinder[,] and lower is fire.' Irmin was slightly mixed up here: it's actually the upper trigram that stands for fire, while the lower represents gentleness, wind and wood. But he rightly pointed out: 'For us it's the most summery and tender record that we've ever done.'[25]

Many writers picked up on that atmosphere, and particularly the sense of movement inherent in the grooves – well in advance of Kraftwerk's classic hymn to European transport, *Autobahn*, and its successor, *Trans-Europe Express*. Steve Lake, in a *Melody Maker* feature, observed: 'There are two ways to consider travel by train. The traveller, you see, is offered two realities. Either he restricts his perspective to the four walls of the carriage, which in themselves are constant and unchanging, or else he extends his outlook to include the continually changing external environment that's viewable from the window. Either approach is all right with Irmin Schmidt.'[26]

Irmin himself used a similar metaphor in another interview promoting the album: 'It's like a train, there's always the same rhythm as it travels along, but when you look out the window the landscape changes all the time.'[27]

For the French critic Jacques LeBlanc, it was 'Spatial and magnificent music from which you come away with the impression of multidimensions, where each musician submerges himself in the ensemble to become Can and express the soul of the group . . . a penetrating, hovering sound which ransacks and annihilates you . . .'[28]

Paul Alessandrini wrote: 'You need to allow yourself to be capsized in order to be intoxicated by these long musical phrases, fragmented, breathless, self-renewing as the spacious environments recover their materiality . . . There are diverse interpretations you could put on this music: an invitation to a voyage, a descent into a kind of musical unconscious, a slow, planetary, cosmic vibration, a psychedelic trip . . . It's not so much an intellectual music, more of a musical appeal to the senses.'[29]

Ian MacDonald of the *NME* considered it 'An immaculate piece of work, the best German rock record so far, apart from Faust. Can have at last found the perfect quality of sound through which to express their very highly-developed internal musical relationships – a sound full of distance and air, halfway between abstract and concrete, sometimes bursting with light, sometimes glowing vaguely as if through a rain-washed window. A bit like a Turner painting.'[30]

If *Future Days* outwardly implied a band with well-adjusted karma, things were as volatile as ever within the circle. This beatific noise had not been achieved without the usual infighting. A large part of Can's appeal lay in its combination of dazzling performance and skilful post-production. But this dichotomy was precisely at the heart of a new factionalism, with Jaki loathing the idea of constructing a track 'artificially' from the best fragments of tape.

'When we started,' he said, 'we thought we have to do very simple things, and no complications, and it went on, but later it became more complicated again, and I think the music died then.' Another time he said: 'It really went off with *Future Days*, I think, it became too symphonic.'[31] In other words, there was too much the feeling of stitched-together 'movements', of long-form 'pieces' moving through different variations and atmospheres, when what Jaki really wanted was to hone down one monotonous rhythm pattern.

Kalle Freynik comments: 'In the later days, when they were already with United Artists, of course the company tried to talk them into becoming more commercial. And this was a discussion between the boys in the band more or less all the time, because they had five different views. I can't remember one day when they were really together and agreed on anything they did. And on that topic they didn't agree either, because becoming commercial meant releasing a single. And a single means to release a three-minute piece, and they said, "We don't have that!" United Artists said, "Do it!" And they said, "We don't want to do it." And then Holger said, "I don't want to do it either, but I can cut a twenty-minute piece down to three!" And they offered to hang him out of the window or push him from a Rhine bridge, or something like that.'

'Holger did the editing,' adds Irmin, 'but the decisions were always made together. Jaki didn't like to take part in this kind of business, and that's why you don't hear edits. Because Jaki would have gone crazy if he had heard the edit and it had destroyed the groove. The groove wouldn't have been right in an edit. And then it had to sound perfectly natural. Which was basically a structural decision first, and then, of course, the craft to do it right.

'Jaki hated symphonic clouds! It was quite often an argument with Jaki. I mean, for Holger and me, who grew up with contemporary music, the techniques of using collage and everything – like Stockhausen – for us it was the most natural thing of structuring the piece, and that's why we did it together, and successfully. But for Jaki, he was a jazz musician; jazz musicians want to play. If he wasn't satisfied, he would play it a thousand times again. Holger and me and Michael, we decided we'd edit something and cut out the less interesting things. That was totally normal.'

°

Psi is the last letter before omega – the end of a phase. Once the *Future Days* sessions were wrapped, Damo's disaffection after his trip to Japan had still not abated, despite the clear skies of the latest recordings. On 25 August the quintet travelled to play a show at the Edinburgh Festival, in the city's Empire Theatre. The show was recorded with the intention of releasing a live album, but when they listened back to the tapes, they found crucial elements missing, such as Michael's guitar and Damo's voice. But in any event, in spirit Damo had practically disappeared already.

Since marrying in late 1972, Damo's behaviour had changed notably. Shortly after the wedding, Irmin remembers, 'a young Japanese woman from Düsseldorf appeared at Damo's place and started working on him. Direction: Jehovah's Witness. She was a very successful missionary.' Damo was drawn further into active membership of the religion. 'After some time Damo got strange,' says Irmin. 'Sitting in dressing rooms, reading the Bible. Got very unconcentrated on the music and objecting more and more to the most ridiculous things.'

Damo accompanied the group on eight live dates in Germany between 1 and 14 October, including three double bills with Amon Düül II. During a fraught studio session shortly after the tour finished, he stuffed the microphone in his pocket and stormed out of the cinema. It was his parting 'Godzilla' explosion: his career with Can was over.

A few months afterwards, Irmin talked about Damo to British journalist Nick Kent. 'He's not painting or creating anything. His wife works and he stays at home. Some of us have received letters from them which are full of Biblical quotes. It's very weird . . . You must remember that German and Japanese cultures are extremely different and we always had a basic difficulty in communicating . . .'[32]

'You have to be able to break stuff,' Damo mused forty years later. 'You build up, break, build up, break, always this kind of process. Look at any painter, they have different periods, they're not always painting the same stuff.'[33] For a long time, Damo wasn't even making music. He moved to the neighbouring city of Düsseldorf, where he worked in a succession of jobs, including road construction, hotel receptionist and exporter of vintage cars, before eventually landing a position at a Japanese technology manufacturer. He had two children and began to re-engage with music in 1985, after a divorce. He also travelled extensively, backpacking alone to off-the-beaten-track locations in West Africa, Asia, the Sahara and elsewhere. 'I love very hot and dry places on the earth,'[34] he told one interviewer.

On the rare occasions Damo has commented about Can since leaving the group, he has tended to downplay or even disown them. 'It was really boring. *Future Days* was musically very good, but it was really distant music for me, and more elemental than at the beginning, not so much of a freak-out.'[35] When I contacted Damo to request his participation in this book, he had just emerged from hospital after a serious illness, and this was his reply: 'I really have no interest to talk about my period with the German band. I had been a season worker, I was and I felt. It's not my home or anywhere I feel comfortable. I still am free person I just have no interest to connect my life again with them. So, if you or people understand me or not, it won't move me anything. I can clearly see my way and as you understand I don't look at passed days.'

Another time he said: '*Future Days* is for me the best album I made with Can. Because it was very easy to quit from Can after that album. I wanted nothing from them after that. Musically I was very satisfied. It was a really good time to begin a new life. I like *Future Days*. Nobody else arrived at such a space. It's just a new dimension. With that album I was really free, it was no longer necessary to make music after. I was not really at the front with *Future Days*. This time I was right in the music landscape. It was pure magic.'[36]

And so Can was once again without a vocalist. But that, of course, was how it had begun. Most groups have the singer at the centre, building an ensemble around him or her. Damo, just as much as

Malcolm, had been an outsider drawn into the band almost by accident, separated by language and culture from the instrumental core. Plus, Can's modus operandi destabilised the role of frontman in a way rock culture was not yet comfortable with. 'If you are a singer with a group,' said Holger, 'you can go to the microphone and say, "Hello, people, how do you feel?" And everybody says, "Yes, all right," and you can clap and say, "Right, let's go into it." This is very obvious and very good, and I like this kind of feeling, and American and English musicians are especially good at this kind of thing. And we make the same kind of thing, but not with words – we never say "hello" and "goodbye" and "how do you feel?" It's beyond the words. I think the people know about this, that they depend on us and we depend on them.'

12

Perpetual Motion

Minus Damo, and with no replacement vocalist, Can nevertheless had tour commitments to fulfil in autumn 1973. After the German dates in early October, there was a free gig, *'un concert surprise'*, at the Grand Studio RTL in Paris on the twenty-third. They were back in France a month later, playing shows at Paris Olympia, Rennes, Bordeaux, Annecy, Troyes and Nanterre.

Their final activity in December was to record music for another TV movie, this time by the radical film-maker Helma Sanders-Brahms – one more director whose world view was shaped by the events of May 1968 in Europe. (Her first feature, *Unter dem Pflaster ist der Strand* (Under the Pavement Lies the Beach), already in preparation but not released until 1975, was set in the immediate aftermath of the Paris riots.) In late 1973 she was completing *Die letzten Tage von Gomorrha* (The Last Days of Gomorrha), a television movie cut from the same entropy/conspiracy/science-fiction cloth as *Soylent Green*, *A Clockwork Orange* and *Fahrenheit 451*. Broadcast only once on WDR in March 1974, and never reissued in any form, *Gomorrha's* Ballardian near-future scenario portrayed a female model fighting for survival in a world dominated by a shadowy mega-retail chain, Gomorrha, Inc., which seems to be in league with the media corporation Noward News. Gomorrha's latest gimmick is the Apparatus, an immersive 'total TV' device that serves (and stimulates) the physical, psychological and erotic desires of its users. A large proportion of the population is hypnotised by the machines' gratifications, while civilisation falls to pieces unheeded. As a speculative fiction it anticipates the themes of films such as *The*

Matrix, and its dark, paranoid atmosphere ended up implying that even revolutionary movements might themselves be initiated and steered by the very forces they claim to oppose. Can's music mainly consisted of a slow, brooding take on their four-chord 'downward steps' signature. The version that opens the *Unlimited Edition* collection is not exactly the one used in the film, which has an even more menacing and tragic intensity.

One evening early in 1974 the studio phone buzzed. A young film director, Wim Wenders, came on the line from Munich. He had finished editing his latest film, *Alice in the Cities*, a low-budget black-and-white German road movie set across the US and Europe, and needed a quick-fix soundtrack. Wenders had wanted to use the moody instrumental 'Colors for Susan' by Country Joe and the Fish, but couldn't afford the rights. Can's old friend Peter Przygodda, who was acting as editor on the movie, had recommended them instead. Hearing that Can were in the studio at that moment, Wenders and Przygodda jumped into the director's Citroën and sped for eight hours to Weilerswist, arriving at around one o'clock in the morning.

Irmin: '[Wenders] rushed to Cologne and said, "Listen, I can't even show you the film. I'll tell you the story. But I need some music, and I need to leave with it tomorrow morning because the studio is booked and I have to mix it."'

Michael, exhausted after an all-night session, listened to the Country Joe track and strummed his guitar for a few minutes. 'Then he announced that we should record it quickly,' recalled Wenders over forty years later. 'From out of nowhere, someone materialized at the console: Holger Czukay.' Michael played a couple of takes, then declared the recording over. 'Then from behind me . . . someone muttered to himself: "There's something missing . . . I'll overdub something!"' It was Irmin, who sat down at his piano and commanded Holger to roll the tape. 'After a while,' Wenders said, 'out of the blue, a whole string orchestra slowly pushed itself into the picture . . . and the little guitar piece was transformed into a massive sound event . . . immediately I could see and hear exactly where this beautiful music would appear in the film. It was beyond my wildest hopes.'[1]

Irmin: 'Basically it was Michael and me, and I played most of my sounds inside the grand piano with Michael and Jaki doing some sounds to it. And Wim said yes, this will fit, and no, this won't, and that was very collaborative in a productive way. And he happily left at about five a.m. for Munich and started to mix. It was not a big score, but it helped the film the way he wanted it.'[2]

Can's muted, largely percussion-free score suits the downbeat tone of the protagonists' peregrinations. The main character, escorting a stranger's young daughter across the US and back to Germany, roams with a kind of purposeful improvisation that chimed with Can's own methods. A mournful, circling acoustic guitar adagio is embedded in synthetic strings from the Alpha 77 and xylophone punctuations. *Alice in the Cities* has become probably the most widely screened film Can ever soundtracked, and their relationship with Wenders continued over the years: they provided music for *Until the End of the World* (1991), while Irmin composed some of the soundtrack for *Lisbon Story* (which also includes Can's 'She Brings the Rain', 1994) and the whole of *Palermo Shooting* (2008).

Many musicians and groups who had surfed on utopian promise since 1968 began to founder after five or six years. By 1974 much counter-cultural energy had burnt out and Europe was suffering from energy shortages, terrorism from without and within, and general recession blues. Can, for its part, still looked busy. After a feted performance for its home crowd at the Cologne Opera House, the group embarked on a twenty-date UK tour, kicking off at Brunel University, Uxbridge, on 25 January. This was prefaced by an appearance in that week's *Melody Maker*, as part of a portmanteau feature canvassing various musicians about Britain's forthcoming general election in February. This gave Irmin another opportunity to make a rare political statement. 'Perhaps it's right that attention should be focused on England, because after all, England is where industrialisation began,' he said. 'I don't believe that England is in any pre-revolutionary state but I'm sure the workers know what they're doing. Crises tend to open people's eyes and if this one makes people one step closer to political awareness, if it makes them more conscious of the way the country is run, then it will have been made worthwhile.

'And once the workers realise that it's they who run the country, and that the country won't run without them, then it's up to them to get to the roots of the crisis and set about curing the disease. I don't think [Conservative prime minister] Mr [Edward] Heath is especially interested in solving the problem.

'It's really impossible for me to say who I'd vote for if I was English, but I can say with some certainty that I wouldn't vote Conservative. I definitely wouldn't vote Conservative.'[3]

The night this was published Can took to the stage at the Corn Exchange in Cambridge. Whatever doldrums might have been affecting the UK economy, and even though Michael could describe the group as 'very frustrated people full of hangups',[4] there was apparently no such sluggishness from the group at this point. A review in *Sounds* implied they had discovered even more focus and equilibrium with their vocal-free line-up. 'It's a four-cornered arrangement and like every rectangle, each player can only alter his own angle of attack by pulling all three of his colleagues out of square. Each piece rises to a pitch where, it would seem, the sky's the limit. Then, on this particular gig, they take it down lower and lower until they could hear the audience's very breathing.'[5]

Here was a perceptive suggestion of equilibrium, of delicately balanced calibration and orbital patterns. For Can in 1974 was all about ascending even higher than the wax-winged glide of *Future Days*, breaking through the stratosphere and exploring deeper space. In this year they would aim to fulfil the promise of cosmic rock translated into their own distinct language, and channel all their research into the mathematical underpinning of harmony and rhythm.

The potency of these ideas, coupled with Can's passing interest in magical effects and their quartz-crystal timekeeping, occasionally seemed to throw the rest of normality out of whack. Witnesses to their session for *The Old Grey Whistle Test* at BBC Television Centre in White City, west London, on 27 January, reported eccentric behaviour from the studio clock. 'At the beginning of a take, Jaki said – "This will make all the clocks stop when it is televised,"' Michael told a journalist a week after the incident. 'And after we finished the song the studio-clock had actually stopped. Just like that. And you should know that studio-clocks never stop!'[6] According to other reports, when Jaki shouted out that he was ready for another take a few moments later, the clock resumed its ticking.

This is not the only story to suggest that a powerful electromagnetic field emanated from Can. From the same tour, Jaki shudderingly remembered 'one of the most terrible concerts we had [at Bradford University on 5 February 1974]. The famous "Bradford crackle" appeared. There was a crackle all the time on the PA system. We couldn't get rid of that crackle, so it became the Bradford crackle. Kssscchk! Nobody knew why – probably they made some technical experiments in the university. It was disgusting! And then Bradford at that time it was a horrible town – and at that time also there was a power crisis. No heating in the hotel. I think it was in winter.' In an interview Irmin gave to the *NME*, he said: 'In the studio, we had an old organ that always made a most peculiar buzzing noise whenever it was switched on. One day Michael became so annoyed with it that he went over and commanded it to stop the noise at once. It stopped! We were all very surprised and so Michael tried the command again, this time saying: "Start the noise!" The noise started up straightaway and Michael carried on ordering it to stop and start and it always obeyed instantly. Since that afternoon it hasn't stopped buzzing ever again.'[7]

The *Whistle Test* track in question was playfully named 'Set the Controls for the Art of the Sun'. (Can generally had fun with the titles they gave their exclusive tracks for the BBC: their session of October that year at the BBC's Maida Vale Studios included 'Return to BB City' and 'Tape Kebab'.) This performance – in the somewhat clinical live-in-the-studio setting, with only the production team for an audience – has not re-emerged since transmission. But several audio recordings of the group from the days immediately afterwards give some idea of their increasingly metronomic precision jamming. There are the two tracks they cut for John Peel's BBC radio show on 29 January at Langham Studio 1, Broadcasting House. The fourteen-minute improvised medley 'Tony Wanna Go' was named no doubt in honour of the duty producer, Tony Wilson (not to be confused with Anthony H. Wilson, Factory Records' founder). It opens with blues-rock ponderousness, but the subdued swing rapidly evolves into a more recognisably Can-like polyrhythmic throb. Particularly notable is Irmin's mastery of his Alpha 77 system. His synthesizers have taken on a far more metallic timbre, keeping up a constant backdrop of groaning steel plates. A new spirit of minimalism seems to have swept over the group; despite managing to take their theme through successive flowing variations, they maintain the pulse they set up at the start, while Holger plays just a single note every four bars and Michael's guitar is little more than a spattering of percussive funk chops fed through a wah-wah pedal.

The group returned to London the following week for a date at the Lyceum, a grand, classically porticoed Regency theatre on the Strand. They played for over two hours and included a forty-seven-minute extemporisation around a theme from 'Bel Air' and a version of 'Spray' that stretched to eighteen minutes. An entranced *Melody*

Maker reviewer glimpsed them in action: 'The group are actually playing tighter, better and more articulate than ever. They seem to have outlawed soloing, and they're probably the only band in rock to actually play spontaneous improvisations all the time.

'Individually, they're like no other musicians on earth. Irmin Schmidt, particularly, is a true innovator, actually using electronic instruments like electronic instruments, something that has occurred to remarkably few electric keyboard players. At one point he contrived to play the same phrasing several times over, using the control boxes to alter the actual nature of the notes so that the sound was never the same twice. At other points he slapped percussively over the top of the organ, with the hand movements of a conga player. The resultant noise was like a curious amalgam of Cecil Taylor and Edmundo Ros.

'Holger Czukay is the most striking. Bass guitar slung near vertical via a strap from shoulder to crutch, Holger bounced from foot to foot and eyes closed his hawk-like features seem to jab jerkily at the air.'[8]

On this tour Can's sound audibly chilled and tautened, while at the same time the component parts assumed ever more discrete identities. The bass is often little more than a single, jutting note; the guitar tone is more piercingly refined, a golden thread with less of the former fuzz attack; and the keyboards surround the band in a sheer fence of cold, industrial blankness. On 19 February, at Golders Green Hippodrome in north London, the 'Mother Sky' riff was superimposed on the descending four-chord motif of 'Bel Air' (on a track that has appeared on one bootleg as 'Tatgirdid Janit'). This British odyssey wrapped up in the north of England and Scotland, including a night at Manchester's impeccably scuzzy freak zone, the Stoneground.

That spring was a time for signing off on several more short-term projects. Alex Wiska arrived at Inner Space ready to record a follow-up album, *That's the Deal*, and as before, Jaki and Holger assisted by playing instruments and producing (Jaki rather poorly disguised behind the pseudonym 'Lee B. Zeit'). On 13 April they appeared at the Festival Equinox in the Parc des Expositions in Poitiers, a stoned hippy gathering headlined by the apocalyptic French progressive outfit Magma. *Melody Maker* writer Steve Lake, who had missed his transport from Paris and had to walk to Poitiers, described the sound balance in the beginning as 'the worst I have ever heard'. After the group walked off, not looking especially happy about their set, they were brought back by 'an unprecedented roar of approval from the same audience that appeared to be dozing throughout their performance . . . the enthusiasm had the required effect. Organist Irmin Schmidt tore into the encore improvisation with more aggression than his smiling face revealed, and in the process whipped off positively the best keyboard solo I've heard in years. The best since Mike Ratledge at the London School of Economics, February 14, 1970, to be precise. Dragging great squeals and screams of white noise from his equipment he propelled the group through a hair-raising fifteen minutes, that sparked off electric moments from all concerned. Superb modern music.'[9]

Shortly afterwards, on a May tour, parts of which were cancelled, Kalle Freynik witnessed a four-hour performance in Augsburg in which Holger fulfilled a long-held ambition to play the same note throughout an entire show.

Now that Can had blazed its trail several times through France and the UK, leaving audiences, fellow musicians and impressed critics in its wake, it was beginning to leave a tangible mark, and to make friends among a wider community. Early touring companions Hawkwind certainly honed their rhythmic rigour after experiencing Can first hand. Perhaps aware of Can's magical dabblings, black-magic-obsessed bandleader Graham Bond warned Irmin not to take Aleister Crowley's pronouncements lightly, while his wife, Diane Stewart, read his Tarot (Venus and the Hermit: love and solitude, Irmin recalls). Can's English friends also included Roxy Music and their recently departed synth player and ideas man, Brian Eno. Hildegard once applied Eno's flamboyant make-up when Can were invited backstage before a Roxy gig in Britain. Eno was so seduced by the new sounds of German experimental rock that, right after leaving Roxy in 1974, he travelled to the woodland retreat of former Cluster members Dieter Möbius and Hans-Joachim Roedelius, at exactly the moment they were joined by Neu! guitarist Michael Rother to form Harmonia. For Eno at that time such music – modern, clean, functional and quietly expressive – was the most promising ladder of escape from simple-minded rock cliché on the one hand and prog-rock pomposity on the other. Such groups – Can included – offered a more mature and fruitful approach. In his profile of Eno in *Chic* magazine, US journalist Michael Gross described meeting 'a visiting member of the German group Can'[10] – almost certainly Holger – lounging on a mattress on the floor of Eno's west London flat. When Michael returned for his summer holiday in the Algarve that year, he went with his sister, Constanze, and his girlfriend Eveline Grunwald. At the same resort they bumped into Bryan Ferry, along with his art director and photographer. As a result, it's Constanze and Eveline who ended up appearing semi-nude on the sleeve of Roxy's 1974 LP *Country Life*.

Although in Britain Can's music remained far outside the standard daytime radio playlist in 1974 (and they weren't particularly a singles band), the group had already been seen on the cult TV show *The Old Grey Whistle Test* and were being championed by the arbiter of credible music taste, John Peel. Youthful ears were tuning in: among them, the teenage John Lydon, later of the Sex Pistols and Public Image Limited (whose bass player, Jah Wobble, would end up working with Jaki Liebezeit), and in Sheffield, the newly founded experimental electronic group Cabaret Voltaire, who would carry their own influence into the story of UK electronica and techno.

*

Since the days of Bach and Beethoven, German music has enjoyed a long and deep connection with notions of universality and the cosmic. In Can's world it was former teacher Karlheinz Stockhausen who had introduced space into the realm of electronic music. His *Sternklang* (1969–71) was designed to be performed outdoors under the stars. The massive operatic cycle *Licht* aimed, in his words, to 'bring Celestial music to Humans, and Human music to celestial beings'.[11] He became interested in the mystical belief that the entire solar system orbits around Sirius, and he publicly associated himself with that star. On one occasion he described the perception of beings from the Dog Star, for whom 'everything is music, or the art of co-ordination and harmony of vibrations . . . every composition on Sirius is related to the rhythms of nature . . . the seasons, the rhythms of the stars'.[12]

Tangerine Dream also appealed to international audiences as the seventies progressed, while their music launched itself further into the distant reaches of space. Their first, landmark album, *Electronic Meditation* (1969), was a gas-giant of a record, votive and solemn in mood, cosmic in scale, yet built of recognisable materials: mellotrons, analogue rumbles and amplified flute. Somewhere between improvised music, contemporary classical and the future direction of progressive rock, the early Tangerine Dream were clear-sighted about what was to come. Subsequent releases *Alpha Centauri* and *Zeit* referred specifically to deep space and time, and reflected Edgar Froese's interest in trying to depict the infinite. Humans, he once said, are 'lost . . . in cycles that span hundreds and thousands of years',[13] but were blind to the environmental fate of the planet because they were too constrained by the tiny scope of their limited life cycles. Both sonically and philosophically, Froese was always seeking the biggest possible picture.

Even Rolf-Ulrich Kaiser, head of the Ohr label, which included Ash Ra Tempel and the Cosmic Couriers, keenly played the space-rock card: a manifesto printed in *Eurock* magazine in 1975 titled 'Discover the Galaxy Sound of Cosmic Music' began: 'Skylab calling

Terra . . .' In the post-hippy fallout, the idea of space was mapped simultaneously onto the literal image of interplanetary travel and galactic exploration, various shades of mystical and religious belief, and the mind-expansion properties of hallucinogenic drugs.

The German philosopher Gottfried Wilhelm Leibniz famously once declared that 'Music is a hidden arithmetic exercise of the mind that is not aware that it is counting.'[14] This touches on a secret history of music as a mathematical code, on its role – from antiquity to the Enlightenment – in illustrating the correspondences between Earth and the heavens. The 'music of the spheres' concept – music whose inherent structures and harmonic relationships act as a gateway to higher forms of knowledge – had preoccupied Michael Karoli in particular since his student days. 'Music is applied mathematics, and I have never seen music as anything else . . . And of course I was very interested in the cosmic harmonies, before we started Can. I spent long nights comparing the revolutions of Mars, trying to work out which chords they were actually making, but I never actually got anywhere. It was only a very strong interest. There was always this idea for me, that there was something behind reality that one tried to understand or guess: there had to be something, some deep secret behind everything.'

'The first thing [Michael] did was my horoscope,' confirms Eveline Grunwald. 'He had metres of . . . books, where, every day, every year . . . you could look it up and say, "What minute are you born? Look it up." They all had these books, and he would do that. At the time I was a bit into that. We read all these books about . . . the typical seventies books talking about mind-wandering, telepathy . . . telekinesis.'

Can rarely indulged in cod-mystical speculation, and even their pronouncements on magic were often couched in ironic disclaimers. But the group's previous connections with Stockhausen and avowed interest in the more esoteric aspects of musical physics and the natural sciences came to the boil around the summer of 1974,

In the Can Studio, Weilerswist, 1973, with roadies Chris Sladdin and René Tinner on the famous beanbag

Jaki, Holger, Irmin and Michael on the swing seat inside the Can Studio, Weilerswist, 1973

Michael Karoli

Irmin Schmidt

Holger Czukay

Jaki Liebezeit

Shortly before he left the band in 1973, Damo is photographed on the famous beanbag that can be heard on the intro to *Future Days*

After the success of their hit single 'Spoon', released in 1971, Can could afford to buy their first proper mixing desk, seen here in the background

Irmin, Holger and Chris Sladdin at the Can Studio, Weilerswist. Holger is changing the tape loops in Irmin's Alpha 77.

when they set out on the recordings that would end up as their sixth studio album, *Soon Over Babaluma*.

On *Future Days*, Can had already successfully evoked the sensation of gliding over the Earth's surface, near enough to descry geographical detail. On *Soon Over Babaluma*, they climbed far higher, breaking through the stratosphere and locking into orbit. The cover collage by Ulli Eichberger sets Can's music in the blue-black of deep space, in benign orbit over a three-dimensional model of a mountain range lit by a distant dwarf star. Its five tracks find their own ideal form, like water turning spherical in zero gravity. Can was still obsessed with repetition, but not so that endless monotony would lead merely to entropy – to the stagnation of an idea through overplay. Technical skill and openness to evolution ensured that energy was continually replaced, not dissipated – a perpetually renewing force, as with the moon upon the tide. Can evolved into a perpetual motion machine.

'There is a lot of hypnotic, repeating stuff in our music,' confirms Irmin, 'and one of the basic difficulties of new contemporary art was denying this physical fact that repetition is one of our basic needs. Everything starts with repetition . . . Our body is something which repeats in cycles, short and bigger ones which superimpose. And all this is music . . . But we never wanted to use this force to get someone asleep, rather it was moving, energising. I prefer that.'

Can refused to embrace the clichéd trappings of 'space music' – the long, throbbing analogue synths and gatefold concept albums of their progressive peers. Much of *Babaluma*'s texture is surprisingly organic and folky – the Balkan violin on 'Come sta, la luna'; the jazz-tipped acoustic piano and hyper-Latin rhythms of 'Splash'. But these flavours merely provide subtle notes grounding Can's habitual liberties with the fundamental structures of song.

Caught up in the Circadian whorl, a drowsy disorientation follows. It's no accident that the opening track on *Soon Over Babaluma* is titled 'Dizzy Dizzy'. Introduced by a drunken sigh across Michael's

Vitar electric violin strings and dry, fluttering drums, the song lurches furtively from shadow to shadow. The lyrics were supplied from a batch sent by their friend Duncan Fallowell, and Michael sings them with particular attention to percussive sibilants – 'Got-t-t-to get-t-it-over' – where the 'T's and 'S's entwine with the artificial hi-hats of a rhythm concocted by Irmin using his slide guitar and a delay effect on the Alpha 77.

'I was very much into free association at the time in a kind of fractalised way, in my own fictional writing,' says Fallowell. 'Mostly unprintable. As well as the lyrics I was doing. It wasn't as if I saw language as unbending: they're very trippy lyrics. I did a lot, sent quite a sheaf to Micky, and never heard anything, then I discovered he's used one for "Dizzy Dizzy".'

'I never enjoyed singing,' Michael commented. 'I never got into a state where I was actually singing the way I play guitar, where the thing happened which Desse and Damo both did. They were drifting in the music, and using their voices, and I never did that. What I did when I was singing with Can as a lead singer was just because I thought, or we thought, that there had to be somebody singing: it was necessary for the music. But I would at any time immediately very happily have stopped singing, if another singer had shown up who had at the same time the power to pick up the whole music with his voice and shift it forward. We had many singers coming here who thought they could perfectly join in. And basically they could join in to the idea, but they could not carry me somewhere.'

The phrase 'come sta, la luna' appears in a notebook of Leonardo da Vinci from 1503. Invoking Leonardo, the artist-mathematician who frequently dreamed of flight and of looking down upon the world while on the wing, is entirely appropriate to Soon Over Babaluma. Featuring the only lyrics Irmin invented for Can (sung-spoken through a slithery phasing effect), 'Come sta, la luna' is a solemn mechanical tango that suggests a drowsy fiddler perambulating from table to table, punctuated at times with neo-romantic flourishes at the bottom end of the grand piano. Its nineteenth-century palm-court ambience was achieved with another loan from the 'restaurant interior' department of the WDR sound effects library. A note of nocturnal melodrama is added by the dropping in of a cawing raven.

> *La luna densa*
> *Ogni densa e grave*
> *Come sta la lu-*
> *Na?*

> [The moon is dense
> What is dense is also heavy
> What is the nature of the moon?]

Playfully extemporising from this text, Irmin cast his eyes across the studio to where Jaki's girlfriend of the time, a woman called Christine, was perched on a sofa with accustomed stillness. 'She had this really mysterious aura around her . . . She could sit there for hours like a cat not moving, or just drawing, or maybe doing nothing,' Irmin recalls. 'So "Come sta, la luna" was about Christine in a way. I'm talking about this girl who is going through walls. I don't remember the words any more and I have never written it down. But there is something very spacey in the words – "Dancer on the rope, in the space" or something. But when I wrote that, she was sitting in the studio and I was looking at her . . . I found her very mysterious and very beautiful.'

Almost by accident, the phrase 'soon over Babaluma' emerged out of this stream of consciousness. 'The word "Babaluma" came out of a conversation with Jaki about the words. He maybe thought I had another word before, and he said, "What did you say? Babaluma?" And because it rhymed with *"luna"*, it was a kind of playing with words – it didn't mean anything. And it's true surrealism. But the whole text is about something happening in space, out there. Seeing the moon and, from there, soon being over Babaluma – which must be another star or something. So it has another story behind it.'

Walking through walls, flying for the moon and ending up looking down on a mysterious landscape. Travel – the earlier sense of looking at the world out of a train window – has become a form of teleportation, dematerialisation, quantum leaps in space and time.

Prefaced by the sounds of dirt bikes roving across a Martian rockscape, 'Chain Reaction' is a premonition of tribal trance. A thunderous stomp constructed from bass drum, flickering hi-hat and tambourine, and various layers of tuned percussion, it travels with a sense of helical rotation, with Michael's guitar dangling off it in languid strands. At 3:44 the energy accumulates to an excess and the track bursts into a disciplined 3/4 plod. Michael's fragmentary text – 'Elephant / Dominating . . . Russian mistress' – repays no analysis; the interplay between the instruments is more eloquent, especially when at 6:26 the group blasts into a thirty-second void of ominous beatings and 'Aumgn'-style bleakness from the Alpha 77, then clicks back into the rhythm in perfect lockstep. With its echoes of tribal drumming, from Burundi to Okinawa, 'Chain Reaction' is also a kind of hyperspatial 'EFS' track.

'Chain Reaction' segues directly into 'Quantum Physics', a throwback to the intense explorations of room space that Can used to conduct at Schloss Nörvenich. All Can's practical craft is drawn into a whole that suggests infinite frontiers without grand operatics. Harmonic plucks on the bass guitar, impressionistic drumming that sketches the lineaments of pulse only, Duncan Fallowell's poetic lyrics ('Dreaming in the autumn . . .') murmured by Michael: all is hushed, tensed, like devoted skywatchers attending an eclipse. Around 4:25 an unearthly chord comes hissing across the sound space, edging the mood from minor to major, from blind stumbling into the unknown to a sense of a certain, ordained destination. It's a flip that echoes the alleged properties of particles: that entire realities might be decided on minuscule atomic vibrations. The final twenty-second drone, as the drums drop away, is one of Can's most beautiful moments, anticipating thousands of electronic ambient recordings to come.

Soon Over Babaluma came out in late 1974. At almost exactly the same time, Kraftwerk issued *Autobahn*, a record that began that group's relentless ascent to the international pop charts in a way Can never managed. 'In many ways,' Michael mused, 'Kraftwerk were very close to us. But from the beginning they were more on the electronic side, more on the mechanical side, whereas we were always on the physical side, doing physical music.' As it was, the world of 1974 still hadn't quite been transformed by the brimming promise of new German music. Nick Kent's *NME* review hedged, 'A deal of the music here does tend to fall on stoney [*sic*] ground, being ultimately rendered fairly obsolete.' Nonplussed by the music, Kent could only make inaccurate comparisons to the Beatles' 'Baby, You're a Rich Man' and the Upsetters. '"Quantum Physics", which ends the side, is so defiantly impenetrable at this juncture that I daren't make some dogmatic statement concerning its merits.'[15] Even back in February Kent prefaced his *NME* Can piece with a sense of ennui: 'Remember back in 1972 when it was the bees knees to get wrapped up in dialectics about how the krauts really knew what was going on and how all those nihilistic electronic landscapes they were droning their way through interminably, were nothing less than the music of the future.'[16]

Citing reggae as the next breakthrough music from outside the Anglo-American axis, Kent had nevertheless defended Can as the only group to have 'motivated themselves out of the Krautrock zone to really merit superlatives as such . . . on a good night they can bristle with a kind of exotically bleak menace . . . The music cannot be pinpointed – it exists for itself and the audience seem bewildered, if occasionally invigorated, by the more exotic passages.'[17] In the same article Kent mocked 'balding intellectuals like Ian MacDonald [who] can be heard occasionally muttering earnestly about the undeveloped potential inherent in the contemporary German music culture'. Yet when MacDonald himself interviewed Can for a long article that came out on the back of *Babaluma*, he concentrated almost entirely on recounting the group's history and prehistory, only glossing the newest material in three final paragraphs.[18] Can still had an audience, one composed of music obsessives, rarefied listeners and rock-critic champions, not casual pop fans. Can's cultivated unpredictability meant that loyalty was difficult to maintain; live shows continued to demand aural stamina. The Hammersmith Palais finale of a sixteen-date UK tour that kicked off on 27 September was advertised in the music press as 'playing for three hours', and included a twenty-five-minute jam on 'Chain Reaction'. A *Top Gear* session, recorded mid-tour at the BBC's Maida Vale Studios, features controlled solar flares of guitar feedback, futuristic synth clouds from the Alpha 77 and distinctly Neu!-influenced riffing on 'Return to BB City'. In 'Tape Kebab', equally tightly paced, Irmin and Michael dive into a spontaneous chord sequence, closing out with a crinkling arpeggiated synth sound. This was superbly disciplined improvisation that refused to lapse into indulgent grandstanding.

There was also the release of a compilation, *Limited Edition*, a collection of thirteen sweepings from Can's cutting-room floor, spanning the earliest experiments with Malcolm, some marvellously dippy Damo moments, a handful of 'EFS' snippets and recent material including 'Gomorrha' and 'E.F.S. No. 36', which was a pastiche of Dixieland jazz with Jaki tootling jauntily on a trumpet. The sleeve was a surreal photograph of a flock of white mice running amok with a metal canister in a doll's house and leaping out of the window into a rural landscape. On a pink poster on the wall, a cartoon woman shrieks. On the reverse, the mice have vanished and the lady has calmed down and smoothed her skirts. Although it didn't present Can in their most powerful light, this interim, budget-price release reflected the commercial need to follow the live activity with a new product, as they had not even begun dedicated work on any kind of new LP. Can's music was becoming ever more improvisational, serendipitously following the whims of the collective group-mind as they extemporised on their extensive archive of motifs or invented entirely new passages in the moment.

Limited Edition was curated by Duncan Fallowell, who at this juncture came close to replacing Damo as Can's new vocalist. He had already acted as a kind of lyric editor and transcriber for publishing purposes, and occasionally helped the group to write press releases and gave other advice. As an Oxford University scholar and man of letters, he found it frustrating that Can seemed to pay little heed to the content of their texts. 'All the Can people were very pure musicians, and they had something of a scorn for words,' he recollects. 'There was a sort of movement; it wasn't an anti-intellectual movement, it was: "Words are a trap, they're too fixed, something we're trying to escape from – it reminds us of school."

'But it was a necessary component if you're going to call yourself a rock band or advance through the rock milieu, rather than an avant-garde concert once a year at Darmstadt. I bridled at this, because words are very important to me, and we had quite a lot of conflict early on because I tried to explain the importance of words, as opposed to sound – the importance of language . . . I said the words are important in the rock world or in opera or lieder or choral music, because it connects the music to humanity. I said, "Think what your albums would be like if they were purely instrumental, with no human voice. They would be quite different. The moment you go on stage and call yourself a rock band, you need that connection with humanity, and it must be direct. You can get away with meaningless noises up to a point . . ."

'I kept banging on about this, and eventually it dawned on them: language has emerged from grunts, and may return to grunts, but nonetheless it has its own validity which I tried to inject.'

With a typically casual invitation, Irmin tried to interest Fallowell in the idea of joining the group, and in some ways the writer's appreciation of both the Dionysian and Apollonian qualities in Can's music made him an ideal candidate. 'I thought about it, and I realised that if I did, I might have ego problems. But more than that, [the question] was: do I want to be sucked into the rock world or do I want to retain my independence as a writer? And I stayed writing. I could have done it . . . I was very into the idea. Part of me still is, regrets not trying, even if it only lasted two months and produced three tracks or something. It was also partly fear. I thought, "I just might take too many drugs and vanish into this pond." So it was partly funk and partly judgement. That's why I refused.'

13

Bumpy Landings

To France, where Can opened the new year with four dates, kicking off in Reims Cathedral on 16 January and including two sold-out nights at the Bataclan in Paris, on the seventeenth and twenty-ninth of the month. These were both colossal performances that spliced extruded versions of 'Chain Reaction' and 'Dizzy Dizzy' with older themes like 'Pinch' and, on the final date, 'Yoo Doo Right'. But much of the material played was one-time-only, never to be repeated. In the French *Rock & Folk* magazine, Paul Alessandrini was moved to rhapsodise: 'The Reims audience, like the one at Bataclan Paris the next day, came to take part in what is, without any doubt whatsoever, the only example of a totally improvised live music, presenting itself as such, running crazily in pursuit of marvellous sounds, novel musical exchanges, starts and stumbles over themes, electroacoustic ruptures and limpid phrases, cool and quasi-Californian.'

Can still left itself open to chance procedures and moment-to-moment musical decisions, even as the music became tighter and more rock-oriented. And its visual manifestation was still unorthodox: Irmin threshing the keys of his organ with his elbows; Jaki's glittering blue drum kit and percussion array; Holger's statue-like poise with occasional bobs of the head, and his newly acquired electric double bass, played with white kid gloves; Michael's subdued, elfin whisper.

Can's entourage was growing, to meet the needs of their scaled-up operations. Their audio set-up, both live and in the studio, was unusual in that it now featured a wall of Altec Lansing speakers, two metres high, spread across the entire backline. The system was designed exclusively for Can by Bob Hickmott, an English plumber who had recently become the band's in-house technician. On their last UK tour, Can had been forced to hire English roadies to comply with union rules. Hickmott stayed on and followed them into Europe. He arrived in Cologne in a three-wheeled Robin Reliant and promptly smashed it. Irmin remembers him picking the coins out of the electric vibrating beds in one Brussels hotel, then organising a round of drinks with the spoils. 'He was a hippy, he didn't care how something looked, as long as it was practical and working,' says Irmin. 'He had no sense of aesthetics!'

'Fantastic person!' remembered Jaki. 'I don't remember how we met him. Because he was a plumber he understood all electrical things, and he thought it's like plumbing. Like water – instead of water, electricity runs. He built crazy things, and I think he was the inventor of this wall [of speakers] we had.'

Meanwhile, a young man named René Tinner, who would end up running the Can Studio after the band split, acted as all-purpose van driver and roadie. He came, coincidentally, from St Gallen, the Swiss town where Holger had met Michael. He remembers seeing Michael about town: 'He had a Beetle with a German licence plate, and everybody told me this guy is awful because he gets all the chicks! I later found out we had hung out in the same club without knowing it.

'I got involved,' says Tinner, 'because I was at art school in Zurich in 1972, '73.' In a pub one night he bumped into Hermi Hogg, the electronics wizard who had designed Irmin's Alpha 77. 'He talked me into helping him out. In those days there were student revolts in Switzerland, and he was a Maoist and built megaphones for the demonstrators. His ambition was they have to be louder than those of the police. And he achieved that ten times over! I helped with soldering the circuit boards. I was unhappy and said I wanted to go somewhere else, and he gave me Can's address and I wrote a letter. Hildegard replied pretty quick, and I went to Cologne.'

In late 1974 another Englishman joined the squad. Peter Gilmour was a writer and journalist who lived in Maida Vale and had friends in the underground scene centred around nearby Ladbroke Grove. He shared a flat with a girlfriend and Michiko 'Michi' Nakao, a Japanese-born artist and photographer who had washed up in London via Paris in the early seventies. She was drawn to the city because of its fashion and music scenes and gained an entrée via one of Japan's biggest international film and music stars, Mickey Curtis. She became close to Roxy Music in the early seventies, and via Brian Eno, who lived round the corner and was her boyfriend for a while, she met and became friends with Holger Czukay in London around 1972 or '73. In 1974 Gilmour started listening to Can in earnest, and on 8 October, a few weeks after he'd bought a copy of *Tago Mago*, Nakao invited her star-struck flatmate to Can's session at the BBC's Maida Vale Studios. 'That was the first time I met them,' says Gilmour, 'and we immediately became friends. Particularly Micky – I was Micky's age and was generally bohemian in thought and attitude.'

Can invited Gilmour to visit them in Cologne. 'Bit by bit I got more and more involved with it,' he says. 'They didn't like the way Bobby Hickmott was mixing the live sound, and because they had such a good rapport with me, they got Bobby to teach me how to use the mixer, which I'd never done before, and I started mixing the live sound. It was a tiny eight-channel mixer, and I used to carry it like a briefcase into gigs. All the other bands would go with these fucking great big twenty-four-channel mixers that took four roadies to carry in, and I had this little thing,' he laughs.

'Hickmott was a lovely bloke and we all got on really well together. But he wasn't particularly keen on their music – he used to prefer folk music. There was a whole bank of speakers across the back of the stage, and nobody else had that, and because he designed it, he ran it. But they felt the sound was a bit wishy-washy, and I felt that I was able to beef it up. I had a fairly natural talent for it. And I had a kind of telepathic communication with them – Micky was walking to the front of the stage and stamping on his loudness pedal, and at the same time, without even thinking or seeing what he was doing, I was pushing up his guitar fader, because I realised he was about to do some kind of solo.' From late 1974 until the middle of 1977 Gilmour became part of Can's inner circle, controlling the live mix, writing lyrics, providing backing vocals and kicking in ideas where needed. 'I was spending about a third of the year in Cologne, and then we were on tour for maybe three months of the year as well. And the rest of the time I was in London. It was great fun. I felt very good about the whole arrangement.' This trio of technically minded odd-balls – Gilmour, Hickmott and Tinner – shared a flat in Cologne for a while. The arrangement wasn't always one of domestic harmony. 'It got difficult,' comments Tinner, 'because Bob was in love with a woman, and Peter had to go and shag her. I never forgot that night Bob came home and smashed all the dishes. That was a difficult situation between the two of them.'

In the mid-seventies the must-have studio item was the MCI JH-16 multitrack tape recorder, which more than doubled the capacity of most recording set-ups and octupled Can's own ancient two-track method. Inner Space took delivery of one of these in February, in time for the group's next bout of recording, which became the album *Landed*. In aural terms it was the equivalent of shifting from painting cameo miniatures to a wall-sized blank canvas, which had its good and bad points. In some respects it caused a general loos-ening of focus in Can's recorded output, as they tried to reconcile the new technology with their own evolving music. For Irmin, the upgrade 'was a natural thing: we had the money to afford it, and that sounded so cool to have our own sixteen-track. But as [is] so often mentioned and talked about already, the thing is, of course, it was a new instrument, and a new instrument you have to learn. So it was something we had to get used to.'

For the past seven years of working together in the studio, even the process of overdubbing – or adding fresh tracks to the initial live take – was of necessity a communal activity, as multiple instruments needed to be added simultaneously, in real time, in order to maximise the capacity of the two-track facility. The set-up allowed for only one extra overdub, so, as Irmin says, 'sometimes we all did it together, or two or three of us did. So you still were aware of the dynamics, you had to listen to it. And while playing, you were part of the mix.' With this, Holger observed, there was somehow more at stake in the moment of musical creation. 'We all felt responsible for the final result. When you play, if someone gets, let's say, over the top and destroys it, he was responsible for a very good recording that was destroyed, so . . . everyone took great care for making everything as good as possible.' With the advent of sixteen tracks, extra material could be added at leisure, and in isolation if necessary. It didn't require the presence of the whole group, so the additions could be more fragmented and solitary. Holger: 'Now [things] could be criticised: the guitar made the mistake, or the bass was doing the mistake. And the effect of it was that the bass player or the guitar player now wanted to do their recordings alone, because they didn't want to get criticised all the time and have someone making bad vibes. No, they wanted to have good vibes, as well as everybody else, but suddenly they were alone. That is the beginning of the end of a community.'

With the new equipment freshly unboxed, these weaknesses in the system had yet to be revealed. The recordings for their next album, which took place all through that winter and into spring, are both more detailed and more dry, claustrophobic in places, as if the group members have drawn themselves into a huddle in the middle of the studio. 'Hunters and Collectors' adds a fidgety, pistoning rhythm to Can's familiar step-down chord sequence, slammed out on piano. The track was used in the crime series *Eurogang*, broadcast in September 1975, and Michael's vocal (backed with

doo-woppish harmonies from the rest) evokes noirish double dealings and secret watchers in nocturnal seediness: 'Thirty leather kids
on the gangbang trail / Catch a brown man in his snakeskin bed . . .
/ Hunters and collectors all come out at night / Hunters and collectors never see the light . . .'

An even more frantic and synth-heavy variation, 'Midnight Men',
appeared on *The Lost Tapes*, in which the guitar motif – five pudgy
notes, sharply picked – is refracted through 'Peter Gunn' and isolated in the mix. Can's sheer subtlety and deftness of touch are
fully displayed in the middle, where Jaki's razor-light, cobwebby
drumming evolves into an effortless moiré of struck fretboards and
ring-modulated piano. A notable detail near the beginning – probably reflecting the ability to flip between multiple channels – is
the weird dialogue between Michael and Irmin around the line 'It
will all be up before the sun is up', in which individual words are
processed in strikingly different ways. As an evocation of the sup-
pressed hysteria and paranoia of street-level gang warfare, 'Hunters
and Collectors' is unrivalled.

'Vernal Equinox', which starts with precisely the same dolorous
piano chord as 'Hunters and Collectors', gallops off at its own pace,
prefaced by a burst of crowd applause taped by the group themselves at a live show. Soon to be a live favourite, 'Vernal Equinox'
is a crazed, exhilarating, two-chord jam taken at breakneck speed
that never quite tips over into a 'Godzilla' moment. At 4:00, a ring-
modulated keyboard percussion interlude opens up, intricate as
gamelan and as precise as a Swiss watch.

Another track where Can let itself off the chain as a rampaging
rock machine was *Landed's* opener, 'Full Moon on the Highway'. A
song played live by the group as far back as 1971 is converted to a
demented punk-style thrash, with fudgy layers of fizzing guitars and
fuzzy basslines. Thumping along with a sped-up 'Mother Sky'-style
tumble, and featuring weird vocodered backing vocals, this was Can

channelling Hawkwind, Neu! and Lynyrd Skynyrd, but turning out as nothing except Can itself. However, the mix had a constrained, boxed-in quality that painted Can in a different light from before.

Although *Landed* was recorded at Inner Space as usual, it was decided to do the final mix elsewhere, since Holger had not yet fully mastered the use of the sixteen-track desk. In Stommeln, a hamlet north-west of Cologne and around forty-five kilometres from Weilerswist, musician and producer Dieter Dierks had established a successful studio in his parents' back garden. Bands enjoying the culinary delights of 'Mama Dierks' while recording classic albums included Tangerine Dream, Ash Ra Tempel, Nektar, Witthüser & Westrupp, Manuel Göttsching, Scorpions, Popol Vuh, Guru Guru, Embryo, Amon Düül, Floh de Cologne and Rolf-Ulrich Kaiser's one-off supergroup Cosmic Jokers. By 1975 the studio was beginning to welcome international artists, including Eric Burdon and Ike and Tina Turner.

Among the floating cadre of producers and engineers stumbling around Dierks Studios' hippy enclave was a young Englishman called Toby Robinson. He ended up there having traced a path through the German music world that overlapped with Can's to some degree. He had already spent time as a sound engineer with Stockhausen and composer Péter Eötvös in Cologne's WDR studios, while his older brother, Mike, was a member of British improvisational group Gentle Fire, which also included another Stockhausen acolyte, Hugh Davies. By 1973 Toby had drifted into the hazy world of underground experimental rock, playing in short-lived bands such as Temple, the Nazgûl and Cozmic Corridors, and running the Pyramid label. He ended up mixing the first four tracks on *Landed*, although his methods proved not entirely compatible with Can's standards. Irmin: 'This guy was listening so loud and mixing so loud and insisting that it's rock that we couldn't really judge what the fuck he was doing. So after that was mixed we came back to our studio, listened to the mixed tape properly in a civilised loudness, and were extremely disappointed. Of course, we had to use it, but it sounds like a satirical version of rock music, which we didn't mean at all. And still I think "Full Moon on the Highway" is one of our worst pieces. Not because of the piece, but because of the sound.' Can ended up mixing the rest of the album back at Inner Space.

With its ska-inspired shuffle and steel-pan percussion, 'Red Hot Indians' pointed to new directions in Can's listening and fresh impulses in their rhythmic range. Still, it sounded as folksy and spontaneously composed as their earlier 'EFS' miniatures, while burbling varispeed background voices, minced through a wobbling tremolo effect, were designed to disguise and dehumanise Michael's vocal. Olaf Kübler, a veteran saxophonist from Jaki's early-sixties bebop years (and producer and manager of Amon Düül), over-dubbed several layers of perky saxophone solo.

With its percussive jitters, pterodactyl violin and fantastic treated-organ interventions, 'Half Past One' is a brilliant piece of Can inter-play. It's also one of Michael's most confident vocal performances. 'Unfinished', by contrast, is a piece that justifies the term 'ambient', made in the year Brian Eno hit upon the word himself to describe the vogue for an atmospheric music that seemed to exist outside human agency. According to Michael, it was 'one of those pieces where we let the atmosphere of the studio impress itself on the tape, it's really a piece composed by the studio'.[1] It is a thirteen-minute edit of sounds Can conjured up in one charmed session they referred to as 'the magic day', when they tried to create the conditions in the studio in which their instruments could practi-cally play themselves. As with 'Soup' in 1972, they came up with this space-filling piece totally spontaneously, in real time, with no post-processing.

Michael: 'Somewhere we had found a very old Selmer organ. It was broken and didn't make ordinary sounds. Suddenly, during the recording of "Unfinished", the organ began to make a great noise by itself. I shouted to the organ to stop. I asked Irmin if I should start again, and he said "carry on", and the organ began to make weird sounds. After that it never worked again. This incident has nothing to do with me, but we were living in the studio . . . every day was so intense that everything started to sync. Different things happening at the same time. That has to do with music – it's what music does."[2]

Michael's electric guitar strings pick up shortwave radio stations and the synth permeates the mix with a beautiful sheen, as if everything is heard through a curtain of mother-of-pearl. On this, the closest they had come to the immersive sonic vortex of 'Aumgn', human actions can be heard – occasional percussive gestures – but all the elements seem to be shifting around each other at different speeds, a throwback to Stockhausen's conception of 'sound masses'. Such constant axial realignment seems to have no beginning and no end; it remains endlessly unfinished.

To pursue larger audiences in accordance with the commerce of rock, changes were afoot. Can's relationship with United Artists came to an end at the start of the year, as Siggi Loch transferred to a new role at EMI Germany, run by Günther Ilgner and Manfred Zumkeller, and brought the band with him. Can's output in foreign territories was still up for grabs, however. And the group's long-standing dispute with former manager Abi Ofarim, which had been grinding away in the background since 1971, was finally brought to a close in the spring of 1975. The lid came down at almost exactly the same time as Hildegard Schmidt was in the UK closing the kind of deal Ofarim could never come up with: a contract with Virgin Records. In the preceding years she had built up and maintained excellent working relationships with the various European branches of United Artists, with particular success in Britain, where it was run by Martin Davis, and along with industry veteran David Platz she had initiated a UK publishing operation, Messer Music. When it came time to hook up with Virgin, she did the deal in person with Richard Branson. 'I signed the contract lying on the floor in his house,' she recalled, 'which, at the time, was close to Virgin Records [in Ladbroke Grove].'³

In the same week Irmin, in Paris, was summoned to Munich, where the lawyers for all parties were gathering to await the final verdict in the Ofarim case. Just before leaving, one of Irmin's Parisian friends suggested he visit a fortune-teller – the real deal, crystal ball and everything. 'She looked at me,' says Irmin, 'put all the cards and stuff away and said, "Oh, I see you don't need that." She took my hand and said, "You can heal with your hands." And I *can* sometimes help a little bit. She was sort of a bit angry with me even. She said, "If you have a gift like this, you have to help."

'She told me exactly the situation: that Hildegard was in London, talking business – she didn't know if it was film or music, but something like this. There was no possibility that she was tricking. She said, "She's with this man that looks like a Viking." Those were her words. Pretty precise. "That will be successful, don't worry."' She told Irmin that he would be meeting his lawyers the next day and that, whatever the outcome, he shouldn't try to contradict or question anything his lawyers told him. 'Think of me when it comes to this point,' she told him, and things came to pass almost exactly as predicted, when Irmin tried to query a small point at the end of the settlement. 'All of a sudden both lawyers said [to me], "Let's go in another room quickly." They said, "Mr Schmidt, please, they don't even realise that they gave everything away. This fucking little detail, just forget it – it's not even worth thinking about." And all of a sudden I remembered that Madame Le Beau had told me this. I shut up and didn't say anything any more, and the thing was finished and we had more or less won.'

Now Can could reap the rewards of a new, lucrative deal, to test out the expanded horizons of multitrack recording, and to build on the audience base the group had assembled over the past six years and finally take their music to American audiences. They were paying themselves a salary of fifteen hundred marks each a month and ploughing the remainder into their studio operation. By signing to Virgin they were now in the company of similarly adventurous acts, appealing to the more intellectual, progressively attuned rock fan: Henry Cow, Gong, Mike Oldfield, Robert Wyatt and even fellow Germans Faust and Tangerine Dream. But was the tide of music and fashion with them or against them?

'When the band was in the throes of creating something, they wouldn't want to be talking to people,' says Peter Gilmour. The few visitors and hangers-on in the studio would have to wait patiently in the lounge area of Inner Space, under a large indoor umbrella, while Can fathomed its music. 'It was boring! I only went there in the beginning, with Hildegard, to go and listen to something,' says Eveline Grunwald. 'They did have long sessions, that's how they worked. There was a lot of arguing. What I witnessed was little things, but there was really heavy screaming going on. But also when it was really good . . .'

Another recent addition to Can's entourage, Englishman Andy Hall, spent many hours in the studio and remembers the atmosphere being more relaxed. 'They were looking for a more refined effect than on stage,' he says. 'I loved it. I would go around 3 p.m. René would already be there. The first member would typically arrive at four or four thirty; by six everyone would have assembled. The group-playing became a bit more integrated by seven. I generally remember there being a relaxed attitude, with some soft-drug-taking. Mostly hashish, as well as alcohol, of course. It all made for a rather soporific atmosphere. They were very at ease with themselves.'

Jaki's girlfriend, the enigmatic Christine, was sometimes found on the Inner Space sofa, painting or sewing Jaki's stage outfits. 'She was very mysterious,' says Grunwald. 'She was a trained tailor, that's why she could do all that. She was very much to herself. She liked to smoke. I remember once she came to our place, and I don't know if she'd bought some [hash] cookies or if she made them . . . oh God, I was paralysed, and they were all laughing, and I sat there and said, "I can't get up any more" – terrible. Christine just ate one after the other. A very quiet person. She had decorated their little flat. They had a lovely, nice little flat. She did all the decorations inside, really comfortable and nice. She was like that.' She had been running Can's fan club, a job recently taken over by Andy Hall. It was a small but dedicated club, with around three or four hundred members. One of the main duties was sending out autographed promotional postcards of the band – a set featuring the portrait photos printed on the back cover of *Soon Over Babaluma*. She began doodling on these postcards and quickly amassed a collection of dozens of defaced portraits – Can tricked out with beards, moustaches, rouged cheeks and lipstick, eyepatches and elaborate bouffantes. Thirty-six of these, collaged into a square, formed the sleeve art for *Landed*. The title denoted nothing more than the touchdown after being 'soon over Babaluma'.

'There are times', opined *Melody Maker*'s reviewer in his consideration of *Landed*, 'when I'm convinced Can enter a recording studio intent on liberating what can only be described as the most homicidal musical tendencies . . . There exists such a fascination with the mechanics and contrivances of a Can performance that the listener is inevitably drawn again and again on the most perilous aural expeditions.' This odd, ambiguous judgement was mostly, perhaps, a reaction to the sonic battering of 'Full Moon on the Highway', because on the evidence of Can's live outings of summer 1975, it was their most beatific tendencies they were more intent on liberating.

Setting out on yet another tour of the UK on 1 May, and sticking mostly to tracks from *Soon Over Babaluma*, *Future Days* and *Ege Bamyası*, Can were clearly out to give their audience variations on material they were already largely familiar with – or perhaps they felt less at home with the material they had recently recorded. On some nights they would summon up a beautiful pastoral motif called 'Meadow Sweet' in surviving set lists, but which they never officially recorded in any form. Other occasions were more gut-wrenching. After an otherwise successful show at the Stadium in Liverpool on 3 May, Michael's Fender Stratocaster, as well as all the band's cables and their live mixing desk, were stolen by someone posing as a roadie. After a night of frantic phone calls to local radio stations and the police, trying to track down the missing items, the band drove to Croydon. The start of their set at the Greyhound was delayed while René Tinner, Andy Hall and Bob Hickmott desperately tried to re-solder all the missing connections, while the in-house DJ played deafening intro music. In the event, with Michael using a Strat borrowed from a friend of Roxy Music's Phil Manzanera, Can displayed a classic example of power under adversity. The dark, crunching version of 'Yoo Doo Right' from that night was later included on the *Can Live* double CD in 1998. The stolen gear was never recovered.

On 17 May they returned to the University of Essex in Colchester, scene of one of their most memorable 1972 gigs. Here they essayed a large chunk of 'Bel Air', as well as streamlined takes on 'Dizzy Dizzy', 'Chain Reaction' and a return to 'Pinch' that segued into 'Mother Sky', whose forceful momentum they relished several times during 1975. A lithe, mercurial version of 'One More Night' closed the set; this was a group that now commanded a treasure box of a back catalogue that they could call up at will.

With Peter Gilmour in charge of the live mix and René Tinner balancing the onstage monitors, Can's sound now had a significantly enhanced stage presence. Even within this engineering conclave there was a degree of internal tension, believes Gilmour. 'René used to do the foldback, mix the stage sound, and it was always a big tussle between him and me because I wanted to influence the sound more than he did. Because we had these speakers all across the back of the stage, what he did affected the sound that I was making, much more than it would do with a normal set-up.'

In response, Tinner calls this version of events 'total rubbish', and for his own part believes Gilmour's fandom and aspirations to write lyrics for Can made him feel he had a superior status to the rest of the crew.

In the middle of the month Can dropped in once more to the BBC's Maida Vale Studios to record two tracks for *Top Gear*. 'Geheim' was a funky foretaste of 'Half Past One', from the forthcoming album, while 'Mighty Girl' (later 'November' on *Out of Reach*) was an expansive synth-rock piece, with the emphasis on cinematic grand piano, that occasionally struggled for momentum. A few days later, the tour wound up at the Roundhouse in Camden Town on 18 May.

Can's only appearances in Austria took place four days apart at the Musik Forum, a festival in the small town of Siegendorf, at the country's easternmost extreme. A recording exists of one track from the 9 July set, and three from the show on the thirteenth. This is Can in freewheeling mode, using only the barest bones of familiar tracks to cast off on long improvised jams. The so-called 'Frenische' is 'Vernal Equinox' with the onboard computers seizing command. The infinity groove of 'Halleluwah' resurfaces on the mighty 'Tunbra', while a space-funk track dubbed 'The Jet' directly anticipates the four-to-the-floor coasting of nineties techno, with the rik-a-tik of Michael's Fender Strat strafed by space age noises from the Alpha 77.

If Siegendorf showed Can was still capable of challenging itself to the limit, two final French concerts rounding out the summer found the group at the zenith of its powers. The outdoor event, attended by around seven thousand people, at the ancient Roman amphitheatre in Arles, in the south of France, on 6 August – with Nico and Kevin Ayers also on the bill – remains one of Irmin's favourite memories of his Can years. 'There were moments like this Arles concert, which was absolutely where I felt that's what . . . you know it in the moment when it happens: the *Glücksgefühl*, the ecstasy. I was looking for that all my life, because it happens every now and then in a different context, and it's those moments where what you do is totally in accordance, in harmony with you. You are in harmony with the world and with what you are doing.'

The surviving tapes are unfortunately pretty low-fidelity, but it is possible to get an inkling of the high flights Can embarked on that day. Running to upwards of ninety minutes (the full concert lasted over two hours), the tape is an almost continuous flow of half-familiar themes: 'Dizzy Dizzy', 'Bel Air', 'Vitamin C', 'Red Hot Indians' and the glorious 'Meadow Sweet' (not Can's title), whose balmy, sun-dappled atmosphere, ushered in with cross-currents of Caribbean percussion, seems tailor-made for an event such as this, singing a swansong for the great European progressive be-in, before the combined waves of disco and punk rock swept music audiences in new directions. A frantic 'Chain Reaction' wobbles so much it ends up spinning off its precarious axis into a sequence unofficially titled 'The Gypsy', where curlicues of churchy organ playfully trace double helixes with spurts and puffs of high-end guitar. This in turn swells and unfurls into a climax that takes an age to burn out, as if the group is reluctant to vacate the stage.

When Can's mercurial music-making collided with a sizeable audience, as here (and at Cannes the day after), spine-tingling effects could still result. 'In every concert,' said Michael, 'about two minutes after the beginning – or sometimes never, unfortunately – was when the hair on the back of the neck started to stand up. Sort of this feeling of goosepimples. That was the feeling when I knew the band had locked. And my technique, one of the techniques to achieve that, was just looking at the audience. I tried not to see the audience as single people, but like a sort of . . . what are they called? Sea anemones, you know, with many arms? I just saw the whole public as a whole thing, and then I would look at the public, and then by playing to get a movement into the public, to start seeing them move as one animal.'

Can drifted back to Weilerswist and rode out the lazy summer with languid dabblings in their upgraded studio. 'Private Nocturnal', an unreleased piece that was eventually issued on *The Lost Tapes*, verges on the cusp of a New Age synth track: a luminous adagio for acoustic guitar, space synth and percussive splats, improvised in the moment. Later in the month, Holger invited Michiko 'Michi' Nakao, his and Gilmour's mutual friend from London, to hang out at Inner Space. Holger had heard her singing one day and asked her to try out for Can, even though she had never undertaken any musical projects before. 'It was my first time in my life to record, so I was excited,' she says.

As a trial run, she was asked to sing over the forty-four-minute unedited take of the track that ended up as 'Unfinished' on *Landed*. Then Holger pulled out the tape of Can's gig at Edinburgh in August 1973 and asked her to extemporise some vocals over the top. This session, never released officially, has been bootlegged, and Nakao's excitable vocals on 'Hot Day in Köln' find her in a time-locked duet with Damo in the opening bars. 'It was very difficult to express myself because of my English,' she remembers, 'but one day there was no one around in the studio. I picked up a synthesizer and played and I found a beautiful melody with my own words. It was like a lullaby of my missing mother to me' – a track known as 'I'm Your Doll'. She also recalls Conny Plank dropping in to play keyboards on one occasion: 'It was a magical time.' Unfortunately, it would not be repeated. Although these impromptu experiments never officially saw the light of day, it's clear Can still felt the lack of a human voice, and they continued their efforts to fill the void.[4]

On 18 November they dropped in for a couple of hours at a London photographic studio, where some of the most frequently reused images of the foursome were immortalised by one of the most cele-brated rock photographers of the time, Mick Rock. Having already captured enduring images of the early-seventies rock aristocracy – David Bowie, the Rolling Stones, Lou Reed, Jim Morrison, Iggy Pop and others – Rock was introduced to Can by the group's short-lived guest vocalist from that summer, Michi Nakao. When Virgin Records' press department realised they had little visual material to offer to editors, Rock was hired at Holger's request.

'I don't remember them being difficult on the session, and I don't remember them showing up late,' recalls Rock of the photo session. 'In those days loads of bands would show up late – that was almost de rigueur.'

Can may have showed up on time, but judging by their attire and demeanour, they were aware that they needed to put a bit more effort than usual into looking like rock stars. In many of these shots they are clad in black leather biker jackets – Holger bare-chested beneath his – and gaze into Rock's lens with 'blue steel' stares. It's the closest Can ever came to being 'styled' in the sev-enties, and they exude an awkward, menacing cool that teeters on the edge of camp.

'Obviously, I had dragooned them to some degree, as you can see from that shot,' says Rock. 'And they were clearly quite attentive. They seemed to be taking it seriously. And maybe that was some-thing to do with the new label, and maybe a desire to be a bit more successful. They were known, but I don't know how many records they had sold up to that point.

'In those days, remember, no one had stylists around. Our mutual friend Michi helped a bit. She probably tidied them up a bit, 'cause she would do make-up in those days. I don't recall them coming and stumbling around; they pretty much did what I asked them to do. And stayed focused on the shoot, which was the whole point of the afternoon. Plus I was getting paid – there was no way they were get-ting out of there without me producing some decent pictures. They weren't necessarily pretty, but then again, it wasn't so long before the ugly characters came along in the form of punk.'

Later that evening, dressed in the same clothes and in a visibly feisty mood, they were at BBC Television Centre to record another live session for *The Old Grey Whistle Test*. The seven-and-a-half-minute 'Vernal Equinox' is one of the most frequently watched pieces of Can footage, and the close-up camerawork with lively cross-fades and intimate angles provides a forensic peek at their methods. Despite being older than the average act on the show, they exude a disciplined glamour – Jaki playing a spangly aquamarine drum kit with double bass drums, Michael sky-kissing in a cream T-shirt with palm trees, and Holger grappling his bass with white gloves on his hands. He had been using these for a couple of years to protect his fingertips for tape editing, and also to absorb sweat. A Ray-Banned Irmin comes out of the shadows on this appearance, wearing a chain-mail waistcoat over his leathers and karate-chopping his Farfisa keyboard. This was evidence of a group described by *Sounds* journalist Vivien Goldman, who interviewed them on this same promotional trip, as having 'a reputation for being heavies of one kind or another. Apart from that boring old rock star mythology of ripping Lamborghinis apart with your bare teeth, throwing your kidney-shaped swimming pool into your hotel room and setting the receptionist on fire. Can have some kind of aura, a mystique about being Scanners Of The Skies, advance guard of a new long-haired breed of Nietzschean super-heroes playing bass by thought-wave control.'[5]

The line-up for that episode of *Whistle Test* also included Jim Capaldi's new group, which had evolved after the guitarist and singer had nominally quit Traffic the previous year, even though this band did include Steve Winwood and Traffic's former bassist, Rosko Gee. Capaldi was promoting a single, 'Love Hurts', which reached number two, although he didn't play it in the TV studio that day.

Founded even earlier than Can, Traffic was another unit with a signature sound that had evolved over long-form improvisation. It had constantly changed its line-up around a small core. Rosko Gee, a British citizen born in Jamaica, had joined in 1974, appearing on the album *When the Eagle Flies*. Behind the scenes at BBC Television Centre, he and Holger struck up an immediate friendship. Within twelve months Holger's new buddy would replace him as Can's bassist.

In this interim period when Can's microphone was open to all comers, they were joined a couple of times on stage by none other than the American folk-rock singer Tim Hardin. This strange meeting was set up by Peter Gilmour, who knew Hardin socially after having been engaged a few times by his manager to act as a chaperone to the drug-addicted singer, to 'make sure he was there on time, that he was feeling OK, that he played the gig'. Hardin was resident in Britain at the time, specifically to take advantage of the methadone freely available on prescription from the National Health Service.

Without thinking they might make music together, Gilmour introduced Can and Hardin at a show on 21 November at Hatfield Polytechnic, and two days later at London's Drury Lane Theatre. A couple of recordings of this extraordinary collaboration survive: on a rehearsal tape in which English voices can be heard haggling for small change, Hardin's grizzled voice sits uneasily with Can's sleek mechanics. Another 'soundcheck' from the London date opens with a weird combination of straight-up blues noodling and a space age synth corona. This piece evolves into some beautifully fluffy funk in which Hardin's guitar seems to pull back towards a more earthbound rootsiness, but Can's ethereality inevitably leaves it floundering in the backdraught.

Michael and Hardin had initially bonded in a mutual search for drugs, and the pair ended up in the same hotel room, chatting and jamming on guitars. 'And then having the idea that next day, he should come with us on stage,' adds Irmin. 'And we said, "Yeah, why not?" During the concert [at Hatfield] then, he went occasionally on stage and sang, and it was all improvised. In a way it fitted and it didn't. He was a very charming and nice person, except that, to put it frankly, knowing that he was a junkie, I was against it. I didn't want to have that trouble in the group. Micky was an occasional, but never a real junkie. He took any drug – also heroin occasionally. But he never brought the group or himself at any moment into trouble. Never ever. You didn't even feel it, except sometimes he was late because he had to wait, which is the normal thing when dealers keep you waiting. But he was late anyway, with or without it!

'But I felt – and I was right – that with Tim there would have been trouble. It was obvious. And we all knew, and even Michael had his doubts. And on one hand he would have been something – as a voice it fitted quite nicely into what we did. But then he was too much a singer-songwriter, and also at that time he was already in incredible trouble with lawyers and stuff for the rights of his songs. It was awful, the stories he told. We didn't want that – not only me. But it was nice to be with him, on stage, in hotel rooms and getting stoned and jamming. Really nice.'

The Drury Lane date occurred shortly after the photo session with Mick Rock, and the photographer remembers 'being surprised going backstage, and there was Tim Hardin sitting there. And later I realised that what they had in common was less the music and more the chemistry. 'Cause I don't know when he died, but not so long afterwards. I think he died later in the seventies. It lasted as long as the chemicals lasted. Those were the days, darling.'

After the London show, Andy Hall says there was a huge bust-up between Hardin and Holger, culminating in the singer throwing a TV set through a car windscreen. The cause of the argument is now forgotten, but it marked the end of their brief alliance.

They were days of impending change, although to what, nobody quite knew or dared admit. The restlessness within Can may be glimpsed in comments by Irmin in his interview with Vivien Goldman, which appeared in one of the final editions of *Sounds* magazine of that year. Having implied that he was dissatisfied with his homeland and would consider leaving Germany altogether, he went on to discuss the wholly unplanned nature of Can's music. 'It sounds strange but in this group everybody is a telepath. Potentially everybody is, it needs acceptance first, and then, like everything else, it needs training. For me there's nothing specially mysterious about telepathy. It's something that happens to everybody every day. If you're looking for somebody's phone number and they call, that's telepathy. They call it coincidence but it's telepathy.

'At the moment, this tension in the new record that makes it different from *Babaluma*, we haven't felt anything like it since *Monster Movie*. You get to a certain level of telepathy and you have to take the next step. That's what I call a crisis point. That's the basis of creativity, it's always crisis. I take the word crisis as something very positive.

'Now, either we'll take that next step or we'll break up. I don't see the end of the breaking down of the walls between people, you get to that kind of level, you know, all living things are one . . .'[6]

Can were reaching some kind of tipping point. They still had formidable powers but were losing, perhaps, the ability to fully harness and control them. Goldman left the hotel with several 'juicy anecdotes' about Can's supernatural powers, but when she listened back to her interview tape, that section was blank.

14

Wanting More

Can underwent big changes in 1976. On New Year's Day they were still the four-piece unit who had made *Landed*. Over the next twelve months they would audition and reject two different lead singers, expand into a sextet with the addition of an entirely new rhythm section, enjoy the biggest international hit single of their career, and record a novelty Christmas track.

They began the year on familiar turf. Dreams of conquering the US had been quashed when Hildegard had tried to persuade Mike Stewart, president of United Artists Music Group, to insert a clause in the contract guaranteeing a tour of the States. Irmin: 'We had made this contract with United Artists in the very naive belief . . . that when we make a new contract, we will make a tour which they will support in the States. And actually . . . the night when we signed the contract we had champagne, and Wim Schut [head of United Artists Germany] called Al Teller [president of the United Artists label in the US] and said, "They are ready, and we are looking forward to the tour." And Al Teller said, "What tour? No, we don't support a tour." So we cancelled the contract the same night. We said, "We cancel, you don't get the tape."'

Shortly afterwards Irmin told a German interviewer: 'We were supposed to do an American tour, but that's completely cancelled. Everything was pretty much arranged, but then we were hit by some very specific agreements about the financing, which then totally fell into the water, and which then led us to look for another record company . . . There are certain cities in America where we nevertheless have an audience: Chicago, Cleveland, Detroit . . . When it's gone, it's gone. Basically for me I don't care whether we do a tour sooner or later. We'll only go to America if it promises to be fun, if we have enough control over it, so that it is run pretty much as we would like it to; there can be some gentle surprises, so long as the surprises don't all come at once and are of an extremely negative nature. You never know, we've seen that on the US tours of other groups, getting on each other's arses all day and still playing well that evening. Luckily the existence of a group doesn't entirely depend on that, whether we play in America or not. Either you do it and get to know what to expect over there, or you just leave it be.'[1]

Each of Can's former singers had joined the group in serendipitous circumstances. On the second live date of the new year, merely ten days into 1976, this pattern appeared about to repeat itself. In Brussels, at the Ancienne Belgique theatre, they fell in with a young singer of Malaysian origin named Thaiga Raj Raja Ratnam. He stepped up to join Can on three songs that night, and again at Grenoble (16 January) and Lyon (17), where he made a fumbling intermission announcement in French and elicited jeers and wolf whistles when he returned to sing 'One More Night'. Undeterred, he joined Can again for a further string of French concerts in early March: at Bordeaux (2 March), Poitiers (3) and Laval (4). At Poitiers, they trialled a track known at the time as 'Goose Egg', an embryonic version of what would become 'I Want More'. Ratnam actually pulled out a convincing Damo-style screech-fest during an improv version of 'Bel Air' that veered into fast thrash territory, but it wasn't sustained. When it became clear that Thaiga could not burn bright enough to compete with Can's fearful symmetry, he bowed out. Irmin's verdict: 'It didn't work. It had no bite, no real character.'

Within a fortnight, Can had taken on yet another vocalist. Michael Cousins entered Can's orbit partly at the suggestion of his acquaintance, Peter Gilmour, and was invited to Cologne by Holger. Cousins picked up the nickname 'Magic Michael' in London's notorious Notting Hill anarcho-hippy squat scene in the late sixties and early seventies, centred around groups/collectives like the Social Deviants and the Pink Fairies. He can be spotted on stage, naked from the waist down, accompanied by a bongo-playing Jesus freak, in Nic Roeg's *Glastonbury Fayre* documentary about the 1971 outdoor festival, and also took a role in another landmark of the UK counterculture: the Greasy Truckers Party at the Roundhouse in 1972 – which was turned into a live album featuring Man, Brinsley Schwarz and Hawkwind – in which he and an acoustic guitar attempted to mobilise the stoned horde with a wandering solo number called 'Music Belongs to the People'. Now, this man who had once claimed to harbour an 'inner TV' and was orbiting around planet Hawkwind was waved through as Can's frontman.

'I always wondered why the bloody hell he was called "Magic", because there was nothing magic about him,' Irmin laughs. 'He at least had some energy . . . and he really wanted to sing with us. But he wasn't good enough as a spontaneous inventor . . .'

For Can's loyal audience in France, the newcomer was an intruder too far. On his second date with the group, at Paris's Salle Wagram on 19 March, he was booed every time he came on stage, even though the rest of Can had tried to ration his appearances.

They persevered with Cousins for a few more weeks. At Langelsheim, Germany, on 10 April, the group sounded almost tribally primitive on 'Made in Japan', as Cousins's blueshound larynx hollered over some of Jaki's most thunderous tom-tom work since 'Yoo Doo Right'. At the same show he scatted the nursery rhyme 'Goosey Goosey Gander' over another fledgling version of 'I Want More'. His crack at the perennial 'Spoon' is more of a scattershot rant that seems to throw Michael's guitar atonally scurrying for cover. The following night at Hannover, he gropes for the foghorn extemporisations Tim Buckley was currently practising in his late funk-driven phase, but somehow missed the mark. While Cousins was the most characterful vocalist Can had adopted since the departure of Damo, the partnership didn't survive the night. 'He put a lot of energy and effort into being our singer. He really wanted it,' says Irmin.

Malcolm Mooney and Damo Suzuki were almost impossible acts to follow. Both of them had managed to channel uncanny texts and declaim them in patterns that connected viscerally with Can's edgy rhythmic sensibility. Few others possessed that magic key, and they ended up singing too conventionally 'over the top' of the music, instead of meshing and embedding within it. Arguably, the challenge was simply too great after all this time.

Holger: 'We tried everything in our power to find someone. But we just didn't have much left. Can functioned like a soccer team. When it was good, then it was a good team that could get the ball, pass it, and eventually get the ball through the goalposts. Our later singers didn't know how to share this basic feeling with us. Maybe they believed they had to prove something, I don't know.'[2] If any new vital organs were to be transplanted into the body of Can and be accepted, it would have to be in a role other than singer.

Critically, Can were still generally respected as purveyors of genuine art, untainted by the business side of operations. A German journalist wrote in 1976: 'The Way of Can is rather a story of musical and personal self-discovery, a progressive direction for finding unique musical expressive forms and reflecting upon them. It has absolutely nothing to do with commercialisation, if they are today making a simpler, more direct music.'[3] Meanwhile, in the real world, there was a record company to placate, requiring some commercial activity. As an interim measure, Virgin licensed the *Limited Edition* compilation, expanded it to a double LP with a further six unreleased tracks, and retitled it *Unlimited Edition*. With these extra pieces, including the seventeen-minute collage 'Cutaway' and the VU-like 'Connection' from 1969, plus two sleek examples of Can's recent style, 'Transcendental Express' and 'Ibis', *Unlimited*

Edition ended up being an entertaining and revelatory album in its own right. 'Cutaway', according to Irmin, was 'a collage of things which run through a period of seven years, partially copied one after another at different speeds, on top of each other and so on. That's one of the possible techniques: to consider the recorded material simply as material, which you can again make more music with. Then you're actually playing *tape* . . . "Cutaway" is a piece where we, in a manner of speaking, have built new houses from the same finished components. I wouldn't be ashamed to reuse a backing tape three times, if it leads to three good tracks.'[4] On the sleeve, the four musicians pose, cloned numerous times, among the Elgin Marbles in the British Museum, in a collage by Trevor Key, designer of Mike Oldfield's *Tubular Bells* and later the creator of iconic sleeves for the Sex Pistols, New Order, Orchestral Manoeuvres in the Dark, Peter Gabriel and Phil Collins.

After bidding *auf Wiedersehen* to Magic Mike, May and June saw Can retreat to Inner Space once again for a spate of new recordings. One of these was the stomping, four-to-the-floor tune that had emerged at various live shows around March, and to which Cousins had attached his 'Goosey Goosey' vocal. In the studio they slowed the pace down a tad, honing the beat to floor tom and hi-hat accents, connected to a wobbling effect on the guitar in a kind of analogue reinterpretation of the new Giorgio Moroder-style arpeggiated synth disco that had recently emerged with Donna Summer's 'I Feel Love'. When they finally fixed upon a lyric, Can picked Gilmour's similarly curt three-syllable hook: 'I Want More'.

Irmin claims 'I Want More' was not initially deliberately crafted as a hit. 'It just came up, this idea, and we developed this song, and it was clear that it becomes a single because the material was asking to be short and not a "Halleluwah" kind of piece. But with a lot of pieces, ideas came, and then you defined the idea more and more precisely, and sometimes it asked for being epic and sometimes it asked for being a haiku. "I Want More" was really asking for not being more than single-length. Anything else would have been too much. So then we realised that it will become a single, and then we really built it as *the* single from this album. It should be a concise three-minute thing. We made it like this.'

The main backing track of 'I Want More' was recorded live, and Irmin claimed there were no edits at all. Michael overdubbed some splatters of wah-wah over the top and the whole group took part in the tune's weird whispered chanting refrain. Once the music was done, it needed words, so they turned to Peter Gilmour: 'Don't care if I / Break the law / I want more and more and more . . .' It's another example of Can's intuitive feel for pop form. The keyboard that jets in at the end of each verse swoops away from the elastic rhythm. Irmin patched in that detail, which he had tried out in concert a few months before, at the very last minute. 'In the last moment, when the song was done and everybody thought it's ready, I said, "The guitar riff is a hook, the rhythm is perfect, but it still needs a melodic hook." So I dubbed this melody on it – "dee, dee dee dee, da da da da dee da". Everybody else said, "Bullshit!" And I did [it], and afterwards everybody was happy I did. So that's how it happened with us. Then when it was on, all of a sudden Micky decided that he will adapt to the melody. And then it had what I imagined about it. When it was done, everybody was happy with it, and it became a hit. So nobody objected to it.'

Gilmour, who worked as a professional hypnotist later in life, believes the 'message of "I Want More" in a way comes into the work I do now. Everybody wants something. People feel there's something missing in their lives. That thing, in my opinion, is happiness. When Virgin promoted it with posters in the UK, they had a beautiful girl in a bikini. And in Germany the posters had a big, overflowing beer stein. So I think that said something about the different cultural approaches. Apparently, in those days in Germany everybody wanted more beer, and in Britain they wanted more sex . . .'

The B-side of the single was an instrumental continuation of the groove, '. . . And More', anticipating the vogue for the extended remixes that would typify twelve-inch singles a few years later. It came in a seven-inch bag featuring Mick Rock's photos. Both halves were also included on *Flow Motion*, the album they completed during the long, hot summer of 1976.

Peter Gilmour remembers that period as a haze of long, garrulous breakfasts with René Tinner, Bob Hickmott, Alex Wiska and others, afternoon dips, heated discussions ('Irmin wasn't the funkiest of musicians, but he was quite brilliant, and he was a typical German intellectual: he always made you think a lot') and nocturnal taping sessions. 'During the day everybody would be baking, and we'd be going out to the gravel pits on the outskirts of Cologne' – the quarries where the filming for *Mädchen . . . nur mit Gewalt* had taken place – 'that were filled with water, and there'd be hardly anybody there and the water was very cold, so we'd swim in the water and sit around talking, and then we'd work during the night in the studio when it was cool.'

Flow Motion sounds almost like a different group from the one you can hear on bootlegs of their live gigs in the first half of 1976. On tour, they retained a good deal of the lean, machine-hungry motorik that had become a trademark of Krautrock. The seven tracks on *Flow Motion* were generally cleaner and more laid-back, ushering in the final phase of Can's existence. 'Cascade Waltz' offered queasy MOR: a glutinous soup of Hawaiian slide guitar, crushed-crystal synths and electric violin, over an old-timey, tea-dance chord sequence. Peter Gilmour's lyrics, spoken by Michael, paint a cartoon reduction of Can's previous themes: approaching the summit of a mountain, looking down on 'a land that flowed with milk and honey / Girls and cars and sex and money', and a passing astronaut cries into his cockpit, 'Does anyone here really understand / What goes on in the heart of a man?'

While the group were playing together, Gilmour – sitting in the little projection room overlooking the studio floor – was channelling the lyrics. 'I used to sit in that room looking out over the fields at the back,' he recalls. 'I used to watch the moon moving through the sky. And I was very aware that when the moon was new, I was very prolific with the writing, and when the moon was full, I'd be taking things in, reading things and thinking about things, and not writing so much. It was an interesting time for me, that.' Irmin or Michael would occasionally look in, flip through his notebooks and cherry-pick some text. 'One of them would say, "I like this or that." Micky wanted very simple things that he could sing, but he wanted the words to be very rhythmic.'

'Laugh Till You Cry, Live Till You Die' is Can's debut stab at reggae, in a singalong style rendered that little bit more folksy by Michael's bağlama. Michael, who also devised the text, recalled being introduced to Jamaican music by none other than Brian Eno, who was himself spending increasing amounts of time in Germany. 'He came with a Lee Perry single, which I have never been able to find afterwards. Which was fantastic, he played it to me . . . Eno played one of the records that really blew my mind . . . I loved the rhythm, and I do think that Lee Perry was not very far off from us.'

'There is one common thing which everybody appreciated from the very first moment,' Holger confided – 'practically jumping up and down in his wrought iron seat with enthusiasm' – to an interviewer a few months afterwards, 'and that is the reggae influence. For me, when it comes to reggae music, I really can get CRAZY!'[5]

'Babylonian Pearl' is another slight piece, with Irmin crooning his way through Gilmour's lyrics hymning a stereotypically exotic, mysterious Old Testament female. Number 59 in the 'EFS', 'Smoke', is a filmic fog of rumbling, ominous drums, saturated with metallic clangs and distant war bugles. It connects the dots between African log rhythms and the approaching metallic tattoos of industrialists like Test Dept, with a nod to the phase music of Steve Reich.

The ten-minute 'Flow Motion' itself is another reggae-based tune, and not a bad one. Jaki halves the speed of his 'I Want More' riff, and Michael overdubs several layers of guitars, a taut upbeat in the manner of Jamaica's legions of dub sessioneers, and solarised, feedbacking flare-ups in the right ear. Half submerged in the mix, he mutters about teeth and ears grinding to the roots, and repeats the title. Holger's sliding fingers never deviate from his two-note perimeter.

Flow Motion – the title was chosen by Irmin and Peter Gilmour using the I Ching – was a hybrid of very disparate styles that, for the first time, didn't hang together very comfortably as a whole. It's inevitable in the life of a group that never ceased to experiment and explore new paths that some of those experiments might be doomed to fail. Like all their recordings from now on, *Flow Motion* was at least a partial success.

René Tinner was by now playing an increasingly crucial role in the studio, and he recalls the eclectic nature of the times. 'With Can it was never ever routine. Every day was always different musically. Completely. And the thing could change within seconds. It's like you have a calm sea and then you have a pounding ocean. All that, in the same day.'

The days of their humble two-track recording set-up were receding faster and faster, and Holger's technical role was also reduced, freeing him up to play more bass. But their expanded studio capacity meant they didn't need to be so fussy about what finally made it onto their tapes. Tinner: 'Since Holger had two jobs to do, being a bass player and a recording engineer at the same time, everybody tried to please him so that he didn't have too much difficulties fiddling around with the knobs during the recording. And when I took over, Holger was more concentrating on the bass, and doing less of the engineering work. They didn't have so much fear that something could have been mistreated, because it was recorded on multitrack. So it was not as bad. With the two tracks, they were quite fussy. For me, it was like a true experience, because nothing was ever really said [about] what's going to be done; it was always what came out of the unexpected, and work with that. If they would record a certain section one million times, but different versions of it, like most people did in those days, it would probably not have been so interesting.'

When Virgin released *Flow Motion* later in the autumn, Vivien Goldman praised its 'android/mechanoid pulsebeat', adding: 'It's fun to listen with creative insanity to this fine example of a mature, imaginative descendant of classical rock. And see what happens . . . The ideal way to appreciate Can is to go limp and flow with the motion.'[6]

When the album was complete, there followed a hot, itchy late summer of dabbling and tinkering. Michael lit out for a couple of weeks in central and east Africa, winding his way through the Congo, Zaïre and Kenya with his new girlfriend. Irmin and Holger holidayed together with Irmin's parents in Yugoslavia. Jaki took up the invitation of guitarist Michael Rother to play drums on a new solo project. Three years earlier, the guitarist of Neu! had teamed up with Hans-Joachim Roedelius and Dieter Möbius of Cluster in a ramshackle house in the forests of Lower Saxony, and together the trio began writing and recording as Harmonia, a name that suggested the very mythical spirit of music itself. At the end of 1973 they recorded *Musik von Harmonia*, a series of sonic vignettes in which the anarchic impulses of Kluster and the incessant forward motion of Neu! were refined and channelled into controlled, Apollonian mechanics, repetitive electronic melodies and soft synthetic textures. This was a wonderfully productive pastoral haven, from which both Harmonia and Cluster pumped out music like a small organic processing plant, assisted from 1976 by Brian Eno, who, having quit Roxy Music, was keenly attuned to new possibilities beyond the realms of rock and pop cliché.

Rother took Jaki into Conny Plank's studio in the rural district of Wolperath, south-east of Cologne. In a sense this was a return for both men: for Rother, it refined the motorik 'Apache' beats of classic Neu!, while Jaki was allowed to indulge that lust for the simple primitive joy of precision percussion that conveyed a smooth sensation of travelling and hovering all at once. With Rother playing all the other instruments, the five tracks were released as *Flammende Herzen* on Sky Records in March 1977, and Jaki would regularly collaborate with Rother on his solo albums over the next few years. Also in 1977 Jaki drummed on the track 'Backwater' on Eno's *Before and After Science*.

'I Want More' – that 'frenzied, jitterbugging, electronified, hypnotic disco ditty with a fetching organ break in the middle, and incomprehensible whispered lyrics'[7] – was released at the end of August. In the summer when drought turned Europe's fields brown and both punk and disco seized the reins of media attention, this was to give Can their biggest share of the limelight, both at home in West Germany and abroad. They mimed the song on a decadent WDR variety show: musical mechanics in make-up among perspiring models, comedians' buffoonery, Greek columns and ferns. They were invited to appear on BBC television's weekly pop show, *Top of the Pops*, on 26 August, a programme with an audience of millions on which artists mimed their current hits to an audience of frugging adolescent invitees. At the time, Holger appeared receptive to the idea of large-scale audiences. 'You should not be on stage for your own pleasure,' he told interviewer Vivien Goldman, 'your pleasure must be the people's pleasure. Otherwise it's not the *right* pleasure, it's just esoteric.'[8]

Certainly, there was no place for the esoteric in the average *Top of the Pops* presentation. On the transmission in question, Can shared the bill with Manfred Mann's Earth Band, Cliff Richard, the Stylistics, Robin Sarstedt and even Bristolian trad jazzer Acker Bilk. Master of ceremonies was ubiquitous BBC linkman Noel Edmonds, who announced them with 'I wonder if Can will get into the top tin?' It was a four-piece Can, with a yellow-trousered Holger on stand-up bass and Irmin resplendent in a silver blazer, but fans might have been puzzled by the stranger on lead guitar, a young white boy with an afro hairdo.

'When it was in the charts we were all on holiday,' explains Irmin. 'Holger and me, at that time everything was very harmonic. Me and a whole bunch of friends of ours, we were in Yugoslavia, and I don't know where Jaki was – probably at home. And, of course, there was a lot of pressure [from Virgin]. They called and said, "You have to do *Top of the Pops!*" So we came, Hildegard and me. Holger and me were together [in London]. Jaki was in Cologne, but no way to find Michael – he was lost somewhere on safari in Kenya. Hildegard said, "You do it and [we will find] a replacement." We said, "OK, then it should be somebody who looks totally different. Please don't put somebody on stage who tries to look like Michael. So everybody should know we didn't find him." It was this guy who moves so English, like [someone in] an English beat group of the early sixties. He doesn't look like he's fitting in with us, that's obvious.' Afterwards, Edmonds couldn't resist quipping that he'd wanted to have them on at the start of the show, but realised he couldn't have a Can opener. Boom boom.

That week 'I Want More' entered the UK charts, where it remained for eight weeks, peaking at number twenty-six. There would be no follow-up single from *Flow Motion*, but it did take Can into the hitherto unfamiliar territory of the student disco and the daytime radio playlist. Whether it made them rich men was debatable. 'I don't know how much it sold,' ponders Irmin, 'but you know, OK, we were a group of people – at that time we were four – but still, that's divided by that, and the whole thing turned towards maintaining the life of a group with a studio and all of that. You don't get rich from it unless you have really million-sellers. And we weren't this kind of group, obviously.'

By now relatively long in the tooth, Can was temperamentally unsuited to high-pressure marketing. Irmin: 'No record company, neither United Artists nor Virgin nor EMI later, ever put pressure on what we did musically. They might have put pressure on a delivering day because the promotion had started and all that business. That is totally normal. But it never came to difficult pressure. The opposite, actually. We might be the exception. But there is always this big myth, this big narrative: artist against industry. And actually we never had that. From the moment we were with United Artists, and worked with Siggi Loch and his stuff, that was brilliant. There was no pressure; there was a lot of real help and encouragement, and it was really good working together. And the same with Virgin: there was no pressure. Here in Europe, the French, the Germans, the British – [it] was always pure peace, astonishingly enough. It was so clear to everybody in these companies that you couldn't put pressure on us without getting the whole thing in a real mess, which didn't help anybody. Because we were so reluctant to give in if we weren't convinced.'

'I Want More' reaching the charts proved that the rest of the music industry, and a significant proportion of the public, was beginning to catch up with Can's tape-based methodology. In the realm of disco and dub reggae, the idea of a long-form, repetitive beat, constructed from tape loops or drum machines, was fast becoming standard practice.

'In the USA, for instance,' noted a German writer, 'in the Hit Factory, any tasty rhythm track that's recorded can get passed around by a producer and sold to anyone else. Then a completely new track can be created out of it, with a new melody. The rhythm could be the current Discotheque rhythm, and afterwards, somewhere else, a different bassline can be placed on top of it. In this way the tape might get altered in five different ways.'[9]

A planned twenty-date tour of the UK in September had to be nixed when Irmin damaged his back while shifting a washing machine down some stairs. The momentum of 'I Want More' was stilled, and *Flow Motion* was left to come out with no touring support. Before his accident Irmin and Jaki had been speaking to writer Karl Lippegaus about the tension between Can's free-form philosophy and the desire to sculpt accessible musical forms, a struggle which came to a head in the live situation, when audiences clamoured for the familiar.

[Irmin:] 'Sometimes we play really old songs and other times we don't play them at all, because in that moment when we play them, they are fairly new. Then sometimes they are so new for the people, that they don't notice that we've played an older track.'

Jaki: 'Sometimes we've played "Yoo Doo Right", and three songs later people call out for "You Doo Right". Horrible.'

Irmin: 'It happens to us as well. Someone starts playing "Yoo Doo Right", and another plays something totally different over it, because he thought it was another track.'

Jaki: 'Improvisation is a shit word, it should be exterminated. It only leads to misunderstandings. So we do *not* improvise!'

Irmin: 'We play shapes every time, we don't make improvisations, unless it gives rise to even newer shapes when we play. It has very clear playing rules and a very comprehensible shape.'[10]

Can itself now shifted its shape. Rosko Gee, the bassist Holger had met the previous November, was recruited to take over on the bass guitar. Having left Jim Capaldi's group soon after that first meeting, during 1976 Rosko, whose signature clothing was a top hat and flowing Doctor Who-like scarf, had been lending his limber bass technique to a fusiony supergroup called Go, which included Steve Winwood, Stomu Yamashta, Al Di Meola, Klaus Schulze and

Michael Shrieve. He had been impressed by watching one of Can's British shows, had a girlfriend living in Bonn, and jumped at the chance to abandon Go's ship of jazz-rock super-egos.

Peter Gilmour remembers that 'Holger got very friendly with Rosko, who wasn't just a rock musician; he used to look for new things, he wanted to do new things and take music to different levels. That's why they became friends.'

'Can at the time were very interesting in their approach,' says Rosko, trying to recall the sequence of events that took him to Germany in 1976. 'Did Holger invite me over? He gave me his address, and when I visited the mother of my daughter [in Bonn], I then contacted him in Cologne. That's how it began. Ah, but there are lots of intrigues, which I suppose I am not supposed to speak about. Because I wasn't meant to be playing with Can; I only went there to meet the guys and say hi, because . . . one has to be open. I suppose it's my Britishness, probably my hopefulness, that made a difference. In the studio it came to the point where they asked if I would play . . .'

Holger's role in Can was always double-barrelled, as he was given responsibility as both an instrumentalist and the member who would manually execute the group's decisions about the mix. Now that they had a resident engineer in René Tinner, and the other musicians were advancing towards new levels of virtuosity, Holger found himself in a quandary. He had taken up the bass in the group almost by default. As the group's music took on more mainstream forms, he now had less of an outlet for his more experimental impulses. Beyond that, the heightened clarity of sixteen-track recording meant his faults were magnified and he was frequently criticised. 'I think the others were on a different trip,' he said. 'They somehow wanted to achieve that Can became a good band of instrumentalists – that means heroes of their own instruments. I could not make it, actually. So they were looking for another bass player, and

I found Rosko during the BBC recording. He came and visited us and played with us, and I thought, "Good, we have a different bass player – I can look out for something new."'

With Holger no longer active on bass, this was one of the most radical shake-ups to hit Can since Damo's arrival back in 1970. For a newcomer like Rosko, integrating with Can's established members was no easy feat, but fortunately the discriminating Jaki found that this was a musician he could work with. 'If the bass player is in the first place a musician, and in the second place a bass player, then there is no problem. But most of the bass players, they just play in the way they have heard from other bass players: it has to be a deep note all the time. It doesn't work. There are only a very few bass players I can work with.' Rosko turned out to be one of those.

The West Runton Pavilion at Cromer on the north Norfolk coast was the first venue treated to Can's expanded live line-up, on 2 December. The next night they travelled to the Free Trade Hall in Manchester, where they received 'an enthusiastic and probably inebriated reception', according to Andy Gill, who reviewed the set for the *NME*. Gill instantly picked up on the altered reality that Holger was 'fiddl[ing] around stage left with his modest array of tape machines and boxes of tricks for a while'. Michael's demeanour was 'bizarre: eyes clenched, face blank, zomboid as those real-life extras in [*One Flew Over the*] *Cuckoo's Nest*, searching, presumably, for that elusive plane where information is rendered only in sound. He appears to be slightly surprised when the piece draws to a close, flashing a bemused smile in the audience's direction and withdrawing to adjust his amplifier.'

Rosko Gee, he observed, 'copes remarkably well on bass, faced as he is with the almost insurmountable task of gelling with a group of musicians, the emphathic [*sic*] nature of whose music is so intense they claim to communicate telepathically on stage. Top-hat bobbing as he jigs funkily along, he stretches and moulds the bass line as the music shifts through its phases, occasionally instigating changes, when he believes the time is right; more often than not, successfully.'[11]

Their show at London's New Victoria Theatre on 4 December was a Can Christmas knees-up to remember: a two-and-a-half-hour set, in an onstage jungle of potted palms, that climaxed with a snow machine and fake wind noises. One reviewer thought they resembled 'twenty first century psychedelic robotic engineers'. Holger, hunched over stage right and operating a table-load of reel-to-reel tape machines, effects boxes and a shortwave radio set, was 'like an eccentric professor busy inventing a doodlebug that would spray the world with LSD'. Rosko enacted 'a beautiful and perpetual funky knee bend in time to his own rich bass lines which were some of the finest I've heard this side of Charlie Haden'.[12] For their first encore they wheeled out a jaunty, ska-style rendition of the Yuletide classic 'Silent Night', which they had recorded the previous month and released as a seasonal single. Reviewer Karl Dallas noted how it was 'played with the same sort of wit that used to invest their Ethnological Forgery Series. Gradually, Michael Karoli mutates the familiar melody, and the band follows him into an unknown region where the theme is barely remembered, and then it slowly re-emerges.'[13]

It was an uncommonly rowdy audience that night, screaming for old favourites like 'Halleluwah' and 'Future Days'. In the middle, during a lull, an Alf Garnett voice screamed out: 'Bloody marvellous! Innit!' However, both reviewers seemed almost exhausted at times by Can's love of flying off at tangents. About 'I Want More', the three-minute wonder that Can extended to more than a quarter of an hour that night, the *Sounds* review chafed: 'Where the single had immediacy, onstage it became just another electronic doodle . . . Can probably think they're breaking new musical territory. To me, they came over like the James Last of the avant garde, all form and no content. If you must have avant garde, go listen to Derek Bailey or, even better, some dub reggae.'[14] *Fröhliche Weihnachten!*

15

Artificial Head Stereo

'When you visit a nightclub in Africa,' Michael told a journalist in 1997, 'where a good highlife band is playing, you feel like a carrot chucked into a boiling soup. You have to move . . . that influence was inevitable on *Saw Delight*.'[1]

Michael's holiday in Africa during the summer of 1976 marked him in profound ways. His personal life was in turmoil in any case. He had recently split up with Eveline Grunwald, his girlfriend since 1971 (they met when Can played at a Hannover nightclub where she was working behind the bar), and now there was a new woman in his life. Michael was never the most faithful partner in any case. 'Micky was the womaniser,' Grunwald says. 'He would swear his love to me, but I think when I wasn't there . . . This is how Shirley came into the whole thing.'

Shirley Argwings-Kodhek, a British woman who had been brought up in Kenya, was led into the Can fold by Peter Gilmour, who had met her by chance on one of his trips to Cologne. 'We took the same ferry and train, and I got talking to her and we started seeing each other, and then Micky sort of admired her from afar, I think. He eventually asked me for permission to . . . I mean, it was only a casual relationship I had with Shirley. That's the way things were in those days.'

Eveline rarely went on tour with Can, and was determined to pursue her own career. She had moved to Cologne to be with Michael in 1971 and was studying to be an illustrator. 'The first year was going on tour, not very satisfying. Later, I decided I didn't want to go on tour any more, I wanted to stay and finish my art school.

You feel a bit like, I was always "the girlfriend of", you know, which is really odd. I suddenly realised I don't want that any more.'

Eveline kept close ties to the Can family: she had become friends with Hildegard and often looked after the Schmidts' young daughter while the parents were on tour. Immediately after the break-up, 'I went off to England because then Shirley was there and I couldn't stand it any more . . . I must say it was really terrible for me, and so I stayed with Simon [Puxley, Can's Virgin press officer] and Polly [Eltes, his girlfriend]. I went to London and I stayed in this little garden shed there . . .' Shirley settled in Cologne and got a job working in what René Tinner calls 'a dodgy nightclub, the Safari in Bad Münstereifel – in the middle of nowhere'.

To the extent that he was ten years younger than the others in the core quartet, Michael was the odd one out in Can. While the past eight years had turned him into a consummate and distinctive guitarist, Eveline hints that on some level he didn't always feel his full expression had space to come through. 'It's difficult terrain,' she confesses. 'How do I put it? . . . He wasn't always happy. He had his problems . . . Sometimes with Jaki. With Irmin there weren't really problems . . . The Schmidts are overwhelming . . . and they love everybody, and everybody's wonderful. I think *he* felt also a bit overwhelmed. And had maybe his own ideas to do certain things and to go different ways . . . on a musical level.

'And Micky was the other one who sometimes had interviews together with Irmin, but I think he wasn't as dominating as Irmin, who is very eloquent. Micky was much more thoughtful – although I don't deny Irmin is thoughtful – but he really looked for words, and he really put it sometimes in a very odd but lovely way. It's really special. I do think that Irmin realised it, but a lot of people didn't, I'm sure.'

In other words, Michael's strength was his reflective spirit, but he could occasionally feel frustrated by his own unassertiveness. The African holiday turned into a cultural and musical pilgrimage, as he was exposed to the continent's astonishing indigenous take on pop music – in particular the pealing, jangly guitars of highlife – on a trail of bars, clubs and discotheques.

'Michael's style of playing may have changed after his trip to Africa,' says Rosko, 'because he must have learned some things. George Harrison went to India and came back and started also in another direction. I believe what he learned from Africa contributed to him becoming a better guitar player, and it's very important.'

'I've always been captivated by the direct, uncontrollable effect of music on the body,' Michael said in 1997. 'I first really learned about dancing when I was in Africa. I had danced a lot before, but there I learned that music can rule the body in such a way that when the music says "go left", you can really only go left. You can't go to the right. I was in Zaïre, in Franco's nightclub,[2] and observed how the people don't jump around like crazy, dislocating their joints; instead they hardly move at all, producing a kind of grind.'[3] Sounds like the perfect way to boogie to Can in 1977.

In the first month of that year, as they began working on new recordings, a distinctly African flavour seeped into Can's music. It wasn't just the explicit, tinkly highlife guitar motifs in 'Sunshine Day and Night' and 'Fly by Night', but also the rippling bongos and rattling percussion tumbling and twirling around Jaki's chronometric drum patterns. This was supplied by yet another new recruit, brought in by Rosko. Anthony 'Reebop' Kwaku Baah was another Traffic alumnus, born in Konongo, Ghana, in 1944. As a child he enthusiastically took up drumming, and in the late sixties he moved to London in an attempt to break into the music business. By 1969 he was slapping congas on a demo of Nick Drake's 'Three Hours' and recording in Paris with jazz pianist Randy Weston's African Rhythms, on an LP called *African Cookbook*. He was recruited as a drummer in Traffic in 1971, before a Swedish tour, and remained a member until 1974. Coincidentally, the group had played on the same Glastonbury

Fayre stage as 'Magic' Michael Cousins back in 1971; they had also been signed to United Artists. Around the same time he appeared on albums by the Rolling Stones (*Goat's Head Soup*), Eric Clapton (*Rainbow Concert*), Viv Stanshall and Free, and solo albums by Steve Winwood and Jim Capaldi, as well as recording his own funky *Kwaku's Thing* in Sweden and a superb LP with Moroccan Gnaoua drummers entitled *Trance*. His ethno-rock credentials, from Can's point of view, were impeccable. When he joined in with Can, Michael said, the result was 'medicine music'.[4] Peter Gilmour had also met him at Island Records' Basing Street Studios in 1971, when he was recording a Swedish film soundtrack with Bob Marley and John 'Rabbit' Bundrick. He knew Reebop as 'a fabulous percussionist . . . highly critical as a musician. There weren't many people he admired, but he used to admire Jaki very much.'

There's no doubt that the double act of Rosko and Reebop, old comrades who enjoyed each other's company, had a revitalising impact on Can in the early months of 1977. '[Reebop] really stimulated the other musicians,' said Irmin, 'and for me he was an extraordinary influence, one of the strongest of my musical life. It was completely magic; a bit like the old days.'[5] The polyrhythmic mesh he layers over Jaki's drums in the fifteen-minute 'Animal Waves' is an effective, organic enhancement of Can's rigour. 'He was full of energy,' enthused Jaki. 'I mean, he would beat his conga drum incredibly and his hands were like wood. Anyone [else] would break his bones if he played like that.'

In this track Rosko also seems to have inherited Holger's obsessive precision on the bass, repeating the same short motif over and over. Holger himself is responsible for the occasional intrusion of a Romanian Gypsy voice, sampled from one of his many ethnic recordings. His role in the group was now as a purveyor of audio esoterica, channelling the unexpected via his effects boxes and a radio set. This symbolised the wider gap that was opening up within Can itself. Even as its horizons were being expanded via the visions of Rosko and Reebop, Holger was returning to the abstract electronic music he had imbibed at the feet of Stockhausen and the WDR. He used his radio set's built-in VFO (variable frequency oscillator) to twist the sound in the same way the composer employed ring modulators.

'Micky started to sing, that was OK, and then I found it was really necessary to get influence from outside,' said Holger. 'This is really why I had suddenly these combined instruments, like a dictaphone, cassette players, a radio, telephone: we had to look for something which came from outside into the group, to get open-minded again.'

Another time he said: 'My idea was to use someone who is in the radio, and make him function as [if] he was playing with Can. The idea was how to manipulate a singer so he becomes our singer. It is more than weird! How can you dare to say something like that?'[6]

On another occasion he explained: 'A short-wave radio is just basically an unpredictable synthesizer. You don't know what it's going to bring from one moment to the next. It surprises you all the time and you have to react spontaneously. The idea came from Stockhausen again. He made a piece called *Short Waves* [*Kurzwellen*, 1968] . . . The musicians were searching for music, for stations or whatever, and he was sitting in the middle of it all and the sounds came into his hands and he made music out of it. He was mixing it live – and composing it live. He had a kind of plan, but didn't know what the plan would bring him. With Can, I would mix stuff in with what the rest of the band were playing. Also, we were searching for a singer and we didn't find one . . . so I thought: why not look to the radio for someone instead. The man inside the radio does not hear us, but we hear him.'[7]

By injecting found sounds into Can's bloodstream, Holger was trying to neutralise any swelling egotism and return to the 'group as machine' ethos of their early days. But could the centre still hold? According to Irmin, it was the beginning of 'a slow transition from the Holger who was fully integrated to one that was slowly fading out with strange noises'.

Meanwhile, there were new and perplexing musical experiences to fathom. Irmin: 'Reebop and Jaki played this incredible complicated polyrhythm, very fast. And I was sitting there trying to get in and couldn't. And I asked Reebop, "Where the bloody hell is the 'one' here?" And he looked at me and said, "Ah, you poor Europeans. The 'one' is where[ver] you start." And that was a revelation. All of a sudden, fuck the "one"! It doesn't exist. Everybody has his cycle. It could have seven units, seventeen units, or four. And he starts and then repeats them, and all together they make a rhythm. And that's actually how it works. And I knew that theoretically, but from that moment on I knew it practically. I could start, and that was my "one".'

Can's next album, a five-track affair called *Saw Delight*, was released – on Harvest/EMI in Germany, and Virgin in the UK and France – as swiftly as March 1977. Although Reebop featured on most tracks and was listed among the personnel in the inner bag, Can was presented as a quintet on the reverse of the album sleeve, with the original foursome plus Rosko arranged in a pentagram formation around a mandala. The front cover's fused image of circular saw, long-player grooves and mystical circle extended the awkward pun of the title. For mixing they took the master tapes to the Delta Acoustic Studio near Hamburg, whose sound engineer, Manfred Schunke, converted it into 'Artificial Head Stereo', essaying a 3D effect that's hard to appreciate at four decades' distance.

'Don't Say No' blatantly revisits Can's 'Moonshake' from four years earlier. Michael sings a lyric by Peter Gilmour and Reebop ('No time to watch / Your life slip away / Forget tomorrow / And do it today'), but at around four minutes Reebop can be heard joining in with some soulful yelps. Rosko wrote and sang the lyrics to 'Call Me', which opens with a windswept tape and crackly orchestral textures from Holger, before the track kicks in. Can was at its most gleamingly polished on *Saw Delight*, and still had moments of freshness. Even though it was a song-based album, their rhythm section upgrade was taking them into areas that clearly foreshadowed musical developments still a long way in the future, as Michael observed: '*Saw Delight* is a hybrid . . . there are long passages of pure rhythm. When you're listening to rhythm, you can do something else in the meantime. If we'd gone further in this direction, it would probably have become a kind of dance music. You can do everything to dance music, not just dance.'[8]

But 1977 was a difficult time for an already veteran group to be releasing album number nine. In May Can's label Virgin signed the Sex Pistols, in a mercenary move that rescued the punks from a short-lived EMI contract. The energy that fired the formation of the early German groups was now owned by the youthful firebrands of punk rock. Can originally wanted to rebuild a nation that was broken. Punk wanted only to destroy, offering nothing beyond the nihilism. In parallel, music criticism had matured, no longer the laid-back accessory to celebrity, but with a new generation of young, post-hippy writers with little patience and less respect for rock's venerable figures. 'I'm into representation, man,' snarled the reviewer for *Sounds* in a scathing critique of *Saw Delight*. 'And Can's solo doodles over regular rhythms always make me think of a one year-old scrawling on a piece of graph paper . . . Unfortunately what ["Fly by Night"] entails is someone doing a weak impression of Kevin Ayers and being moreover so embarrassed by the thing that he's had to sellotape a wad of Kleenex over his mouth whilst doing it . . . It's a turkey.'[9]

Melody Maker, at least, took a more charitable view. '*Saw Delight* has an assurance and determination absent (to my mind) on its predecessor,' it said, noting that the African stylings were 'inviting and effervescent', and 'a communication of Can's optimism and their revived delight in their music'.[10]

Mercifully, the negative reviews had not been published by the time Can – as a five-piece, minus Reebop – took to the road for what would prove to be their final sequence of concerts. Opening on 1 March in Canterbury, they travelled through Great Britain for almost the whole of that month, from Keele and Aston Universities to the Coatham Bowl in Redcar and the Winter Gardens in Bournemouth. Long lost tapes from their Nottingham show, recorded for the local station Radio Trent, surfaced in 2018. Two dates at London venue Sound Circus (at the former Royalty Theatre in Aldwych[11]) on 23 and 24 March were the last occasions Can played live in Britain.

They played several German dates in late April, including an appearance in Cologne, where old buddy Manni Löhe turned up on stage. Around the same time they recorded a live set for WDR television's *Musik Extra* in front of a respectfully seated audience. The one track that has emerged on YouTube – a splashy, reggaefied jam on the 'Dizzy Dizzy' chord sequence – shows a confident, tight band hard at work, with Rosko by far the most animated member. The camerawork gives a good close-up of Holger's stage-side set-up at the time, including his radio and a grey telephone – another telemetric device he was using to dial up extraneous sound sources and patch them into Can's mix. With the aid of a Morse code tapper, he could play these noises in a rhythmical fashion in bursts of disruptive sound.

However, Holger was now less than a month away from taking the stage with Can for the last time.

'Towards the end, before I got out, that was really scary,' Holger said. 'If you don't feel understood any more by your nearest friends, then it is scary somehow. And I myself felt very useless suddenly, like going along with my car to the studio on the autobahn, there was like a big power which pushed me back – I didn't want to go to the studio any more. Live, it was not wanted by the others – this idea of bringing a parallel music world into what you do at the moment . . .' Can's former battles to keep the music as progressive as possible had gradually tipped over into more vindictive clashes.

'As long as we keep fighting for the material,' said Holger, 'it's fine. But as soon as the struggle becomes personal, and people are criticised in such a way that they don't dare take on the instrument, then I would say it is not only for the music any more, it is something else which comes on top of that. That happens with every band, as we know. Can is no exception.'

In a television interview recorded alongside Klaus Schulze just before the group's *Musik Extra* performance, the cracks begin to show. Holger is proudly demonstrating his shortwave radio and Morse tapper. Earnestly, the interviewer turns to Irmin and asks, 'Does that mean he is trying to electrify on a greater scale?' 'Holger, perhaps, but not necessarily us,' he replies with an awkward smirk. Nervous laughter also accompanies the suggestion that musicians like Can and Schulze have arisen from the late-sixties underground in Germany to become successful, critically respected and wealthy artists. 'Not with a radio like that,' retorts Holger. Misunderstanding, the host remarks that perhaps only those in the overground can afford it. 'But this gear doesn't cost a thing, you can buy it for two marks fifty,' comes Holger's beatific reply.

Most of Can's existence had been dominated by the tension between its constituent parts – between spontaneity and construction, between the expressionist moment and the collagist's detachment. Purely from a musical standpoint these differences were now becoming insurmountable. There was less of the team spirit of the early years. 'There *were* often arguments,' agrees Peter Gilmour, 'but these were German intellectuals with a passionate . . . they weren't just a rock 'n' roll band playing music, they were breaking new boundaries. That's why I was interested in it and spent time with them. Because we were taking things to a different level, breaking boundaries, not just living in our comfort zone. When you have that situation, people do have disagreements, and sometimes very passionate disagreements, and there was a lot of that going on. We were pretty stoned most of the time as well, of course.'

'In music we understood each other very well,' said Holger. 'As personal, we tried to do everyone living in his own flat. That was completely against the hippy syndrome of the time. We make music together yes, like crazy, but we never stay together, after that it was private.'[12]

One curious fact about Can was that for most of their existence, they never shared a common tour bus, but drove themselves to each concert under their own steam. 'It was nice,' Jaki said. 'Each of us had his own car – there was a lorry with the roadies and equipment, and at least two or three private cars would go. We never went together in one car always. Individual car, everywhere.' In such circumstances, professional though they seemed, small rivalries and resentments could grow.

'There was sometimes a problem with Micky's guitar,' believes Duncan Fallowell. 'I associated this with him taking too much smack. He'd float off on long guitar solos, which went too far away from the collective effort, from the *unum*. In a way it's like plaiting a rope – his strings were moving too far away from the line of the rope. And I never ever felt that with Jaki, Holger or Irmin, but sometimes Micky floated off into overlong guitar solos. And I don't ever remember anybody telling him not to. I think if I'd been in the band and taken up that singing role, I would have told him not to . . .'

As he has pointed out, flaws in Holger's performances were being singled out for criticism. 'Holger was always being accused of being too loud, too heavy, too late . . .' says Irmin. 'Many times I had problems with Holger too,' said Jaki. 'Rhythmical problems too, a little bit. With his bass he had huge bass loudspeakers, and it could be very loud and destroy me. Holger was always a complicated character.'

Now his sideways shift to electronics and radios destabilised his position in the group, and the ebullience of Rosko and Reebop was fundamentally altering the internal ambience of Can. Reebop, in particular, couldn't stand Holger's electrical interventions, says Irmin, 'First of all because rhythmically it often interfered with what Jaki and Reebop did. But not only this: he had some ideological [issue] about stealing others' voices and all that.'

'Oh, Reebop was the tormentor of Holger,' agrees Rosko. 'Reebop was worldly. And very open. One of those who you don't find so often. He doesn't take fools lightly, or easily. And he reacts where most of us would probably be a little reserved. He was not. He would say things direct, because he felt it. He comes from Ghana. Maybe that was a bit different – he didn't grow up in Britain. When we as individuals regard ourselves as important, Reebop could not understand that, and he would say that. And not everyone can accept the truth. So that's probably one of the reasons he couldn't get along with Holger so easily.

'It was very difficult. But it must have been more difficult for Holger, because he was trying to invent something new. I can feel his pain. Wherever we are, we learn something about people and culture. Then somebody like Reebop comes, and we don't know how to take him. For example, in Britain we laugh about ourselves easily. In Germany it's not so. And I believe someone like Holger . . . finds things not so easily funny. And Reebop would react to these things. And, of course, I have lots of memories of Reebop, not only with Can. But his contribution to Can . . . the time we spent together, the power he gave, was amazing. Jaki and Reebop – wow. It didn't last long enough perhaps to break the barrier, the world. But the little we did together was amazing, magic.'

Since 1968, authorship of Can's songs had always been credited to the whole group, with lyrics attributed separately to commissioned writers like Peter Gilmour and Duncan Fallowell where appropriate. Within Can's self-created bubble, this was always tacitly understood to be totally in tune with the group's democratic objectives. Rosko and Reebop had taken the harder route through many groups, sessions and engagements, and had experienced the exploitative side of the music business, which saw them uncredited and unrewarded for their individual contributions to the identity of a song. In Can, beginning with *Saw Delight*, they began to insist on separate credits, explains Irmin. 'It's quite a pity that when Holger started with his experimental sounds, the group was already in so much of a confusional state, which was partly the reason [for adding] these two fantastic musicians, but they didn't, in a way, fit absolutely. They didn't fit with the ideological background Can had – sharing everything. They all of a sudden wanted their own authorship.'

For his part, Rosko denies that he had ever been ripped off in Britain before joining Can, but admits: 'I may have said something . . . I don't know what I said, or what I asked for. I may have made a mistake. In Britain, if you contributed to the song, you would get credit for it. But I look back now and see that in Can it was not the same, the management and set-up was not the same as we had in Britain, and I can well imagine the antagonism that may have caused. I realise today that as a band, it makes no difference. You can work together and share.'

On top of that came one final catastrophe that would make it impossible for Irmin and Holger, at least, to work together in the immediate future. Irmin had been having an affair with a psychotherapist who lived in Paris. She would sometimes accompany Irmin on tour, including to the UK. For a while it was so serious that Irmin even wondered whether it might lead to him and Hildegard separating. 'I kept it going because I was so insecure about how that would develop,' he says now, 'and I didn't want to tell Hildegard before I was sure what it actually means. And then one day we came back to the hotel in London from tour, and Hildegard had arrived, and of course, this girl wasn't with me any more. And Hildegard came with a friend of ours . . . They told me that Holger had told them that since two years ago, there was a woman on tour.'

The friend was Michael's ex, Eveline Grunwald, who says, 'I remember exactly where we were: in some pub in London, outside in the summer. It was all beautiful. I sat there with Hildegard, we'd been shopping, and Holger came and brought it all up.'

Holger had been struggling with his conscience for a long time now, in a high-stakes personal–professional dilemma, having to conceal this transgression from his manager, who was also the wife of his friend and colleague. Revelation might well mean the dissolution of a group that was providing many people's livelihoods. In the end, though, with the group tangibly fraying at the seams, he couldn't hold on to the secret any longer. 'I think for him, I did sacrilege,' admits Irmin, contrite after forty years. 'This was treason. I committed treason against Hildegard. And Hildegard was a kind of mother substitute for him. So I committed treason against the mother of the group. Which meant a real sacrilege. I think that was the thing. The second was that he probably felt "looked into" by a professional psychiatrist, because [Véronique, Irmin's mistress] could explain every move he made.'

'It was a serious affair, it wasn't a bit on the side,' confirms Duncan Fallowell. 'He went through a very bad period . . . and stayed with Hildegard. I suppose the main rivalry in the group was always between Holger and Irmin, as the co-founders,' he continues, although he agrees that Can would have terminated anyway without this incident. 'I think the band split up because they'd said all that they could say under those circumstances. I don't think it was anybody's fault. It wasn't anybody's attempt to destroy Can from the inside or anything like that.'

'It was an earthquake,' adds Grunwald, 'but they had so much in common too. If Hildegard had gone away and left him, it would have been a disaster for Can. Hildegard *is* Can – she's keeping that together. Her mind is constantly going round the idea of Can, how to keep that going. There she is, fighting like a lion.'

After dropping this bombshell at the end of Can's last UK tour,

Holger 'didn't show up in the next two days, he was hidden', says Irmin. 'And I swear, if he weren't hidden he would have spent the next two weeks in hospital. Because it wasn't his business to tell that to Hildegard. From then on there was something broken between us.'

Irmin claims he and Michael were usually the mediating figures in the group, the ones used to moderate the various conflicts, especially when Holger and Jaki argued over instrument levels or the viability of a recording. 'Well, from that moment I no longer cared if he was in trouble with others,' says Irmin. For the first time, in his bitterness he decided not to intervene in any more disputes, whatever they might be, as the group's intermittent tour threaded its way in and out of Germany, France and Switzerland. 'And [Holger] got into trouble with Reebop – a lot – and there was the last concert before he left' – in Geneva, on 20 March – 'where they started beating each other up. They had a real fight. And Holger was biting Reebop and screaming. I was sitting on this sofa, watching them the whole time, and against all my normal behaviour – before, I would have gone between – I watched it and didn't move. Let them do [what they wanted].' Peter Gilmour thinks this argument began when Reebop became so infuriated with Holger's electronics that he yanked the plugs out of the wall.

Minus Holger, Can played its final live shows in Spain and Portugal at the end of May, appearing for the first and last times in the cities of Madrid, Barcelona, Porto and Lisbon. The arena in Lisbon was packed with a crowd of ten thousand, with many thousands more rioting outside as they tried to storm their way in. The disturbances marking the end of Can's live career affected the remaining group members too, as its parts splintered and fell away. After the show, Irmin and Hildegard were woken in the middle of the night by Reebop, naked, having staggered back to the hotel with a bottle of cognac in hand. 'You're my brother,' he mumbled to the drowsy Irmin, 'and I need to sleep with your wife . . .' After being gently dissuaded from that notion, Reebop handed over a bag of cash – his share of the takings from that night's gig – asking the couple to look after it for him as he was afraid he might do something terrible with it if left to his own devices. The following morning, Hildegard received a phone call from the hotel's front desk. Reebop had accused one of the housemaids – who had spent the night in his room – of stealing his money, and now she had come sobbing to the management. Hildegard called Reebop to the telephone and reminded him that he had entrusted it to them for safe keeping.

Meanwhile, René Tinner got into an argument with Peter Gilmour over where to go next. Tinner was responsible for getting Can's truck full of gear back to Cologne, while Gilmour suggested driving first to the coast to soak up some sun. 'He wouldn't take no for an answer,' says Tinner. 'He just didn't understand what it was all about – if we have fun on the beach and the car is stolen . . . that was beyond his mind. We had a routine how to get the gear in and out of the truck, and you couldn't leave it without a person being there. We had had a terrible experience in Liverpool once, when Michael's guitar got stolen.' The incident was the cue for Gilmour to part ways with Can.

'Can function as a geometry of people,' Michael once said, 'it may be a triangle, a rectangle, or a quincunx figure, but there is never someone . . . who is leading the others, never.'[13] When Can – Irmin, Michael, Jaki, Rosko and Reebop – eventually regrouped in October 1977 to find out what could be salvaged from the wreckage, they found a tough haul ahead. The Virgin contract was over, and their next record would come out on EMI's Harvest subsidiary. The music the five created in the dark final months of 1977 is probably the least loved music Can ever made, and also possibly the least heard too, as the album, *Out of Reach*, was the only one they kept out of print for many years and left out of official discographies. In rock's history, there are many recordings unjustly forgotten in the vaults and spoken of in terms of hushed awe. In the case of *Out of Reach*, that would never be deserved.

'November' is a typical example. There is little sense of space, inner or outer, in its production. Plangent grand piano comps around grouchy chords, as congas and Jaki's busy snare keep up an unvarying chatter. Everyone is always on, there appears to be little dialogue happening on a musical level, and it is all to no obvious purpose or destination. 'Seven Days Awake' is another hollow-eyed jam, dominated by a muddy pile-up of hand drums and bowel-straining high-end guitar streaks.

Of the two songs credited solely to 'Gee', 'Pauper's Daughter and I' tumbles along with Michael's highlife-style guitar, but all Rosko can muster for the opening lines is the nursery rhyme 'Jack and Jill'. Jaki's drumsticks are reduced to disco timekeeping. 'Give Me No "Roses"' is a straight ahead Can boogie, more like Rosko and Reebop's former band Traffic. Rosko takes lead vocal, with Reebop chipping in on background harmonies. Irmin is practically inaudible, apart from a dab of squelchily inappropriate, grouchy synth in the final minute. 'Like Inobe God' is a 'Kwaku Baah' joint, and is a contender for the nadir of Can's entire output. A sluggish disco groove underpins it without any real heart, and Rosko and Reebop's frankly diabolical vocal double act is a drunken ramble, often straining painfully above and below comfortable registers. There's some incoherent burbling about Philadelphia, and near the end the words 'Giving, taking but never getting anywhere . . .' emerge out of the curdled, buttery mix.

Of the seven tracks that wound up on *Out of Reach*, only the opener, 'Serpentine', and the closer, 'One More Day', seem anything like the former spirit of Can in both title and feel. With such agile drums and percussion bubbling away in the foreground, Irmin resorted to his piano to cut through 'Serpentine''s dense mulch, and Michael's guitar has more of a trumpet-y timbre. As with every other track here, 'One More Day' refuses to open up any space, though it's the most experimental piece sonically, with wibbly synthetic effects applied to the drums and grinding atonal synth, although the whole thing is done after less than two minutes.

Irmin: 'The climax of confusion was reached in *Out of Reach*. I mean, this is really a prophetic title. I hate this record. It's just a document of total confusion. Musically and psychologically, and in every sense, it's bad.

'Reebop . . . seduced Jaki to start playing very fast . . . You hear it already on *Saw Delight* – Jaki gets very nervous. Which could be marvellous . . . but with Reebop, and on *Out of Reach*, it really got out of reach and control.'

The tapes were handed to Conny Plank to mix, but even his magic couldn't clean up the mess. 'I said no I don't want to participate,' said Holger. 'Conny Plank got very angry that I said "I don't touch with my hands this music"! And they said to Conny, can you mix this? Conny was saying to me later, why have you done that? Now I have to take on my shoulders all the shit.'[14]

At exactly this moment, the profile of German rock enjoyed a brief upswing in credibility. David Bowie's 1977 'Berlin albums' *Low* and *'Heroes'* channelled the rhythmic rigour and experimental energy of Can and Neu! (Michael Rother was even shortlisted to play guitar). Bowie's collaborator on those albums, Brian Eno, was in the middle of his collaborations in the forest with Cluster and Harmonia, which helped him refine his ambient concept. The robotically groomed Kraftwerk began to penetrate the British and American charts with 'Trans-Europe Express' and 'Showroom Dummies'. Can should have been in a prime position to capitalise on the situation. Instead, when *Out of Reach* finally appeared in summer 1978, an invisible hand clenched at nothingness on a bleached sleeve that exuded impotent frustration. The writer Ian Penman, assessing this 'tangled, intriguing, infuriating music' in the *NME*, picked up on its sense of exhausted ideas. These were 'Songs which do not caress sentiment: they go straight for the nerves, the darkness of the heart . . . (The prevalent mood of the whole album is one of melancholy; it should have been released in autumn, methinks). A feeling, not surprisingly, of moving into shadows and not emerging again. An inflexion of warmth ready to snap, love ready to hate (always felt that way with Can?) – abstract lyrical.' For Penman, the brief 'One More Day' represented 'what Can were all about: structured such that play might be limitless. Yet it is a stab, no more. A shooting star. The demise. Suddenly, no more.

'Goodnight.'[15]

16

Can Will Eat Itself

It wasn't quite time for goodnight, not yet. Before *Out of Reach* had even been released, in the early months of 1978, Can had completed one more album's worth of material and had put together the *Cannibalism* compilation, which was to be the point of entry for many new listeners. Beginning around February 1978, they recorded the eight-track album known simply as *Can*, featuring their name compressed into a hexagonal nut that is being raised aloft to the heavens in the embrace of a spanner. Released on Harvest Germany and the short-lived Laser label in the UK, *Can* sounds far more unclenched than the previous album, and to a certain extent it picks up where *Landed* left off. Even Holger was partly back on board, helping out with the editing of the tracks, although he did not play any sounds. 'We gave Holger the final tapes to edit,' said Michael. 'It was like in the *Tago Mago* days.'[1] Holger added: 'The band had made it through the vale of shadows.'[2]

Only three or four months after the disastrously misjudged *Out of Reach*, something of a change seems to have swept over the group. On opener 'All Gates Open' the collective sounds as though it has taken a firm grip on its output again. The track sweeps majestically along with the kind of simplified yet muscular groove Jaki had been churning out with Michael Rother. The production too is cleaner, more spacious. Rosko's bass has much more of the character of Holger's early-seventies work, and the group with sound engineer René Tinner have learned how to accommodate the extra elements brought in by Reebop: by keeping his contributions lower in the mix. A harmonica adds some unexpected rootsiness over the opening bars, before Michael begins to sing lyrics that directly reference the process of constructing sound: 'Sometimes it is hard to say where the songs come from / Especially when there are so many around / The breathing sound is usually just below the gate / It has to be much louder to be heard . . . By the time we realise the way we've got to play / All gates are open now, it seems . . .' With a 'manifesto song' such as this, the group seem aware they are constructing their own epitaph. That phrase 'all gates open', redolent of inclusiveness, takes on a double meaning here: when the gates are open, things can slip outwards as well as be allowed in. That is a precise analysis of the state Can found themselves in during the early part of 1978. Even if they knew it would soon be over, Can nevertheless sound majestic, dignified, even triumphant.

'This is a greeting message to all those who try their best to make everything quite easy and who aren't sure either which is the right way / To them this is the safe way, safe as the mighty flower and all his friends roaming as they roam where they roam . . .' Michael's gabbled intro to 'Safe' – a track perched on the cusp of reggae and rock – is repeated halfway through the eight-minute track, this time through a vocoder. 'Safe' regains some of the mystery of the early Can tracks, where something powerful is being invoked, although its rules of engagement are still obscure. 'This is how we roll / This is how we used to roll,' he chants. Can certainly has its groove back here, and Jaki's frequencies are married up with Rosko's bass in a more integrated fashion. Like the best Can tracks, this is a dynamo which could go on for ever if it was left to run by itself. Irmin: 'It has a real Jaki rhythm, it has a very nice groove, and it has these dense, strange kind of sounds, and I always imagined if that had been a new starting point and Holger again coming in, playing all his crazy stuff, it would have worked wonderfully, it could have developed into something. But it was too late.'

Aspekte was the flagship arts review programme on Germany's ZDF television channel, disseminating 'information and opinions from cultural life' since 1965. During the mid-seventies the show had become increasingly esoteric and frequently featured avant-garde arts and themes relating to youth protest. In 1978 the show was given an overhaul in an attempt to open it to a wider public, and Can were invited to contribute a new theme tune. They came up with a funky sixteen-beat shuffle, beefing up Michael's choppy wah-wah in the mix. For the relaunch, Can (including Holger, huffing away on a set of pan pipes) were filmed playing the track at Inner Space: the last extant moving images of this particular ensemble. A six-minute version of the tune, complete with vocal line sung by Rosko, appears on the *Can* LP, titled 'Aspectacle'.

Can also included one of the last of the long-running 'EFS' – number ninety-nine (in total, there were over a hundred). Appropriately enough – Jaki called it 'a compulsory exercise'[3] – this was a bonkers reading of Jacques Offenbach's 'Infernal Galop', from his 1858 opera *Orpheus in the Underworld*, popularly known as the 'Cancan'. In serving up this student-bop-friendly slice of Dada disco, there was method in the madness. Although a Frenchman, Offenbach was born and raised in Cologne (the city still contains an Offenbachplatz). The wild and erotic cancan dance had become a part of western Europe's cultural folklore, and Offenbach's has come to be the one tune by which this berserk dance form, prevalent from the 1840s onwards, is remembered. With rasping electronic tones and a ska clatter, Can play the piece as good-time mayhem with an amphetamine aftertaste, a last *Totentanz* before the gravediggers move in. 'Offenbach would have liked it,' said Irmin. 'He had a feel for the vulgar.'[4] It was Can's final single of the seventies.

Considering this was a group on the brink of disintegration, the remaining tracks on *Can* were perfectly respectable: the rainbow glide of 'Sunday Jam'; 'Sodom', like a piece of Stockhausen *elektronische Musik* over plodding rock, and which even included a tiny snippet of sproingy sounds from a ping-pong table, a staple of early electroacoustic music. The album rides into the sunset with 'Can

Be', an instrumental reprise of the eternal 'Cancan'. At least there was no gloomy coda to Can's ten-year run.

It's not clear that Can knew it was the end, anyway. In the first half of the year Duncan Fallowell came over to help put together *Cannibalism*, a new compilation of material from the United Artists years. This involved selecting fourteen tracks for a double album, some of which ('Halleluwah', 'Soup', etc.) had to be edited down to fit the double-LP format. 'Yoo Doo Right', though, proved uncuttable and appeared in its full twenty-minute length. Fallowell published a florid diary of his trip in the German *Sounds* paper a few months later, describing how he found himself 'In the big, big studio, with glinting black and silver machines, and lights alternatively blinking red/green/orange, level meters twitch like tortured nerves, whole rows of colourful switches, levers and buttons, which on the mixing desk turn on and off and on the mixing desk are slipped in and out, which are equipped with numbers, titles and temporary controls. Fountains of black cable gush out of this mixing board and stream into every corner of this big, obscenely big studio (hung with lurid flags), in order to couple with other complex equipment, from which even more cables spill to reveal a visual chaos of instruments, junk, technology, sofas and a parasol, which eventually flows into a blooming, pulsating earthquake of massive syncopated noise . . .'[5]

He also gave thumbnail sketches of the band members who were hanging around the studio:

1) Irmin Schmidt, keyboards and carnivore, drinks rather less since losing his driver's licence. Alternates between Cologne and the south of France, where he owns some land and is planning to build a crazy house.
2) Michael Karoli, guitar, although his favourite guitar has been stolen. Would the thief kindly return it. There's a huge reward, the police won't be informed, naturally, it merely requires a solid, unbureaucratic solution.

3) Jaki Liebezeit, drums and percussion. Seems to be the healthiest one in the whole group. That could be a mistake though. Surely has some secret vices.

4) Rosko Gee, occasional member. Born in Jamaica, grew up in England. Was the former bassist in Traffic, but has spent the last 18 months in Can. Likes to wear a top hat, but I believe he is almost over that phase.

5) Reebop, occasional member. Congos, bongoes, congas, born in Ghana, has been with the Rolling Stones etc. . . .[6]

Cannibalism was released in 1978, with an electric blue face starring grimly out of the cover under a haze of strange, alien-style typography. The album has been reissued several times with different artwork, including a grisly pencil drawing of a mouth wedged open with a toothgrinder, and a primitivist painting by artist Kay Kassel that defaced an indistinct family Polaroid. Significantly, this album introduced Can's early, rawest material to a younger audience that was not weaned on psychedelia and progressive rock but heard early Krautrock through the lens of punk and new wave. To cement that impression, the liner notes were written by Pete Shelley, guitarist and vocalist of Manchester punks the Buzzcocks. In his brief text, dated 16 August 1978, he described how he 'used to play "Halleluwah" in the bath and "Yoo Doo Right" in the dark at neighbour-hating levels. Listen to "Father Cannot Yell" on headphones and the middle-section twines itself around the brain. Other things at first hearing I've hated, but later I've had to admit that first hearings are always misleading.

'I've only one criticism to make of this compilation – the amount of material left off. The only way to treat this album is as a mouthwatering hors d'oeuvre, although it does make a tasty meal by itself.

'. . . I would never have played guitar had it not been for the late Marc Bolan and Michael Karoli of Can. I hope this makes you, too, curious to hear more.'

Although punk rock in Britain had launched itself under a banner of tearing down the entire pantheon of former rock heroes, some of its key representatives were nevertheless happy to cite German music as an influence. On Tommy Vance's Capital Radio show on 16 July 1977, the Sex Pistols' Johnny Rotten gave an interview that has passed into punk infamy, in which he played twenty-four of his favourite tracks, demonstrating a much more eclectic and catholic music taste than anyone expected. Alongside Neil Young, Tim Buckley, Nico, John Cale and plentiful Jamaican dub, he closed out the show with the full eighteen-minute bludgeon of Can's 'Halleluwah'. Weary after a two-hour interview, his only comment was 'They've got the most amazing drummer I've ever heard. He keeps the beat and plays two at once and he's just . . . good.' But in this context – with the formation of Public Image Limited around the corner – the music sounded leaner and more brutal than ever before. A year or two later, Lydon even phoned the Can office to offer his services as a vocalist, insisting that he would be the ideal singer for the group. Unfortunately, this was after the band had called it quits, but apparently it took several calls to convince Lydon that this was true. Around the same time, incidentally, Mark E. Smith of The Fall also got in touch, wanting to arrange a gig in which first his group would play, then Can, and finally the two groups would improvise together. Too late.

Inner Space hardly enjoyed a moment's silence during the bulk of 1978. Whenever Can vacated the studio, Holger would move in – 'I was practically the nightwatchman there'[7] – to continue working on his first solo project since *Canaxis*, ten years earlier. In fact, since 1977 he had been privately tinkering with some of Can's own back catalogue and out-takes, re-recording and remixing them to amplify different details and frequencies, overdubbing and reshaping the material via thousands of micro-edits. His early solo music often has the perfume of half-remembered Can drifting through it, as if Can refused to entirely let go. A thirteen-minute piece called 'Oh

Lord Give Us More Money', for instance, uses the rhythm track and chord sequence of 'Hunters and Collectors', splurge-gunning it with samples of a TV evangelist, car horns, thunderclaps and concrete noises and audio clips from films; Holger sings in a hysterical whisper. 'Persian Love' is sparkling synthpop taking its cue from ravishing extracts of Iranian vocal music. Holger's guitar, tightly tinkling, was recorded at half speed. 'Hollywood Symphony' is a masterclass in the art of cut-up movie dialogue, over a gentle lollop of drums from Jaki and a transcendent synth coda that enters the realms of 'Bel Air'. There was even a single, 'Cool in the Pool', a tongue-in-cheek celebration of the high life – featuring 'chicken organ' by Reebop – in which a saxophone solo taped off the radio falls into perfect alignment with the middle eight. Duncan Fallowell described it as 'the Temptations collide in a Disney sound-cyclotron with Radio Moscow and the Invading All Stars'.[8]

Recorded at Inner Space using Can tapes and personnel, and mixed at Conny Plank's studio, *Movies* can be thought of as the first seed transplanted from Can into a new garden. Its collage of found elements has become second nature – and sounds utterly natural – to subsequent generations of producers working in various branches of electronic music, hip hop and sampladelia, but it was among the first to propose such an approach and package it as pop. In the immediate term it inspired another influential landmark in early sampling aesthetics: David Byrne and Brian Eno's *My Life in the Bush of Ghosts* (1981). Holger had been a friend of Eno's since the early seventies, and their paths had recently crossed again in Cluster's woodland studio. Now Eno was working with Irmin's former lodger, trumpeter Jon Hassell, on their *Possible Musics* album, one that introduced Hassell's concept of the Fourth World – a magic-realist musical zone in which all the world's music could be fluidly recombined and transmuted. Holger's solo music fitted right in with this notion, and there was a logic about these former connections circling around each other once more. Like on *Canaxis* ten years earlier, Holger returned to his work-intensive methods of handling tapes. And just as 'Boat-Woman-Song' spun a golden thread from the folk music of war-torn sixties Vietnam, so 'Persian Love' alchemised the music of Iran, whose revolution at the end of 1978 made it the most serious international flashpoint at the time.

'When I was 39 it was a very special year for me,' he later reminisced to the writer Biba Kopf. 'Big things happened in my life. Finishing with Can was a big break, I learned to laugh at W. C. Fields and discovered telepathy with plants. This discovery made me feel like a newborn child. I could have stayed talking with plants forever. It took me two years to ask myself, what do you want? Do you want to talk to plants all your life? The break came one winter's morning. I went out about five o'clock, stood in front of a bush and said, OK, you have roots, you don't need to walk anymore. But I have legs and I'm running away! I set off running and ran as fast and as far as I could. Which is where I came back to music.'[9]

Right after Holger's last Can gig in Geneva, Hildegard, with the agreement of the rest of the group, had agreed to maintain financial support for him and his work. She had initially borrowed funds from her family so that he could take a holiday to recuperate, and he remained on the same Can salary for years afterwards. 'Nobody in the group would've simply let me fall,' he said, 'even though the entire affair was very painful. That was simply Can's way.'[10]

*

As the present flies away
The future is diminished
The night is really over
The past is all just finished.

The verse in 'Laugh Till You Cry, Live Till You Die' had already foreseen the inevitable. There is no law stating that innovators shall remain innovative indefinitely. In the arts as in human history, pioneers open the ways for others to follow, and what was once virgin land is developed and settled by those who follow. A complex of causes – interpersonal, technological, ideological, financial – meant that at the end of 1978, the remaining members of the group decided their time in Can was at an end.

'My theory', mused Jaki, 'is that a group lives about as long as a dog. After ten years at the most, it's over. Like in a marriage. At some time the excitement wanes.'[11] 'It's like a piece of rubber that's always under maximum tension. One day it gets floppy,' was how Irmin once described Can's demise[12] – an image Jaki had originally used. From the very beginning, Can was an entity that thrived on its constantly fluctuating tensions. The internal dynamics of improvisation, premeditation and mechanical post-production were mirrored in the interrelationships between its human components.

'We were so much older than normal rock groups who start,' Irmin tells me, 'but the group was not made by friends. It's a chamber orchestra! Like any orchestra, or a string quartet, most of them come together because they are the best in the university or the academy. They are not necessarily friends. But still they have to grow together. And musically we grew to an extreme together, which is rare. An extreme which became telepathic. Then, if that becomes routine – if you know anyway what the other will do – it has the opposite effect.'

'The first five albums were enough,' commented Jaki many years later. 'The band could've then broken up in peace.'[13]

What had begun as a music woven into solid air out of the collective subconscious had ended up as a clash of competing egos and financial disputes. For Rosko and Reebop it had always been difficult to suppress an innate suspicion that this band might be ripping them off. 'They wanted to bring in their own compositions,' Jaki explained, 'but they didn't understand. They simply didn't get it, the ideology in the group. That the old style of songwriting didn't function. We were never in our lives songwriters, the way it is in ninety-nine per cent of the bands. There's a completely different ideology behind that . . . Nobody was replaceable in our band. We always made sure that nobody became the boss or Number One.'[14]

Rosko states that he decided independently to leave the group. 'I believe today it was the distance between the musicians, between the band members. For me there was too much distance. It just seems to happen. I didn't want to carry on. Perhaps I may even have thought that we are *not* going further. It was not a calculated decision on my part. For a start, we were taking a year to make a record. And I'm coming from a culture where we would make a record in six weeks. But with Can it was a different process, and this I had to get used to. The time between when we were in the studio together was so long that sometimes one forgets – "What am I doing?" But I cannot blame anyone for that. I have nothing bad to say about the band.'

With Hildegard as manager, Can was something of a family affair. A situation like that could have been problematic in itself for some personalities, although everyone now agrees the arrangement worked well. '*Any* manager – even if it hadn't been my wife – would have been part of the group,' insists Irmin. 'I mean, a *real* part of the group, because we functioned like this. But Hildegard was so much able – I still admire that – to separate our family from the quarrels inside the group. She never ever took my part, and nobody in the group had the feeling that because she's my wife I have more influence or whatever.'

Jaki added: 'We spent all the money on equipment and all kinds of things. We had to buy bigger cars and bigger lorries . . . It got bigger and bigger, and the money we had was not much more. But we always had to spend it – partly for tax reasons – or invest it [in new equipment] . . . but we thought we must be stupid to spend all the money on all this equipment, which will be scrap anyway in five years! And so we gave up . . .'

Irmin doesn't remember any specific day or instant when the

group officially parted company. But he had been unhappy with the situation for quite some time. The falling out with Holger had left a nasty aftertaste, and 'there was a point . . . especially mixing *Out of Reach*, I thought, "That's it, I can't stand this confusion any more. It's the end, it doesn't make sense any more, either musically or . . ." I was still close to Michael, but Jaki . . . he was always at that time all day long criticising and . . . he was not satisfied with whatever was going on. It could get on your nerves. And when the music was good, and he was in a good mood, it would be wonderful. But, yeah, I had the feeling it didn't work any more.

'Also, a very important thing for me was I had a wife and a daughter, who was ten years old, and I hadn't lived with her much. During Can there was no family life, very little. Actually, I saw my daughter at four o'clock in the morning, when I came home from the studio, and then she woke up and I made a kind of pancake with chocolate, and we sat there for an hour between four and five in the morning, when she was four or five years old, and we talked about our day, and that was wonderful. And that was about it. Wonderful memory, but not enough for family life. And so I thought it's time to arrange my life so that there is a place for family.

'Of course, if the group had been flourishing like hell, it would have gone on, but it wasn't. I can't even pinpoint a special moment . . . In Germany we say if something doesn't work any more, *"die Luft ist raus"*. Like when a balloon has deflated.'

An epitaph, of sorts, ran in the *NME* in January 1979, in the form of a one-page interview with Holger, who 'spent most of Christmas week longshanking the streets of London town in search of a record company'. The article confirmed that Can had definitively ceased activities, and pronounced a verdict many would agree with in subsequent years. 'Can, understandably but unrealistically, remained aloof from the promotional process, valuing privacy over publicity.

'At the same time, perhaps encouraged by the surprising single success of "I Want More" in 76, they attempted rather hesitantly and nebulously to coin a more extrovert, accessible, "populist" currency (best exemplified by parts of *Flow Motion*): an experiment that ultimately failed to convince. Old Can fans were mildly disillusioned; new Can fans simply weren't secured.' Furthermore, *Saw Delight* and *Out of Reach* 'swung the Canometer with alarming lethargy and, worse still, a near-total lack of mysterioso travelling'.[15]

17

One Last Rite

==========

'Anything happening where I can sing?'[1]

The voice grating down the phone line from the US was unmistakable. Malcolm Mooney had sporadically made contact via post or telephone over the past fifteen years, but now, when he dialled Irmin and Hildegard's French telephone number in the middle of 1986, there seemed to be the chance of a genuine reunion.

In the seven years that had elapsed since the Can members had jumped into their escape pods, they had not separated entirely – apart from Reebop, who died of a heart attack while playing on stage in Sweden in 1983. While they had not reunited en masse, molecular bonds remained between certain members. After a couple of years of slightly dazed fallout, Holger picked up the thread of his own compositions with instruments and tape, bought himself a French horn and got himself back to Inner Space, where he recorded *On the Way to the Peak of Normal* (1981). Jaki played drums on several tracks, and it included the brief 'Two Bass Hit', recorded at Inner Space in 1976, with Holger playing both drums and guitar. The mildly skanking title track featured a German new-wave band, S.Y.P.H., whom Holger had met and invited for a session at Weilerswist. 'Hiss 'n' Listen' featured Jah Wobble, bassist with John Lydon's Public Image Limited, with whom Holger and Jaki also recorded the six-track *Full Circle* at the same time, a dub-infused LP with considerably more urgency about it than much of what Can had achieved in a while. Holger's journey, through the early eighties, was as a kind of shamanic mentor to a number of fellow artisan-popsters, who seemed to require extraneous outlets beyond their more commercially successful ventures. He popped up with Wobble and U2 guitarist the Edge on *Snake Charmer*, an EP produced by French electronic musician François Kevorkian, in 1983; and was a key contributor to *Brilliant Trees*, the debut solo album of atmospheric song by David Sylvian, who had recently fled from the New Romantic band Japan. The pair discovered a certain affinity, and it wouldn't be the only time they worked together.

By the mid-eighties Holger had an ongoing Virgin Records contract, and he released his fourth solo album, *Der Osten ist rot*, in 1984. Although he had all but retired from the live stage, his cultivated image as a puckish Mitteleuropean audio scientist was largely paying off, and his music – appearing presciently postmodern in an age of sequenced cut 'n' paste hits – was still regarded highly in the British music press.

Irmin had built a house on a large plot of land, purchased in the late seventies in the Luberon district in the south of France. He was now free to work as the professional composer he was destined to be in the years pre-Can. When the group folded, he immediately reconnected with his contacts in the film and television world and began composing and recording soundtracks almost full-time. One of the first was the Reinhard Hauff movie *Messer im Kopf* (*Knife in the Head*, 1978) starring Bruno Ganz and edited by Peter Przygodda. Irmin played every instrument, apart from a Turkish bağlama strummed by Can's old accomplice Alex Wiska.

The house in France was also the headquarters of Spoon Records, an independent label, and its sister publishing operation Messer Music, set up by Hildegard in the aftermath of the Can break-up. While attending the Midem festival in Cannes in 1979, Hildegard decided to take control of Can's back catalogue. Setting up Spoon, she first secured the rights to the United Artists recordings and set plans in motion to reissue them on vinyl. Spoon also issued two volumes of Irmin's collected *Filmmusik* in 1980 and '81, as well as *Toy Planet* (1981), an enjoyable electronic pop collaboration with Bruno

Spoerri, a Swiss electronic composer and jazz saxophonist. Spoerri ran his own electronic music studio in Zurich, and Irmin produced several albums by other artists there in the early eighties.

Further volumes of soundtracks followed, as well as Irmin's music for *Rote Erde* (1983), Klaus Emmerich's celebrated TV series covering around seven decades of life in Germany's mining communities in the Ruhrgebiet, from the late nineteenth to the mid-twentieth century. These becalmed and elegiac pieces, salted with yearning accordion and harmonica, are some of the best of Irmin's career and featured Michael on guitars, Manfred Schoof and Gerd Dudek on trumpet and saxophone, British drummer John Marshall and a full string section.

Right from the start, Irmin frequently called in Jaki and Michael (and Rosko until 1981) to work on his soundtrack recordings, and on many of these occasions Jaki was reunited with his erstwhile jazz colleagues. In 1986 Irmin invited Manfred Schoof and Gerd Dudek, as well as Duncan Fallowell as lyricist, to record a new batch of songs with Jaki and Michael that would be released as Irmin's solo LP *Musk at Dusk* the following year. Jaki had continued to work with Michael Rother right after Can disbanded, releasing *Sterntaler* and *Katzenmusik* (1979) and *Fernwärme* (1982). Sky Records also released the first two LPs by Jaki's new Phantomband in 1980. On the first, Rosko turned up on bass, Holger tooted a few horn dribbles and mixed the record at Conny's studio, and the group included new friends Dominik von Senger (guitar), Olek Gelba (percussion) and Helmut Zerlett (keyboards). The latter three remained for 1981's *Freedom of Speech*. *Nowhere*, Phantomband's third album, from 1984, added Sheldon Ancel on vocals, who would later turn up on Holger's 1989 LP *Moving Pictures*. In the post-Can universe, the degrees of separation remained small.

Holger was involved in mastering *Deluge*, Michael's first non-Can project. Like Irmin, Michael invested in property in southern France after leaving Can, in a former olive oil mill near Nice.

He married Shirley in 1981, established his own recording studio
at home, which he dubbed Outer Space, and spent the next three
years working intermittently on the material that became the duo
album *Deluge*, which came out on Spoon in 1984 and was recorded
with Polly Eltes (wife of Simon Puxley and an amateur vocalist who
had recently taken part in 'Voodoo', an obscure twelve-inch single
by Jah Wobble and Ollie Marland). It's an undemonstrative collection of songs that don't sound out of place in the post-punk galaxy,
with a few nods towards Michael's interest in reggae. In the same
time frame he was studying African rhythm and dance with the
drummer Seni Camara, and in around 1985 added guitar to a number of Holger's tracks, which eventually surfaced on 1991's *Radio
Wave Surfer* album.

Somehow, though, none of these drifting particles of the atomised
Can quite added up to an entirely convincing whole. And there was
a lingering sense that the various members couldn't let go of each
other entirely. Malcolm's beam-in from New York opened up the
possibility of finding out if there was any of the old telepathic energy
still floating out there. A reminder of that energy had bubbled up in
1982, when Spoon Records issued *Delay 1968*, a collection of raw
Can tracks from the first year at Schloss Nörvenich – mostly the
material from the abandoned *Prepared to Meet Thy Pnoom* project. At the time the album slipped out widely unnoticed, and not
always loved when it was, although Richard Cook in the *NME* took
the opportunity to eulogise Can's 'sleepless drift, its freezing beauty,
its motionless erosion of convention, its rehabilitation of folklore,
its respectful bow to art, its ignorance of starting and stopping, its
passageway into dream, its unconscious passion and its indifference
to simple spirituality, [which] makes it kind of intimidating'.[2] Apart
from *Monster Movie* and half of *Soundtracks*, Malcolm's tenure in
Can had always seemed like a brief prologue, but the *Delay* tracks
fleshed out the picture considerably.

Just as in the early days of Schloss Nörvenich, when Can had been kick-started with support from the art world, now Hildegard secured sponsorship from George Reinhart, film producer, photographer and nephew of the wealthy Swiss art collector Oskar Reinhart. George was interested in investing part of the family fortune in the arts – he would later open a photographic museum in the Swiss town of Winterthur – and knew Bruno Spoerri, Irmin's collaborator on *Toy Planet*. (Reinhart once funded the recording of an album by Swiss guitarist Hardy Hepp, aka Hand in Hand, in Spoerri's studio, which Irmin produced.) Later in the eighties, this generous patron founded a production company called Fink & Star, which employed Hildegard and financed Irmin's LPs *Musk at Dusk* and *Impossible Holidays*.

When a new Can recording was proposed in the mid-eighties, Fink & Star's financing paid for the musicians, technicians and various friends (including Duncan Fallowell and Simon Puxley, the Virgin press officer who had become close to Can in the mid-seventies) to assemble at Michael's studio to write and record new material, and covered travel costs, accommodation and studio time. Malcolm arrived too. 'Two letters crossed,' he remembers, 'one from Hildegard, one from me. "Can we get together and do something?" And Hildegard was writing and saying the same thing. It seemed coincidental.'

They met up just after Thanksgiving in 1986. Malcolm bounced into the middle of it all after seventeen years away, dapperly dressed, upright and outgoing, a different man from the fearful and paranoid Desse of the late sixties. 'He was a rather suave New Yorker, with an arty pedigree, and still very jolly,' says Fallowell, who had not met him first time around. With everything paid for, and with nothing to prove, this was potentially an easygoing experience, and a social one too, with all the group members accommodated in Michael's spacious abode.

'It's always touch and go if you try and resuscitate something,' says Fallowell. 'I spent a lot of time there while they were recording it . . . There was no structure; if one was there or not there, it didn't seem to affect the fact that life would continue. People would drop in . . . this ongoing thing. The *moulin* at Lantosque was quite big; you could set up beds in odd places without people falling over each other. It was all stone and semi-underground. Actually like living in a chink of museum or monastery or something. [Michael] liked it because he wanted to go back to the womb, and this was the nearest thing. Of course, synchronising the timing was very difficult: it always took ages for anything to begin, because different people would be going out or washing, having breakfast, feeling dreadful – you know, whatever it might be. Shirley and I would be the first ones up, and there was that somnolent silence which says nobody's going to appear for another three hours.

'Then Michael would suddenly get it into his head that he had to have some sushi. So everybody was going to Nice to a Japanese sushi bar. This would take most of the day to organise, forty minutes down an autoroute, and they'd come back and record something, and it would be built up like a coral reef.'

'It was not a good working atmosphere there, it was a holiday atmosphere,' Jaki confirmed. 'Working was not so intense. [Everybody] would prefer to eat something there and have a nice time. But there was not a group feeling. Holger was completely gaga. He would come in with this horn, he only wanted to blow this horn. That was his contribution.'

Malcolm, on the other hand, calls it 'a really wonderful time – very good memories. We did a bunch of sixteen-minute takes, and out of thirty-three of those came *Rite Time*.'[3]

'It was nice to see Malcolm again, but there were a lot of fights. It was the wrong time,' Michael said.[4]

Irmin confesses he's not a fan of *Rite Time*. 'There's too much routine in it. Like, doing what we anyway can do. And it's not very new. We didn't invent a new Can. When we started, I thought this will be a chance for a new Can, for something totally . . . like we always were. But *Rite Time* is a Can record like any one before. It's nothing surprising. Not that I dislike the record – it's OK, and there are some nice pieces on there, but it's just a good record. Not like, say, the difference between each of the first four or five Can records to the next – [then] it was a totally new point of view of what this kind of group could do. Between *Ege Bamyası* and *Future Days* there are worlds, they are totally different. But *Rite Time* is a good Can record. And there is one song, "Below This Level", I love. It's the strangest one on it . . . It has a kind of rock normality [*laughs*] to me, which is OK. But it's not enough!'

Listening beyond the members' personal reservations, *Rite Time* has stood the test of time rather better than many of their late-seventies records. In Michael's studio Can sounded bigger than ever before. The drums are beefy and widely separated, the spaces between instruments are more clearly defined with digital effects, and the whole sound horizon is flooded by a corona of brightness, as if a glowing sun is setting behind it. To save the production from becoming too pristine, Malcolm's sandpapery, confident holler is the perfect foil. Many tracks include a weird chorus of ethereal backing vocals, occasionally featuring Hildegard and Shirley. Whether or not it was the right direction for the group at that point, it didn't sound exactly like any previous Can album and landed like a gleaming UFO among the other alternative music appearing in 1989. '[The album] is typical,' opined Holger, 'not a youngster's, a beginner's work – it is a good work and there is no need to be ashamed of it.'[5]

Most of all, it sounded as though Can was persuading its musicians to actually listen to each other again. 'On the Beautiful Side of a Romance' came out of the dock surging and tossing on a sea of lopsided reggae. Jaki's complex time signature prefigured his rhythmic experimentations of the years to come. 'The Withoutlaw Man' was a spiky silly-walk, whose closest cousin was perhaps the quirky

Beefheart boogie of British indie band Stump. Malcolm's abstract 'chow-chow diddley-dow' vamps, and his repeated invocation of the outlaw Jesse James, recall his nonsensical chewing-the-fat back in 1969, while Irmin thrummed an African thumb piano. On 'Movin' Right Along' Holger's cut-and-paste approach can be heard, as he splices together echoing French horn and shortwave fragments, and the voice is punched in and out in a variety of different echo chambers. 'Give the Drummer Some' is a loping dub, with chicken-scratch guitar and atonal clusters from Irmin. Holger's one-note bass is always on the money, though the track itself remains some-how forgettable. 'Hoolah Hoolah' is an agitated robo-rockabilly can-can dance, as antic as this Can line-up would get. 'They do wear pants in the southern side of France . . .'

The blithe backing vocals of 'Below This Level (Patient's Song)' belie the fact that Malcolm is referring to his time in a mental ward. 'Psych-i-atric must I do,' he recites Yoda-like, but this genially detached piece is a reckoning with his and Can's past, recalling a point in his life when he had reached the bottom of his mental ele-vator shaft. According to Irmin, the track 'reflects the nuthouse, actually. It's not me who has the right to say that, but he said it. He mentions "psychiatric" in the song, and it's reflecting his experience with the psychiatrist and psychiatric therapy and all the rest of it.' Like Nurse Ratched on the warpath, Can's music force-marches him down a cubist corridor of mirrors.

As well as this poignant song, there were two tracks where Can outreached themselves and slipped into another dimension, strange and wondrous, as they had done in their early years. 'Like a New Child' fades in on an otherworldly plane, an onyx pre-dawn hush as Michael taps the back of his guitar neck. Jaki's drums etch out a slow, inexorable sleepwalk through a dreamy tunnel lit by lumi-nous harmonic guitar overtones. This indeed is the 'rite time' at the heart of the record; you feel as though Can is conveying you somewhere transcendent, to a state, as the title suggests, of rebirth.

Holger blares unsettling fanfares along the way, and Malcolm sings from the depths of a mesmeric trance. 'Don't pay no attention to me / I'm just a silent partner in your mystery . . .'

'I think the way Can record and make music has something to do with rite,' said Holger. 'It's more a sort of ceremony actually than performing a task.'[6]

Rite Time's sporadic ambient passages bore the hallmarks of some of the work Holger had recently accomplished with David Sylvian. In early 1987 they had hooked up for a few days at the Can Studio and, with radios, sampled and prepared piano, harmonium, vibes, synthesizers and 'environmental treatments', generated enough material for an album of unsettling, wordless textural music. *Plight and Premonition* was released on Virgin in March 1988, featuring two long tracks, and it co-credited Jaki for 'infra-sound' and even music journalist Karl Lippegaus for turning the radio dial. Inspired by this collaboration, Holger and Sylvian reconvened at Weilerswist in December 1988, around the same period *Rite Time* was being pieced together, and recorded *Flux + Mutability*, whose 'buzzes and fluctuations' made for an even richer, more elegiac brew than the previous one. Side one, 'Flux (A Big, Bright, Colourful World)', managed to unite various Can-related elements all at once: Holger, Michael and Jaki were involved, plus vocals by Michi Nakao, and even Markus Stockhausen, son of Irmin and Holger's former mentor, was on board, on flugelhorn. Jaki's African flute on 'Mutability (A New Beginning Is in the Offing)' is a ghost from the 'EFS' returning for one last whistle.

On one level this music might serve as a reverent elegy, waving off the soul of Can as it departs for shores unknown. At the same time records like this announced a new world, proposing an alternative to the enforced camaraderie of a group-as-football-team – the dream Can lived in its heyday – and instead treating music as art, with musicians, samples, instruments and conceptual ideas chosen and splashed over a sonic canvas. Never mind the bollocks – make way for the Pollocks.

The other outstanding track from this period didn't appear on the original *Rite Time* vinyl LP, but was an extra track on the CD. 'In the Distance Lies the Future' is the most unconventionally structured of all these songs, raw and off-the-cuff rock, with a tension between Malcolm's untrammelled roar and the clipped interplay of the instrumentalists. Holger's octave-leaping bassline and Michael's gnat-in-a-jam-jar guitar teleport the listener right back to the judder of 'Mother Sky'. The last sounds of this version of Can simply fade out, with the future unresolved.

True to Can's form, *Rite Time* was a product of extensive post-production. Once the sessions were wrapped, the master tapes were mixed in 1988 at the Can Studio by Michael, Holger and René Tinner, and Holger performed one last edit at his 'Lab for Degenerated Music' – actually a room at his Cologne apartment – before the album was delivered for release.

'After not seeing each other for some time, or not so frequently, when everybody showed up to do the record it was like those years had not even taken place,' says Tinner. 'Maybe a bit more respectfully than before, because it was now some time in between and there was some more knowledge about, "Why should I get angry now because of this or that?" And with the presence of Malcolm there's always a different thing. No, with Can it's never boring. Because the ideas are wide-angle! You're not pinpointed.'

The quintet assembled in France once more, where a German TV crew directed by Hannes Rossacher made a documentary that wasn't broadcast until 1999. With a mix of fly-on-the-wall camerawork, live run-throughs of the *Rite Time* repertoire in Nice and Weilerswist, and footage out and about in the south of France and Cologne, it's an interesting peek into Can's working methods and social interactions. Several times the group are filmed having supper and chatting at a local bistro: they discuss the nature of revolutions and laugh at the news that a Can fan club has sprung up in Texas. Malcolm, in white slacks and a straw trilby, appears to have fully found himself. He gets his first glimpse of the Inner Space cinema studio and the camera even records his historic introduction to Damo Suzuki. The two greet each other like old comrades-in-arms and saunter around the streets of Cologne. Malcolm, towering over him, tells Damo he has been waiting to meet him for twenty years but knows he must have a strong heart, as that's what it takes to work in Can. Malcolm says he himself feels as if he spent two years with the band, then a twenty-year break, and now another two years. Everything moved too fast in the late sixties, he continues, leaving too many unfinished goals – but he denies that Can's music was the factor that drove him crazy. We even see him in New York, teaching clay modelling to kids at the Children's Art Carnival. For Damo's part, he has started a new group and has few thoughts of the past with Can. Irmin is seen commenting that everything about this project is paid for (with the Reinhart donations), so he feels no pressure and no expectations – they have nothing to prove – and the reunion is an easygoing one.

Mercury Records released *Rite Time* in the late summer of 1989, and it was reviewed in more publications simultaneously than any previous Can release. At the end of that year a hole was finally punched in the Berlin Wall, and the process of German reunification began. It was a time for the German media to begin to celebrate Can's legacy, and they were profiled in a wide variety of publications, from the music magazine *Spex* to the German edition of *Cosmopolitan*. Can presented a united front to the UK press too, with features in the weekly music papers. *Rite Time* emerged into a world in which Can were becoming a point of reference for many younger musicians. John Peel's beloved band The Fall issued a song entitled 'I Am Damo Suzuki' on 1985's *This Nation's Saving*

Grace. The track was a shambolic riff on Can's familiar descending four-chord trademark, although in execution all the instruments never quite managed to get in sync. Notorious for their feedback-drenched, riotous concerts, Scottish band the Jesus and Mary Chain featured a white-noise take on 'Mushroom' in their live set, and included it on their 1987 *April Skies* EP. By the end of the decade a wave of mostly British experimental guitar-based groups – including Spacemen 3, My Bloody Valentine, Loop – were namechecking Can as an inspiration for a minimalist, riff- and texture-based rock form that also looked back, as Can did, to the Velvet Underground and the Stooges. Stephen Malkmus of US alt-rock outfit Pavement claimed to have spent three years listening to *Ege Bamyası* every night before falling asleep.

All this was further bolstered when Spoon Records did a deal with Mute in the UK, an independent label with a decidedly German/Europhile angle to its catalogue, and by the end of the decade the whole of Can's back catalogue, on vinyl and CD, became more visible and accessible in retail stores than at any point in the past. Sealing the deal, the first book exclusively on Can was published in English. *The Can Book*, by French music journalist Pascal Bussy and the group's old associate Andy Hall, felt like more of a scrapbook than a digested biography, consisting of individual Q&As with the founders, plus Malcolm, Damo and Hildegard, but it collected in one place more information about the group than had appeared before. All of this activity, coupled with the optimistic and historic events sweeping East and West Germany in the dying days of the eighties, would have made this the perfect moment for a reformed Can to strike out on a last tour, or the long-desired push in America. But everyone knew there would not and could not be a Can stage show any more. *Rite Time* was left in orbit, an eccentric satellite joining the existing cluster of Can emissions. Once more, transmissions fell silent.

With a couple of small exceptions, *Rite Time* proved to be the last broadcast from Can's collapsed star. In 1991 Wim Wenders was putting together his flawed sci-fi movie *Until the End of the World*. Since *Alice in the Cities* Wenders had become a world-respected international film-maker, and his musical connections extended from Ry Cooder to U2. For this movie, set forward in time in 1999, he invited many of his favourite musicians to supply a track they imagined they might produce in that year. Can's last communal recording session at the Can Studio generated 'Last Night Sleep', a three-minute piece with a sinuous log-drum beat and a soporific blanket of synths and guitars. Malcolm was there too, with a more restrained vocal than on *Rite Time*, yet the track has all the quiet intensity of vintage Can, with its uncanny image of a girl holding green onions in her hand, listening to the sound of the band. He explains: 'It was dedicated to the daughter of my friend Frederick Brown [an American abstract expressionist painter] and his wife Megan . . . They had just moved to Arizona and their daughter had just picked green onions out in the yard . . . that's how the whole thing started. And it was written actually on the plane on the way to Cologne, and I think it was the first time Can and I had worked and done a song within two or three hours.' While he was in France, Malcolm confides, 'There are some takes we did with Jaki, me, Micky and an African bass player. We did five songs that have never been released at Micky's place, Outer Space.' The opening verse of 'Last Night Sleep', playing off a running theme of the film, had to suffice as an epitaph for this most telepathic of units.

> Dreams seen by a man-made machine
> How does it seem, how does it seem
> That we can see each other's dreams . . .

18

In the Distance Lies the Future

What the Beatles were to the sixties, and punk/disco was to the seventies, so house and techno were to the eighties: new paradigms in the production, scope, aesthetics and fanbase of contemporary pop music. Into the nineties electronic music and hip hop spawned a multitude of strange flora and fauna, not all of it dance music as such, but all sharing the common factor that they no longer required the traditional structure of a recording studio, a manager, an album-tour schedule, even a record deal. As music went digital, it also went DIY. A thousand global music-makers could install their own Inner Space studio within the silicon chips of their personal computers. In addition, this type of music featured almost no lyrical content, which made it accessible to any pair of ears in any nation or culture on the planet.

In the terms dictated by the music industry over most of the twentieth century, this was a form of sacrilege. Equally heretical was the notion, pervasive in the mid-nineties, of the remix. Just because they *could*, people *did*, offering up the master tapes or tracks of their own music to be reconstructed, re-edited and reshaped by a third party. This had the commercial logic of adding a high-profile remixer's name to an otherwise obscure release, or acted as a form of mutual cap-doffing between like-minded artists.

It was appropriate, then, that *Sacrilege* became the title of Can's next promoted project. Initiated in 1996 by the head of Mute Records, Daniel Miller, this was a double CD of sixteen remixes commissioned from an array of artists, both old friends of the group and admirers from a younger generation: Brian Eno, Pete Shelley, Sonic Youth, the Orb, A Guy Called Gerald, UNKLE, Carl Craig. Miller himself, teaming up with Gareth Jones as Sunroof, rendered 'Oh Yeah' almost unrecognisable as ferocious drum 'n' bass. German artists included the commercial dance outfit Westbam, Cologne duo Air Liquide and experimental samplist Holger Hiller. Steve Hillage of System 7, former guitarist in Gong, praised Can's 'deeply artistic anarchy'. Bruce Gilbert from the British art-rock band Wire, who arguably retained something of Can's angularity in their bloodstream, turned a stray sample of 'TV Spot' into a Noh drama. Eno stated he was disappointed with his own effort: 'turning things into loops destroys the delicate balance you always kept between the mechanical and the human . . . A word of advice: if you want to make records for people to remix, make less brilliant records in the first place.'[1] Kris Needs, who saw Can live in 1973 and wrote about them in *Zigzag* magazine in 1976, was now a club DJ and techno producer working under the name Secret Knowledge, and his mix of 'Oh Yeah' – it began with the atom bomb, but actually it was more like a trippy version of 'Halleluwah' – included a new bassline from Jah Wobble. Featured on a documentary filmed by Spoon at the time, Needs spoke warmly of his generation's attraction to Can: 'There was an organic current going through the group which connected the individuals. It was like a bunch of lunatics let loose on instruments, and they weren't conventional instruments. Irmin's keyboard sounded like a flying saucer going off half the time; Holger played bass with his gloves. The singers just used to make it up as they went along. The guitarist just sounded like he was playing on the moon. You know, it was just alien funk, really.'[2]

Remix culture was finally catching up with and infecting the corpus of avant-garde contemporary music: remix albums of Iannis Xenakis and Pierre Henry also came out in 1997. If nothing else, remix culture was opening up audiences to new and more challenging forms of music. *Sacrilege* was no improvement on Can's originals, but it was a refreshing revitalisation of their catalogue at a timely moment, its best tracks were a reminder of Can's continuing relevance, and the members themselves publicly embraced the project warmly. 'They have done us great justice,' Michael told me. 'I stood there after dinner and listened to the tapes, and I danced the whole way through. From the beginning to the end I was on my feet.'

For all the united front Can presented in 1997, there was an undertone of discomfort with dwelling too much on the past. Rock and pop was entering a nostalgic phase, with celebrations of classic canonical albums and a mound of reissues piling up monthly. By contrast, Can talked of the present and the future, and there was never any suggestion that they would re-form. They began popping up in unexpected contexts. One night in 1998 I was attending a massive underground techno event at a Cologne warehouse. In the ultraviolet-lit bar I met Holger and his wife, the singer U-She (aka Ursula Kloss), who were checking out the latest examples of minimalist, primary-coloured Cologne techno. Around this time Holger was actually collaborating on stage and on record with Dr Walker and others from the techno collective Liquid Sky. A few minutes later I stumbled up the wrong concrete stairwell and burst in on some kind of practice room. Jaki was sitting there at his drums, with a handful of electronic musicians including Burnt Friedman (aka Bernd Friedmann). Friedman was one of the more imaginative of Cologne's electronica producers, with a strong feel for unconventional, Latin-influenced time signatures. He and Jaki began working together around the late nineties, and the partnership continued for years afterwards, with a fascinating series of releases and performances under the name Secret Rhythms.

Both Michael and Jaki had been working with Damo Suzuki the previous year. Still living in Cologne, Damo had slowly found his way back into music, first with a band called Dunkelziffer in the mid-eighties, and later hooking up with Mani Neumeier of Guru

Guru and Michael Karoli for some concerts in Japan and the US in 1997–8 as Damo Suzuki's NETWORK, an improvised rock unit. At the end of the century Damo came up with the ingenious notion of travelling around the world picking up impromptu groups of musicians, amateur and professional, trained and untrained, in every location he played. In this way he kept his own inventive powers continually renewed, making friends all over the world, and he was still conducting his 'Neverending Tour' well into the second decade of the twenty-first century.

Jaki had been effectively working as a jobbing drummer. He still kept a seat in Jah Wobble's innumerable groups, including Invaders of the Heart, and was beginning to venture out with his own electro-rhythmic trio, Club Off Chaos, formed in 1996 with Boris Polonski and Dirk Herweg. This later mutated into Drums Off Chaos, a collective that sucked in many of Cologne's younger percussionists who were looking to deepen their understanding of rhythmic principles. In this configuration he had radically rethought the conventional drum kit, and was now playing what he called a 'drum set', without any kick drum, cymbals or hi-hat. In a phone interview with me at the time he explained how he was making a scientific study of rhythm, creating his own Morse code-like beat system based on a mathematical combination of small rhythmic cells. 'I'm preparing a book about this kind of drumming,' he told me – though this publication has yet to materialise. He called this system 'E-T', corresponding to the dash and the dot at the heart of the method. The dot was a one-handed strike; the dash was two strikes with one hand, the second never as loud as the first. Dots and dashes had to be played by alternate hands. Aligning this dogma with the physical laws of stick weight, drum tension, gravity and the proportions of the human body, Jaki and his colleagues discovered an open-ended system that allowed real-time composition based on mathematics and geometric patterns, fractal accumulation and ancient classical proportions.

Irmin's big achievement was the completion and premiere of his first opera. Since around 1994–5 he had been labouring over a full-scale 'fantasy opera' adaptation of Mervyn Peake's *Gormenghast* trilogy, a weird Gothic labyrinth of English phantasmagorical fiction published between 1946 and 1959. Duncan Fallowell, who introduced Irmin to Peake's work as an alternative to Tolkien, wrote a libretto that transplanted Irmin's ritualistic scenarios, shaped around incidents in Peake's books, into his own words. (Although the author's literary estate finally granted the rights to adapt the work, they did not give permission to quote from it directly.) Lasting upwards of three hours, *Gormenghast* premiered at Wuppertal Opera House in November 1998, scored for orchestra, string quartet, percussion, samples, and classical and rock singers.

Set in an enormous, crumbling castle symbolising a decaying tyranny, and with its main protagonist Steerpike the rebellious kitchen boy, *Gormenghast* condensed artistic preoccupations Irmin had held all his life. 'Steerpike is . . . a mythical hero, who, akin to the trickster, provokes chaos in order to bring about the transformation of an exhausted system,' Irmin wrote in the opera's programme notes. There was something of the anarchic spirit of 1968 in Steerpike, even when transplanted to the macabre, grotesque atmosphere of Peake's alternative universe.

Irmin's son-in-law, British electronic musician Jono Podmore (aka Kumo), assisted with the music production, especially in constructing electronic beats and rhythms that contributed to the work's swift-flowing pace and sense of barely repressed hysteria. Operatic voices, orchestral, chamber and drum 'n' bass elements became surprisingly sensual bedfellows. Between 1999 and 2004 it was staged at several other venues in Germany and Luxembourg, and a CD of highlights came out on Spoon in 2000.

The closest thing to a Can reunion came in 1999, when several 'Can Solo Projects' concerts were presented at a handful of European halls. This was no nostalgic reunion, but a showcase for the individual musical endeavours of Irmin, Holger, Michael and Jaki, showing how all four had continued to expand their parameters, tracing their own connections and networks.

The concerts began in Berlin in March 1999, travelling to Hamburg, Cologne and Frankfurt in the same month. Holger, working with the techno artist Gvoon, opened the evenings with long ambient passages that coalesced into more beat-driven work. Midway through his set, U-She entered the stage to sing the Velvet Underground's 'Sunday Morning'. 'He loves the new media,' wrote one reviewer of the show at Berlin's Columbiahalle, 'and it seems a lot more fun in his pixilated [*sic*] hands than in the dour world of Microsoft accountancy.'[3]

Sofortkontakt (Instant Contact) was Michael's current group, named after a late-night TV ad for a sex hotline. With Felix Gutierrez and Alexander Schoenert making up the trio, they played ponderous rock, with Michael alternating between violin and guitar. Jaki unleashed the long rhythmic DNA spirals of his Club Off Chaos percussion group. Irmin appeared as part of a new duo he had formed with Kumo. Both live and on record (2008's *Axolotl Eyes*), in this pairing Irmin once more found an outlet for his more aggressive and spontaneous keyboard and sound-processing wizardry. The older man's feel for cinematic atmospheres and keyboard virtuosity could now be supplemented with more contemporary beats and rhythms and occasional vocals. Holger said his last goodbyes at the Berlin 'Solo Project' concert, when the four Can founders took a final collective bow at around one o'clock in the morning. It was the last time that quartet would be seen together on stage in public.

One final, little-known Can recording was made in 1999. As a millennial project, the Grönland label, run by former pop star Herbert Grönemeyer, commissioned German artists to record cover versions of significant *Deutsche* songs from the twentieth century for a compilation entitled *Pop 2000 – Das gibt's nur einmal*. Blixa Bargeld of

Einstürzende Neubauten chose 'Soul Desert', and Can – perhaps as one final 'EFS' – chose an electronic version of the theme from Carol Reed's classic movie *The Third Man* from 1949. It was almost Can, at any rate: Irmin, Michael and Jaki, with Jono Podmore taking Holger's place on the bass.

Holger was, therefore, absent from further Can solo concerts between August and October 1999, which took them from Cologne to Dublin, the Hague and London's Barbican. The music writer Mike Barnes, who attended the latter show, remembers how Jaki, 'as he sat upright, impassive, reminded me of the idea of the Zen calligrapher, who has amassed years of experience but then makes his best work by stilling his mind before executing the "one breath, one stroke".' As for the Irmin Schmidt/Kumo duo, 'Some of the music was quite pastoral, with Irmin playing lyrical piano to a largely ambient accompaniment, but then it all raced off into techno velocity sequences, with untempered noise and rich timbral effects. There was clearly an empathy between them, and their set was always absorbing and sometimes exciting. Each of the sets had an integrity, but it was the most exploratory of the three.' Michael, meanwhile, spent his set 'sauntering around onstage, his guitar slung casually across his back and playing his violin'. Out of sight, he was performing with a medical drip attached. He had recently been diagnosed with terminal cancer.

On 17 November 2001 Michael died in Essen, the town where he had spent much of his youthful life. He had been in Germany for the previous weeks and even made an informal recording session in Dortmund with some of his new friends, drummer Thomas Hopf and electronic musician Mark Spybey. The youngest of Can's originators – he was fifty-three – was the first to depart the planet, and he apparently did so suddenly, while in the act of playing his guitar. He left behind his wife Shirley and two daughters. On the Spoon Records website, tributes piled in from all over the world.

The ensuing years were ones of renewal and consolidation. Can was presented with a Lifetime Achievement Award at Germany's Echo Awards in 2003. Herbert Grönemeyer introduced the surviving members with a five-minute speech, and the trophy was handed over by members of the Red Hot Chili Peppers. Remastered editions of the whole Can catalogue appeared on Spoon/Mute in 2004. This was the first wholesale restoration of Can's recorded legacy since the original releases, and despite the difficulty of dealing with the early two-track recordings, a surprising amount of clarity and detail emerged. Reviewing the new editions for *The Wire*, I pointed out that 'each album is about one third louder, exposing far more detail and amplifying the sense of acoustic space'.[4] A layer of murk had been rubbed off in the restoration; if you listened hard enough, you could hear birds tweeting outside Schloss Nörvenich during 'Yoo Doo Right'.

In 2007 the interior of the Can Studio was sold to the RocknPop Museum in Gronau, in the Westphalia region of north-western Germany. Holger and U-She moved into the shell of the cinema at Weilerswist. As a musician Holger slowly faded from view, though CDs on his own label, Dignose, occasionally surfaced featuring his electronic music, such as *La Luna* (2000), *Linear City* (2001) and *21st Century* (2007). The sleeve of the last one showed Holger and U-She seated, talking on mobile phones, on a pair of canary-yellow chairs in the middle of the main space in the Can Studio, which now resembled a vast loft-style living room. Since the late nineties he had been running a personal website, czukay.de, containing a typically humorous and eclectic range of commentary, and retrospective nods to his past and his former colleagues. The site, which also contained sound samples, a shop and video clips, dried up but remains online. During his tenure of Can's former studio, rumours occasionally surfaced that he was re-recording all of his solo albums, but the originals received an official re-release in 2015.

When the studio was cleared out, it finally became imperative to address the problem of Can's master tapes, which had been stashed in a small utility room at Weilerswist for decades. Irmin enlisted Jono Podmore to help sift and assess the fifty hours of material on the reels, much of it unheard by the Can members since it was first recorded. There were tracks dating right back to the group's residence at Schloss Nörvenich, featuring saxophonist Gerd Dudek, various film soundtracks, live versions of familiar songs and abstractions such as 'Evening All Day', constructed from the ambient sounds of a room and accidental contact with the instruments within it. There were seven tracks featuring Malcolm Mooney that even the group had forgotten existed. And there were several examples of works in progress, giving a clear insight into how much the LP versions of Can tracks were only one possible outcome from a soup of alternatives. The restoration process ended up with thirty tracks, dating between 1968 and 1977, which came out on Spoon/Mute as *The Lost Tapes* in 2012. In 2015 a box set of the complete Can catalogue, including a first-time reissue of the much-maligned *Out of Reach*, was issued on vinyl, while a collected set of Can singles was assembled in 2017. With these events, the officially sanctioned body of Can's recorded traces has been set in order.

On 8 April 2017, a full house at a major London arts venue had the chance to see Irmin Schmidt the orchestral conductor. *The Can Project* was a one-off event at the Barbican Centre at which Can's music could be shown extending back into the orchestral realm where Irmin (and Holger) began, and also featured a reconstructive tribute to the band's raw electric power by a specially assembled supergroup. Irmin strode onto the stage in tie and tails to lead the London Symphony Orchestra in his *Can Dialog*, a new composition with the younger composer Gregor Schwellenbach. Lasting around twenty-five minutes, this piece swarmed and seethed like a restless ocean, occasionally allowing chunks of half-recognisable songs such as 'Sing Swan Song', 'Spoon' and 'Halleluwah' to float to the surface. Far from a kitsch orchestral medley, this was an attempt to make new, to retain Can's spirit of transformation, squeezing this Establishment symphony orchestra into unfamiliar patterns and textures.

After the interval, two drum kits, amplifiers and keyboards were wheeled on stage. The group calling itself The Can Project was nominally led by Thurston Moore, former guitarist with Sonic Youth. He had called in a dream team of associates: fellow Sonic Youth member Steve Shelley on drums (Valentina Magaletti played the other set); Deb Googe of My Bloody Valentine on bass; British improviser Pat Thomas on keyboards; James Sedwards on guitar; and Tom Relleen on electronics. The vocalist, making a triumphant and coherent return after so many years, was none other than Malcolm Mooney.

The Can Project stuck to familiar songs almost exclusively from Mooney's heyday, and the singer seldom deviated from the script, turning in an exuberant and self-confident performance. By zoning in on Can's monolithic essence, the instrumentalists gave possibly the closest approximation of a genuine Can live show it was possible to hear in the twenty-first century.

However, tragic absence loomed over the evening. It should have been Jaki in Steve Shelley's drum seat, but three months earlier, on 22 January 2017, Jaki had died after a brief but intense bout of pneumonia. The illness had come upon him suddenly; he had been looking forward to a year of drumming engagements, and particularly this Barbican show, where he would have been reunited musically with Malcolm after so many years. He refused medication, but after becoming delirious his wife, Birgit Berger, and son Ben took him to a Cologne hospital, where he said his goodbyes and passed away in his sleep. Can's mainspring, unwound at the age of seventy-eight.

Absent from the funeral was Holger, who had recently suffered a fall which had injured his femoral neck. For most of the 2000s his wife U-She had been permanently ill, with a condition that left her confined to a wheelchair. According to Irmin, the couple largely rejected conventional medicine or treatment, so Holger was her de facto full-time carer. Now approaching eighty, he was continually exhausted. He hardly travelled outside of Weilerswist and received few visitors. His final communication with me – an email response to a request to drop by the studio – read: 'Dear Rob, Sorry – I'm afraid. TIME WENT ON ALL THE TIME. I got old and they plaster me with interviews like never before. CAN became old now as nothing really new had happened.' He batted away almost all interview requests, except for one from *Mojo* journalist Ian Harrison in mid-2016, who reported that Holger had aged dramatically and seemed mentally distracted, although he did eventually focus his mind on the earlier years.

U-She passed away on 28 July 2017, her fifty-fifth birthday. Holger was, of course, devastated, but he made efforts to pick up his life, buying a new sofa and TV in readiness to move back to his flat in Cologne. He planned to archive his tapes and hard drives and anticipated a 'Czukay 80' tour to accompany a collected-works box set Grönland had planned for 2018. However, on 5 September 2017 he was found dead in the studio, apparently of natural causes. His funeral took place on 14 September in Cologne.

What epitaph can you lay on a shapeshifter? I recall him in 1997, gleefully quoting Katharine Hepburn: 'The people can write about me what they want, as long as it's not the truth.'

Cologne to Gronau

Raindrops pelt the windscreen as I dodge the heavy trucks heading north on the autobahn out of Cologne. With *Future Days* on the car stereo, the journey flies by, and just over an hour later I'm locking the vehicle in a waterlogged car park surrounded by artificial gardens planted in child-friendly floral patterns. Gronau is well off Germany's tourist trail: a medium-sized provincial medieval town, with obligatory post-war pedestrianised shopping centre, just inside the border with the Netherlands. What brings people from out of town is the RocknPop Museum, the huge modernist building that squats in between these ornate pleasure gardens at 1 Udo-Lindenberg-Platz. The address takes its name from one of the museum's co-founders, German rock star Udo Lindenberg, who was born in Gronau and has contributed to the creation of a legacy that celebrates a century of German popular music history.

Eight euros get you through the turnstile. I stroll around the huge basement exhibition space, its timeline starting with the arrival of American jazz in Germany, the evolution of popular song in the Weimar age, the Nazification of popular song in wartime propaganda, the outlawing of various forms of improvised and otherwise degenerate music, proto-*Deutsch* rock 'n' roll, and the inevitable visit of the Beatles and other western groups (the museum displays one of the vocal mics used at the infamous Shea Stadium concert and the Gibson Flying V guitar photographed on the cover of Pete Townshend's *All the Best Cowboys Have Chinese Eyes* LP). From then on West and East German music artefacts from different eras and subcultures are given their own glass cases: mid-sixties pop, psychedelia and hippy music, the Krautrock bands, Kraftwerk, punk and the *Neue Deutsche Welle*, the Scorpions, techno and club music, various domestically famous German rock stars, including one Udo Lindenberg, and so on. A school trip here wouldn't get a bad picture of the nation's main contributions to pop. On this weekday I have the place almost to myself.

But this is not what I've come here to see. In a corner of the foyer is a large industrial elevator. Inside, there are only two buttons to press. The gleaming steel doors slide shut and I lift off for the second floor. Moments later, they slide apart, and you step into Inner Space.

The Can Studio occupies a floor all to itself. Although the space where it's installed is smaller than the original, and the ceiling lower, the initial impression is not so far from my experience at the actual cinema in Weilerswist, nearly twenty years ago. The calm, the thickened quality of the air, the sense of space intuitively divided and mapped for optimised acoustics. The lighting is subdued, but the atmosphere is vivid and optically revitalising. This is mainly due to the white-painted parquet floor, which reflects the coloured lighting, and the vibrant painted wall hangings. Only a couple of the sound-damping mattresses have remained, and even they had to be placed in huge deep-freeze cabinets for a few days to kill off an infestation of bedbugs before they could be hung in the museum. At one end is a giant tapestry of colourful home-made flags from imaginary nations. A new sonic republic welcomes careful listeners.

Whatever equipment wasn't salvaged by the band members when René Tinner closed the studio has wound up on display in Gronau. Much of it is rare and idiosyncratic. There's a hexagonal wooden table on wheels called an '*Abhörtisch*' that seems to have been some kind of group monitoring hub for multiple headphone inputs. Cables and connectors hang coiled on a massive wall rack. Collections of percussion and exotic instruments lie around on tabletops: cowbells, bamboo rattles, brass finger-cymbals, an African talking drum, bells from Vietnam, Indonesia, China and Japan. Hand-painted castanets surely picked up from a tourist stall in Ibiza. Pan pipes, wood flutes and tambourines: the instruments of Greek mythology. A gong, its iron hub engraved with a pentagram. The tools of the musician, waiting to be flooded with magic.

Glass partitions on wheels separate the different instrumental zones. A drum kit and a pair of congas, black paint flaking, lurk in a semi-sealed booth. Fender guitars and Marshall amps huddle under the flags. A grand piano sprawls in the centre. Beyond it is a keyboard fetishist's dream corner: an enormous vintage Hammond organ, with a bench big enough for two and a yellowing copy of the original instruction manual; a rotating Leslie speaker; a Fender Rhodes electric piano; and a cream Farfisa organ with grey and white keyboard. An even rarer-looking device called a Crumar

Organiser 2 features a double keyboard, plastic drawbars and an electronic 'nerve centre' with an enigmatic parade of grey, black and red buttons for selecting rhythms.

Hollow concrete breeze blocks support the studio monitors and double as bookshelves for all the equipment manuals in fat ring binders. This leads you to the heart of the operation: the extraordinary mixing console. Constructed from rare African redwood, this carcass is utterly unique and was built to house the Can Studio's array of mixing desks and effects racks. The original mixing desk was recently replaced, as no one could be found to repair it, but many of the other military-grade rack effects clearly date from the early seventies. The two suitcase-sized Telefunken reel-to-reel tape recorders, housed in square wooden boxes, might be even older. This studio has been deliberately remade as a fully functional replica that can be used for events, recording sessions and occasional online transmissions. The flashing amber lamp, dating back to Can's first studio in Schloss Nörvenich, has found its place on top of the mixer.

In another corner is a workshop and maintenance area, with soldering iron, tools and cupboards lined with old files and storage units. A TV monitor plays back live footage of Can and a touch screen gives a history of the band and the studio, as well as recent interview clips. It's a lot to take in, and thankfully the old relaxation area has been recreated just as it was, with the crescent-shaped beige velveteen sofa and coffee table. In places the fabric has worn thin: band members sat themselves down here countless times after takes, to smoke, drink and chat, sign promotional photos, read the papers, entertain friends and journalists, or just zone out, rest the ears and let the mind wander among the mattresses.

As I sink into the sofa I watch other, mostly German visitors to the museum passing through. One couple in their thirties have clearly come specifically on a Can pilgrimage: they ask questions to the museum attendant who is on hand in the room, and stare reverently around at all the gear and decorations. Almost all the others who poke their noses in have a puzzled expression; they have to ask what it is they are looking at. Despite the video screen showing clips of Can in performance, and the information touch screen, the notion of a Can Studio simply draws a blank. They may have seen movies featuring the group's music; might, if pushed, own up to recognising 'Spoon' or 'I Want More'; but Can is clearly still not a household name in Germany.

That remains true of the wider world, too. You could argue that Can was a group of cognoscenti making music for other cognoscenti – but that doesn't quite pan out, especially when you look at the large-scale tours of the mid-seventies, the critical acclaim, the huge crowds at the Cologne Sporthalle, the Arles festival, the final concert in Lisbon. Their enormous potential to rock the US was never given its opportunity. For ten years or so after they split up, Can kept a relatively low profile, even while exerting a covert influence on some of the decade's outstanding alternative music: Joy Division, The Fall, Talking Heads' *Fear of Music* and *Remain in Light* (compare with *Soon Over Babaluma*), Cabaret Voltaire, 23 Skidoo, Happy Mondays.

I began picking up on Can in the very late eighties, a time when little of the back catalogue was easily available in shops. In the music press, Can began to be a name dropped with increasing frequency by artists in both the indie-rock and acid-house/techno sectors. Then came the release of *Rite Time* in 1989, and the band itself emerged briefly back in the spotlight. That was surprisingly good timing. Loop, the British guitar group, recorded a monolithic, nerve-shredding cover of 'Mother Sky', complete with explosions, on their 1989 EP *Black Sun*. Credible alternative figures such as Julian Cope and Genesis P-Orridge became more vocal cheerleaders of German rock, and Bobby Gillespie of Primal Scream often mentioned Can as one of his favourite groups. The 1997 Primal

Scream single 'Kowalski' sampled drums from 'Halleluwah', and Jaki Liebezeit eventually guested, uncredited, on their *XTRMNTR* album of 2000. The spaciousness, rhythmic delicacy, near-inaudible lyrics and sonic experimentation of Talk Talk's farewell album *Laughing Stock* (1991) owed a big debt to Can's sound. Stereolab's Farfisa-driven metronomic rock, with sloganeering lyrics that harked back to a pseudo-1968 sensibility, helped turn younger listeners on to the historic motorik of Neu! and Can. Their Chicago-based contemporaries, the instrumental group Tortoise, concocted a mix of surging polyrhythms, egoless soloing, electronics and electric guitars, bred from a similar hothouse of jazz, rock and avant-garde sensibility. Meanwhile, in New York James Murphy of the US group LCD Soundsystem wore a *Future Days* T-shirt on stage and in photo shoots; the group deployed the meta-consciousness of Can even as it delivered seductive and overwhelmingly infectious rhythmic heft.

Can continues to reach a wider public through the medium of cinema. The films Can soundtracked in its early years were mostly obscure cult movies and porn flicks. Recently, more mainstream music editors have included Can tracks in various cinema releases: *Broken Embraces*, *Norwegian Wood*, *The Bling Ring*, *Inherent Vice*, *Life After Beth*, *High Rise*. In Germany 'She Brings the Rain' was placed in both Wim Wenders's *Lisbon Story* (1994) and Oskar Roehler's *Die Unberührbare* (2000), while Can music was used to brilliant, jarring effect in a BBC documentary on the Baader-Meinhof group, *In Love with Terror*, in 2002. Jonny Greenwood, guitarist in Radiohead and accomplished soundtrack composer, selected the Can tracks in *Norwegian Wood* (Tran Anh Hung, 2010) and *Inherent Vice* (Paul Thomas Anderson, 2015). Radiohead (as well as John Frusciante of the Red Hot Chili Peppers) have been one of the highest-profile champions of Can's music, often including a cover of 'The Thief' in their live sets, and throughout Radiohead's international tour of 2017 their rhythm section – two drummers and a bassist – sounded markedly Can-like in its mechanised discipline. The Scottish author Alan Warner has dedicated novels to Holger Czukay and Michael Karoli, and Lynne Ramsay's 2002 film adaptation of Warner's book *Morvern Callar* featured two Can tunes, as well as a couple by Holger Czukay. (Warner even published a short book on *Tago Mago* in 2015.[5])

Meanwhile, at least five groups have named themselves with an overt nod to Can: Moonshake, Spoon, Hunters and Collectors, Ege Bamyası and the Mooney Suzuki. In the hip-hop sphere, Kanye West's *Graduation* (2007) included a rap reboot of 'Sing Swan Song' entitled 'Drunk and Hot Girls', while a cover of 'Vitamin C' by young rappers Raury and Jaden Smith snuck its way into the soundtrack of the Netflix series *The Get Down* (2016).

It's tempting to place Can within a deep, innovative, Germanic music and art tradition that would include J. S. Bach, Ludwig van Beethoven, Arnold Schönberg, Kurt Schwitters, Karlheinz Stockhausen, Joseph Beuys, Kraftwerk, Einstürzende Neubauten and others. That is to say, a lineage that has a connection with process, structure, monotony, rhythmic rigour, communication beyond language, universalism, material heaviness, technological advance. The nineties and onwards, with its huge technological leaps in music production and the dawn of the digital age, has seen a younger, united Germany embrace electronic music, forging close connections with parallel developments in Detroit, Chicago, London, Tokyo and elsewhere, while honing its own identity. In Cologne itself the artists around the Kompakt label concocted minimalist repetitive beats with laser precision, while the Cologne/Düsseldorf-based duo Mouse on Mars playfully sculpted infectious electronic grooves and seductive textures, informed by more avant-garde and contemporary music practice (member Jan St. Werner later became head of the STEIM institute in Amsterdam). In Berlin the floating collective of producers around the Basic Channel/Chain Reaction/

Rhythm and Sound labels devised intoxicating, billowing clouds of transforming sound around quartz vibrations. Like Can in the late seventies, Rhythm and Sound absorbed reggae and dub – a rare opening up from a German act to the influence of the Caribbean. Austrian four-piece Elektro Guzzi came out around 2010 playing a form of minutely calibrated techno using only acoustic instruments, taking Can's idea of playing like a telepathic machine to new quantum levels of musicianship and endurance.

There are similarities and points of connection here, even if the music doesn't sound precisely like Can. No one can do that. More important is the permission Can clearly gave for Germanic music to embrace the machine, to thieve the Promethean fire of technology and make it human. To put forward a distinctive German musical sensibility without shame, unhindered by the calamities of the past.

Now a genre-tag in its own right, 'Krautrock' has become press-release shorthand for any kind of vaguely mechanical beat coupled with unusual sounds, a combination that was prevalent with the dual rise of 'post-rock' and electronic/digital music. Kraftwerk, of course, was the one group that broke through into the international pop market. By refining the banality of automation, consumerism and primitive computer culture into a series of hit singles in the late seventies, their music chimed with a notion of the new Germany rebuilding itself as a centre of technological excellence, to which individuality was sacrificed to efficiency and precision. Aside from Nena's '99 Luftballons', few German acts matched their success.

Krautrock connoisseurship grew during the nineties. Julian Cope's book *Krautrocksampler* (1995) overflowed with hyperbolic purple prose, but acted as a handy primer to a wide and wacky range of Teutonic hippies and mavericks. CD reissues brought hitherto obscure music back into the frame. The problem was that you didn't have to move very far outside the circle of 'core' groups – Can, Faust, Cluster/Harmonia, Ash Ra Tempel, Amon Düül I and II,

Popol Vuh, Neu!, Guru Guru, Tangerine Dream – before the quality rapidly went downhill. With enough exceptions to prove the rule,
the central encampment was ringed with low-burning fires, straggly
scenesters, stoned opportunists and mediocre minstrels. Even the
cream of the crop tended to have fairly mono-dimensional qualities. Kraftwerk were micro-electronic efficiency gurus. Amon Düül,
Amon Düül II, Guru Guru and Ash Ra Tempel kept things spontaneous and frayed at the edges. (Mani Neumeier, drummer in Guru
Guru, was in a similar position to Jaki in the late sixties, a free jazz
drummer (with the Globe Unity Orchestra, Irène Schweizer and
others) who aspired to play rock. Yet he never totally shed the jazz
looseness.) Faust's cheerfully destructive impulses were bolstered
by the post-1968 spirit, but they refused to bring them under control in neat song forms, nor tailor them to fit film soundtracks, nor
write hit singles. Cluster, Popol Vuh and Tangerine Dream opened
up vast dreamworlds of sound, painting ambient atmospherics with
a composer's ears. Neu! will forever be associated with pistoning,
mechanical beats along the endless autobahn.

With hindsight, Can stands apart from all of its contemporaries by encompassing all these qualities in some measure. Like this
rebuilt studio on the upper floor of a musical museum, it is separated from the rest of German rock history, located literally above
it all. In Can's music there are strong connections with everything
that's exhibited downstairs, and yet it somehow doesn't quite fit anywhere in that story. It's both part of it and apart from it.

The musicians' broad combined experience as individuals made
them harmonically and rhythmically the most sophisticated and/or
most primitive. Noise, rock, free improvisation, avant-garde and
ethnic music, even reggae travelled through Can's wires in vivid
hybrid combinations. It could open up to total abstraction, lock
into exhilarating, pulsing monotony, sparkle with effervescent
textures and invent radiant atmospheres of beauty and mystery.
And when the urge struck, it could compress all of this down to

a perfectly turned three-minute wonder. Can did not so much lead the pack as keep its distance from the rest. It achieved its difference by remaining apart, untroubled by fashion and zeitgeist, largely unpressured by commercial necessity. Can found its ideal membership, and together they built a universe in a shell and filled it with sound.

Contemplating what remains of that shell, in a sofa on the second floor of a rock museum in the top-left-hand corner of Germany, it would be too easy to survey the gradually loosening mutual bonds, the stripping of the Can Studio, and the recent deaths of various members, and feel a leadening sense of melancholy. But that would be against the spirit of Can, and I refuse to do so. Unlike so much other music from its era, Can has armoured itself with a force field that has resisted getting old. It does not belong to the dust heap of rock obscurity or the increasingly desperate revival industry. It is no longer locked to a place, or to material objects like old amps and drum skins. Its ecstasies and enigmas continue to thrill listeners and inspire musicians, but none of them can ever quite explain its mysterious marvels nor replicate its dizzy sonic webs. The sites significant to Can – Schloss Nörvenich, Inner Space – are historically charged, but there is no sense of loss associated with revisiting them now that they have been abandoned. Like Can itself, the present day has found other uses for them.

In the end, what Can sounded like at any given time is not important. What it stands for, at both its zenith and nadir, is a philosophy and a practice that applies to music, to human society, to life itself. Can does not choose the route to stagnation, as a ghost stuck in a forgotten time warp. It stays alive, electric, liquid, seeking the path of least resistance, the swiftest course towards the future.

For all time, the gates remain open.

Notes

Quotes are taken from interviews with the author, unless indicated.

2 *Pandemonium Manifestos*

1 Bruce Tantum, 'Vanguard: Irmin Schmidt', *XLR8R*, 11 December 2015

2 Hans Mayer went on to become an internationally renowned gallerist, representing artists including Andy Warhol, Joseph Beuys, Christian Boltanski, Anthony Caro, Tony Cragg, Liam Gillick, Keith Haring, Nam June Paik, Robert Rauschenberg and more

3 Michael Kurtz and Richard Toop, *Stockhausen: A Biography* (London: Faber and Faber, 1994), p 36. Quoted in Martin Iddon, *New Music at Darmstadt: Nono, Stockhausen, Cage, Boulez* (Cambridge: Cambridge University Press, 2013)

4 On another occasion Irmin described the run-through as lasting 'one whole afternoon and night. [Holger] was trying to teach me the percussion part of a composition he wanted [to] have performed. It wasn't really percussion: I had to rub with foam rubber . . . in a real complicated way: with the left hand I had to do nine, with an accent on the five, where in the right I had to do eleven with an accent on the five and the third. So that was really heavy work, you know.' Andrew Graham-Stewart, Can interview (unpublished transcript), July 1973

5 D. Straus, 'I'm So Green: Can's Holger Czukay on his Berlin Youth', *Exberliner* (September 2006), archived at http://www.exberliner. com/nightlife/reviews--interviews/interview-holger-czukay/

6 Oliver Lowenstein, 'Science Music and the Angel Radar: Being Holger Czukay', *Fourth Door Review*, no. 1, 1996

7 Ian Harrison, Holger Czukay interview, *Mojo* 273 (August 2016) (quote from complete transcript)

8 http://media.hyperreal.org/zines/est/intervs/czukay.html

9 Harrison, Holger Czukay interview

10 Jason Gross, Holger Czukay interview, *Perfect Sound Forever*, February 1997; http://www.furious.com/perfect/holger.html

11 Arno Frank, 'Can-Musiker Holger Czukay im interview: "Musik hat immer etwas Absolutes"', *Der Spiegel*, 1 January 2014 (author's translation)

12 Damon Krukowski, Can interview, *Ptolemaic Terrascope*, 1998. http://www.terrascope.co.uk/MyBackPages/Can.htm

13 M. J. Grant, *Serial Music, Serial Aesthetics: Compositional Theory in Post-War Europe* (Cambridge: Cambridge University Press, 2005)

14 Robert Beyer, 'Das Problem der "Kommenden Musik"' (1928), quoted in Grant, 2005

15 Karlheinz Stockhausen, Programme notes, *Hymnen*, New York Philharmonic at Lincoln Center, 1971

16 Cornelius Cardew, *Stockhausen Serves Imperialism* (London: Latimer New Dimensions Limited, 1974)

17 On the CD of the soundtrack to the film *Agilok & Blubbo*. It's a rare recording (taken from a 1967 WDR TV broadcast of a new music concert in Frankfurt) of Irmin's *Hexapussy* – a spectral improvisation, full of gaping spaces of near silence, that falls somewhere between the total free music of groups like AMM and the Spontaneous Music Ensemble, and the BBC's music for cosmic kids' animation *The Clangers*, made a few years afterwards

18 Diane Waldman, 'Georg Baselitz: Art on the Edge', in *Georg Baselitz* (Guggenheim Museum exhibition catalogue) (New York: Guggenheim Museum Publications, 1995)

19 Georg Baselitz and Eugen Schönebeck, *Second Pandemonium (Manifesto)* (1962)

20 Thomas Mann, 'The Tragedy of Germany', in Ben Raeburn (Ed.), *Treasury for the Free World* (New York: Arco Publishing Company, 1945)

21 Daniel Cohn-Bendit (trans. Arnold Pomerans), *Obsolete Communism: The Left-Wing Alternative* (London: Penguin, 1969)

22 The full title of Weiss's play is *Discourse on the Progress of the*

Can concert in Soest, Germany, 1970

The band's first tour without Damo, 1973, travelling from Montpellier to Marseille

Jaki, Michael, Hildegard, Holger and Irmin, 1975 (Michael von Gimbut)

Promotional booklet for 'I Want More', with sheet music (overleaf), 1975

have to say no more you know what I'm aim-ing for Don't care

E Bm7 E Bm7 E Bm7 E Bm7

if I break a law I want more and more and

E Bm7 E Bm7 E Bm7 E Bm7

more.

E E D

E D

Meru 2 by Malcolm Mooney

DIETER MEIER CAN VISUALISE TAGO MAGO BY EAR, 2011, produced for the 'Halleluwah: An Hommage to Can' exhibition

Irmin found this book at a car boot sale in Joucas, southern France

On top of the mountains by the Madonna of Utelle, behind Michael's house, near Nice (Michael Karoli)

Michael, Damo, Jaki, Malcolm, Irmin and Holger at the Can Studio, Weilerswist. This was the last photograph taken of all the band members together.

Prolonged War of Liberation in Viet Nam and the Events Leading Up to It as Illustration of the Necessity for Armed Resistance Against Oppression and on the Attempts of the United States of America to Destroy the Foundations of Revolution

23 Kommune 1 letter (1 June 1967), quoted in Peter Stansill and David Zane Mairowitz (Eds), *BAMN: Outlaw Manifestos and Ephemera 1965–70* (London: Penguin, 1971)

24 Uncredited report and cartoon, *Der Spiegel*, 5/1968 (29 January 1968)

3 *Mutter(ing)s of Invention*

1 'Kek-w', 'Holger Czukay: "I was fired for being too . . . *intriguing*"', *Fact Magazine*, 6 May 2012; http://www.factmag.com/2012/05/06/holger-czukay-on-can-marriage-and-learning-from-stockhausen/

2 Wolf Kampmann, 'A Kick Out of the Cold' (Michael Karoli interview), in Hildegard Schmidt and Wolf Kampmann (Eds), *Can Box: Book* (Münster: Medium Music Books, 1998)

3 Harrison, Holger Czukay interview

4 Biba Kopf, 'The Lunatic Has Taken over the Asylum', *New Musical Express*, 12 May 1984

5 The Remo Four's main claim to fame would come a couple of years later, when George Harrison, working on his first solo album *Wonderwall*, chose the group to act as his backing band. Tony Ashton would go on in the seventies to work with former Deep Purple member Jon Lord

6 'Kek-w', 'Holger Czukay. . .'

7 Pascal Bussy and Andy Hall, *The Can Book* (Harrow: SAF Publishing, 1989)

8 Ian MacDonald, 'Can: They Have Ways of Making You Listen', *New Musical Express*, 9 November 1974

9 Ralf Krämer, 'Techno, im Prinzip ein flotterer Marsch', *Spex*, 10 December 2008

10 Montoliu toured Germany in May 1961. A recording exists from 20–22 May 1961 at the Deutsche Jazz-Salon Berlin, although Jaki is not the drummer on these dates

11 Bernd-Alois Zimmermann (trans. unknown), 'Commentaries to *Die*

Befristeten (The Numbered)', sleeve notes to Wergo/Heliodor LP, 1967

12 Fred Mills, 'Recycled Cans', *Harp*, May 2006

4 *A Castle with Better Equipment*

1 Quoted in unidentified newspaper clipping, found in Can archive
2 Tom Doyle, 'Finding the Lost Can Tapes', *Sound on Sound*, July 2012
3 Aaron Copland, Preface to *Inscape* score (New York: Boosey & Hawkes, 1967)
4 Bussy and Hall, *The Can Book*
5 Kenneth Ansell, Can interview, *Impetus*, May 1976
6 Damon Krukowski, Can interview, 1998
7 *Can Documentary*, compiled by Rudi Dolezal and Hannes Rossacher, prod. DoRo Productions, 1998. Included in Can DVD (Spoon/Mute Records, 2003)
8 Bussy and Hall, *The Can Book*
9 On Tago Mago, an independent label run by Pascal Bussy
10 Irmin Schmidt, sleeve notes, *The Lost Tapes* (Spoon/Mute Records, 2012)

5 *The Last Kick Towards Rock*

1 Archie Patterson, Malcolm Mooney interview (full transcript), 1980
2 Unknown radio interviewer, Malcolm Mooney interview, *Charmer's Almanac*, CJSW 90.9FM (Calgary), January 2014; https://soundcloud.com/cjsw-90-9-fm/malcolm-mooney-interview-on-charmers-almanac
3 Unknown radio interviewer, Mooney interview, January 2014
4 Patterson, Mooney interview
5 Joshua Zim pursued the spiritual life and worked as First Information Officer for the Tibetan Buddhist meditation master Trungpa Rinpoche. He died of Lou Gehrig's disease on 22 October 1985
6 Patterson, Mooney interview
7 Patterson, Mooney interview

Notes

8 Cited in Ansell, Can interview

9 *Popwatch* #9 (March 1998)

10 MacDonald, 'Can: They Have Ways of Making You Listen . . .'

11 Krukowski, Can interview, 1998

12 Bussy and Hall, *The Can Book*

13 John Doran, 'The Lost Tapes by Can: An Oral History', *The Quietus*, 18 July 2012; http://thequietus.com/articles/09376-can-the-lost-tapes-interview

14 Patterson, Mooney interview

15 Bussy and Hall, *The Can Book*

16 Patterson, Mooney interview

17 Patterson, Mooney interview

6 *Thieves of Fire*

1 Wolf Kampmann, 'Endless Madness' (Irmin Schmidt interview), in Schmidt and Kampmann (Eds), *Can Box: Book*

2 Lowenstein, 'Science Music and the Angel Radar'

3 Tom Doyle, 'Finding the Lost Can Tapes', *Sound on Sound*, July 2012

4 Wolf Kampmann, 'Singer from the Ether' (Holger Czukay interview), in Schmidt and Kampmann (Eds), *Can Box: Book*

5 Patterson, Mooney interview

6 Harrison, Holger Czukay interview

7 http://www.geraldjenkins.co.uk/journal/2014/10/19/malcolm-mooney

8 Holger Czukay, 'A Short History of the Can – Discography', *Perfect Sound Forever*, May 1997; http://www.furious.com/perfect/hysterie2.html

9 Patterson, Mooney interview

10 Kopf, 'Holger Czukay: The Lunatic Has Taken Over the Asylum'

11 Patterson, Mooney interview

12 Patterson, Mooney interview

13 Archie Patterson, 'Malcolm R. Mooney: An Interview', in *Eurock*, 1983

14 Richard Williams, 'The Can: *Monster Movie* review', *New Musical Express*, 30 May 1970

15 Markus Schurr (trans. Matt Goodluck), sleeve notes, Technical Space Composer's Crew, *Canaxis 5* reissue (Revisited Records, 2006)

16 Holger Czukay, Can history; www.czukay.de

17 Patterson, Mooney interview

18 Patterson, Mooney interview

19 Uncredited writer, *Der Spiegel* 29/1969 (22 September 1969)

20 Harrison, Holger Czukay interview

21 Johannes Jacobi, 'Neuer Anfang in Zürich', *Die Zeit*, 26 September 1969

22 *Der Spiegel* 29/1969

7 *Truth at 33 rpm*

1 Kampmann, 'Endless Madness', pp. 73–5

2 Patterson, Mooney interview

3 Josiah Hughes, 'Malcolm Mooney: Visual Artist, Poet, Original Can Vocalist', in *FFWD* (*Fast Forward Weekly*); http://www.ffwdweekly.com/life/your-face-here/malcolm-mooney-visual-artist-poet-original-can-vocalist-8658/#sthash.uBJpsZMm.dpuf

4 Patterson, Mooney interview

5 Patterson, Mooney interview

6 Patterson, Mooney interview

7 Richard Williams, 'Burnin' Red Ivanhoe, Can, Amon Düül et al: Is It Euro-Rock Next?' *Melody Maker*, 13 June 1970

8 Claudia Littmann was, ironically, the daughter of the president of the Frankfurt police force at the time. In 1974 she became involved in the Divine Light Mission religious cult and married one of its leaders, Rajaji Rawat, in 1974. Their daughter, Navi Rawat, became a successful film and TV actress in LA. *Mein schönes kurzes Leben* displays one of the largest (and perhaps only) bongs ever to have been broadcast on national television in Germany, and production crew members complained to their unions about passive smoke intake. Lead actor Schwankhart was arrested immediately after shooting for possession of hashish

9 Lee Gates returned to the US and became a moderately successful blues singer

10 Uncredited writer, 'Abi war hier', *Der Abend*, September 1971

8 *In at the Deep End*

1 Norman Crossland, 'Long Hair a German Badge of Courage', *Guardian*, 14 July 1970

2 Another Can connection was that their old associate Kalle Freynik was responsible for *Hair*'s German libretto

3 Robert Greer, 'Being Damo Suzuki: The Man Who Practically Invented Post-Punk and Ambient Music', *Noisey*, 15 September 2014; http://noisey.vice.com/blog/damo-suzuki-interview

4 Greer, 'Being Damo Suzuki'

5 Mike Barnes, 'The Accidental Anarchist', *The Wire* 245 (July 2004)

6 Ian Martin, 'Damo Suzuki Sees Promise in Young Artists', *Japan Times*, 29 October 2013

7 Martin, 'Damo Suzuki Sees Promise in Young Artists'

8 Greer, 'Being Damo Suzuki'

9 Greer, 'Being Damo Suzuki'

10 Kernan Andrews, 'Damo Suzuki: 21st Century Nomad', *Galway Advertiser*, 29 July 2010; http://www.advertiser.ie/galway/article/29122/damo-suzuki-21st-cettury-nomad

11 Greer, 'Being Damo Suzuki'

12 Doran, 'The Lost Tapes by Can: An Oral History'

13 Jeff Fitzgerald, 'Damo Suzuki Interview', *Aural Innovations*, 17 May 2012; http://www.aural-innovations.com/issues/issue20/damoo3.html

14 Doran, 'The Lost Tapes by Can: An Oral History'

15 Kampmann, 'A Kick Out of the Cold'

16 Bussy and Hall, *The Can Book*

17 Damo Suzuki, Letter to Gittan, 11 November 1970, in Simon Torssel Lerin and Bettina Hvidevold Hystad with Damo Suzuki, untitled book accompanying *Ripple Effects and the Impossible Loopholes* LP (Clouds Hill Records, 2013

9 *Witchy Surprisings*

1 James Johnson, 'Can Can . . . And They Will', *New Musical Express*, 5 February 1972

2 Krukowski, Can interview, 1998

Notes

3 Nick Kent, 'Can: Ve Give Ze Orders Here', *New Musical Express*, 16 February 1974

4 Erik Quint, transcript of Michael Karoli interview appearing in 'Can heeft ons gevormd', *De Haagsche Courant*, [May?] 1997

5 Andrew Graham-Stewart, Can interview (unpublished transcript), July 1973

6 Kampmann, 'A Kick Out of the Cold'

7 Reproduced in *Sounds* 26 (Germany), February 1971

8 Kampmann, 'Endless Madness'

9 Holger Czukay, untitled text at www.czukay.de

10 Johnson, 'Can Can . . .'

11 Ansell, Can interview

12 Translation by Jay and Mika Young

13 Ian MacDonald, 'Can: Automation for the People', *Uncut*, August 1997

14 Wolf Kampmann, 'Listening and Opinionated' (Hildegard Schmidt interview), in Schmidt and Kampmann (Eds), *Can Box: Book*

15 Bussy and Hall, *The Can Book*

16 Lowenstein, 'Science Music and the Angel Radar'

17 Johnson, 'Can Can . . .'

18 Kampmann, 'A Kick Out of the Cold'

19 Kampmann, 'A Kick Out of the Cold'

20 Kampmann, 'A Kick Out of the Cold'

21 Kampmann, Hildegard Schmidt interview, 1998

22 Michael Watts, *Tago Mago* review, *Melody Maker*, 29 January 1972

23 Johnson, 'Can Can . . .'

24 Duncan Fallowell, 'Pop Records: Playing Fair', *The Spectator*, 27 November 1971

25 Suzuki, Letter to Gittan

26 Suzuki, Letter to Gittan

10 *Concord of Sounds*

1 Jon Dieringer, 'An Interview with Can's Irmin Schmidt', *Screen Slate*, June 2012; http://www.screenslate.com/screen-slate-presents/an-interview-with-cans-irmin-schmidt

2 Lowenstein, 'Science Music and the Angel Radar'

3 Manfred Weiss, *Bernds Berliner Rockwiki*, July 2013; http://www. rockinberlin.de/index.php?title=9._Januar_1972_Can

4 'News', *Sounds* (Germany) 38 (April 1972)

5 James Johnson, 'Row Reviews', *New Musical Express* 'What's On' pull-out, May 1972

6 Johnson, 'Can Can . . .'

7 Williams, 'Burnin' Red Ivanhoe . . .'

8 Michael Watts, 'Deutsch Rock', *Melody Maker*, 15 April 1972

9 Michael Watts, unknown article, *Melody Maker* [1972?]

10 Andy Hall, sleeve notes, *Can Box: Music* CD (Spoon/Mute Records, 1998)

11 Schmidt, sleeve notes, *The Lost Tapes* CD

12 Unknown writer, Jaki Liebezeit interview, unknown publication (cutting in Can archive), May 1972

13 Schmidt, sleeve notes, *The Lost Tapes* CD

14 Howard Wuelfling, 'Rock on the Rhine', *Zoo World*, 13 September 1973

15 Graham-Stewart, Can interview

16 Steve Hanson, Damo Suzuki interview, *Ptolemaic Terrascope*, 2002; http://www.terrascope.co.uk/MyBackPages/Can-Damo.htm

17 'J.M./W.T.', 'Abi Ofarim stoppt die Kölner Can', *Kölner Stadt-Anzeiger* 286/25 (9–10 December 1972)

18 Ian MacDonald, 'Germany Calling Part 2: Bomb Blasts and the Beat', *New Musical Express*, 16 December 1972

19 Duncan Fallowell, pop column, *The Spectator*, 24 February 1973

11 *Wanderers in the Fog*

1 Schopenhauer, *The World as Will and Idea* (1818), III, §52

2 Biba Kopf, 'The Autobahn Goes on Forever. Kings of the Road: The Motorik Pulse of Kraftwerk and Neu!', in Rob Young (Ed.), *Undercurrents: The Hidden Wiring of Modern Music* (London: Bloomsbury, 2003)

3 David Cavanagh, 'Lifting the Lid on Can', *Q*, 1989

4 Richard Williams, 'Can Do', *Melody Maker*, date unknown, 1973

5 *Sic* – Irmin was actually expelled from his high school

6 Paul Alessandrini, untitled article, *Rock & Folk* 76 (May 1973)

7 Uncredited writer, *Sounds* (Germany) 50, April 1973

8 Alessandrini, *Rock & Folk*, 1973

9 'Yes, They Can!' EMI Electrola press release for *Flow Motion*, 1977

10 Graham-Stewart, Can interview

11 Alessandrini, *Rock & Folk*, 1973

12 I'm grateful to Jay and Mika Young for transcribing and translating the entire thirty-five-minute track

13 Bussy and Hall, *The Can Book*

14 Ansell, Can interview

15 Lawrence Gowing, essay on Caspar David Friedrich in *Paintings in the Louvre* (New York: Stewart, Tabori and Chang, 1994)

16 Ian MacDonald, *Future Days* review, *New Musical Express* (undated)

17 Cavanagh, 'Lifting the Lid on Can'

18 Andy Gill, 'Can: Future Days', *Mojo* 112 (March 2003)

19 John Payne, sleeve notes to *Future Days* (remastered edition) (Spoon Records, 2005)

20 Martin Hayman, 'Can: Communism, Anarchism, Nihilism', *Sounds*, 24 February 1973

21 Lowenstein, 'Science Music and the Angel Radar'

22 Martin Hayman, 'Future Days: Games Deep Inside the Can', *Sounds*, 24 November 1973

23 Kampmann, 'A Kick Out Of the Cold'

24 John Peel, Singles review of 'Moonshake', *Sounds*, 6 October 1973

25 Hayman, 'Future Days: Games Deep Inside the Can'

26 Steve Lake, 'Can You Dig It?' *Melody Maker*, 17 November 1973

27 Hayman, 'Future Days: Games Deep Inside the Can'

28 Jacques LeBlanc, *Future Days* review, *Extra*, December 1973

29 Paul Alessandrini, *Future Days* review, *Rock & Folk*, December 1973

30 MacDonald, *Future Days* review

31 Bussy and Hall, *The Can Book*

32 Kent, 'Can: Ve Give Ze Orders Here'

33 Martin, 'Damo Suzuki Sees Promise in Young Artists'

34 Hanson, Damo Suzuki interview

Notes

35 Gill, 'Can: Future Days'

36 Hanson, Damo Suzuki interview

12 *Perpetual Motion*

1 Wim Wenders, untitled sleeve note in Irmin Schmidt, *Villa Wunderbar* CD (Spoon Records, 2016)

2 Dieringer, 'An Interview with Can's Irmin Schmidt'

3 *Melody Maker*, 26 January 1974

4 Kent, 'Can: Ve Give Ze Orders Here'

5 Martin Hayman, 'Can in a Square Chamber', *Sounds*, 9 February 1974

6 Kent, 'Can: Ve Give Ze Orders Here'

7 Vivien Goldman, 'Tales of the Supernatural', *Sounds*, 6 December 1975

8 Steve Lake, 'Free Rock in the Can', *Melody Maker*, 16 February 1974

9 Steve Lake, 'Blues From an Aircraft Hangar', *Melody Maker*, May[?] 1974

10 Michael Gross, 'Brian Eno: Mind Over Music', *Chic*, July 1979

11 Karlheinz Stockhausen, *Donnerstag aus Licht*, 1977–80

12 Karlheinz Stockhausen (selected and trans. Tim Nevill), *Towards a Cosmic Music* (Longmead (Shaftesbury, Dorset): Element Books, 1989)

13 1982 interview, quoted in David Stubbs, *Future Days: Krautrock and the Building of Modern Germany* (London: Faber and Faber, 2014)

14 G. W. Leibniz, Letter to Christian Goldbach (17 April 1712), in *Opera Omnia*, vol. III (Geneva, 1768)

15 Nick Kent, 'Can: Obsolete, Impenetrable, Enticing', in 'Platters' (preview column), *New Musical Express*, undated

16 Kent, 'Can: Ve Give Ze Orders Here'

17 Kent, 'Can: Ve Give Ze Orders Here'

18 MacDonald, 'Can: They Have Ways of Making You Listen'

13 *Bumpy Landings*

1 Bussy and Hall, *The Can Book*

2 Quint, transcript of Michael Karoli interview

3 Kampmann, 'Listening and Opinionated'

4 This date is sometimes erroneously credited to a different singer, Hiromi Moritani, aka Phew. It's not her, but Phew did collaborate with Can members in the late seventies, after Can had split up

5 Goldman, 'Tales of the Supernatural'

6 Goldman, 'Tales of the Supernatural'

14 *Wanting More*

1 Karl Lippegaus, 'Can aus dem Inner Space Studio', *Sounds* (Germany) 91 (September 1976)

2 Kampmann, 'Singer from the Ether'

3 Lippegaus, 'Can aus dem Inner Space Studio'

4 Lippegaus, 'Can aus dem Inner Space Studio'

5 Vivien Goldman, 'Can Laundered', *Sounds*, 23 October 1976

6 Vivien Goldman, *Flow Motion* LP review, *Sounds*, 23 October 1976

7 Goldman, 'Can Laundered'

8 Goldman, 'Can Laundered'

9 Lippegaus, 'Can aus dem Inner Space Studio'

10 Lippegaus, 'Can aus dem Inner Space Studio'

11 Andy Gill, 'Can: Free Trade Hall, Manchester', *New Musical Express*, 18 December 1976

12 Peter Silverton, 'Can: New Victoria, London', *Sounds*, 11 December 1976

13 Karl Dallas, 'Can: New Victoria Theatre, London', *Melody Maker*, 18 December 1976

14 Silverton, 'Can: New Victoria, London'

15 *Artificial Head Stereo*

1 Quint, transcript of Michael Karoli interview

2 Franco, aka François Luambo Luanzo Makiadi (1938–89), earned the nickname the 'sorcerer of the guitar' in his native Congo on account of his trebly, flowing, clear guitar style. Based in Kinshasa, he led the group OK Jazz (later TPOK Jazz) and ran several night-clubs, including Un-Deux-Trois every Saturday in the mid-seventies.

He became one of the most popular and wealthy musicians in the former Congo/Zaïre (now Democratic Republic of Congo)

3 Kampmann, 'A Kick Out of the Cold'

4 Kampmann, 'A Kick Out of the Cold'

5 Bussy and Hall, *The Can Book*

6 Harrison, transcript of Holger Czukay interview

7 'Kek-w', 'Holger Czukay . . .'

8 Kampmann, 'A Kick Out of the Cold'

9 Giovanni Dadomo, 'Can: *Saw Delight*' (LP review), *Sounds*, 4 June 1977. Dadomo, incidentally, was a music journalist turned punk musician, noted for his leading role in minor punk outfit the Snivelling Shits

10 Unknown writer, 'Can: *Saw Delight*' (LP review), *Melody Maker*, [April?] 1977 (reproduced on Harvest Records press release)

11 Later renamed the Peacock Theatre

12 Harrison, Holger Czukay interview

13 Bussy and Hall, *The Can Book*

14 Harrison, transcript of Holger Czukay interview

15 Ian Penman, 'Reach Out, We'll Be There (Ha Ha – Fooled You)' (Can: *Out of Reach* LP review), *New Musical Express*, 15 July 1978

16 *Can Will Eat Itself*

1 Kampmann, 'A Kick Out of the Cold'

2 Kampmann, 'Singer from the Ether'

3 Wolf Kampmann, 'The Ghost in the Can' (Jaki Liebezeit interview), in Schmidt and Kampmann (Eds), *Can Box: Book*

4 Kampmann, 'Endless Madness'

5 Duncan Fallowell, 'Cannibalism, or Seven Long Nights in Cologne', *Sounds* (Germany) 115 (September 1978)

6 Fallowell, 'Cannibalism, or Seven Long Nights in Cologne'

7 Kampmann, 'Singer from the Ether'

8 Fallowell, 'Cannibalism, or Seven Long Nights in Cologne'

9 Kopf, 'The Lunatic Has Taken Over the Asylum'

10 Kampmann, 'Singer from the Ether'

11 Kampmann, 'The Ghost in the Can'

12 Mills, 'Recycled Cans'

13 Kampmann, 'The Ghost in the Can'

14 Kampmann, 'The Ghost in the Can'

15 Angus Mackinnon, 'Last Bean Bails Out of Can', *New Musical Express*, January [?] 1979

17 *One Last Rite*

1 Cavanagh, 'Lifting the Lid on Can'

2 Richard Cook, 'A Trance in Tatters: Krautrock und Beyond' (*Delay 1968* LP review), *New Musical Express*, 27 November 1982

3 One of Malcolm's favourite songs from the session was not used on *Rite Time*. 'Irmin played such beautiful piano on it, and I wanted to do it with Irmin again, but I didn't know if it would ever work. I called Hildegard and said, "Do you mind if I use this song?"' It appeared in 2012 on a vinyl release by Malcolm, *The Sound of White Columns*, released by White Columns Gallery in New York

4 Quint, transcript of Michael Karoli interview

5 Harrison, Holger Czukay interview

6 Cavanagh, 'Lifting the Lid on Can'

18 *In the Distance Lies the Future*

1 *Sacrilege* sleeve notes

2 *Can Documentary*, compiled by Dolezal and Rossacher

3 Richard Cook, 'The Can Founders: Columbiahalle, Berlin' (live review), *Mojo* 66 (May 1999)

4 Rob Young, 'The Boomerang' (Can remasters review), *The Wire* 249 (November 2004)

5 Alan Warner, *Tago Mago* (London: Bloomsbury Academic, 2015)

Bibliography

Bussy, Pascal and Hall, Andy, *The Can Book* (Harrow: SAF Publishing, 1989)

Kurlansky, Mark, *1968: The Year that Rocked the World* (London: Jonathan Cape, 2004)

Schmidt, Hildegard and Kampmann, Wolf (Eds), *Can Box: Book* (Münster: Medium Music Books, 1998)

Stubbs, David, *Future Days: Krautrock and the Building of Modern Germany* (London: Faber and Faber, 2014)

Watson, Peter, *The German Genius: Europe's Third Renaissance, the Second Scientific Revolution, and the Twentieth Century* (London: Simon & Schuster, 2010)

Acknowledgements

In a lifetime of listening, the music of Can has remained a rock to cling to and an ocean to bathe in. For that, and for sharing the memories chronicled in this book, my deepest gratitude to its four permanent members: Holger Czukay, Michael Karoli, Jaki Liebezeit, Irmin Schmidt; and to Reebop Kwaku Baah, Rosko Gee, David Johnson, Malcolm Mooney, Damo Suzuki.

Thanks to Hildegard Schmidt and Sandra Podmore at Spoon Records for help and hospitality.

For additional interviews and source material, halleluwahs to: Duncan Fallowell, Kalle Freynik, Peter Gilmour, Andrew Graham-Stewart, Eveline Grunwald, Andy Hall, Jon Hassell, Katrina Krimsky, Michiko Nakao, Mick Rock, Manfred Schoof, Serge Tcherepnin, René Tinner.

A heartfelt 'Aumgn' to my agent Sam Copeland and to the movers and moonshakers at Faber & Faber: Lee Brackstone, Dan Papps, David Watkins, Ian Bahrami, Paul Baillie-Lane.

For shared listening, hunting and collecting, inspiration, useful links or essential assistance and general vitamin C in the soul desert: David Barbenel, Mike Barnes, Dean Belcher, Chris Bohn, Max Dax, Michel Faber, Lukas Foerster, Ian Harrison, Joakim Haugland, Kim Hiorthøy, Bettina Hvidevold Hystad, Tamara Karoli, David Keenan, Zoe Miller, Leon Muraglia, Jono Podmore, Edwin Pouncey, Erik Quint, David Stubbs, Pat Thomas.

Ethno-forgery consultants (Japanese translations): Jay Young and Mika Young.

My sunshine day and night: Anne Hilde, Axel, Mathilde.

Can Kiosk

Althoff, Kai (b.1966 in Cologne) is a German visual artist and musician who creates imaginary environments in which paintings, sculpture, drawing, video, sound and found objects interact.

Arbeit, Jochen (b.26 June 1961) is a German sound artist, most notably as a member of the bands Die Haut, Einstürzende Neubauten and Automat.

Barrow, Geoff (b.9 December 1971) is an English music producer, composer and disc jockey, and is the founding member, instrumentalist and producer of the band Portishead.

Brücker, Wolf-Dietrich (b.1945) is a German film producer who worked at WDR Cologne from 1970 to 2010.

Emmerich, Klaus (b.10 August 1943) is a German film director and screenwriter. Irmin composed the music to most of his films and TV series.

Empire, Alec (b.2 May 1972) is a German musician best known for being a founding member of the band Atari Teenage Riot.

Fallowell, Duncan (b.26 September 1948) is an English novelist, travel writer, journalist and critic. He wrote the very first UK article about Can in *Melody Maker*: 'Wagner in Black Leather', in 1970. He went on to become a close friend of the band and wrote the lyrics for all of Irmin's solo work, as well as the libretto to his opera *Gormenghast*.

Gillespie, Bobby (b.22 June 1962) is a Scottish musician and singer-songwriter. He is the lead singer and founding member of the avant-garde rock band Primal Scream.

Hey, Ans (1932–2010) is a Dutch sculptor.

Hey, Jozef (b.1962) is a Dutch audio-visual artist, working under his company name, Beam Systems.

Innes, Andrew (b.16 May 1962) is a Scottish-born, London-based musician. He is best known for being the rhythm guitarist in Primal Scream since 1987.

Irmler, Hans-Joachim (b.1950) is a musician and electronic-sound artist. He is a founding member of Faust – one of the most influential bands of the Krautrock era.

Kent, Nick (b.24 December 1951) is a prolific British rock critic and musician.

Malkovich, John (b.9 December 1953) is an American actor, director and producer.

Nicolai, Carsten (b.18 September 1965 in Karl-Marx-Stadt) is a German artist and musician (performing under the name alva noto) who is dedicated to the exploration and expansion of the boundaries between music and non-music.

Obrist, Hans Ulrich (b.21 May 1968) is a curator, critic and historian of art. He is a co-director at the Serpentine Galleries, London.

Reihse, Andreas (b.21 January 1968) is a founding member of the German post-electronica quartet Kreidler, who are widely regarded as the abstract successors to the Dusseldorf sound of Kraftwerk.

Richter, Werner (1942) is a German graphic designer and painter who designed the covers for Can's *Rite Time*, as well as Irmin

Schmidt's *Musk at Dusk*, *Impossible Holidays*, *Gormenghast* and *Masters of Confusion*.

Saville, Peter (b.9 October 1955) is an English art director and graphic designer. He rose to fame by designing countless Joy Division and New Order record sleeves for Factory Records, of which he was a part-owner.

Sheehy, Michael J. (b.1972) is a singer-songwriter and founding member of the bands Dream City Film Club, Miraculous Mule, The Hired Mourners and United Sound of Joy.

Silvester, Hans (b.2 October 1938 in Lörrach) is a German photographer and environmentalist.

Smith, Mark E. (b.5 March 1957–d.24 January 2018) was an English singer, songwriter and musician. He was the lead singer, lyricist, frontman and founding member of the post-punk group The Fall. He was born in Prestwich, Manchester.

Urhausen, Romain (b.1930) is a photographer, designer and architect from Luxembourg.

Wenders, Wim (b.14 August 1945) is a German film-maker, playwright, author and photographer. Can made the music for his film *Alice in the Cities* and contributed to the soundtracks of *Until the End of the World* and *Lisbon Story*. Irmin also made the soundtrack to Wenders's *Palermo Shooting*.

Wolfertz, Herbert (b.1939) is a German painter who lives and works in Provence.

I: Hands on the Table

'Musical bars are like prison bars. Playing without notes means that you must play repetitively, and repetition is rhythm. At the same time repetition does not really exist here, because you never quite play the same thing twice.'

Jaki Liebezeit,
26 May 1938–22 January 2017

'Cyclic rhythms and harmonic relationships generated by the number five'

Drawing by Jaki Liebezeit, taken from *Jaki Leibezeit: Life, Theory and Practice of a Master Drummer*, Podmore, Jono (ed.). Courtesy of the Jaki Liebezeit Foundation.

Foreword

After a delicious dinner, the view over the dazzling landscapes of Provence expands, gliding over fragrant fields of lavender, which glimmer to a dark purple in the final strains of the sunset, interspersed with stone buildings that have been standing there for centuries. 'I love to listen to the silence,' notes Irmin Schmidt, who together with his wife and manager Hildegard has settled in the small Provence village of Roussillon. Here is where the lightning struck, there is where the neighbours once planted a hedge, and in between Hildegard and Irmin Schmidt built their own house. Yet from the seeming arbitrariness of individual struggles and coincidences of a landscape, a collage emerges in which the personal, familiar, strange, contradictory and resistant meld into a whole.

In Berlin, the telephone rings. In the summer of 2015 we received the call from Hildegard Schmidt in France. It was the beginning of a trans-European express tour through occidental musical history, from its ritualistic beginnings to the modernism of new music, the repetitive grooves of James Brown all the way to the loose ends of the future. *Can Kiosk* is a collection of texts centred on a question posed by Irmin Schmidt: What does music mean in the twenty-first century, and what does it mean to be an artist today? We discussed this question with Irmin, together with musicians, artists and authors such as Geoff Barrow, Hans Ulrich Obrist, Bobby Gillespie, Alec Empire and Peter Saville.

From the very beginning it was clear that in this work we would refer to the principle of collage, which is the inspiration for the creation of one of the most influential bands of the second half of the last century: Can, founded in 1967 by the young conductor Irmin Schmidt. The oral history of *Can Kiosk*, consisting of six chapters, can also be read as such: as a collage of various free associations from a total of fifteen speakers on the question of music and what it means to be an artist these days – with repeated reference to Can. After we had put all these conversations down in writing, we built a narrative by connecting around five thousand snippets of paper.

The result is a virtual round-table discussion, in which the answers and recollections of the speakers follow a logic based on their content, but which are sometimes also associatively collaged as in a cut-up. Thus we follow not only the method by which Can worked musically, but also a central structural principle of modern art.

The second major narrative block in *Can Kiosk* is Irmin Schmidt's notebook from the years 2013–14, in which, at irregular intervals, he wrote down everyday observations, alongside dream portraits, image descriptions, epiphanies, reflections, memories and theoretical explanations regarding music, art and, of course, collage.

In the opening chapter of his notebook, Irmin goes on a dream journey to the immediate post-war period in Germany. The country is in ruins, and children play among the rubble. Here we read the words of someone who not only looks back on eighty years of a life rich in experiences and endeavours, but above all, a person who views the world rhizomatically. Everything seems connected with everything: the cooking recipe with the composer, the music with the philosophers, Marcel Proust's *In Search of Lost Time* with Can.

A text by Kai Althoff and conversations between Irmin Schmidt and Wim Wenders, Jozef Hay, Herbert Wolfertz, Wolf-Dietrich Brücker, Romain Urhausen, Hans Silvester, Klaus Emmerich, Werner Richter and John Malkovich finally round off *Can Kiosk* – a collage of conversation in several acts and from different angles.

Max Dax and Robert Defcon,
Berlin, March 2017

1

'A Schmidt-Smith from Germany'

Mark E. Smith and Irmin Schmidt meet in a crowded craft-beer brewery near Highbury and Islington, London.

Mark E. Smith: How are you, Irmin?

Irmin Schmidt: Fine. Still.

MES: That's like a shock. I am finally meeting you. I was told that you wanted to meet me. I thought it was a joke.

IS: Do you remember that you once called me? That was in the seventies.

MES: What are you suggesting here?! I don't think so.

IS: Maybe you'll remember when I mention what you proposed: you said that we should do a gig together. That must have been in 1977. Long ago . . .

MES: Fuck me! That's fucking right!

IS: But it didn't happen.

MES: I was an insane fan of yours back then. I had just begun and formed a band. I had formed The Fall in 1976. Ah! Here comes the beer!

IS: I like the temperature of the beer in England. In Germany they usually serve it way too cold.

MES: These microbreweries brewing craft beer in the backyards are the biggest-growing business in the country. Four years ago there were only sixty, and now there are over two thousand. They're popping up like mushrooms. The people who are running these are fucking shit, certainly. In Manchester and Liverpool they wouldn't let people like me in.

IS: I'm more into wine. But I read in your book that wine isn't your thing, is it?

MES: I also drink wine – if it has to be. But why are we meeting anyways? What is this interview good for?

IS: We are doing a book.

MES: About what?

IS: It's about Can. Actually, it's less about Can and more a book about music and being an artist.

MES: So it's a book floating between Can and music. I like it when it's floating and when everything suddenly changes.

IS: Did you ever see Can perform?

MES: No, never.

IS: Do you remember when you first heard of Can?

MES: I recently saw a vinyl re-release of *Monster Movie* in a record shop in Manchester. It's hip to buy Can records nowadays.

IS: That was our first album. It was released in 1969. You must have been twelve years old back then. You were born in 1957, weren't you?

MES: Yep. Do you still play live?

IS: Sure I do! I recently did a collaborative concert with Thurston Moore. In 2017 I will turn eighty years old.

MES: So what? That's no age.

IS: Exactly!

MES: It is an honour to finally know another Smith. A Schmidt-Smith from Germany.

IS: Welcome to the club.

MES: You know what Can's problem is? Many people just pretend that they like Can. But they don't. For them it's just a hipness thing to buy your records. You could have called your band 'Coffee Table'. Then your records would be considered 'coffee-table records'. For most of the Britons, Can were consisting of Damo Suzuki and the bass player, Holger Czukay. But I know that Can were Irmin and Jaki. People in Britain and America pretend to know the Can. But what they don't understand is Irmin. And the problem with the Germans is that they are like fucking English people. They pretend to know you, but they don't have a clue. The Germans never do appreciate what's on their own doorstep.

IS: That's why I'm living in France.

MES: I bet you did this one right.

IS: Still, I'd be interested in your first encounter with 'the' Can . . .

MES: I heard it then.

IS: You heard it on the radio?

MES: No, I ordered it by post. It was called mail order. The first record I bought was *Tago Mago*. When I was fifteen, I was a hard-core Velvet Underground fan. And other friends of mine who were also listening to the Velvet Underground told me that I should listen to Can. So I filled out a postcard, and two weeks later I got back a Can record – from London.

IS: And did *Tago Mago* live up to your expectations?

MES: Fucking yes. It formed my skills listening to it. I went to grammar school at that time and everybody was listening to Pink fucking Floyd and the Beatles. They were shit. But Can were great. As was Gary Glitter. And the Velvet Underground. Manchester people always liked Can. That's why we are called 'The Can People' since 1973. To earn some money I was working on the docks. All music during that period was fucking shite – David Bowie, Genesis, Pink Floyd and James Taylor. Crap. Can saved my life. Irmin, you fucking saved my life! And because you saved my life I even bought *Soon Over Babaluma*.

IS: I actually still quite like *Soon Over Babaluma*. At least to me, that was the last of the good Can records. After that we somehow lost the focus, I'd say. But that happens to a lot of bands.

MES: We could have had this conversation in 1977.

IS: I listened to The Fall's records during the eighties. But I never saw you live.

MES: You are joking. This is a cruel joke.

IS: But it was me who wanted to meet you. Don't you remember?

MES: I should play the south of France more often then.

IS: And we played Manchester quite a few times.

MES: *Ja, ja, ja.* That was in the early and mid-seventies. You had to be a student to get in. You had to be academic. But I was working at the docks.

IS: We'd never have allowed only students at our gigs.

MES: Didn't you get it? That was a joke, Irmin.

IS: We played for everybody.

MES: Fuck the seventies. I don't want to go back in time. Never ever, ever. But I would like to have a jukebox in this micro-draught-beer brewery to spin a Can record. In Manchester there is a bar with a jukebox that has tracks by Can in it. I always go there. I always spin 'Yoo Doo Right'. Once I even played it twice.

IS: You know, I recently read your book again, *Renegade*.

MES: Oh, that was written a long time ago.

IS: I loved the story about how you kicked out your band in America.

MES: I have a new band now. Not like you.

IS: I would probably come to see a show if you were playing Marseille.

MES: I won't go there. The French hate The Fall.

IS: I don't think so. The French actually love music like The Fall are doing.

MES: But we played Marseille. And they fucking hated us.

IS: Can were never well received in Marseille either.

MES: We played there three years ago and it was a disaster.

IS: We played there twice in the early seventies and stopped playing there thereafter for the same reasons. But in other French cities we'd always have a great time. In Bordeaux they even opened a club and called it Tago Mago.

MES: It's funny because we have a promoter in Paris. But he books us in cities like Nantes. I had to look at the map to find out where this city was supposed to be. You know, I'm English. It's in the blood. I have a hate relationship with the French. I'm not a Londoner. I'm a real Englishman. I am allergic to France. Of course, I try to be nice. But they don't like me and I don't like them. And let me add that I get along very well with anyone else. The Japanese, the fucking Londoners, even you Germans.

IS: Do you regularly play in Germany?

MES: We often play Berlin. Almost every year we play there. And we've been very warmly received in Israel the other day. Before going there I received letters from London not to play there.

IS: Why?

MES: Because of the Palestinians.

IS: It's stupid, because as a musician you play for people – and not to political parties. I would try to play in Palestine and in Israel on the same tour.

MES: I even got blacklisted by the Londoners because I played in Israel. You know what? We should play together in Israel. I might need a new keyboard player by then.

IS: But I don't play rock music any more.

2

'This Record Does Not Contain Interfering Noise'

Jochen Arbeit, Max Dax, Duncan Fallowell, Bobby Gillespie, Andrew Innes, Daniel Miller, Carsten Nicolai, Hans Ulrich Obrist, Andreas Reihse and Irmin Schmidt virtually meet in various places, among them the Santa Lucia Galerie der Gespräche, Berlin, the Serpentine Gallery and the Grosvenor Hotel in Victoria, London.

Irmin Schmidt: I was born in Berlin and I still have some vivid memories of the bombings. I can remember the Deutschlandhalle burning. It was made out of wood and I was as happy as ever to see the sky glowing red with the flames. I had been there just a week before, to the circus, and I was afraid of the clowns. 'The circus is burning!' That, in my opinion, was suitable revenge. I particularly remember one attack. I must have been five years old. We had to remain in the bomb shelter for quite some time, after which we were eventually allowed to go back into the garden. My grandparents and my uncle were with me and some other members of the family. Two of them were militant Nazis. It was during the night. Flak spotlights were combing through the dark sky. At a certain point, they seemed to have located one of the attacking airplanes. When my uncle applauded, I kicked him hard against his shin bone, and then I cried and screamed like I was insane. I had just realised that they were about to kill a human being.

Jochen Arbeit: You realised it at that very moment?

IS: Yes. I had tin soldiers and tanks too. As a boy I played war. And I remember that specific war-related terms, such as *Kesselschlacht* – an encirclement battle – sounded completely common to me. After this episode another uncle of mine gave me a toy ambulance as a present. I remember him saying, 'This is for all your wounded and dead soldiers.'

Max Dax: Did you start to play differently with your tin army?

IS: I drowned them all in a little creek. I can still hear the wind in the trees and the water flowing when I recall that scene. And then we were evacuated – my mother and three children. It was August 1943. I had turned six in May. We went to Austria. For the rest of the war and in the first post-war years I was far away, in a small village up in the Tauern. It was nice there.

JA: And when did you return?

IS: It was after the war, in 1946, that we left Austria, where I hadn't seen a single bombed city, and returned to Germany. It was an adventurous journey, riding on freight trains. We landed in Nuremberg, which was utterly destroyed. We lived in one of the ruins for fourteen days. It was summer, and the building was completely open. Across from it stood a burned-out church, but the bells still rung and they always woke me up terribly early. Strangely, I have no memory of anything else there, although I can remember many other details from that trip. Perhaps the shock was preserved in my dreams.

MD: Your family then moved to Dortmund. In your diary you mention a reoccurring dream: you are walking through a city that has almost entirely been wiped out by air raids.

IS: When we came to Dortmund in 1946 we were very poor. My parents had lost everything and we lived in just two small rooms as a family with three children. The family lived in Dortmund until I was twenty-six years old. By the time I was eleven we had a neighbour who was an organist. He had a piano and offered to give me piano lessons for free. But being a boy of eleven years, practising the piano in someone else's house is not the most comfortable thing. So I didn't work on it very much. It was only later, when I was fourteen or fifteen, that I had my first piano and a proper teacher – a fantastic teacher. I really owe it to him that I became a musician. At fourteen I had already decided that I'd either become a conductor or an architect. In hindsight, many things seem predestined . . .

Duncan Fallowell: Did you know that all the great composers have been pianists? I can only think of one very great composer who couldn't play the piano: Berlioz. He used to work it all out on a guitar. That's why he has this fantastically weird and original string and orchestral sound, which owes nothing to Beethoven. There may be others who also couldn't play the piano, but I think he is the only great composer. But you are talking about learning the piano in the ruins of Germany. Did your war experience play a role in deciding to become a composer?

IS: I don't know. My artistic perception actually came from being aware of my acoustical environment as a young child – much more than being attracted by music. I turned sounds into something interesting in my head. It started like that. That was the beginning of the composer in me, and it began with environmental sounds. It was only then that I started to make music. I think the reason I ended up doing a project like Can was because I wasn't born as a composer who would start composing in a classical tradition. It's very natural for me to turn my environment into music. I only fully realised this in 2000, when I had a brain haemorrhage. It put me out of commission for an entire year, so I couldn't make music. The first ten days in hospital were among the most awful things I've ever had to experience. I was in terrible pain for the first five days. From the sixth day it was bearable, but then I realised that I could no longer hear any music in my head at all. Usually, when I'm awake, but also in my dreams, I have music in my head. But when I tried to think of Beethoven's Seventh Symphony or Schumann's Fourth, I couldn't imagine a single tone. On the eleventh day I slept properly for the first time again and woke up with a violin concerto in my ears. It didn't leave me for nine hours. That violin cheered, scratched, screamed, cried and wept. There was this violin concerto with a great orchestra in my head for hours. Through this one violin concerto, all kinds of other violin concertos were illuminated, but it wasn't a concerto that I knew. That was an epiphany. Suddenly my life fell into place again. I didn't give a damn that I would immediately fall over whenever I stood up or that I was half blind. The most important thing was that I had music in my head. Then I decided that I would definitely write a violin concerto again. The thought has been hanging around with me ever since. If I live long enough, I'll write it.

MD: You've heard music in your head ever since you were a child?

IS: Yes, all the time.

MD: But how consciously can a young boy listen to concrete sounds and surrounding noises and understand it as music?

IS: Very consciously! I know that I hallucinated choirs and orchestral sounds to the repetitive groove of the train. A later song of mine that appeared on my first record after Can, which I wrote together with the Swiss artist Bruno Spoerri, has the title 'Rapido de noir'. For this particular track we took one of Bruno's field recordings from a train ride, edited it and gave it a structure. Then I played the Prophet-5 synthesizer over it – treated heavily with guitar distortion and wah-wah pedals. Even though that childhood memory is actually quite a sweet one, the song itself turned out to be rather dark.

MD: One of the beautiful things about train noise is its sonic spectrum. A moving train features almost all the frequencies the human ear can hear. I don't know any other machine that has such a rich sound.

IS: There is another aspect that fascinates me when it comes to trains, which is that every moment sounds different. It's like watching a river flow: you'll never see the same river, just as you never hear the same train sound twice. The other day, I lingered under a railway bridge. Hell, it was a moment of beauty whenever a train passed.

Carsten Nicolai: And yet we only rarely ever hear the entire sonic spectrum on a CD. It always amazes me how little you have to do differently in order to drive people crazy. I've never understood it. The CD standard goes from 20 to 20,000 Hz. If you try to exhaust that spectrum, then you're considered a freak. I always thought, 'What's the problem? The CD standard allows it, so why doesn't anyone do it?' We hear these frequencies. They're around us every day. Of course, they're filtered, but if they are used in music or in a sound structure, then everyone is surprised. In that sense I belong to a generation where notes have become insufficient when it comes to defining the syncrisis of a sound. Any given sound that Olaf Bender – my partner in crime at our label raster-noton – and I are working with cannot be limited to the fact that it was played in the key of C, for instance. Almost all of the sounds we generate have a prototypical quality. Space, time, temperature, the instrument the sound was played on, the amount of noise inherent – a sound is like a cosmic event. What I mean is, how would you notate white noise? But white noise is a key element in almost all of our compositions. I'd say that the vocabulary of sounds has increased enormously during the last one hundred years, whereas the vocabulary for defining and notating these sounds has not. To me, this shows how much growing up with abstract music – if not electronic music – has altered the way we perceive sound.

IS: After 1945, composing with concrete sounds from nature and the environment became a very important element of music: in France, with Pierre Henry and Pierre Schaeffer and the musique concrète of the late twenties and thirties; in Italy, with the futurists based around Luigi Russolo, who wrote his manifesto *L'arte dei rumori* in 1913, it was even much earlier. That music is clearly one of the central movements of the twentieth century. I learned a lot from my meetings with John Cage and from his way of thinking.

MD: The Austrian singer-songwriter Andreas Spechtl has begun to replace his lyrics with concrete sounds. With the kind of music he's currently making, he sees the concrete moments, such as field recordings and other recorded sounds, almost as equivalent to lyrics. When he writes lyrics, he tends to go for a walk. He strolls through cities and processes that in some form as a text. Or he sometimes even just takes what he hears. Then an intermediate step is simply eliminated. Concrete sounds have a very narrative quality.

IS: That is very familiar to me. The Can piece 'Future Days' was created when Damo sat down on a cushioned seat made out of artificial leather and filled with tiny plastic balls, as was modern in the seventies. As he sat down, the seat made a certain noise. The microphone was already up and we all had headphones on, then we heard this rustling, crackling sound. Then Damo continued to produce that sound while making rhythmic sliding movements. The track came from that. We played around with the sound for a long time, then Holger added some reverb, I started playing something to it and the piece was built up like that. The guitar picked up a radio signal: a little Musette waltz on the accordion, very quietly from afar. Jaki and I were talking, and Holger distorted our voices with a telephone filter, and so on. That piece came together from all kinds of strange noises. I still love to do that kind of thing.

CN: What used to be perceived as noise, today we hear as a tone or sound. Our listening habits seem to have changed completely. Of course, to pay attention to a noise at all, to appreciate that it has a musical quality, is actually quite an achievement. So why do people actually get upset about it?

IS: It really is strange. One would think that it had gradually gained acceptance. But actually, it's only a matter for a particular 'serious music' audience.

CN: One of my favourite songs is 'Scream' by Michael and Janet Jackson. The track starts off with this crazy noise, like a machine scream. It could be from a track by Einstürzende Neubauten. It may only appear as a tiny element, but that's a sign, an advance. Something has happened. But perhaps that's just my faith in progress.

IS: We pressed the first five hundred copies of our album *Monster Movie* with a sticker that said, 'This record does not contain interfering noise' – simply because we didn't consider background noise as interference.

CN: I grew up in the GDR. When I think about it, my musical education actually comes from the radio. I always listened to the radio, with very bad quality, of course. Listening to the radio was always combined with a lot of static, and the signal was rather eroded because the radio receivers were faulty. At one frequency, entire columns of figures would suddenly be transmitted in Russian for a quarter of an hour, and you had to wait for them to pass by. Of course, you still sat in front of the radio listening to that. And those strange, entirely uncomposed collages coming out of the ether then seeped into my subconscious. Some years ago, it occurred to me that in a certain way I am reconstructing those series of numbers that I heard back then, because they obviously shaped me. I was actually waiting for the music that I wanted to hear and listened just as closely to the noises as the radio programme. When I hear something like that today, I immediately feel right at home.

IS: I spent night after night glued to the radio when electronic music was invented in the fifties. Initially I thought that most of the things were just ugly. Then one night they played *Gesang der Jünglinge im Feuerofen* by Stockhausen. That's when lightning struck. It was a masterpiece. I wanted to study with him.

MD: You heard *Gesang der Jünglinge* on the radio and then enrolled with Stockhausen?

IS: It didn't happen quite that fast. I first heard him on the radio, long before I studied with him. I was probably even still in school. I was already totally fascinated by him. This was, in my opinion, the first time that a real piece of music had been made with electronics. I don't know of any other piece from that time that has such lustre.

CN: And that epiphany was the motivation to study with him? I can see it the same way. Listening to music can entirely change the course of one's life and steer it in a new direction.

IS: *Gesang der Jünglinge* was definitely the reason why I began to further investigate this strange music, and Stockhausen in particular. At first it was merely through repeated listening – over and over again. Before I enrolled with Stockhausen, however, I dutifully studied music for six years. I only went to him after that. He was already on to *Hymnen* and *Kontakte* by then. In *Hymnen*, there are people blabbing away in the middle of the piece, there are field recordings and purely electronic noises. Wonderful.

Andreas Reihse: You had all this knowledge about new music, you could play an instrument, and the others as well, you had all studied music – was it the case with Can that you had to start off by forgetting everything?

IS: Yes, somehow it was about forgetting everything we were capable of musically, because otherwise it would have just resulted in more new music. The attempt to forget about our background – and that also meant no longer striving for virtuosity – led to a certain kind of acoustic violence. I was also fascinated by Fluxus at the time. Cologne and Düsseldorf were the centre of the German art scene, including Fluxus. Wolf Vostell lived in Cologne. He tried to convince me that his pictures were scores. Scores for happenings. I very much liked his pictures, those collages, as pictures. But why scores? We argued very heatedly about it from time to time. At one Flux Festival, he spent hours in silent concentration while sticking pins into huge chunks of raw meat. Right beside him, a naked and completely wasted Charlotte Moorman played the cello, wrapped in cellophane. She passed out and Nam June Paik and I moved her onto a sofa and used cold compresses to bring her back to Fluxus life. The first of the nine tracks from *Album für Mogli* – entitled 'ObSzene' – is very clearly a reply to Charlotte's performance. *Album für Mogli*, my last and still unfinished composition prior to Can, was heavily influenced by Fluxus. And also those first, sometimes quite aggressive performances by Can at the Schloss Nörvenich still had a certain relation to Fluxus.

Hans Ulrich Obrist: There was an insane Fluxus scene in Germany. It also had a lot to do with the war, and people like Emmett Williams and Nam June Paik came to Germany. This was the unbelievable post-war modernity, which Kasper König examined very well in the exhibition *From Here – Two Months of New German Art in Düsseldorf*. He showed that Fluxus is post-national German art.

IS: For me, Fluxus was also a kind of protest against serialism. I got into squabbles with Stockhausen now and then, even though I loved his music and working with him was wonderful. The problem, however, was his dogmatism. Fluxus was truly the opposite of dogmatic.

Andrew Innes: Did you openly rebel against Stockhausen, then?

IS: In a way, I did. I had many discussions with him when I studied and worked with him. Unlike Holger Czukay. He was some kind of father figure for Holger. But I learned a lot from him. His analyses of his music were really fantastic! But at the time, in the early sixties, he was so dogmatic! Later, he lost his dogmatism.

AI: I only got into Stockhausen a couple of years ago and went to see him at the Barbican in 2009. By then he had evolved into a rock 'n' roll star and he seemed very closed-minded. I knew he was important, sure, but I'd never listened to his compositions.

Daniel Miller: Stockhausen was very cool for a certain group of people in those days. People wouldn't listen to his records, but he was still considered to be very cool. They'd drop his name. I was kind of like that too, but at least I had heard some recordings of his. It made sense that this was one of the roots of Can's music. There was the more blues-oriented music, coming from the Afro-American sources of blues and soul – which I loved and still love – and there was the prog-rock stuff coming more from classical music. But the music that Can made was something that came from some-where else. Stockhausen was definitely somewhere else.

IS: Stockhausen's music still came from a European and especially a German tradition. There is still a lot of nineteenth century in it.

AI: I'd just never been exposed to Stockhausen. Or any other mod-ern classical music, to be honest. Sure, if somebody would buy me a ticket to see Stravinsky, I'd go. There was a concert recently of work by a French futurist which had an aircraft engine, telephone bells, some sirens – it's a piece from 1924. I went to see that and it was wild. They had half an aircraft engine on stage. You could sense why it caused a riot in Paris back in the day. But then again, they say that about everything in Paris. He also wrote a manifesto about music. It was such a radical piece, about how melodies were history, how they were a thing of the past. The futurists were beyond punk. I think the futurists must have taken a lot from the Russian revolution, as it was only a few years before.

IS: Do you remember which composition of Stockhausen you went to?

AI: It was a piece with helicopters – and it was just beautiful.

IS: That's his string quartet with four helicopters. Each of the four musicians plays inside one of the helicopters. And they communicate with each other, as far as they can communicate, through that noise.

Bobby Gillespie: My dad doesn't drink any more, but before he went to this pub in Glasgow every Friday night. And one Friday night a helicopter crashed into the pub. There was a band on stage which was in the middle of playing, and some dust came down from the ceiling. The boys in the band said, 'Wow, it looks like we brought the house down.' Then the bar collapsed and eight people died. My dad didn't go to the pub on that night, because there was something wrong with his car. Normally he went to this pub exactly around the time when that helicopter crashed there.

IS: Andrew, you mentioned Stravinsky. Did that mean something to your musical thinking and musical practice? Did that nourish you in a way?

AI: I was actually more taken by a piece by Edgar Varèse. When I first saw it, it really blew me away. When you are at school and you get taught about classical music, then you can end up easily quite bored. Some guys are trying to tell you that Bach is great, but you really aren't interested, because at that point, when you are twelve or thirteen, you want to hear some rock 'n' roll. And then to find out later that some of these guys were really revolutionary, that's great.

But it's wasted on the young. When you're really young, you don't want to be taught about Bach. But if you go to hear some Beethoven later in your life in a real concert hall, then you might have antennae for the sheer power that this music has. I had never heard a proper symphony by Beethoven, and so I thought, 'I have got to do this.' And it was heavier than Black Sabbath at some point, it was louder than the Who. And at one point it had this riff, and I thought, 'Wow, that is Beethoven?! That's just wild!'

IS: Beethoven composed great rhythms. He is extremely interesting rhythmically. In the Fifth Symphony there is this little riff, and it goes on and on.

BG: Did you ever take any of the classical stuff and put it in Can? You know, the way that in rock people steal riffs from other rock guys? Like, they copy and paste?

IS: I have never been especially interested in quoting or sampling others. This music is so deep inside of me because I grew up with it and I practised it for so long. Part of Can's music is the consciousness of a long history of music. Jaki started to play jazz at thirteen or fourteen. He started with Dixieland, of course, and he ended up with free jazz. So he drummed his way through the entire history of jazz. I studied all the last six hundred years of music, so it's not that you actively want to quote that, it's just there. And it's physically still there. You can buy records with music from the fourteenth century; Guillaume de Machaut, for instance. And you can buy all the American music of more than a hundred years of jazz and blues, and behind that is a history of African music. The music of the Dogon, for instance, is blues. It's there. And you can listen to the old Japanese court music, to *gagaku*, and to traditional Bejing opera and to Balinese music . . . And rarely any rock musician even listens to 'our' classical music.

BG: When they composed and played their music, it wasn't considered 'classical' music either. It was rather contemporary music, wasn't it?

IS: Guillaume de Machaut and the group of composers around him called their music *'ars nova'* – new art, new music. For me, this music is still contemporary, it still sounds new each time I listen to it. History has become more of a space that we inhabit rather than a timeline that fades into the forgotten.

HUO: It's also interesting how the new is defined.

IS: For me, it was in 1967, when I started to make rock music. That was a new experience for me as a musician.

HUO: Tell me more about your encounters with Cage.

IS: Cage taught me a lot, just through conversations. He also showed me how he prepared the piano. I then often organised piano evenings with two pianos: a prepared and a normal piano. In the first part of the evening I played on the unprepared piano – Webern, Debussy or something like that. In the second part I would play Cage compositions and sometimes my own things on the prepared piano. When I planned to play a prepared piano, I always told the organisers: 'Take a grand piano that isn't your most precious concert piano, because you simply don't know whether something will have changed with the instrument afterwards.' When I performed one of my own pieces in Heidelberg, I used a Remington electric razor and ran it across the bass strings of the grand piano – an incredible sound. I put the razor away and began playing normally again – and someone jumped up onto the stage, slammed the lid down on my hands and smacked me across the face. He shouted at me that Gieseking had played on this piano the previous week.

JA: Jesus . . .! At Einstürzende Neubauten concerts, for a time, bottles and cans were regularly thrown on the stage. It was often quite dangerous. I wasn't the guitarist yet at the time, but we were friends.

I saw it from the audience. That was exciting. You also always had to be careful in the audience. You were always nervous that something would come flying at you or a fire would break out. N. U. Unruh, one of the two steel drummers of the Neubauten, was a bit of a pyromaniac. He lit fires on the stage. It got really hot. You couldn't really relax at those concerts. But it was never boring.

BG: Irmin, how did you manage to become a student of Stockhausen? Were you assigned to him at university?

IS: No, it was active on my part. I wanted to study with him. Simple as that. Because I had heard his *Gesang der Jünglinge* on the radio. Before that, however, I studied composition and conducting at the Folkwang Academy in Essen, and also piano in the masterclass. This study wasn't free, but I had a scholarship, so I didn't have to pay anything. But it was almost taken away from me when I spent an entire semester with Marcel Proust's *In Search of Lost Time* – reading, thinking about what I had read, going out, dreaming . . . Thank God my conducting professor understood this literary escapade. After my conducting exam, I finally went to Cologne in 1964 to study with Stockhausen at his Cologne Courses for New Music. Earle Brown, Luciano Berio and Henri Pousseur also taught there. But for me it was mainly about Stockhausen and the WDR Studio for Electronic Music.

BG: What most attracted you to Stockhausen?

IS: In addition to his music, it was Stockhausen himself as a character, as a person, a teacher and a thinker. That reminds me of this incredible story which Stockhausen told me in the dressing room at the Barbican Centre. He had wanted to go back to the original version of *Telemusik* in order to digitise it. He didn't want to do it from the first score, but from the original tapes. And he insisted that no one except he himself should undertake this digitisation. So he sat down at the machine, put up the tape and rewound it at full speed. And suddenly thousands of tape snippets were flying around the studio. It happened so fast that he couldn't press the 'stop' button in time. So the original version of *Telemusik* was lying scattered throughout the room. Of course, nobody could put it back together.

BG: Did you ever play the music of Can for Stockhausen?

IS: Not personally. But one time Stockhausen was supposed to evaluate rock music from Germany for a German music journalist – it must have been around 1970 or '71. He listened to it all and found everything terrible – except for 'Aumgn' by Can. He thought that was really good. He asked the journalist who it was – it was a kind of musical blind date. And when he told him, Stockhausen said, 'No wonder. They were my students.'

BG: My boys . . .

IS: Exactly. That was sensational for us, because he didn't really appreciate anything after Monteverdi.

CN: What kind of figure was Stockhausen for you?

IS: For me, despite all admiration, he was a controversial figure. At one of his Courses for New Music, Stockhausen analysed *Gruppen*, the orchestral piece for three orchestras. It had a certain madness. He was obsessed to the core with his faith in structure. Everything related to everything. That fascinated me and repelled me at the same time. His courses were consistently incredibly exciting. As a teacher, he was very rigid, but he also brought his students to his home, and we would party at his house for nights on end. One sometimes has an image of him that he was this strict, authoritarian figure. As a teacher and composer he had that, but he wasn't that way at all in private – on the contrary, he could be very funny. I've learned amazing amounts about the architecture of music from him. His sense of relations was so complex that it was bordering on madness. He was someone who did what he did with incredible conviction. I admired that very much. Also later, when he allowed improvisation, though he didn't call it 'improvisation'. Just like us. I've always avoided that term. The concepts of 'jamming' and 'improvisation' are closely associated with jazz, and secondly, they imply a kind of abandon. Stockhausen called this kind of improvisation 'intuitive music', which corresponds to the meditative, to listening, and not playing anything before you have something to say. Alertness and concentration. For me, the term 'intuitive music' has always been very illuminating.

3

'He Wanted to Make Stone Age Music'

Jochen Arbeit, Geoff Barrow, Max Dax, Alec Empire, Bobby Gillespie, Andrew Innes, Hans-Joachim Irmler, Nick Kent, Carsten Nicolai, Michael Sheehy and Irmin Schmidt virtually meet in various places, among them the Santa Lucia Galerie der Gespräche, Berlin, the Grosvenor Hotel in Victoria, London, and a pub in Bristol.

Geoff Barrow: Can was massively important for me – even though my relationship started only in about 1991. I was working in London on the demos for the first Portishead album at someone's house, which had a studio in it. In the kitchen there was a radio that was always playing. It was at night when I went to the kitchen to grab a beer, and there was a track playing on the radio that immediately attracted my attention. To me it sounded like Public Enemy with a bit of A Tribe Called Quest, but someone was singing instead of rapping. Rhythmically it was really hard, and I thought it was a track from a brand-new band. More than that: I literally thought it was the best band in the world. I honestly thought that this was the music that was made for me. So I grabbed a cassette, banged it into the tape recorder unit of the radio and started to record. The song was already about three-quarters of the way through. Mark E. Smith was hosting the show on Radio 1 and he mumbled something about 'Can' and 'Vitamin C'. I didn't know whether the band was called Vitamin C and the track 'Can' – or vice versa. I had no clue. The next morning, I drove back to Bristol, where I went to this record shop and asked for a track called 'Can' by Vitamin C. The guy at the record store was a real asshole. He knew exactly what I was looking for, but he said he'd never heard of it. He was one of those typical, sort of anal record-collector guys. He owned a record shop, but he wouldn't sell me a record. But there was a customer in the store who lifted the secret. So I went over to the shelf, pulled it out and there it was: *Ege Bamyası*. I ran home, put it on and I just couldn't comprehend it. Especially when I read in the credits that this was a recording from 1972. I thought it couldn't be. My brain works in a way so that I overanalyse everything. As soon as I had heard the tune again I was trying to analyse it. I was like a robot, trying to work out information. When someone sees a painting, they go, 'Oh, it's from this-and-this period of time.' But my brain just couldn't comprehend it. The song just sounded so futuristic, but incredibly modern at the same time. When I found out it was from 1972, I was stunned, because I was a massive Hendrix fan. When you look at what his drummer Mitch Mitchell was playing, for instance, it was comparable, but there was less blues in your song. It was European. And I fell in love with Can.

Nick Kent: Can's music has aged in a very good way. I loved it then and I love it now. Can's music is timeless in a literal sense. Normally, when you listen to music, the era it was written in is usually evoked – maybe in a nostalgic way, but you could tell if it's from the seventies or from the eighties. But with Can's music, still nobody has caught up. I've not heard one group that has really managed to do so. I've read in the music press and I've heard groups that claim to be influenced by Can. There are an awful lot of them around. But I've not heard anyone who has even caught up to you – even now, after forty years. I have also never heard anyone who has caught up to Jimi Hendrix. If you think about it, nobody has actually caught up. It's not a case of advancing, but they have not even caught up to what has been done forty or fifty years ago. And that's what timeless means. That's your music. It rises above the formulaic stuff.

GB: I am one of these people who can get absolutely obsessed about one record. I don't go out and buy every record. I just obsess about this one record. But I've obviously bought your other records since. I investigated you all like some weird stalker – like we all do. The funniest thing about it was the fact that musically, I couldn't comprehend what you were doing on that record. I'm primarily a drummer. But it took me ten years before my brain was ready to actually work out what you guys were doing. I just couldn't take it in at the time.

Irmin Schmidt: What exactly was the difficulty?

GB: It was your ability to avoid standard patterns. Maybe that's a weird thing to say. The concept that you were naturally or not naturally pulling in a creative direction without resorting to standard procedures was so strange. There was unusual harmony. There were melody lines in a key that otherwise doesn't exist in the track – in a key that shouldn't exist. It was the complete opposite of root-note music. You didn't go to the automatic place. If you had 99 per cent of all musicians in the world in one room to play music, they would try to make music that would be recognisable. That can be great, but most of the time it's just boring. But you guys were somewhere else. It felt like you didn't actually write like that and that you were composing instantaneously. I hate the word 'jamming', but that's kind of what I mean.

IS: Somebody starts with something and the others try to fit in. There is always something that could lead to something. But you were right: nobody wrote anything. Even the words were invented on the spot. I mean, Damo Suzuki didn't really sing words; or rather, he sang words, but not lyrics. When something was growing, we used to say, 'That's a good idea, we have to follow it!' Simply by doing, something was created, and then you had this moment where the ignition started and something became electrified. Then we knew that we'd have to chase the piece that had just emerged. We didn't like the word 'jamming' very much either – to create something, you need a constant focus. Even if nobody knows where it is going. But every now and then, something magic happens. And since you are focused and constantly listening to the others while playing – or should I say, while composing – you follow the trail, and sooner or later you realise that you are working on a new composition. We couldn't fix anything afterwards. In our formative years we had a studio that we understood and used as an instrument, but we still could only record on a two-track tape machine. What we heard on our headphones was the final balance already. We couldn't fix anything later.

GB: Did you discuss the music before you played it?

IS: No. We'd discuss everything only after we had played it. We'd play and then we'd stop at some point, and then somebody might have commented on it. But we didn't talk that much. Rather, we played. Of course, sometimes there were also fights. But we would only argue about music. Jaki would sometimes insist that we shouldn't change a harmony because it would destroy the groove. But in between recording sessions we talked about music that we were listening to. And this, of course, included a lot of classical music, African and Asian music, et cetera. Every time we listened to music together, it also was about getting to know each other.

GB: My first record with Portishead turned twenty years old this year. My knowledge of music history is incredibly limited, though. I was thinking about this the other day: There are a lot of people who are incredibly versed in musical history and in art and film, et cetera. They are collectors, they consume and they study and compare. Pretty much all my musical life I have spent making music, and I had very little time listening to it. I find very little music that excites me. I don't feel like I really ever have the time to listen to stuff.

IS: I've also always listened to relatively little music. At night, I usually find it more exciting to listen to the silence. It was like that in

Cologne back in those days, and it's still the case today in Provence, when I sit out on the terrace at night and listen to the crickets chirping. When I listen to music, I always listen very consciously – never just peripherally. It was the same for the others in the band. For me, the conscious perception of rock music began with Jimi Hendrix, with Captain Beefheart and with James Brown. The Velvet Underground were also important. Before that, I listened to beat music at parties. I would dance to it, but somehow I didn't really get it. Yet I've listened to a huge amount of jazz – that was a very early influence. However, there was never a single time that I played some kinds of jazz pieces on the piano. I just couldn't do it.

NK: Captain Beefheart was really crazy. Talk about thinking outside the box! For this guy, the box didn't exist in the first place. But there was a method to the madness. If you were standing there and you looked at him doing his thing . . . For example, he'd tell his band, 'You can't go to the toilet before we go on stage. I want your bladders full, so you'll play with more urgency!' And they'd go along with him. I'm not saying that this was a brilliant idea, but it was just one of his many crazy ideas. So many of them worked. He was crazy with these ideas, but they worked. He had two bass players, not just one. And the drummer will have the smallest kit in the world – like a child's toy kit. So there will be two bassists, there will be two guitar players, one playing Delta blues. And he will be in the middle doing this Howling-Wolf-being-abducted-by-aliens type of vocal. And normally that would be a recipe for complete cacophony. But what he actually created from this complete madness was brilliant!

IS: With us it could never have become a recipe. You can't do that kind of concert with a recipe. It only works for those kinds of people.

NK: I just think that each of you as players was individualistic enough, so that each one of you could start it, and the others could lock in and bring their own stuff to it. It wasn't a case of, 'OK, I hear a slow blues here. Let's play it like B. B. King.' The time we are talking about is 1969 through to the seventies – there were still the old blues-rock clichés. There was a load of soul and funk clichés. There was a method to your madness. It's like James Brown. When you look at what James Brown was doing in 1967 – you could argue that he invented funk with 'Cold Sweat' and songs like that. And people were saying, 'What? He's just staying on one chord?' There was not really a verse–chorus, verse–chorus scheme. There was not a bridge. There was only one chord, and he was just making noises half of the time. But there was fucking supreme method to his madness. He created a new music.

IS: In 1969, 1970, when we'd tell music journalists that we loved Captain Beefheart, they often hadn't even heard of that band. So we'd play his music to them, and they'd say, 'Oh, you're crazy! That's not music!' There was this guy from San Francisco who came over to visit us in 1970, and he had a live tape of a Captain Beefheart gig. He told us that Beefheart detuned his musicians' guitars right before they went on stage. That is so wild and great! Imagine these four people playing the blues all wrong on detuned instruments. All of a sudden it was in a completely different universe. It was alien and wonderful – absolutely great!

NK: In that period there was some great music coming out. I don't want to become nostalgic here, but those were the days of a particular kind of electric music outside the whole rock thing, and even outside the progressive-rock thing. It all existed in its own world.

IS: One of the reasons we weren't a real rock or pop group is that nobody was interested in us as people. There was nothing about the personalities. When you are young and impressionable, you want to be like Mick Jagger or you want to be like Keith Richards. Nobody was interested in us. We kept ourselves almost secret. That's not really rock.

Max Dax: How did the studio, the personalities, the musical tastes, the contradictions merge when you started recording together?

IS: We recorded *Tago Mago* in the third year of Can's existence. The album is a prime example of how it all came together. Every single track on the album had a completely different genesis. And in its entirety the album shows almost every aspect of what this whole adventure was all about. Probably the most important thing when it comes to playing and recording music is to build and to think in structures. Our structure was the collage. The collage is one of the central stylistic principles of the twentieth century. That was especially the case in literature, film and visual arts, but also to a certain degree in music. If you watch movies frequently, you sooner or later get used to the concept of editing and harsh cuts. The same goes for the modern contemporary classical music that I grew up with. Take, for instance, the central piece of *Tago Mago*, 'Halleluwah': that track is almost twenty minutes long. It took ages until we had the groove finalised. But only when we had agreed on the groove did we start to record tunes that were based on this groove – some of them good, some of them bad. The final version that you can hear on *Tago Mago* is a collage of several late takes. Holger, Michael Karoli and I had built this architecture, whereas Jaki just wanted to play.

MD: You mean he wasn't interested in the idea of the collage?

IS: No, not at all! He just wanted to play. But every time we presented him the cut-ups we'd done, he'd always listen to them extra carefully. How often did he reject an edit that we had painfully cut together because he had heard a slightly slower beat here or a dragging groove there . . . But considering that 'Halleluwah' is one of our most popular songs, I suppose he was right.

MD: Let's talk about the importance of what you just called 'architecture' in music.

IS: Thanks to our studies under Stockhausen, Holger and I had quite a similar understanding of music as architecture. It was a common practice in so-called new music to collage pieces of taped music by cutting the tape. Stockhausen encouraged us to do so and to take apart and reassemble tape music at the Studio for Electronic Music in Cologne.

MD: Who did the cut-ups?

IS: Holger Czukay was the most gifted of us all when it came to editing the tapes. Like with some of the pieces by Miles Davis, you wouldn't hear that they were edits.

MD: 'Halleluwah' has one of the most incisive breaks in the history of pop music. Was this break the result of such an editing process?

IS: Yes. Like Sergei Eisenstein, who also edited his films radically, as if he was using a sword. And you can find an equally radical cut in the song 'Mother Sky'. Or take 'Oh Yeah' – you hear Damo Suzuki's voice played backwards at the beginning. But all the thinking and all the theory is worth nothing at all if you don't have someone like Holger Czukay – someone who knows the deep secrets of editing. I would go so far as to call collage a central pillar of our work. You could even consider the band itself a collage of people that don't fit together.

GB: I think that you guys knowingly invented the remix by working that way. I think our connection is in harmony. We all know the standard way to write a song, I guess: someone sings a melody, and you'd play the chord that goes with that melody and when the text part comes you'd play the matching chord again. But both our bands really don't have that. The note of the harmony that the melody sits on is actually an unusual phenomenon in our music. It's rare. That is what remixes do as well. In the late seventies and the eighties remixes were mostly disco versions of songs. They'd take the beat and put a bassline on it, and it would be something like an extended version for the disco. Later on, when a song would be remixed, you'd maybe have a string section from Wagner and a hip-hop beat put under a traditional pop song. It would be in the same key, but because it was Wagner there would be this strange harmonic tension between the melody and the strings – it would work but it would be strange. And you guys did this first. This is something that I always loved about Can. It was unusual.

IS: Yes, and I hear that in Portishead's music too.

GB: But it was first in Can. And you did it naturally. And I think that this is what most musicians are trying to work out: how did it happen naturally? It's not supposed to happen naturally, but in Can's case it did.

Alec Empire: I have always been excited by modern classical music. I have to add that I didn't start as a DJ and producer of DJ music. I played instruments and had played in bands before. But it was the mixing console of the DJ that really drew my attention. With this machine you could radically blend all kinds of music together. You actually could blend Messiaen's organ with a funk beat by James Brown. Not many DJs have ever done this really, but at least in the early hip-hop days the DJs were radically cutting up music and collaging it on the spot – and maybe they had it from Can, who basically tried the same as a band. I also really like remembering the early nineties, when jungle music suddenly was exploding. Other examples of musicians using cut-up methods were the dub reggae people, like Lee 'Scratch' Perry, who'd use the studio like an instrument. As we all know, jungle music heavily drew from dub music.

IS: Playing together in Can was like a constant clash of erratic sources. Different styles and musical ideas would clash in the moment when we'd record. Nobody in the group insisted on his ideas being superior to those of the others. Can did a couple of songs in which the harmonies are really pure. Nothing disturbs them – they are very conventional. But when you really listen carefully, then you find out that the changes in harmony are sometimes weird. There are some logical harmonic progressions, and all of a sudden it jumps somewhere else. In itself it is again logical, but it has nothing to do with the rest, really – a chorus, for instance, that seems to come from another world.

GB: But that's what we're talking about. That's why I talk about Public Enemy too. They'd take a piece of music from somewhere and they'd take a second piece of music from somewhere else, and they'd cram it in together, and it would create this powerful new song.

MD: Primal Scream later adapted this method. The album *Vanishing Point* contains the song 'Kowalski' – which is nothing other than a friendly appropriation of 'Halleluwah'.

Bobby Gillespie: Exactly. It has the same drums. Do you still remember, Irmin? Back in 1997 I met you, Holger and Jaki in Cologne. We had dinner together. I handed Jaki a CD with new demo recordings by Primal Scream. I knew he would be in London three weeks later, so I asked him if he wouldn't mind recording with us in the studio. On that demo CD there was also an early version of 'Kowalski'. When he visited us in the studio, I asked him how he liked the songs. He said that he especially liked the drums on 'Kowalski'. I replied that I wasn't surprised – after all, we had simply sampled his drum track. You might have even thought he hadn't noticed. I've asked myself a few of times since then whether he didn't just have an extremely dry sense of humour.

IS: He did! People always refer to what's come before, by the way. One is always influenced by something or by someone. We were influenced by James Brown, and I have been told that my melodies are reminiscent of Kurt Weill.

GB: It's interesting that you say that, because it was kind of a similar thing with Portishead. We had been influenced massively by American black music. But we are not black Americans. We were white people from Bristol. The city is traditionally culturally very mixed. Bristol was one of the largest slave-trading cities in Europe. Everything that you see in the city is pretty much built on the death of ten million Africans. It's horrendous. The councils have only now just started to work it up and commemorate. There has also always been a big West Indian culture in Bristol. But there has also been somewhat of a punk presence. Pirates came from Bristol. In Bristol's history you have Blackbeard the pirate and you have Banksy, and they're pretty much the same characters: they're humorous, they don't respect authority and they are trying to cause trouble. There has always been a huge reggae influence in Bristol, so the music we listened to has always been fairly slow. But we're not Jamaicans, so it was out of the question to play such music ourselves. And we wouldn't try to emulate American hip hop. We just try to write songs by using our version of American black-music production techniques. Like sampling.

IS: We actually sampled before anything like a sampler existed. Mostly we sampled our own stuff. But I sampled also before Can. I was fooling around with tapes, editing all kinds of snippets from classical music, from pop to environmental sounds.

GB: Were you aware of any other bands from other countries making interesting music that went in your direction? Bands like Plastic People of the Universe in Czechoslovakia or the Silver Apples in New York come to mind.

IS: I had heard things by Plastic People. I didn't know Silver Apples, although most of the things that interested me came from America: Stooges, Zappa, the Doors, Sly Stone, also MC5, the Holy Modal Rounders, among others. But I also loved Juliette Gréco and I found Cornelius Cardew exciting.

GB: All those records that you mentioned, I would not have guessed that they would have been important to Can. I wouldn't have guessed that the Velvet Underground, for instance, had been important for you. Possibly Zappa. The thing is, I've worked a lot with hip-hop artists from America, and we always talked about James Brown. And I asked every one of them if they knew Can. Mostly they didn't. So I'd put it on, and these guys would just freak out, because Can to them was like a mirror: Europe and black America. It was so interesting as a comparison – the way you worked and how hard and aggressive you were rhythmically. It was just this groove that was quite hard. It was exciting.

AE: I once read a text by William S. Burroughs called 'Riots Produce Riots'. He basically said that every sound is loaded in that sense. You could do a field recording of a street riot and later play it loud in a concert, for example, to a crowd. And you'd certainly have had a different crowd reaction without the riot sounds. You basically raise the energy level. Imagine playing riot sounds very loud in a shopping mall. Something would happen. Don't you think so?

IS: Something could happen, for sure. It actually sounds like a Fluxus idea.

AE: There are also plenty of examples when it comes to recorded music. I would, for instance, call Billie Holiday's 'Strange Fruit' a loaded song. Or there are the key songs of the Civil Rights Movement that were sung on the March on Washington. Songs by Aretha Franklin come to mind too. If you edit these songs or their atmospheres or little snippets of them – like a sample of a single drum beat – into your music, you automatically implement into them some of the source music's history, narration and weight. The music is literally inherited, on more than one level: on a musical and a political level, to name just two. And making music always involves at least two people: the musician and the listener. It is a form of communication that can use conceptual methods from literature or film as well.

IS: Maybe the aggressiveness and our tendency towards radical editing came from our shared childhood memories growing up in the ruins of post-war Germany.

Jochen Arbeit: Did Holger learn how to splice tape during his time with Stockhausen, at WDR, in the Studio for Electronic Music? Where could one even learn to do that? Was editing even a common practice back then?

IS: It was common in electronic music! And then Holger and I both learned a lot at the electronic studio at WDR. They were constantly editing there. We spliced miles of loops. Holger was more talented at splicing than I was. I wasn't so fascinated by that. He did it with great love and enthusiasm. Even when he was just fourteen, Holger earned money by repairing the radio for the neighbours. I never had that affinity for technology. But I had already made musical collages before Can. Can's film music for *A Big Grey-Blue Bird* by Thomas Schamoni is a veritable frenzy of splicing. It has a film within a film: the gangsters film the good guys, and they also film back. These films appear in the film on monitors. Everything is very intricate, and no one really understands what's going on. Thomas Schamoni wanted those films on the monitors to have their own sound world. For that, I recorded shortwave radio at home for hours. I cut it into loops, and then we played to them in the studio. I then edited those recordings again with the editor, Peter Przygodda. The short-wave sounds became motor sounds, from which a groove arises. It becomes music, into which we again mixed shortwave sounds, and so on and so on.

JA: Miles Davis did it at the same time, with Teo Macero, in the early seventies. They broke with the rigid song structures in jazz. Through collage techniques, through these long grooves, you could suddenly make a completely different kind of music. One might also mention Ennio Morricone here. Not only did he have a free-jazz band, he also questioned typical structures in his scores, experimented with sounds and long-lasting grooves.

IS: Morricone has written film scores that I still love to this day. There is a film music from him which I especially have in mind – one night I was slightly drunk and already pretty sleepy listening to it. Unfortunately, I can't recall the title of the film . . . It was some kind of crime film . . . There was just one little theme – it really burned itself into my memory – with four notes and two harmonies. It was as if he had just used a snippet of tape that he took from somewhere – a coincidental discovery. It doesn't even have a beginning or an end. And this turns up in the film again and again, quite abruptly, almost at random, while people are talking, but also when the villain drives around the corner. The music had no comprehensible dramaturgy at all. It was totally fascinating and lifted the entire film into a surreal sphere, because the music was so different. Of course, you notice it all the more if you also make film music. Then you think, 'Is he crazy?! What is he doing there?'

Hans-Joachim Irmler: The seventies were also a time of social experimentation – naturally aided by the absence of the Internet and modern communications media. We didn't know what others were doing at the very same time. It occurs to me that we are talking today for the first time in more than forty years! I remember that every time Can was touring in England, we [Faust] weren't in England, and whenever we went over to England, you had already left. Obviously we were always booked alternately.

IS: That wasn't only the case with Faust and Can. In the seventies people generally didn't know each other. There wasn't any exchange if you didn't happen to live in the same city. There wasn't, in that sense, a metropolis in Germany that could have been a magnet like

Berlin is today. There were many centres – Hamburg, Cologne, Munich, Frankfurt, Berlin. In that sense there was a sort of 'safety gap' between Faust and Can, which amounted to about 500 kilometres. The same applied to Amon Düül, who lived in Munich. But I had more contact with them, because I did theatre and film music in Munich. But what happened in Berlin was really a long way away – and you also had to make this adventurous journey through the GDR. That was rather torturous every time – our car smelled so suspicious. The dogs were always tumbling about inside it, looking for something. **MD:** Which musicians did you have contact with? In what cities?

IS: It was comparatively easy with Kraftwerk and Neu! They lived just 40 kilometres away from us, in Düsseldorf. But Faust, Tangerine Dream and Amon Düül – it was like travelling around the world to get to those cities and those bands. Of all the German groups, Faust was the only one we never encountered. How could that have been possible?

HJI: We not only lived far away from Cologne, we escaped civilisation and fled to the country. Then, after the seclusion of the German province, we went to England in 1972. We always carried the idea of encapsulation around with us. For a while, we tried to eliminate the influence of other civilising elements – and that is best done in the middle of nowhere. We followed through with it quite seriously by living in the countryside as if we were in a monastery. We had no contact with the outside world at all. No one from Hamburg was allowed to enter our retreat on Lüneburg Heath. It was a social experiment. We took it upon ourselves to get everything from ourselves. We thought that it wouldn't have worked in the big city.

IS: That's exactly why it's strange that all of the important groups that emerged in Germany in the late sixties and early seventies all had a common denominator: they experimented in order not to copy anything. And Faust, just like us, were determined to make something of their own, something that could only be created here in Germany. And then you flee to England. I don't understand that.

HJI: It was simply the case that out in the countryside in Germany, we no longer had the right input any more. We no longer got along so well with our German record company at the time. Then we received an offer from England, so we left.

MD: What role did your record company play back then?

HJI: A big one. It was the bank which financed our retreat on Lüneburg Heath. The story of Faust began with the idea that we were looking for a wealthy sponsor who could enable our life in the countryside. And we found that partner in the record company Polydor. But of course, for their money they wanted to see a success on the order of the Beatles. We couldn't deliver that, however. After two years, we no longer got along so well.

MD: How much money had the bank invested in Faust?

HJI: We were playing for high stakes – half a million Deutschmarks. We're still paying it off today.

IS: That's interesting. We wanted to keep total control over our music. That meant that we recorded our music with only two Revox stereo machines, yet it was our own means of production. We didn't want to get into a situation in which anybody could place demands on us.

HJI: We had no inhibitions in taking the money from Polydor. It was the largest record company in Germany at the time. Even if the deal was, of course, a little blue-eyed on both sides in retrospect. We never were the German Beatles, and we didn't want to be, anyway. But it was tempting to accept the money in order to finance our social experiment and the special music of Faust.

IS: I definitely understand why you withdrew. That was a very natural process, which we also went through. We often had to listen to beat fans telling us that we didn't make real music.

HJI: That's difficult to comprehend today, because Jaki Liebezeit is a great master of polyrhythm. He loves everything with odd rhythms. You have greater freedom with odd rhythms. You can dance better, you can make better associations. Jaki's grooves had something shamanistic.

IS: Absolutely. Repetitive grooves are part of rituals all around the globe. Jaki sometimes said – only half joking – he wanted to make Stone Age music. He wanted to get closer to the origins of music, something primordial in our body and brain. The suggestive, hypnotic energy of repetition and monotony. Cognitive neuroscience also deals with this.

Andrew Innes: If you talk to a neuroscientist, ask how repetition affects your brain. It seems like Can music just lures you into a different state. You can get lost in Can music. It drags you to this other place. It must affect the chemistry in your brain in some way.

BG: I recently watched some Can videos on YouTube. I found a set of you playing in Paris in 1973 at Bataclan. I had never seen that footage before. Especially in Michael Karoli's guitar figures I could hear James Brown. I was wondering how you arrived at doing the repetitive thing?

IS: It was there from the very first moment. Jaki's drumming has always been based on finding the one pattern that sort of defines a piece of music. Such a pattern sets up a rule, like a law, that determines the piece. One pattern that goes on and on in cycles, not necessarily absolutely identical, always slightly changing in volume, colour, intensity, et cetera.

AI: That is an amazing thing in your music. It is very hard to do a long song without it being boring. But your music has it all. Within that repetition it has these peaks – highs and lows, all the emotion.

BG: I think it is meditative. The repetition of Can's music puts me into some kind of meditative state. And apart from that, it's really interesting for me to realise that you dug Sly Stone and James Brown so much. That's probably the reason why there is so much space in Can's music. It is important to have rhythm and space.

IS: I think that is one big mystery of all art – that you leave space for the listener, the viewer or the reader. Leave the space, so they can beam themselves into it.

AI: But that is probably one of the hardest things to achieve, because there is an urge in most musicians to fill out space. If you hear a gap, you always tend to fill it up.

IS: I know that temptation. When the rhythmical structure leaves space, you feel tempted to put a wall of sound on top of it. It suffocates the music.

AI: But in the case of Can, the whole band is the rhythm section, even the singer is part of it. Usually it's just the bass player and the drummer.

BG: I learned a very important thing from Can: I don't have to be the melodic lead singer. I could write songs and sing rhythmically, and that could be a hook in itself.

IS: Sun Ra once said that in the whole Arkestra they were all percussionists. And that is exactly what Jaki was always saying, that he was not the one who makes the rhythm – everybody is a drummer, whether he is singing or playing the piano. Everybody is a percussionist.

HJI: I've recorded together with Jaki a lot in the past years. He once told me how he went from being a free jazzer to the drummer of Can. He told me that he learned from Malcolm Mooney that with a continuous beat you can achieve a completely different intensity than with a jazz beat, where one is rather playing a permanent sequence of little phrases.

AI: I recently became very sad when I noticed that rhythm sections are a dying phenomenon. The great rhythm sections are dying out. The great reggae rhythm sections, as well as the funk ones.

IS: It's a sign of the times that people think you can do it now with computers and sequencers. But could they replace Sly and Robbie?

BG: There can be a recklessness to it when a human being plays. That can be so exciting. And sexy as well.

IS: Yes, that is exactly it! There is a dynamic that you can never get from the machine. Even if Jaki is like a machine in terms of control. It's subtle, but if you watch how he treats the drums, you'll notice. Not every hit is directed to the same spot on the skin of the drum. It varies by maybe only a centimetre, but it makes a hell of a difference. It makes the drums melodic. Jaki's drums are singing.

BG: Twenty-one years ago, we once played with the Muscle Shoals Rhythm Section in Alabama. They had recorded for everybody, from Aretha Franklin to Arthur Conley and Wilson Pickett. We were rehearsing with them. At this point we didn't have a rhythm section, so it was just us two, a guitarist and a piano player. And their drummer, Roger Hawkins, kept looking at me for the entire two days we were playing together. So eventually I asked him, 'Why do you keep looking at me?' And he said, 'I am listening to what you are singing and I will play as soft as you sing or as hard as you sing. I am taking my cues from you because you are the singer.' And I was amazed, because any drummer we had worked with previous to that moment, any garage-rock drummer, would just beat away, no matter if it was a slow song or a hard song. But Roger was just like Jaki, except that he was a groove drummer, but it was the same kind of sensitivity. He was amazing. I was singing softly and he was playing softly, and because of that all the guys played softly. So the whole thing became more sensitive and beautiful. I learned so much playing with those guys.

MD: This touches on an interesting point: Can rejected blues and gospel music.

IS: I think it depends on what you understand by the term 'blues'. I recently listened again to 'Stranger Blues' by Michael Sheehy's band the Dream City Film Club, and I totally identify with it. First of all, there is the killer groove. It has nothing to do with what I usually mean when I say 'blues'. There aren't twelve bars; you guys are playing on one chord all the time. This to me is an absolutely genius way to play blues nowadays.

Michael Sheehy: Ha! But you noticed that it is basically an adaption of Jaki's groove from 'Halleluwah', didn't you?

IS: But your singing has a deep blues feeling to it. I was amazed to realise how blues music and Can's idea of composing could finally amalgamate. Your singing is so beautiful and humble on that song. You grew up in a tradition that I don't relate to. In Germany there was no blues tradition and no real legacy of pop and rock music when we started. Now it's different, of course.

MS: Did you ever feel tempted to engage with blues music?

IS: No. Jaki refused to pick up any blues references even more fiercely. Whenever Michael Karoli dared to get bluesy on the guitar, Jaki stopped playing immediately and shouted, 'Can you please stop playing that fucking blues?!'

MS: I can understand that, though. And there was no need at all to become like all the others. There were so many bands doing it well.

Whether you like them or not, the Stones were good at what they did. I doubt that I would have become a fan of Can if you had been a German band copying them. Listening to Can, on the other hand, fed into the way that our own music came out. I'm glad that we took those other influences. There really is nothing original under the sun, but I think that you can sometimes find original combinations. If you take two disparate ideas and put them together, you can get something strange, unique and interesting.

IS: But there is a flip side to what you've just said. If you are collaging diverse styles, you might be less successful because you can't be related to any of the main musical genres. You don't deliver to whatever market. You do your own thing. It sometimes takes quite a long time until the world finally recognises what you've created. At the same time, there has probably never been a time in which our culture has accepted so much diversity. But even nowadays you are more likely to be accepted if your music corresponds to a category.

MS: But there was a category called Krautrock. What did you guys make of that?

IS: I am totally indifferent about the term. It came up at a time when Kraftwerk and Neu! and Can were already established. I don't even know who came up with it.

Carsten Nicolai: Did you ever feel offended by the term 'Krautrock'?

IS: No. Actually, only Jaki was angry when he heard that term for the first time. The 'Krauts' were us Germans, of course. They could have said 'Boche', like the French do. In French, by the way, there is an even better term: *'les chleuhs'*. 'Chleuhrock' would have been wonderful. But unfortunately nobody ever thought of it.

GB: Obviously the media needed a term to tag the modern progressive German music scene: 'Wow, there is this sound coming from

Germany, and we don't really know these guys and we don't know if it's a movement – so, how we gonna call it?' How did you feel about the fact that you were loved in England?

IS: It was surprising for us when it happened. When we first came to Britain in 1971, we were really welcomed. People seemed to like us from the first moment – they even freaked out. In Glasgow someone broke me a rib hugging me hard. The journalists were also really approving. They probably respected that we weren't imitating British rock. Also, there weren't many bands from Germany who'd tour the UK back then. We were sort of the first ones – among Kraftwerk and Faust, of course. How did Portishead cope with being labelled trip hop?

GB: The label to us didn't mean anything. But everywhere in this world people would say, 'Portishead do trip hop – just like Massive Attack and Tricky from Bristol.' I would consider them friends, but we make music for completely different reasons. And there was never a movement. And unlike Massive Attack and Tricky, the very first Portishead record had blues elements to it. I think this came out of my naivety of songwriting. I didn't really understand the concept of songwriting, but I liked Public Enemy, who would use a heavy rhythm track with layers of audio together. And then they'd have a political message on top of that. So it was interesting that you could have this non-tuned form of music. The discordancy was exciting to me.

IS: There is something that I particularly like about Beth Gibbons: she sings these melodies that never seem to find an end. They start with the beginning of the piece, and only when the piece is over the melody also comes to a halt. Even if there are pauses in it, the melody silently continues. It just goes and goes and goes on. Was Beth ever into classical music?

GB: No. But it happens that she starts singing on the wrong beat.

And then she is amazing, because she can sing perfectly in tune a semitone down from her melody.

IS: That's one of the things that amaze me about Portishead. There is a chord and she is singing a melody over it, and all of a sudden she is a half-tone higher than the harmony actually allows. And that makes your music so wonderful. Apropos starting on the wrong note: once, Jaki and Reebop were playing a very complicated rhythm. I couldn't get into it and asked where the hell the *one* is. Reebop said, 'What a funny European concept, what a silly question! The *one* is where you start. It's your *one*.' It was a revelation to me.

GB: Some artists sing in the third person. It's their job and they sing for money, for fame, or whatever. But Beth doesn't. It's not in question. She cannot write a false song about someone else's life. She just can't do it. She has to write only from her pure self and honesty. It's incredible to work with her for that reason. She's never ambiguous. We didn't record a Portishead album in ten years because we couldn't. We couldn't write it because there was nothing to say. That's one of the reasons why I founded a new band called Beak> – to release these problems that I have with creating music. With Beak> we just play and we find ourselves somewhere. But with Portishead we end up not creating anything. The problem with me is that I analyse every single note that I put down. And because I do that it stops me from doing anything. Adrian Utley has the same problem. That makes it tough.

IS: Your music doesn't sound at all like there had been a difficult process to get to the final result.

GB: Our music might not sound like that because once we get going, we're fine. Can has dug a tiny little pathway that you can escape through. Can is the band where all these people end up. I think what you have created was a pathway.

IS: Thank you for saying that. That was what I really wanted to do when I gathered the people to form the band. I really wanted these different streams you are talking about to come together and become one.

4

'It Was a Conscious Discordance'

Geoff Barrow, Max Dax, Duncan Falloway, Bobby Gillespie, Hans-Joachim Irmler, Daniel Miller, Andreas Reihse and Irmin Schmidt virtually meet in various places, among them the Santa Lucia Galerie der Gespräche, Berlin, the Grosvenor Hotel in Victoria, London, and a pub in Bristol.

Irmin Schmidt: It is with discomfort that I remember the old times, when you had to spend an hour and a half at passport control every time you crossed a border. Those were the days when there was still the 'Carnet ATA' in use – a document that listed your valuable goods such as instruments, cameras, clothes, et cetera. Every time you crossed a border, the border police would check if you were still travelling with all the listed equipment. It seemed like they were thinking we'd sell our gear abroad. It was a nightmare and not glamorous at all. When we wanted to go on tour to the UK, we had to go from Cologne, where we were living at the time, through Belgium or France to come to Britain. Sometimes you even had to go through both countries. You had to cross at least two borders, and every time you spent an hour or two with paperwork, depending on the mood of the officers. I remember one day we arrived in Dover. After we had done the usual paperwork, we were sent off, and when we were 20 metres into the UK some border-police officer came running after us: 'Stop! Stop! You are a rock group, I saw you on television. You must be full of drugs!'

Daniel Miller: I saw Can soon after Damo Suzuki had left the band, in 1974 or '75. I might have even booked the tickets when he was still in the band. That was the first time I saw you live. It was an unbelievable concert. It was in the Drury Lane theatre.

IS: In England no one wanted to listen to imitations of British bands. They heard something in Can that was totally crazy and quite different. That was fascinating for them.

Hans-Joachim Irmler: And the presentation was also different. I imagine that you went on stage quite similarly to us, in completely normal outfits.

IS: We weren't at all glamorous, although we did have long hair and I wore dark-green round sunglasses with mother-of-pearl frames. Holger wore white gloves for a period. But above all, we were focused on the music. The lack of style didn't disturb anyone.

DM: Holger wasn't wearing his white gloves that night. My memory is that you played a long show, continuously, without a break. It felt explosive and alive and musical and machine-like in a good way – things working and moving together, not mechanical, but very organism-esque. It was one thing coming together rather than separate players. I had heard that on the record and I saw it live.

IS: When we came on stage, everything was very loose. Michael sometimes had to go to the loo at the last moment. It could happen that somebody would walk out first and then suddenly realise that he'd be all alone on stage. And then you had to start playing something.

Andreas Reihse: Was it about creating a trance-like state?

IS: A rhythmic sound will always set your body into some kind of movement. Even if you are sitting, your body will vibrate with the rhythm. A functioning groove is energy. Something is coming right at you. And because it's so incredibly physical, it's also impassioned.

It's a physical thing. It's such a powerful experience when a groove really grabs you and starts affecting you, and there is also that great sonic density. I can really enjoy that. I can bathe in it. Then it has a violent aspect, a lustful violence. Producing that pressure was important to us. In fact, I consider Can's music quite spiritual.

Duncan Falloway: All music is, in a way. The act of making music goes back to these ancient religious dances.

IS: So many rituals in religion are based on repetition and monotony. It also connects to healing. I remember a concert in Bristol, when this gang of heavy-metal rockers came into the dressing room before the show. One of them was stuttering. They came to visit us again after the concert and the guy was crying because he didn't stutter any more. They said that it was a miracle – that we had healed him with our music. A few days later, he of course was stuttering again. He wasn't healed for ever.

DF: I hope he bought your record and played it every few days!

IS: They started following us all over Britain. They were wonderful guys. In England we had groups of people who were there for almost every night of a tour.

DF: I remember those tours you did in the seventies. I didn't go to all of the concerts, but I went to quite a lot of them as you did a lot of touring in the UK, probably more than anywhere else.

IS: We definitely played there more often than in Germany. From 1971 we regularly toured in England. With great success and fantastic reviews. Sometimes we did two tours per year. On every tour we did about twenty concerts.

AR: Did you rehearse for your tours?

IS: Never. We always just played.

AR: It's the same for us with Kreidler.

IS: The stage situation didn't differ from the studio situation: the music emerged spontaneously. At the moment of the performance. That is an incredibly exciting situation, a permanent state of risk. Our pieces were not rehearsed and not reproduced. Specifically, there were no songs and no set list. Essentially, there was no set at all. Sometimes things happened that can only happen in that state. Then something magical develops. You're standing there on the stage and it takes off. You don't know exactly why and just watch your hands doing something. You're really only listening to the music and you are happy. Those moments are the reason why we did it.

AR: Was it ever about something like virtuosity?

IS: Our live performances were never about virtuosity. There is not a single Can piece on which I ever really showed off my abilities as a pianist. There is a part on 'Halleluwah' where the organ really starts chirping away and gets incredibly fast. But it doesn't happen in the foreground at all – I hid it behind clouds of sound. We all knew exactly what virtuosity is. Holger, who was, of course, himself a virtuoso, has always asserted in interviews that what we did was pure dilettantism. In a group in which listening to each other is the central element, any selfishly displayed instrumental virtuosity would be false.

Geoff Barrow: Were there times of you playing together when the guitar started playing a fifth harmony and you unknowingly went down there and just went, 'Wow!'?

IS: Yeah, or the opposite. The result could also be terrible.

GB: I think feeling comfortable within music is boring. We can all sit in a room and generally find a note to play on with which we feel comfortable – lots of people do. They hire rehearsal rooms, they get together with their friends, they have a couple of beers and they play accordion music and folk music and reggae music and rock music and whatever. It makes them feel comfortable. But then there are musicians who feel incredibly uncomfortable playing comfortable music.

IS: There is this particular balance between feeling uncomfortable and realising that you need to feel uncomfortable. At least that was the case with us. We had to feel uncomfortable to keep on pushing the music to the limits.

GB: You must have been aware of the excitement of discordance.

IS: There were beautiful moments of discordance on stage. Everybody was playing something, and let's say I played a chord and Holger played a bass to it. He'd change the chord from a C to an E7, and as a reaction I would do something totally different. We were interpreting each other in unexpected ways and we could go on like that for ever. It was a totally conscious discordance.

GB: Even if it went wrong, you still trusted each other enough to create and to be respectful of each other. So you still had strength within you as a group of musicians to support each other. Most bands play it safe and basically recreate the recording sessions, almost note for note. That's because there's a fear of being terrible in front of the people who have paid good money to come and see you.

IS: We could play terrible concerts. There were also concerts that failed. If you go onto the stage and don't know what will happen, then the atmosphere, the audience, your own mood and whether there might be strains within the group are decisive. It's absolutely clear that not everything will always succeed if you're not falling back on routines but inventing things on the spot. The strange thing was, that while we suffered through the bad music we were playing, the audience suffered with us – in an empathetic way. There was

417

this strange bond between the audience and us. There was no anger. It was more like the audience tried to help us get it right. The seventies were a time in which risk-taking, in a way, wasn't that risky. It wouldn't be an immediate catastrophe if you failed. Audiences to an extent even expected the unexpected from a performer. Can merely took risk-taking to a higher level. But today it's different: if you take a risk and fail, you might be written off immediately. Imagine a young and emerging band that is doing something that nobody wants to listen to. Imagine them doing that for a number of years – it's so much more difficult to do that nowadays because there is nobody out there who will help you. With us it happened more than once that we might deliver a first half of a concert where we didn't really click. But when we'd enter the stage to play the second half we'd realise that everybody was still there. Nobody had left. We were regularly surprised about our empathetic audiences. And it helped us to play a strong second set. Then all of a sudden it'd click and the magic was there. The good feeling took over.

GB: I'm sure that when Can had more of a name, it became even more difficult, because the expectations were much higher.

IS: Of course.

GB: But nobody whispered, 'Let's play something that they know'?

IS: No, with us it was never intended like that. Each piece by Can is available in a version on a record, and if we used material from this version onstage, then it was only to make something new out of it.

GB: So how did you play something like 'Sing Swan Song' or 'Vitamin C' live?

IS: We reproduced elements of the recorded tracks. We sometimes played three pieces at the same time. Because when Holger played the bass of 'Vitamin C', I didn't necessarily think of playing the barrel-organ melody from the recording, but I would play something quite different – something which might have appeared in another piece. So we played around with that. Things like that didn't happen accidentally. There were evenings when Damo sang 'Mushroom' – but no one else was playing that piece.

GB: Didn't you find that frustrating at times?

IS: No, the opposite was the case. We would have found it bizarre to reproduce the original arrangements. We maybe used elements and grooves, and then we'd get lost in the music and arrive somewhere else. And all of a sudden, we had a new piece. If you listen to 'Spoon' live, it has almost nothing in common with the original arrangement on the record. It's totally different. We didn't rehearse the live version. It just happened. There are concerts we did where we just played straight through for an hour and a half. During that hour and a half the riffs and elements from other songs appeared and then disappeared again. From time to time we played our pieces, but hardly anyone recognised them, because they had simply changed completely. Ending pieces was sometimes difficult. Two of us would think, 'That's it,' and finish playing. But Jaki would simply keep on drumming.

AR: And the fact that the audience knew tracks like 'Spoon' didn't trigger any expectations?

IS: We did sometimes play 'Spoon'. In 1999 Can released a compilation of live recordings that spanned the years 1972–7, and on it you can find a live version of 'Spoon'. And Peter Przygodda filmed us live in 1972 at the Sporthalle in Cologne. The film is called *Free Concert*. There we play 'Spoon' again. And on the *Lost Tapes* compilation you can find yet another live version of 'Spoon'. But if you compare these three versions with each other, you'll notice that there are almost no similarities. The only reoccurring motif is the opening keyboard riff. That's why the audience always recognises the song. The rest is reinvention.

BG: How long did you play for?

IS: We played long concerts. At least two and a half hours, and often longer. Most of the time our shows consisted of two sets. We'd play one hour, then we'd have a break of twenty minutes, and after that we'd play another two hours. The longest concert we ever played was six and a half hours long. That was in 1971, when we played in a university hall in Berlin during the time of the sometimes very fierce student protests. There was a lot of smoke in the air. On one side of the hall there were huge windows, so the audience could see the police waiting outside for the gig to end.

BG: Did the police actively interfere?

IS: No, they were not allowed by law to enter the university. But they were waiting for us to finish the concert, and everybody was giving them the finger. We had started playing at around nine o'clock and it was in the depths of winter and about −18°C outside. Together with the audience we decided that we would let them freeze their asses off. We wouldn't stop playing until the police would leave. They should see how we got drunk, how people would come on stage and give us spliffs. We also made short breaks every now and then and talked with members from the audience, then we'd have another spliff and go back on stage again to play for another one and a half hours. With all the breaks, our show went on for nearly seven hours. And at some point the police went home, because it just was unbearably cold outside. That was a nice night, with the audience responding and being so much a part of it. And we played good music.

HJI: At first I didn't want to perform live with Faust. I was only concerned with the studio. It was only later that I realised that playing live is also fun. I was the youngest in the band and for me it was all about the possibilities we had in the studio to change sounds and expand the music. It was only when Polydor urged us

– if not forced us – to play live that we dared to go on stage. We then did a furious concert in 1971, in Hamburg at the Musikhalle – one of the best concerts Faust ever played. There simply was nothing at all that was determined by what we had done before. We wanted to create a spatial sound in the Hamburg Musikhalle that would be capable of overcoming the shitty acoustics of the hall. Despite everything, the Musikhalle is a representative hall for serious music – with stucco and gold and columns – but we absolutely wanted to play there, motivated by our rebellious attitude. We then conceived a concert that was intended to create this specific *raumklang* – a sound that could only be created in this particular room. Playing in a hall like that came way too early in our career. Three hours before the concert I went to an electrical supply shop to buy the missing cables for our intended reinvention of spatial sound. We had set our minds on having a colour TV onstage for each band member – they had come onto the market in 1968 and were still quite expensive and small. So we set them up onstage, and when the concert was due to start at eight o'clock, nothing was ready yet. Except the TVs. So we were able to offer our audience the evening news, while we musicians were still soldering away in the background. A little later we suggested that the audience should visit the surrounding restaurants and maybe come back between ten and eleven o'clock. At one o'clock at night the whole thing ended with the caretaker of the Musikhalle bursting onto the stage and pulling the plug: 'That's enough! My wife says I have to come home!' It was a phenomenal concert.

IS: So it was a kind of expanded musical concept?

HJI: It wasn't just our intention to make music, but the whole event should have meaning. It was also during the time of the happenings.

IS: So it was actually Fluxus? As such, that would have been quite normal – if it had been announced as a Fluxus event.

HJI: Fortunately it was not announced as such. But it was exciting from A to Z. The expectations were indeed huge – even journalists from England had been flown in. And then nothing matched the expectations. It required a complete rethink. It was so exciting for me because there weren't any of the clichés of a rock concert during our gig. It was poetic.

BG: There's no longer any space for poetry when you see and comprehend the potentially fascist dimensions of a rock concert.

Max Dax: At the Glastonbury Festival in 2005 you did a Nazi salute to your audience during the concert and upon leaving the stage. In Germany you would possibly have been arrested. What was the background?

BG: First of all, we were very wasted that evening. And it was hardly 'our' audience! When I saw that mass of people, I just thought, 'You would all have been part of the Reichsparteitag in Nuremberg.' The masses were slavish consumers who threw themselves to the stars like fodder. So I displayed the gesture. I was fucking wasted.

MD: Isn't any rock festival with enough people in the audience potentially fascistic?

BG: Glastonbury is in some respects the end point of the festival culture. People buy the tickets one year in advance – at a time when they don't even know who is going to perform at all. In 2005 Kylie Minogue was supposed to be the headliner. When she cancelled the performance after her breast-cancer diagnosis, we were asked to play in her place. Of course, we agreed. At the time, we were in the midst of producing our album *Riot City Blues*. Before Glastonbury, we had perhaps not given a concert for a year and a half. We were completely worn out by all the amphetamines we had taken in the studio. Above all, we were constantly eating a kind of glue, which had a stimulating effect. We didn't sniff it – we swallowed the stuff.

You couldn't predict exactly how the substance would work; it was some kind of methamphetamine derivative. You had to drink a lot to come down again. And when we were on the main stage on Sunday evening, we were wasted. We probably offended a lot of people, because they wanted Kylie and got us instead. In addition, people were so far away from the high stage – maybe thirteen metres. And between us and the people there were dozens of BBC cameras set up. It had the effect that we were no longer playing for the people but for the cameras. The festival is broadcast live on television by the BBC. Due to the great distance between us and the audience, any communication was difficult. So I kept on insulting the people, until I was finally escorted off the stage by security. But the show itself was great. You can still watch it on YouTube. Perhaps we were also so loaded because right before the show our time was shortened: from sixty minutes to fifty-five, then finally forty-five. It was actually disrespectful.

MD: Did Can ever experience similar concert situations?

IS: Not often. Mainly because we hardly played at festivals at that time. Only right at the beginning, and that had nothing to do with festival culture as it is today. For example, I don't recall that we ever had to play so far away from the audience. Nevertheless, our concerts were often aggressive, even if our aggression was never directed against our audience. I remember a concert in Cheltenham in England. Immediately before we were due to go on stage, the door of our dressing room opens. And three guys are standing there: in the middle is some kind of Steve McQueen copy, and to the left and right of him are two very bad imitations from Mafia films, wearing sunglasses and thinking themselves so incredibly cool: 'Hands on the table! We are the drug squad!' So we put our hands on the table and allowed ourselves to be searched. But they didn't find anything. Except for one joint, a gift from a fan, which Jaki handed over right away. So we were instructed to accompany them to the station.

However, I was permitted to make an announcement beforehand. I went onto the stage and said, 'The drug squad is here. We have to go to the police station. So there will be no concert.' That made people really aggressive. And I heated that mood up vigorously. They began to demolish the hall. The promoter almost went mad, but he managed to convince the police. And then we played an extremely aggressive show.

MD: And the police just went home?

IS: We had to go to the station after the concert, but just to annoy them we played a ridiculously long set.

BG: There simply is a difference, whether the audience participates in the event or only consumes it. Glastonbury was also charged because it had been raining buckets from Thursday to Sunday, and it was only on Sunday evening, just before we went on the stage, that the sun came out. This clash between an audience, which had been soaked to the bone for four days, and a band that was no longer able to function from all those amphetamines was pretty remarkable. Of all the bands that played in Glastonbury that year, we got the most publicity by far. Two years earlier we had already played as headliners on the small stage. We were a lot tighter, in a better mood and possibly also more relevant than in 2005, but nobody talks about that gig any more. But playing on occasions such as Glastonbury also means that you see the way the UK looks and feels – grey and damp and sick and old. A bit oppressive.

IS: Do you still think of Britain like that?

BG: When I was younger, it felt a bit more oppressed. But maybe that was just a side effect of being young, of being a teenager. The second album that John Lydon made with Public Image Ltd in 1979 really feels like it felt like back then. It was a good piece of art. It was true to its time. Still, it is kind of depressive.

IS: Your latest record doesn't sound that depressed.

BG: That's because some of it was done in Los Angeles. We were out in the sunshine. And I feel a lot better now, anyhow. Is it true that when the Sex Pistols split up, you received a call from Johnny Lydon?

IS: That was in around 1977. He wanted to be our singer. A few years earlier we would have invited him to come along, play a few concerts with us and see what happens – as we always did when somebody wanted to sing with us and we considered it a good idea. We invited people to the studio and did sessions, but mostly we invited people to do concerts on the spot, to get right into it and see how they behaved. Unfortunately, it was too late. Can was already in the process of breaking up.

BG: Johnny was an idol for us as teenagers. And when the Sex Pistols split up, we all wondered what he would do next. I can well imagine that he was asked by Richard Branson to be the singer of a kick-ass rock 'n' roll band. That would have been the success formula of the day. Instead, he preferred to play this very strange and, what's more, very personal and also painful music with Public Image Ltd. 'Theme', the first song on PiL's first album *Public Image*, was over nine minutes long, and John Lydon repeated the line again and again: 'I wish I could die!' I loved that song, but he didn't exactly make it easy for himself. His music and singing were pure, unconstrained expression. The song had an incredible power. And let's not forget: it was Lydon's first sign of life after the end of the Sex Pistols. It was the record that everyone had been waiting for. He showed it to all those who were looking forward to three-minute rock 'n' roll. The story about the call makes total sense: John Lydon kind of formed his own version of Can with Public Image Ltd. It's a great fusion. And it sounds really British, as well. Do you remember what time he called you?

IS: At around three o'clock in the morning. 'Think about it! Think about it!' he kept on saying. I do believe he would have fit in rather well. He should have called two or three years earlier.

5

'Not Playing Was My Contribution to the Song'

═══════════════

Jochen Arbeit, Max Dax, Alec Empire, Daniel Miller, Carsten Nicolai, Hans Ulrich Obrist, Peter Saville and Irmin Schmidt virtually meet in various places, among them the Santa Lucia Galerie der Gespräche, Berlin, the Grosvenor Hotel in Victoria, London, and the Serpentine Gallery in London.

Peter Saville: I have to confess that the first album I had to go and buy for myself was Kraftwerk's *Autobahn*. Sorry, but it's true.

Irmin Schmidt: There is nothing to be sorry about. With Kraftwerk, I did feel a kinship. But it's like that: we were sort of expressionists and they are more like Mondrian – they are constructivists. There is something very original in what they did.

PS: I first of all liked the cover. I remember I liked the single edit and eventually found out that the track was much longer on the album. So I had to have the album. And all these albums – from Kraftwerk and Neu! to Can – had something about them because they were a culture coming from another place that was very interesting to me. But I was most interested in images, the surfaces and the look of things. Visually the Kraftwerk albums did appeal to me more than the Can covers. Of course, back then I liked the cover artwork of Roxy Music. The first concert I went to was David Bowie in 1969. He was the support act, but he looked great. As I said, I was interested in the look of things.

427

IS: Today I regret that we were not careful enough with our covers. There is not much that is stylish about Can.

PS: I was stylish and that was a handicap, and then I made it my job. But you learn. And it's always the same: you start somewhere and then you learn.

IS: You have become a style icon.

PS: I would never have thought that you'd know of me. I had to ask Max why you wanted to meet me. I felt flattered and honoured.

IS: When I discovered your cover art, I had to think of Can's cover artwork, and I figured that we did exactly the opposite of what you were doing. Our first record, *Monster Movie*, had a monster on the cover. I was imagining artwork that wouldn't relate to the album title at all. In that sense I really love your work for New Order. Some of your artwork literally has nothing to do with the album title or the music. It stands for itself. I always admired that.

PS: If you don't mind, since you mentioned them let me say how I came to do the covers for New Order. When I was at school, the pop movement was like a window to another world. In Manchester there was no contemporary art in our local universe. Magazines and record-shop windows were our sources of information. The record cover was art for us. And the record shop was the gallery that we were aware of. So this is what we emulated. At school our art teacher encouraged some of us to consider studying graphic design, so I attended art school from 1974 to 1978. Punk happened in the middle of my degree. And as you know, punk was like a *coup d'état* in youth culture. What we call the second generation of rock had become quite corrupt and self-serving – like a political administration that has eventually lost connection with its electorate. By the time you are floating inflatable pigs over Battersea Power Station and philharmonic orchestras are playing with Deep Purple, you are

428

not connecting with the fifteen-year-olds on housing estates any more. Punk was a *coup d'état* – young people taking their culture back. I remember one particular night in 1976. I was in a basement in Manchester in a small club with maybe thirty people and a band playing – it was visceral, it was immediate. In my mind I thought, 'Maybe this is what rock 'n' roll was like at the beginning, something that you could feel and touch.' By the time I was fifteen or sixteen, rock had become an entertainment spectacle. And punk brought it right back next to you. And you could also be part of it. All you had to do was get an instrument, shout a lot, take a picture or write something – basically it was a potentially inclusive experience. You only had to contribute something.

IS: How did you get involved with Factory Records, where you eventually developed your own graphical style?

PS: A local television personality, the regional *Granada Reports* TV host Tony Wilson, organised a venue. It was what young people nowadays call 'a night'. By 1978 all the punk and new-wave clubs that had existed in Manchester had been closed by the police or the city council. So Tony, as a champion of the new music that he was, booked a venue. And I had heard of this and went to the Granada TV station and asked to see him. I told him that I would like to contribute. I hadn't really done anything to this point, I had nothing to show to him. But I had found my way into the canon of graphic design going back to revolutionary Russia and pre-war Germany, to Malevich's *Black Square* and to the Bauhaus and ultimately to the typography of Jan Tschichold. I had borrowed the books from the library and I noticed that I was almost the only person to have ever taken them out. A universe opened. I remember the moment as if it was yesterday. I was twenty-one, sitting in the refectory of the art school and my life had just begun. I was introduced to what I didn't know. And that was vast. I was already in the final year at art school, but my real education started at this moment when I realised what

I wanted to learn. I showed Tony Wilson a book by the very ascetic Jan Tschichold. Tschichold's hyper-cool was the one place beyond Bauhaus and Russian constructivism that my contemporaries had not gone. For me, he was the Kraftwerk of typography. *Die Neue Typographie* was Tschichold's manifesto from 1919 about how communications in the new industrial age should be. Tony Wilson, like most British intellectuals, didn't have a particularly visual culture at all, but he said, 'That looks good, do a poster.' So I did the first poster for the Factory. From there on, and through sheer wilfulness, we released a record. It turned out that some really good new groups didn't have a deal: for example, Cabaret Voltaire from Sheffield or the Durutti Column from Manchester. And Joy Division didn't have a contract either. It was Tony's suggestion that we should release a record to help these bands get a 'real' record deal. The idea was to give them more exposure.

IS: Like a dummy?

PS: Exactly. Like a springboard. And of course the first question that arose was: 'But how can we do this?' In 1977/8 people were only just starting to realise that you didn't have to sell your soul to EMI or Columbia to release a record.

IS: We started like that too.

PS: It seemed doable to us. I had seen my poster on Manchester's streets. That felt good. And I knew that a record sleeve would even go further, as it would be in the windows of the record stores – our art galleries. So we started Factory Records, but I wouldn't say that Factory was ever a real record company. We just released records. The result of that, some months later, was that Joy Division asked Factory to release their debut album independently. And they asked us to really release it – and not just as a springboard. And as I had put an address on the back sleeve of our first release, hundreds of demo tapes had come in. And that's how we found Orchestral Manoeuvres in the Dark from Liverpool. They had sent us a demo tape. So what started then was genuinely a collective. Nobody really knew anything. Tony was in charge because he was the most grown-up. But it wasn't his professional job. He was a well-paid reporter on Granada Television. At Factory he was kind of playing the boss in a pop Svengalian way. I was doing graphics the way I thought you did graphics. And the groups were being the way they thought being a group was. And Rob Gretton, who managed Joy Division, was managing the group in a way he thought a group is managed. There was no actual experience. In the industry, the moment of reality usually comes when you sign a record contract and you take the advance. But that never happened at Factory. There never were any advances paid. There was never a contract. There was not even any money for promotion. There was nothing. So the collective started as an autonomous entity, and it continued in that way. No one was really in charge. But we all would be giving something. And that was Factory, and it stayed like that for the next fourteen years. Everyone did things the way they thought it was done. It was extraordinary that it worked for such a long time.

IS: Can were exactly like that. And the way you describe Factory Records reminds me of anarchism – in the most positive sense.

PS: Factory Records was an organised anarchy. And no one necessarily liked what the others did, but they did not presume to tell them what to do. It is very interesting when you hear Peter Hook and Bernard Sumner talk about Joy Division's first album, *Unknown Pleasures*, which Martin Hannett produced. They recorded in the studio, and at a certain point Martin told the band to leave him alone as he had an album to produce! So off they went, and Martin produced the album. And Joy Division didn't really like it. When you read interviews with Peter and Bernard, you'll notice that they don't actually like *Unknown Pleasures*. They say, 'It's not what we wanted.' Martin had done it his way. And the same thing applied to

431

me. I did what I wanted to do. For the cover of *Unknown Pleasures* they had found this amazing wave image in a book. They said, 'We would like it black on white.' I said, 'Fine.' They left, and I did it white on black. They did not see it until they had the finished album in their hands. I did the covers for Joy Division and for New Order relatively on my own, and they don't particularly like them.

IS: They still don't like them?!

PS: No, not really.

IS: I like your artworks for New Order because they have a narration that does not necessarily relate to the music.

PS: They don't relate to the music.

IS: I hated our first album cover because its motif was so stupidly related to the album's title, *Monster Movie*. It is a great album, but it didn't need a monster on the cover. In hindsight, it would have been very interesting to have worked together with you.

PS: If the group are involved, you can often end up with the consequences of a disagreement: a compromise. Ultimately, most bands are a hierarchy and one person decides. With all the other record covers that I have done, I was working with that one person. If you do a Pulp cover, you converse with Jarvis. You do a Roxy Music cover, it's with Bryan. You do a Suede cover, it's with Brett Anderson. It's very simple.

IS: Can didn't have that kind of a hierarchy. In Can there was no one person who was in charge. It was always the anarchist collective. But of course, when decisions had to be made, the processes sometimes became annoyingly slow.

PS: Can would have needed yet another member in the group that was responsible for the graphic design and the covers.

Daniel Miller: I must say, I really like the English sleeve of *Tago Mago*. It has a shot of the band at a concert on it.

IS: The photo is a still from the Can film about the free concert in Cologne by Peter Przygodda. Robbie Müller was one of three cameramen who shot the film, and this particular still is by him. Both worked intensely with Wim Wenders – Peter as a cutter and Robbie as the director of photography. I still think he is one of the best cameramen ever. We didn't like the German cover image of *Tago Mago*. We called it '*Kotzkopf*' – 'vomit head'. The graphics department of the record company had taken care of the graphic design. And they had to do it because we didn't provide any ideas. We were very inexperienced in dealing with record companies. They had no right to say anything about the music. They had to take what we provided, and we never discussed the music with them.

DM: There was definitely a lack of consistency among the artwork. I was pretty much into sleeves. I would buy records on the basis of how the sleeves looked.

IS: I quite liked the cover for 'Blue Monday' that you did for New Order. You converted all the language on the cover into a colour code. There is literally nothing else on the cover. What does the code actually say?

PS: It says: FAC 73 BLUE MONDAY AND THE BEACH NEW ORDER. It's actually quite easy, if you know the code! I used the same code on 'Confusion' and *Power, Corruption and Lies*. The real point is, there was nothing written on it, and no record company in the world would have released something like this in 1983. No sticker, no shrink-wrap, no nothing. And don't forget, the single was seven minutes long, that's why we had to release it as a twelve-inch. It wasn't even going to be played on the radio. And then it sold two million copies. It became the biggest-selling twelve-inch single of all time. It proved me right that you don't have to write anything on a record sleeve. When has anyone ever failed to find a record they want in a shop? If you don't find it, you ask someone where it is. 'Blue Monday' is the ultimate proof that you don't need any of that stuff. But it was only because Factory was this autonomous collective. That's how I was able to do what I did. Otherwise it could have never happened. And then it proved that a cultured object can be part of the everyday. If you can do a record cover like this, you can also do a bus ticket like that. You can do a cigarette packet like that. You can do anything. It is not limited to the context of museums and galleries. I always ask myself, 'Why can't art exist in our everyday?'

IS: Kurt Schwitters took Hannover bus tickets and glued them on paper. He – among others – was groundbreaking as he introduced the concept of collage into art. And that's the way Can bricolaged their music – it originated from the art world. Can were a collage band. You make non-fitting elements fit together.

PS: The cover to *Power, Corruption and Lies* is still my favourite work, because for me it is the most biographic. In hindsight, it took me almost twenty years to understand exactly what I'd done. I finally saw it when sitting in my mother's living room. She had to move into a much smaller flat when she retired, and there were many of the family possessions in one room. I realised that the family home was the front cover of *Power, Corruption and Lies* – the nineteenth-century oil painting by Henri Fantin-Latour was the epitome of the environment that I had grown up in. The painting was home and the colour code on the back cover was the industrial north-west outside. The front and the back are the two poles of my childhood. It has nothing to do with the music, but there is a synergy of the pastoral and the industrial.

IS: But was there also an epiphany in the case of 'Blue Monday'?

PS: It is 'Blue Monday' that defines New Order after Joy Division. And being into Kraftwerk I liked the transition. It took the band eighteen months to find who they would be without Ian Curtis, the talismanic writer and poet. Very rarely does a group continue after they lose the singer/songwriter. They usually dissolve, as the Doors did after Jim Morrison. New Order had to answer the specific question of who they really were after Ian had died. They were a punk band and they didn't really have a voice. But what they had was a sensibility of convergence. They did like disco. They liked Giorgio Moroder. They liked Kraftwerk. They liked Chic. But they were a post-punk new-wave band. At that time you had long hair or short hair. You either listened to rock or to dance music. And with 'Blue Monday' they just made a very courageous statement and said, 'Yes, we are a post-punk rock group – but we like sequencers!' It was extraordinary to hear 'Blue Monday' then because so many wanted to hear electronic music, but it just hadn't been 'allowed' before. It was a mixed marriage. It was fusion. And 'Blue Monday' is the beginning of what then happened to music. Since then everything has merged.

IS: But how did you come up with the idea for such an elegant and black futuristic cover?

PS: When I went to the rehearsal room, I spotted a black object that immediately caught my attention. 'That's a floppy disk,' said Stephen [Morris]. I had heard of floppy disks but I'd never seen one. It was computer technology. And in 1983 you didn't have computers. So I asked Stephen if I could have it, and he said, 'You can't take that one. There's "Blue Monday" on it.' But he opened a box and gave me an empty one. And this floppy disk looked great. I transferred that look onto a record sleeve like a matrix.

Max Dax: When I spoke to Jean-Michel Jarre the other day, he told me that when he was a child, his mother used to sew at home and that she was using a sewing machine. The rhythm that machine made was music to his ears. As we all know, he later became a scholar of Pierre Schaeffer and Pierre Henry. It is interesting how the concept of collage or of adapting ideas and patterns seems to be a driving and reoccurring factor within the realm of music.

IS: Some say that looming machines were literally the first computers, because they used punch cards to operate the patterns of the looms.

Carsten Nicolai: The first textile machines were basically mechanical computers. The cartridge paper is a stamped series of patterned holes which function as the schematic representation for the patterns fed into and woven by the textile machines.

PS: And where were these machines invented? In Manchester! The north of England was the centre of the world's cotton-looming industry. The connection is obvious. There is a direct link from looming-machine patterns to computers to digital and to New Order.

CN: I remember some day after the reunification of Germany, I wandered into one of those defunct looming factories in Chemnitz – during the Industrial Revolution, Chemnitz was Germany's industrial powerhouse, like Manchester – and happened to find a massive collection of cartridge-paper punch cards. Those were remarkable patterns drawn onto this really thick paper. These were beautiful, sometimes simple, sometimes highly complex weaving patterns – to me they looked like historic sheet music of the future.

Hans Ulrich Obrist: Do you still have them?

CN: Yes, there are more than one thousand drawings that I have in my archive. I'm still waiting to incorporate them into my work in the future – it's sort of a sketch pad, in a way.

HUO: And what are the drawings like? Are they geometrical?

CN: Yes, very geometrical and very beautiful. The industrial weaving machines produced these great abstract motifs – sometimes just huge ovals or other really simple forms. And because they were made bigger, they ended up looking like ornaments.

HUO: When were they from?

CN: The drawings themselves were done in the sixties, but I found them in the early nineties.

HUO: For me this invokes the history of the digital.

CN: Sure, it's the history of ones and zeros. In Germany the centre of the looming industry was in Chemnitz and Jena. Historically, there's a huge concentration of patents that were registered in the area, which was the result of industrialisation and the importance placed on technological advancement. It truly was a city of inventions. And I, of course, was interested in how such punch cards would translate into music.

PS: Didn't Stockhausen follow the same trail?

IS: No, Stockhausen claimed that in every atomic particle, in every smallest musical unit, the DNA of the whole musical piece should be defined. What he did in *Gruppen* and in his early works was exactly that: in every second of the music all parameters are already defined. But Stockhausen did indeed compose a piece called *Trans*, where he incorporated the sound of the weaver's shuttle going stereo from one loudspeaker to the other. The orchestra, meanwhile, is hidden behind a curtain.

PS: When I was twenty-three, I found a book in the library about avant-garde music scores. I really liked the book. When the first demo tape from Orchestral Manoeuvres in the Dark turned up, I immediately thought of it. I liked the look of the scores. For the band's first single, 'Electricity', I asked them to write their instrumental instructions in a similar way. So they drew a score, and I used that as the basis for the cover – remade with Letraset. We printed it black on black, and I remember the printer telling me that this wouldn't work, that it'd be impossible to print it that way. And of course it worked out very well.

IS: I am very bad with the technical aspects when it comes to studio work. So I often suggest things where the sound engineer will tell me that 'It wouldn't work.' That is exactly the point when it starts to get interesting.

PS: Sometimes experts are very quick to say that something 'wouldn't work'. And also we learn when we make a mistake. When something goes wrong, that's when we learn something.

IS: A mistake can be magical, it can be most exciting. Especially when you force machines to make mistakes.

PS: Yes, you have to use them wrongly. You see something – or in your case, you hear something – that you've never ever imagined. A mistake. It's the machine making a mistake. And I love it when the machine is doing it wrong.

IS: What about the other cover you did for Joy Division?

PS: The truly profound, if slightly spiritual, moment was the second Joy Division album, *Closer* – the one with the tomb on the cover. Joy Division were in London recording *Closer*, and I was in London too. I had a new job there. So Rob Gretton brought the band to my studio and said to me that they hadn't had the time to find anything for their cover themselves. He asked me what I would like to see, and the only thing that had really impressed me at that time was a series of photos by Bernard Pierre Wolff in *Zoom* magazine of a cemetery in Genoa.

IS: In what context did the magazine present these photos?

PS: I understood them as post-modernist photography. I didn't expect the group to be interested. The uncanny and strange thing is

Photograph taken by Werner Richter, who designed the cover for *Rite Time* and many of Irmin's solo albums

Opening for the Schulze-Vellinghausen collection in the Haus Kley, Dortmund, with Dieter Schönbach performing John Cage, 1964 (Anne Hubert)

Preparing the piano for the John Cage performance, with Hildegard, 1964 (Anne Hubert)

At school, 1955

At home, *c.*1964

During a conducting course, *c.*1964

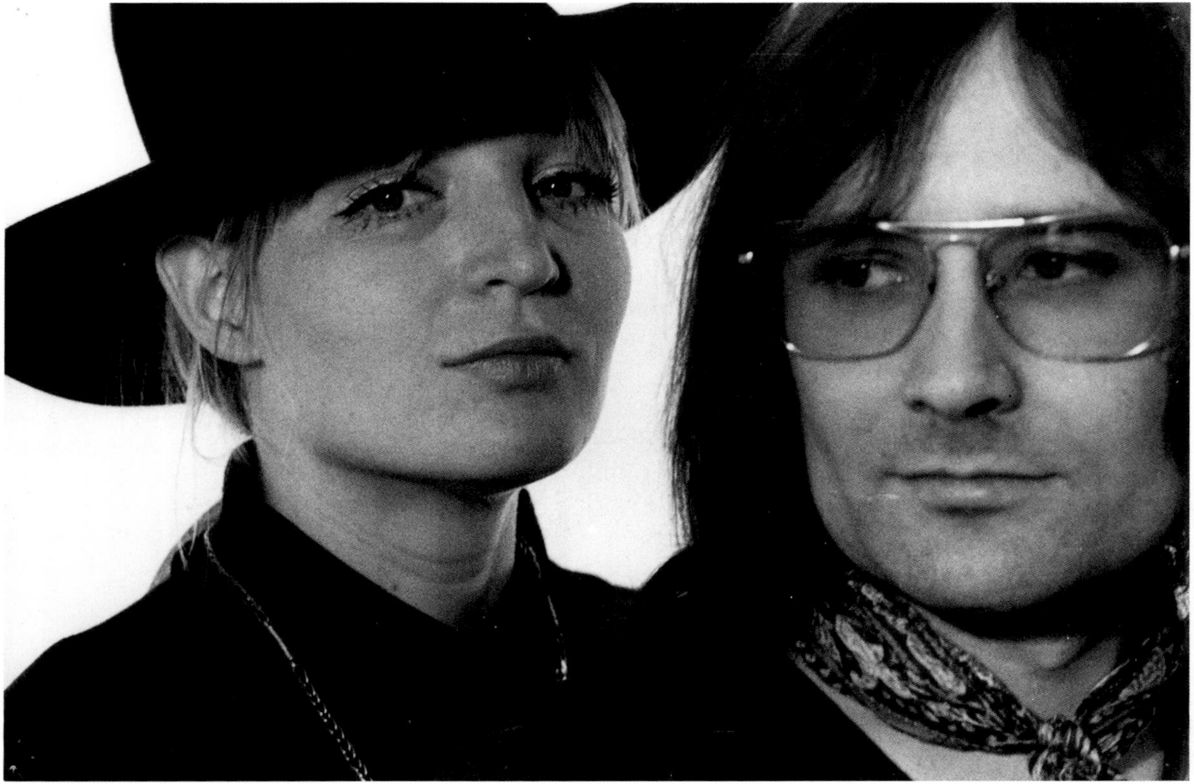

Irmin and Hildegard, 1970 (Romain Urhausen)

Irmin and his daughter, Sandra, in the Averard Hotel, London, during a Can tour of the UK, c.1973

Irmin and Sandra (with her favourite food, scampi) at La Coupole, during a Can tour of France, c.1973

Irmin Schmidt
Album für Mogli

7.01ml(g)

Für Jackson MacLow
(für Jackson MacLow)

sprechen wie ein Wurm sprechen würde oder der zurückhaltende aber
sehr beharrliche Drehorgelmann durch ein geöffnetes Fenster oder hinter

demolieren einige etwas Albernes
aber wissen auch nicht so recht
& stehen rum
& sind eine Einheit
& reagieren heftig
auf unseriös erscheinende Vorgänge

oder unschlüssig & auf Kunst treffen sie

und
sich
treffen
& eine andere Sprache einsetzen sitzt eines Abgeschlossenes

setzt eine Geschichte allerhand Schmähungen zwischen
reagiert einer auf etwas Abgeschlossenes

während einige rumstehen wie eine Einheit
& etwas Albernes demolieren
& heftig auf unseriös erscheinende
Vorgänge reagieren
& auch nicht so recht wissen

© Copyright 1967 by edition modern, München 13

Composition
No. 7 from
*Album für
Mogli* by Irmin
Schmidt, 1966

Premiere of Irmin's opera, *Gormenghast*, based on Mervyn Peake's trilogy, in Wuppertal, 1998 (gormenghastopera.com)

Ethiopia (Hans Silvester)

In Lacoste, France, standing between the sculptures of his dear friend, Ans Hey (Hans Silvester)

that Ian Curtis was writing in the daytime and recording the vocal tracks at night with Martin. The others in the group didn't know what he was singing. Annik, his Belgian girlfriend, knew what he was writing and was very concerned about his state of mind. She told Tony, and he told her not to worry, as it was 'only his art'. Ian was part of the group decision to show a tomb on the cover. Then some months later he was dead – well, actually maybe less, as the cover was still at the printer when Ian died. I remember this so well because I was the first person to realise that we might have a problem with the image. There was a serious discussion whether we change it or not. In the end we agreed that Ian had been part of choosing it, so we left it as it was. Everyone involved – but me in particular – had to wonder what had been going on in his mind when I showed them those pictures.

DM: It's an interesting question how the dynamic or the perception of Can would have changed if there had been more consistent or more appropriate artwork.

MD: You witnessed a more consistent and very successful approach when Anton Corbijn started to direct the covers and the graphical language for Depeche Mode. You can judge the kind of impact such an approach can have.

DM: A lot of things indeed came together with Depeche Mode when Anton Corbijn became involved. They became a brand. He created something that was instantly identifiable and consistent.

MD: Up to the point that people started saying, 'Oh, there's the new Anton Corbijn album.'

IS: He would have been good for Can.

DM: I think it made a lot of difference to Depeche Mode, because people started to take them a lot more seriously. At the time Anton Corbijn joined the band, everybody thought that Depeche Mode were a teeny pop band. But their music had changed quite quickly, and I think that this was eventually emphasised and amplified by Anton's artwork. It went from something that wasn't taken very seriously to people saying, 'Maybe there actually is something worth listening to here.' Can, on the other hand, were taken very seriously from the beginning. I am trying to remember what I thought of the artwork at the time. I definitely liked the English cover of *Tago Mago*. I kind of liked *Ege Bamyası* too. It's super-literal, but I still like it.

IS: The can on the cover of *Ege Bamyası* was one of the few exceptions, where the idea for a record cover came from the band and not from the record company. I saw the can of okra pods in a Turkish shop window. The cover is a photograph of the original can, and not a painting. When I had finally convinced the record company to use it, I sent a dummy of the cover to the Turkish company, whose brand name was 'CAN' – the Turkish word for 'life'. I wrote to them: 'We are a rock group, our name is Can, and we will use a photograph of your product on our record sleeve. That's a good promotion for you in Germany. We don't want anything for it, but could you allow the shop in Cologne where I saw the can first to give us fifty cans for free?' A letter from the company's lawyer came back, prohibiting us from using the name 'CAN' at all. So we bought about eighty or a hundred cans to send to journalists as a gift – we paid for them on our own. We never heard from them again. The letter must be still somewhere, but I have no idea where that could be.

DM: I had an entirely different experience with the cover of my first single. I wrote to the Motor Industry Research Bureau – they do crash tests – and I asked them if I could use some of their photographs. They were so happy to let me use their pictures. They were very excited about being in the music business.

IS: The only other cover that I sort of was involved in was the one for *Landed*. At our record company they all thought it was the most disgusting idea for a record cover they had ever come across.

DM: Well, what do you expect from record companies?!

PS: This is one of the things that I have never really understood: why do music people stay in the music world? And art people stay in the art world? Why don't they cross over more? I was really surprised when I went to college in the seventies to discover that there were such distinct camps. The convergent sensibility that is more common now was not happening at all.

IS: Funnily enough, that was one of the reasons why I founded Can in the first place. I was frustrated because of this camp mentality. I knew people from both worlds and couldn't understand why they were not interested in each other at all. For instance, the new music scene – that was a circle of approximately three hundred wise men – would gather twice a year in Stockholm or Palermo at their new music festivals. But if you asked one of them about modern pop or rock music or art, they wouldn't have a clue. The same could be said about pop or rock music. And the record industry was another camp and had little connection with the art world. Before Can, in the sixties, most of my friends were painters. I organised exhibitions for them – nowadays you'd call it 'curating' – and wrote about their work. But using their paintings – that's what the rest of the group thought – would come across as too intellectual and too pretentious. And I wasn't sure myself. What if they were right? I remember that for the cover of *Tago Mago* I proposed a painting by Cy Twombly. Ever since I had seen some of his paintings in an exhibition in 1963 at Haus am Waldsee in Berlin, I was totally fascinated by his work. But nobody agreed with me: too strange, too pretentious, like quoting Marcel Proust in a press release.

DM: Was there an anti-intellectual sentiment?

IS: There kind of was. We denied our musical virtuosity and consciously didn't show off. That included a ban on showing off intellectually. There was some anti-intellectual resentment within the band, even though our music is considered by many as being quite intellectual. For instance, Holger once stated in an interview that he had read only one book in his entire life – in a way, that was pretentious too. But Michael read a lot. I remember when I gave him Thomas Mann's *Joseph and His Brothers* he got totally excited. I read it again, just to accompany him, and we had a continuous conversation about the book for almost half a year. Jaki wouldn't have exhibited his knowledge anyway – and he knew a lot! I mean, he taught himself Sanskrit.

PS: A Can album in a Twombly cover is a much more interesting proposition. It would have been iconic. People like myself would have become more aware of Can, in the same way I had become aware of Kraftwerk through the *Autobahn* cover. My covers are never about music but in parallel. In that light, it seems weird to me that your other group members were against using a painting by Twombly, and that's intolerable. In the end, you took the path of least resistance because it is just too painful to always argue.

IS: It was already stressful enough to bring five people coming from five different musical disciplines under one umbrella.

PS: Autocracies can work better in the field of art, as it actually means that somebody with a vision gets something done. I don't have anything against group decisions per se, but they can go terribly wrong. With New Order, they would just disagree in principle. I once presented a logo in black and white and asked them what colour they'd like it to be. And Bernard said blue. Which was fine with me as I love blue. Hooky: red. Stephen: green. Gillian [Gilbert]: what about yellow? And I realised that they were not saying what they thought; they were just saying something different to what the others said. There was no attempt at an agreement. The opposite was the case. So I turned to Rob as their manager to possibly resolve things. And he suggested black. End of meeting. So they left. And as Rob was the last person out of the door, I asked, 'What am I supposed to do?' And he said, 'Just fucking do it.' That was the moment when I appreciated that I had to do as I wanted because I would never get them to agree on anything. So that's how I did the covers.

Alec Empire: How were the group dynamics within Can?

IS: We worked as a collective. Playing together in Can was like a constant clash of erratic sources. Different styles and musical ideas would clash in the moment when we would record. Nobody in the group insisted on his ideas being superior to those of the others. Nobody gave directions. On the contrary, we were listening to each other and each of us was contributing his bits and pieces. I don't remember any discussions about daily politics. Or money.

AE: How did you split up the money?

IS: Hildegard, as our manager, would handle all the money and all our business affairs. She'd split up the dough equally among the band members. To the exact pfennig. In all the years we never had a discussion about who'd written which melody or bassline, or who'd written the lyrics. And this even counted for songs like 'She Brings the Rain', in which Jaki and I don't even play. Jaki always said, 'Not playing was my contribution to this song.'

MD: How political was Can?

IS: We didn't ever address topics from daily politics in our music. But the fact that we worked consistently as a collective, without any hierarchy, without a bandleader, and always credited Can as author of our pieces and not any individual, so everyone got the same money, was a political act. And in order to remain independent, we also insisted on recording only with our own production resources, even if it was just four microphones and two Revox stereo tape machines.

AE: And you recorded everything all the time when you were playing?

IS: We recorded almost everything. And because we did that, our playing was very disciplined! We knew that sooner or later a situation would occur that would catch all of us like a spell. And from there we had to push the music further. Only later would we edit the tape to cut songs or albums from the material.

CN: How democratic were you as a collective?

IS: Very. Let me give you an example. There was a big lump of hashish in the studio,, so we didn't have to go out and buy it ourselves. Then everyone took as much as they liked. No one ever said, 'Hey, you've had 30 grams more than I did!'

Jochen Arbeit: That also saves studio time. No one needs to run out and get something, while the others have to sit around for half the day and wait for him to return.

CN: Whether you actually save studio time that way is another question . . .

IS: We were at our own studio. We didn't have to be stingy about time.

JA: Beginning in the eighties, access to certain devices became easier; the devices became cheaper and more powerful. And suddenly it was possible for everyone who did not normally have access to an electronic studio to make that kind of music at home. In that sense, the digital revolution was also a big step for many people.

CN: Of course, the democratisation of the tools has made many things possible. When you started with Can, there was the big recording studio – anybody who wanted to make music back then needed a lot of money. It was a completely elitist situation.

IS: That's why we didn't do it in a rented studio, but in our own space. On the other hand, the democratisation of the tools entails the danger that one too quickly thinks that something is already music, even though it's only a preset pattern. It's as if someone thinks a piano is already music. Computers are instruments today. You have to learn them, practise and master them. And finally, you have to have the imagination to do something worthwhile. Software can make you think you just have to fiddle a bit with a preset and then it's music.

CN: The question regarding the software I use to produce music is one of the most common questions I'm asked. I always try to answer indirectly. I know, of course, where the question is leading. People think that if they own the software, then they could also make this music.

IS: The idea that it's possible to make good music if you simply have the right tools began with synthesizers.

CN: Many bands I admire emerged from a situation where they would see a band and say, 'Oh, we can do that too.' The feeling that the means are simple, and of course the enthusiasm, but at the same time that you can find such an easy way in – that you can dare to take that step and make music yourself – is very important. It's the moment when people say, 'I want to do that too! I want to give it a try!' – whether it's free jazz or punk or electronic music.

IS: Free jazz is not like punk. Free-jazzers can be very dogmatic. That was actually always more of an intellectual and exclusive scene.

CN: There was a huge free-jazz scene in the GDR. It was the most authentic type of music that we in the east had access to. But it was also very much based on virtuosity. I was always afraid of that virtuosity in jazz.

IS: Jazz always has something very professional about it.

CN: Exactly. And I took a stance against that. When the computer appeared, I thought, 'Now I can finally make what I hear in my head, very precisely. Now I can cut the groove and let it run through for an hour.' What you always had to play, with Jaki as a 'living drum machine', I could now do with the computer. The deliberate decision to break that down and not to want any swing in the pieces, but for the groove to stupidly always be the same . . .

IS: But no way in hell would Jaki ever have been willing to program his grooves.

CN: You pioneered that with Can, and only with the rise of techno was it finally understood as an evolutionary step in the history of music – though many years later.

AE: In 1994 I left Berlin for New York, where I started to hang around in the East Village and got soaked up in the downtown noise and independent scene. There I met Matt Sweeney, J. Mascis, Will Oldham, Jon Spencer, Sonic Youth and the Beastie Boys, among others. It was a pretty intense mix of people, and they were all hanging out together. And basically everybody I met told me, 'You are from Germany – how do you like Can?' They sort of talked me into listening to your music. And then it clicked. It was like Can opened a lot of doors for me. I suddenly started to look at music from a different perspective. This is especially important when you feel stuck as a musician. And it wasn't only me – I had the impression that the whole techno movement had come to a standstill by 1994.

IS: What element of Can specifically helped you out of your isolation?

AE: First of all, it struck me that Can didn't seem to care about beaten tracks. A typical Can song didn't follow any known compositional rules. Their sound aesthetics must have been groundbreaking in the seventies too. And last but not least, I was also blown away by the way you guys had recorded and mixed the music. I immediately realised that Can had been far ahead of their time. I basically discovered Can's proclamation of a musical future with almost twenty-five years of delay. And the other interesting and uplifting thing in New York – as opposed to Germany – was that nobody would draw a line of demarcation between 'tasteful' music on the one hand and 'aggressive' music on the other. In Germany aggressive techno music was still considered proletarian and dirty, whereas any kind of introverted music was considered culturally valuable. A year later I came back to Detroit and New York, where I got stuck in my apartment over New Year's Eve and was literally listening to every record by Can. This time around I was carrying test pressings of my new album *Low on Ice* with me – that was my attempt to escape the deadlocked situation in Germany's techno scene. And playing that album to the Beastie Boys and the other aforementioned musicians, everybody was suddenly hearing the influence of Can too.

IS: I know exactly what you mean. You can listen to music all your life, but it needs a specific trigger for you to really connect to it.

MD: Between 1967 and 1970 there were a number of groups in Germany working on a similar idea, although the individual projects usually had nothing to do with each other.

IS: The English were the first to recognise the connection between the different German projects of the seventies – and to label it as Krautrock.

CN: It's sometimes the case that the view from outside provides a clearer picture than when you are inside the machine yourself. You can't really get the context of what's happening. With us, it was the case that at some point we realised that there are people in Finland, Sweden, America or Japan all working on the same concept. But that only happened at the moment we were invited to a festival and then realised that other people had also been invited, and together you form a kind of wave. I think there is something like parallelism: there isn't a direct connection, but similar things happen at the same time in different places.

6

'The World Itself Becomes a Staging'

Hans Ulrich Obrist and Irmin Schmidt meet at the Serpentine Gallery in London.

Hans Ulrich Obrist: You have finally released a CD box set spanning your entire career after Can, *Electro Violet*. It includes your solo albums, but also film music and even your opera *Gormenghast*. Can you tell us more about this publication?

Irmin Schmidt: As you just said, the publication compiles the work I did after Can. So it's the music after 1979. The first album was *Toy Planet*, which I recorded in Zurich with Bruno Spoerri, a jazz musician who was very much into electronic music. *Electro Violet* includes two real solo records, *Musk at Dusk* and *Impossible Holidays*, but these solo records also feature Jaki Liebezeit and Michael Karoli, who were both members of Can. There are the two records I did with Kumo on *Electro Violet*, and excerpts of the opera *Gormenghast* – it doesn't feature the entire opera. This makes six CDs. There are also six additional CDs with my film music in the box. Already before Can, with Can and especially after Can, I produced a lot of film music. One album of the film music, *Volume VI*, is exclusively released as part of the box; *Volumes I–V* have been published a while ago already. I put only those pieces of my film music on these records that can live on their own. It's not necessary to know the films in order to understand the music. It is music in its own right. That's why I never put the entire music I did for films on a record – there is too much stuff that only works together with the actual film images. What I put on the records are pieces which also work as standalones.

HUO: Let's talk about your epiphanies. How did you get into music? Was it a sudden awakening or a gradual process?

IS: There was no epiphany. There were moments. Again and again there was noise, which in my head became music. Sounds have accompanied me throughout my life. And now, while we're talking here, as I push my coffee cup back and forth on the table, then we've captured that noise on tape. Another moment is the cultural influences of the fifties and sixties in Germany. All the important developments of the post-war period came from the outside, as a result of the cultural devastation by the Nazis – Fluxus, jazz, pop music. In new music, too, aside from the old things, we listened to what was coming from outside. All of Stockhausen's generation went to Paris for Nadia Boulanger and Olivier Messiaen, and didn't study in Germany. Until I was thirty years old, I listened almost exclusively to classical music – from the Middle Ages to Webern and Stockhausen. And then came Jimi Hendrix, and the way he improvised 'The Star-Spangled Banner' at the Woodstock Festival. That experience continues to accompany me to this day. For me, it was one of the greatest moments of spontaneous music discovery in the second half of the twentieth century. Another revelation came from literature. Reading Antonin Artaud, I came across the idea of drama being improvised onstage, being created during the very moment of performance. His description gave me an image of how live music could be made.

HUO: In his book on quantum physics, *The Fabric of Reality*, David Deutsch describes parallel realities. My impression is that parallel realities continually combine to fertilise each other. My work is to mediate between those parallel realities, to enable connections. The Vietnamese general Võ Nguyên Giáp, who died a few years ago at the age of 103, said, 'What we gain in territory, we lose in concentration. What we gain in concentration, we lose in territory.' Mario Merz has often quoted this. Jacques Delors, on the other hand, once referred to the European Community, 'It is both about expanding and deepening.' The more parallel realities there are, the more these realities relate to each other and the more reciprocal fertilisation takes place. As Alexander Dorner said in the early twentieth century, 'Assuming that we want to understand the forces in a field' – in my case, this is the visual arts – 'it is important to understand what is in the neighbouring fields of music, literature, science or architecture.' That's why I delve into these fields. This alleged 'outside' is constantly fertilising my own field. I have made that my work.

IS: In order to participate in all these parallel realities, one needs to be everywhere at the same time. How do you do that?

HUO: Rituals are important to me. I have a night producer who comes every night at midnight. Then we work together until seven in the morning. In between I go to sleep. Every morning after getting up I always read the same author for fifteen minutes: Édouard Glissant. I am very inspired by those monasteries that wanted to acquire all knowledge. If you work with science, with architecture, literature and music, you will be invited to enter these fields and can deepen your knowledge. This leads to new connections. That always helps with the creation of new formats. As an intermediary, I do a very different job than you do as an artist. In my first conversation of the day something happens, which then connects with the second conversation. It's always about those connections. The work somehow develops from those connections. They arise and create a kind of inspiration.

IS: My morning ritual begins with tea. Hildegard brings tea to my bedside. She gets up at least one if not two hours before me. I'm utterly incapable of getting out of bed before nine o'clock. What I cannot stand is when I have to talk or I have to listen to someone else talk. So Hildegard brings me the teapot without a word. I need silence. It's almost obsessive. I need plenty of silence.

HUO: It is interesting that you start the day with silence. I once had a conversation with Hans-Georg Gadamer in Heidelberg. He was a hundred years old at the time and he fell asleep during our conversation. At some point he woke up again and said, 'You won't be able to transcribe my silence.'

IS: For me, silence is one of the most important places. Silence always has something spatial about it. I need spaces where it is quiet. My bedroom, for example. Or my studio. It has two sets of double windows. It's directly connected to the large living room. When you go in there and close the door, then it's suddenly much quieter than before. That's necessary for recording anyway, but I also like it. At night, out on the terrace, when everything is already asleep, there might be a dog barking in the distance, but otherwise you actually don't hear anything at all. That is wonderful.

HUO: And in the morning there is this awakening – and then there are those 'sparks', if you will.

IS: Many of the works that I like best have arisen at such moments. I wake up and in my half-sleep I go to the piano, which is in the bedroom. Then I watch what my hands are doing. When I realise that it is playing me – when I hear something that electrifies me – then I'm suddenly extremely awake from one second to the next. Then there is no transition at all, but suddenly my heart is racing and I have to hold onto the idea because it's so good. Trying to capture that is always a big deal. Because I don't like to record things in a hurry, I have to write everything down in notation. That's how scores are produced. There are stacks of those sketches in pencil lying around – and I've always loved handwritten notation. For me, technological elements are not compatible with the piano. I like to write it down.

HUO: Some of the pieces you write are very long – there's even an opera with *Gormenghast*. Such long pieces surely don't arise in a few minutes in the morning. How do you get from one of those morning moments to an opera?

IS: I heard a radio interview with Stravinsky about fifty or sixty years ago in which he was asked about intuition: 'Young man, what do you mean by intuition? I sit at the desk at half past eight every morning, then I compose until twelve. Then I go for lunch, have a nap, answer my letters, then go to the opera or a concert and meet friends. But from half past eight to twelve I compose. *Basta.*' That spoke to me from the soul. I have a very Prussian attitude. My mother raised me like this: 'If you want to be a musician, you have to practise six, seven, eight hours every day. Otherwise you can forget it.'

HUO: So where Gerhard Richter talks about the daily practice of painting, here one can speak of the daily practice of playing.

IS: Yes, and of composing. For an opera, one develops strategies to come to terms with such a large form. I stuck the score up on the walls. Suddenly one can see what curves the score takes. That's why I can't work on a computer. I need to be able to visualise the chronological development of longer sections.

HUO: For the Vienna Opera, we regularly produce a large picture with Vienna's museum in progress [an art association]. Artists are invited to produce a large-format picture to cover the safety curtain in the opera house. While working on this opera mural, we looked at the opera's schedule, and I noticed that almost no operas from the twentieth and twenty-first centuries are ever performed – they play an entirely old repertoire. So it would be interesting to add new things to this repertoire. That is why I did an artist opera with

Philippe Parreno. We gave each artist a fifteen-minute piece, so the artists received time instead of space. This resulted in a group exhibition in the opera. One thing that was particularly important to me was the attempt at a complete work of art, but not in the sense of the late Wagner, but rather in the sense of the early one. Late Wagner diminishes the listener. It's overpowering. My interest is that they made an opera in the twenty-first century. Was it also the opposite of late Wagner? How did you approach that?

IS: *Gormenghast* has – at least in places – a great pathos, and the narrative does have something quite Wagnerian. An initially sympathetic youth works his way up and becomes a murderous tyrant. This has the dimensions of great opera. But because it is sometimes very funny, boldly and formally broken into fragments that do not really fit together, it is also the opposite. There is a chef who sings reggae, but in the bel canto style. A tiny fragment is in twelve-tone, but shortly afterwards the crazy twins chirp their way through music history. It doesn't have a Wagnerian narrative. *Gormenghast* is more of a number opera.

HUO: How does the process look, from the score to the finished work?

IS: When I finished the score, the goal was to meld the orchestra into the electronics together with Kumo and to incorporate concrete sounds. We poured large river pebbles down a stone staircase in front of my terrace, and Jaki played all our kitchen utensils. I dropped whole piles of porcelain plates from the mezzanine in my studio onto the tile floor that is laid there. We recorded the sound of them smashing. Hildegard filmed it. The model of the stage set stood in my studio like a big box. When I removed the stage settings from the model, there was only the theatre box with the stage. That's what we threw the plates into.

HUO: The fascination for noises has accompanied you since childhood. In the fine arts, the beginnings of a work of an artist are often clarified in the catalogue raisonné. At some point, such a catalogue is created and then it is numbered, and the number 1 is clarified. Everything coming before that are student works, but there begins the actual work and thus the catalogue raisonné. Number 1 is often the work where an artist found his language. What is the number 1 in Irmin Schmidt's catalogue raisonné?

IS: There is an unfinished album entitled *Album für Mogli* – that's my nickname for my wife. This album is still very Fluxus-related, a sort of Fluxus score that actually consists of nine pieces – but de facto there are only four. I have never written down the others. There are only drawings or playing instructions. It has a lot to do with game theory, which has always fascinated me. So there isn't any classical notation. It was my first composition to be released.

HUO: And with it you had found your language?

IS: No. In retrospect it was the first piece on the first Can record: 'Father Cannot Yell'. At that moment, the music I had dreamed of came into being. But the funny thing was, there was no concrete idea prior to it. The music just happened, and suddenly you knew, 'That's it!' For me, it was about no longer composing something myself, but letting the composition happen in a collective musical process. 'Father Cannot Yell' is a piece that simply fell into place. It was on tape, and when we listened to it, we were all actually speechless. That was the first real work.

HUO: James Abbott McNeill Whistler said, 'Art happens.' It simply occurs.

IS: Yes, it happens. You can really say, 'It plays me.' But I do not have a religious feeling about it. Rather, I think the brain just works that way, so that it plays me.

HUO: I once asked Benoit Mandelbrot how he discovered fractals.

When you talk to scientists, they always say something like, 'It was a rainy Wednesday and on a blackboard I saw blurred chalk trails, and suddenly they were fractals.' He could describe it like that. Can you tell me about the day in 1968 on which Can originated? Do you remember the hour or the day when it came into being?

IS: I wanted to form a group that made music similar to the way Frederic Rzewski did. So that was still entirely in the field of new music. But I didn't want any instrumental virtuosos from classical music. Rather, I imagined that musicians from all the new musics of the twentieth century should take part, from new music in the narrower sense, as well as from jazz and rock. Also, it should be musicians with practical experience. So I simply approached a few people: for example, Holger Czukay, who had studied with Stockhausen together with me. I asked Jaki Liebezeit if he knew a suitable drummer – I imagined someone like Max Roach. He said he'd take care of it. We met at my apartment in Cologne. Holger brought along Michael Karoli, who had just graduated from high school, a young rock musician and Holger's guitar student. A fantastic guitarist. I wanted something just like that. Jaki came to the meeting a little later: 'Count me in!' Initially I wasn't all right with that. Starting at the age of fourteen, Jaki had played his way through jazz history and had finally landed at free jazz. And I did not want a free-jazz drummer. That was far too close to new music for me. But it turned out that he was frustrated with free jazz and wanted to play proper rhythms again. That was the first meeting of Can. From that day on, we stayed together for ten years – which is really amazing, because I was looking for people with whom I was not close friends, not even with Holger. I only knew him as a crazy composer. He had once asked me to perform a drum piece he had written. We both cracked up laughing! It was simply unplayable. Hildegard had met the painter and sculptor Malcolm Mooney in Paris through Serge Tcherepnin, and she brought him to Cologne to introduce him to gallery owners, because we were friends with quite a few. At first there was no thought of him becoming our singer. Since I usually spent the whole day in the studio, he came along once and immediately started singing. Suddenly we had a singer. The amazing thing was that from the moment Malcolm started singing, we were a rock group. Something strange happened between Malcolm and Jaki. There were sparks. Something illuminated the two of them through rhythm. We edited the recordings like the devil. Both Holger and I came from Stockhausen's electronic studio, where they spliced away like crazy. So we did the same thing with Can, but all together. Except Jaki, who hated that process. But he was the one to whom we had to play the results, and if there was a break in the rhythm, in the groove, then he wouldn't allow it. In that way he was also involved in the post-production.

HUO: I am always interested in the things that inspire artists. Because, on the one hand, there is this idea that 'art happens', as Whistler said, but there are also things that influence you, of course. The BBC has the programme *Desert Island Discs*, where public figures in Britain are invited to present their favourite pieces of music. For example, they invited Zaha Hadid, who had distinctly mainstream musical tastes. She picked Adele and Drake. What would it be if you could only take a few records to a desert island?

IS: It depends so much on the day and my mood. For reading, I would bring Raymond Chandler, and the next day Nietzsche. Georges Simenon, in any case. It depends how you're feeling. It's the same with music. Perhaps I would take the *Messe de Nostre Dame* by Machaut. I also especially like the madrigals of Gesualdo. But my preferences go throughout the entire history of music. Sometimes that includes mainstream things: Schumann's piano concerto, no matter how often it is played, is simply a wonderful piece. Today I might take *Images* by Debussy.

HUO: That's also the case with works of art – one can view a picture again and again. With Beethoven there are the *Diabelli Variations*: one can listen to it again and again and it's amazing every time.

IS: That's what makes a great work of art – it always has a secret that one can never quite grasp and which always reappears. How do you explain, however, that contemporary fine art has a huge audience intake, but that audience disregards contemporary 'serious music' or *'musique savante'* or whatever you want to call it?

HUO: Music is lacking a museum. If we had a museum for experimental sound today, in which the *Polytopes* by Iannis Xenakis, the early pieces by Karlheinz Stockhausen – which also had a spatial aspect – to Fluxus and up to the present would be exhibited in thousands of square metres, it would receive just as much attention. I think such a place is simply missing. It is so often the case that one also has to perceive these works spatially. That isn't possible with CDs. These are spaces. An institution is lacking. As Ernst Bloch said, 'Something is missing.'

IS: Many compositions need personnel, from the string quartet to the symphony orchestra. It's not something you can simply install. I often notice that some people even leave concerts. My sister-in-law goes to a Brahms violin concerto, then comes Bartók and half of the people walk out. How do you explain that?

HUO: I think that would also happen if you were to force people to watch an art video. Many would probably also walk out. What makes the museum so attractive is that it is a ritual in which everyone defines their own time. In that sense, it's not a mass experience. Millions of people come to the museums, but everyone comes alone or only in small groups, and part of experiencing the works is based on one's own decision about how long the experience will last. That was Xenakis's idea with the *Polytopes*: you didn't have to listen to a concert for two hours. Not at Fluxus concerts, either.

IS: Maybe that's why. The history of pop music goes back only a hundred or a hundred and fifty years. But here one actually grows up with a cityscape that is hundreds of years old. But history within music is lost. It is only there for a small audience.

HUO: It is also the question of what continues to be performed. This in effect is also the case with art: it is not known whether a work, once it has been in a museum, will go into historical custody. So it's important that something is performed again and again.

IS: Quite a lot is lost actually. I have just stood enthusiastically before the self-portrait of Anna Dorothea Therbusch in the Gemäldegalerie in Berlin. It's a fascinating picture by a painter who is not really in the general consciousness.

HUO: That is why Eric Hobsbawm speaks of protest against forgetting. When I asked you to write something for my Instagram, you wrote: 'If you want to change the world, make better music.'

IS: That just came into my head. It's a quote from somebody, but I don't remember who – maybe Sun Ra.

HUO: I wanted to tell the story of Oskar Sala. Sala was rediscovered in the early nineties because of the techno movement. He was a pupil of Paul Hindemith and the inventor of the Trautonium. At the time, as a young curator, I was excited about techno, and I went to Oskar Sala, who was already over ninety years old. He showed me his Trautonium and we did an interview. Mr Sala then described how Alfred Hitchcock came to him because of *The Birds*. Hitchcock was desperate because nobody could record the sound of threatening birds – which meant they had to produce their screams synthetically. That was why Hitchcock had turned to him. Sala then produced the bird sounds for the film using the Trautonium. By the time I visited him, however, the instrument had long since ceased to function – it was only a kind of relic in the studio. Then Sala, with his voice, tried to imitate how this Trautonium synthesized the birds' voices. That was one of the greatest moments ever for me. I then gave that recording of Sala's Trautonium imitation to Mika Vainio, who with Pan Sonic then created a sound piece from this verbal imitation of an electronically generated bird sound.

IS: Every film music creates an artificial environment, even when a reality is being told. Even if there are cars driving and trees rustling in the wind, it is rarely the actual sounds from cars or trees, but rather manipulated, artificial sounds. How does that change our perception? Do we hear the rustling of the leaves with ears that have been conditioned that way? Do we hear artificial sounds? When I look out the window now and see the wintery trees there, I think of Emil Schumacher's late gouaches. When I see a lake with a meadow in front of it or a forest path, I see it through the eyes of Corot. These images have shaped my vision. I often sit on the terrace in the evening and look at the poplar tree in front of my house. If the wind is still and nothing moves, then I see a Perugino in front of me. But what has happened with our hearing since the second half of the twentieth century? Is it a similar phenomenon? Do we now listen through the ears of Stockhausen or John Cage? The audible world is superimposed with a whole artificial world that we ourselves have created. Do we hear that yet? I hear passing cars as if I were watching a film. This change of hearing fascinates me. Music becomes mimetic and listening a kind of animism.

HUO: It's interesting to think of that in connection with 'augmented reality'. In the meantime, we can see things in nature or in urban spaces that we cannot see in reality. They appear magically – and only on our glasses. It's no longer like 'virtual reality', where we are looking into a box, but now I can curate a park and we see things through glasses that are there and are not there at the same time. We hear what is there and we suddenly hear something that is not there.

IS: Then we experience nature as an installation.

HUO: Exactly, suddenly it becomes a kind of exhibition. Everything is curated. The world itself becomes a staging.

II: From My Notebook

Roussillon

Large new buildings. Hotels, perhaps. Bulky and unattractive, they stand disconnected from one another, contextless within the urban landscape. I say to someone, 'Typical Cologne. It's not like the buildings make the city seem any more metropolitan.'

I'm looking for my ruins. There has to be something left of them.

It's like a calling. And a bidding farewell. The entire street of ruins is – or will be – demolished. In its place: a housing complex. I actually like the architecture. As I turn to leave, walking past building rubble and wooden planks, I discover a hole. Deep down inside are basement rooms and arched cellars of my ruins. Loose sand trickles in. Should I pee into the hole? No, I'll let it be. I cover it instead with a large rock, and that's when I wake up. I desperately have to pee.

Slowly it dawns on me that I've dreamed about this street and these ruins before. Indeed, it's a reoccurring dream that I've had every few years since the early days of my youth, where I find myself all alone on a narrow street, surrounded on both sides by the looming, palatial facades of buildings whose copper tones glow in the setting sun. The window panes and doorways to the buildings are empty. Inside are large halls and fallen walls strewn with rubble and devastation. They too are covered in the glow of dusk.

I'm not allowed inside, as tempting and bewitching as it seems. No, I'm not allowed inside. I'm left spellbound and strangely mournful. I sense a deep, profound love for these ruins, but mixed with an awful and mysterious dread.

This dream was precious to me. I longed for it during dry spells and would sometimes try to recall the details before going to sleep in order to dream my way inside. But it never worked. It only appeared without warning.

And now, despite having actually buried it inside of another dream, I still feel drawn towards its oddly enchanting vortex.

Occasionally, when standing in front of certain paintings by Claude Lorrain, I experience a feeling similar to that dream. In Lorrain's images I find not people but souls, bathed in an Arcadian light, a light that contains a veiled horror. On the periphery of his images, inside, beyond the facades of palaces, stretches an endless void.

I imagine that perhaps Poussin's *Et in Arcadia ego* is a response to his friend Claude's world of souls aglow.

Nuremberg

Andreas[*] is staging Engelbert Humperdinck's *Hansel and Gretel*. Tonight is the premiere. Before we go, Mogli and I take a walk. There's the castle and a few well-restored half-timbered houses, but I just don't feel comfortable in this city. I'd prefer to leave immediately. There is something uncanny about Nuremberg.

This feeling accompanies me into the opera. But when I listen to the music, in all of its harmless charm, beautifully sung and played, I start enjoying the little sonic gems, especially in the sound of the orchestra. (When I was twenty-five years old, we were supposed to have rejected it all: Richard Strauss, Puccini, Rachmaninov, Sibelius, all the late Romantics. Hallelujah to the post-modernists.)

[*] Andreas Bäsler, German opera director who directed the second production of my opera *Gormenghast*.

Anyhow, Andreas's staging does away with *Hansel and Gretel*'s grand fairy-tale magic, and the results are more dry. While the staging maintains a balance and tension to the music, it in no way betrays the music. At the party after the premiere, we're surrounded by friends and champagne: Andreas, Harald, Tanja. *Cin cin*, here's to the epigones and the unfashionable.

The next day we visit Waltraud. She is almost ninety and the last time I saw her was seventy years ago. She started out as our maid in 1942 in Berlin, but as the bombing got worse, we were evacuated to Austria, and she came with us. She left our family in 1945, after the end of the war, in order to marry her fiancé Fritz, who survived because he was employed as a fireman and was sorely needed on the home front.

In the summer of 1946 I travelled with my mother and my two sisters back home. I was eight, my younger sisters were five and four. It was a horrible week-long train ride back to Dortmund, where my father awaited our arrival. The train emerged from the idyllic valleys of the Austrian Alps, where we had lived for the past three years, into an absolutely devastated Germany. Train cars extremely overfilled and awful scenes at the stations along the route, where we some-times waited days for the trip to continue. Occasionally we travelled in freight trains that would stop for hours on end in the middle of the tracks. We stayed for a few days with Waltraud in Nuremberg, in a house that was half bombed-out, half in reconstruction. We were surrounded by ruins, rubble and debris as far as the eye could see.

She still has pictures of us as kids. She tells us that when we lived in Berlin, my mother would occasionally take breaks from doing the daily housework to sing and play the piano. Waltraud would have to sit down and listen.

Waltraud now lives alone in a charming, spacious apartment. Fritz died several years ago. He was a wonderful man, she says. She started taking piano lessons at seventy and now owns an electronic keyboard, with which she plays popular ballads and folk songs at family gatherings and in old people's homes. She recorded a CD, which she gives to me as a gift. She isn't interested in taking my CD. She doesn't like rock and roll.

❋

In the Kolumba art museum of the Archdiocese of Cologne there is a corner chapel named 'Madonna in den Trümmern' ['Madonna in the Ruins'].

In Orange in the sixteenth century they built the church Notre-Dame la Massacreuse ['Our Lady the Slaughterer'].

'La nature a des perfections pour montrer qu'elle est l'image de Dieu, et des défauts pour montrer qu'elle n'en est que l'image' ['Nature has perfections to show that she is the image of God, and defects to show that she is only His image'] – Blaise Pascal.

Everything OK? Perfect!

'Der Messias wird erst kommen, wenn es nicht mehr nötig sein wird, er wird erst einen Tag nach seiner Ankunft kommen, er wird nicht am letzten Tag kommen, sondern am allerletzten' ['The Messiah will appear only when it is no longer necessary. He will appear one day after he arrives; he will not come on the last day, but on the very last.'] – Kafka, cited in W. G. Sebald, *Kafka – Das Schloss*.

Roussillon

I sit at my desk and stare at the photo of the beautiful young woman. I don't know her. The picture in the round art deco frame has been here for years. The woman is gazing over her right shoulder, directly into the camera, her hair tousled from turning her head so quickly.

Her expression is slightly shocked, vaguely amused and extremely self-confident. Her lips are slightly parted. She is enchanting. And strange. No past, no common ground. And at the same time I know that I love her, and have loved her since this photo was taken more than fifty years ago by Walter Kirchberger. Perhaps in a few minutes it will transform again into the familiar photo I love so much.

With my school class by the seaside. At night I could hear my fellow students softly weeping. Homesickness. I didn't have it. I imagined what it would be like if I was never allowed to go back to my parents and my sisters, even though I loved them. This was unsettlingly tempting. That's when I also began to cry bitterly, ashamed by my own heartlessness.

The lizard on the cornice of the terrace, its front leg twitching ever so slightly. Suddenly, in a single lightning-fast motion, it scurries down headfirst and disappears from the middle of the smoothly plastered wall.

The raspy conversation between two magpies.

A single shivering leaf on the otherwise motionless willow tree.

Suddenly it all means something: it's about me.

An omen, a promise, a threat: symbols that have dissolved before I can consider them. Symbols which leave me behind within a dull hopelessness, a feeling of having missed a big chance.

The moment of horror when, the glass to my lips, I realise I no longer know how to swallow. Like before, or almost in, sudden death. Or the moment of mortality itself.

Moments in which everything appears beautiful and enigmatic; feelings of detachment, mild euphoria and subdued horror, not unlike the light trips Michael and I would take while driving on tour. A strangely serene consent to the state of alienation.

'Misfitting together'. We didn't fit together. And we invented a music in which we were all strangers, each in his own way. Holger called it 'dilettanting'. On the one hand I tried to incorporate my knowledge. On the other, I strongly rebelled against it. 'Reject skill. Do away with it' (Louise Bourgeois). Our very beings were fractured and contradictory. Michael, who wanted to make dance music, was fascinated by Michael von Biel and his electronic piece *Fassung*, as well as his wild, untameable and skilful cello playing, which disregarded all the rules. Perhaps only Jaki returned home from a foreign place, a return to the groove. He was never really so into free jazz. And so he too escaped – just like the rest of us.

That especially applied to our singers! Malcolm had often spoken of the foreignness of being black in America. With us, he was doubly foreign. He reacted to this with a spontaneity and radical presence of mind, which lured us inside with his charisma but, in its anarchic intensity, became a threat to himself.

And then there was Damo, a stranger par excellence. Never at home in any language, he sings in his own foreign tongue. That somehow works everywhere. With his 'Never-Ending Tour', he is at home all over the world.

'I feel comfortable as a foreigner,' said Georges Didi-Huberman, in an interview about his life conducted in his home town of Paris. The same goes for me: here in the Provence, in rock music, in *'musique savante'*, in Berlin. Living life as a foreigner is liberating. It's not about a break, but about distance. *'Le regard éloigné'* – 'The view from afar'. In a sense, this foreignness excludes theatricality, homing in instead on concentration, immersion.

'Foreign and strange is he who asserts his own being in a world that surrounds him' – Vilém Flusser.

Years ago in Berlin, in an overcrowded train. A chunky, pimple-faced punk girl packed in tight black leather and with a red mohawk comb-over. Parts of her shaved head had razor rash. From a safety pin in one of her ears dangled a chain, onto which clung a white rat with pink paws. Occasionally it would nibble on her ear or disappear into the black leather and cleavage, occasionally popping its head out between her breasts. Despite the throngs packed into the train, people kept their distance, respecting her space. A motionless, untouchable, stony-faced queen of the night. It was an image of such unique and unexpected beauty that not even the normally cheeky Berliners could muster up any commentary. Total silence.

Vienna, 26 November 2013

With Mogli and Michael Sturminger in the Kunsthistorisches Museum for the Lucian Freud retrospective. One of the exhibit's panels describes the Freud family's escape to London. I'm thrown for a loop again, this time by the word *'Reichsfluchtsteuer'*,[*] and find myself fighting back the tears, even though the word itself is monstrous, comically absurd.

Lucian Freud. No other artist painted people like he did, infusing renderings of our meat and bones – our fundamentally vulnerable, mortal make-up – with such dignity. His is a lesson in love, both brutal and tender. It doesn't exclude a 'small amount of poison that every good image must contain', as he put it. A lesson about beauty.

'My music is not beautiful,' Schönberg claimed, though beauty always has to be redefined (at least according to the Western or European notion of art and culture). Schönberg did just that. So did

---

[*] Reich Flight Tax, originally a law created to stem capital flight from the Weimar Republic. During the 3rd Reich it was used to confiscate the property of Jews who fled.

Lucian Freud, his paintings containing a poignant and never-before-seen beauty. Freud's are images of human beings whose nakedness is an annunciation: this is who we are. Man, as the Upanishads say, is a wound.

The museum will close shortly, but I still need to pay a quick visit to a friend: *Young Woman at Her Toilette* by Giovanni Bellini. It's not easy to find in this enormous labyrinth of a building, but friendly exhibit attendants help us out.

The painting, this woman touch me as wondrously as a song – one which, when heard or recalled, create an undefinable *Sehnsucht*° (still such a beautiful word).

Bellini painted the picture in 1515, when he was eighty-five. They say it was his last. That was five hundred years ago. And yet how close it seems, Bellini and Freud.

'You've entered the winter of your life.' So ends Paul Auster's *Winter Journal*. He was sixty-four then, and I was sixty-four when I started recovering from my stroke, full of plans to pursue the gift of my new life. Not a trace of winter. Today, it's only three and a half years until my eightieth birthday, and the air smells like snow. Winter music.

London, December 2013

Jenny tells me about a song sung by a woman with a voice so deep, it had mesmerised her as a one-year-old. She says that her parents told her she would sit completely still with tears streaming down her face. The song is 'Blow the Wind Southerly', sung by Kathleen Ferrier. It still touches her deeply. To this day she still occasionally has to put it on and cry a little.

° Translator's note: in German, *Sehnsucht*, or 'longing', can be broken down etymologically to mean the desperate need or addiction (*Sucht*) to see (*sehen*).

At Sandra's. Drinking my morning tea in bed next to the window, outside the bushes and trees stand bare under grey skies. The light is dull and expressionless, but I still want to look out the window for hours and marvel at the variety in this shrubby world. A moment of tranquil desirelessness. It doesn't take a special place. Actually, it may be the opposite: the transformation can happen in any banal location and at any time.

Right now, while writing this, I suddenly remember my attempts at regularly keeping a diary, sometime around 1967–8. I was trying to change my life and form a group. No idea what would come out of it.

My first notebook was stolen along with my leather jacket during an opening at the Reckermann Gallery. The notebook was almost full. After that, the second mostly contained observations on the trials and experiments surrounding the collective creation of our own music, but also quite a bit about the musicians themselves, who, at the time, I didn't know very well. Michael, Jaki, Holger – their moods, quirks and sensitivities.

I wake up at 5 a.m. – the notebook! Shit, I left it on the organ. Worried that one of the members would read it, I sped in a panic to Nörvenich. I got there shortly before 6 a.m. It was an incredibly sunny summer morning, and Holger was in an equally sunny mood, cleaning up and organising things in the studio. He cheerily informed me that he had taken out the trash. It had already been picked up. The notebook was gone. 'On the organ? Nope, there was nothing there.' I saw it as an omen. It wasn't meant to be. That was pretty much the end of my diaries – for a long time.

°

Tea in bed again next to the window. Above the brush, in the grey soup, a helicopter flies. I can't hear it, the guppy in my aquarium, the last of eighteen, all of whom died on a single day, most likely after I attempted to feed them water fleas from the opaque green liquid I found in the bomb craters, though now the helicopter is very close and very loud; a horrifying, never-before-seen aircraft, low above our heads, the field full of marsh marigolds glowing yellow, slowly it's floating through the valley amidst the deafening rattle of metal. So the war isn't over, and a horror has furrowed into my brain – a horror that still reappears in my dreams, and in new, threatening forms of aircraft. But in my dreams they're always silent.

Roussillon, December 2013

Tonight I dreamed not of frightening aircraft, but of Holger. I am pulling him out of the water on a lakefront. He's unconscious. I do the whole cardiac-massage thing. His chest expands but can also be compressed like a plastic bag. In a minute I'll have to give him mouth-to-mouth, though the thought fills me with dread. I'm disgusted. Then, thank God, he wakes up. Was it an accident or attempted suicide? Either way, I'm not allowed to talk to anyone about it . . . at the party. It would be impossibly embarrassing for him, Holger insists. I do as I'm told, but I'm not sure if later on I'll eventually have to discuss it with someone.

I'm cold and about to get into bed when I spot an ant walking along the bookshelf. I angrily swat at it with the paperback I have in my hand, Georges Perec's *Thoughts of Sorts*. Shit, thoughts of murder. Slowly, the ant rises up from its chest, standing almost perpendicular to its abdomen. It freezes, a threatening little ant-sphinx. I know that tonight I'll be visited in my dreams by the ant god. What can I offer it? Nothing.

Bandol, January 2014

The half-moon casts a bright, shimmering stripe across a deeply dark sea. Suddenly a spot near the dyke begins to sparkle for a few minutes, then it goes back to being completely still. Nymphs and ocean spirits.

Munich, January 2014

On the street one afternoon I hear the beautiful bells of St Martin's church. Minutes pass. The ringing subsumes all the sounds of the city around me, coalescing them into a single sonic space. Harmonies and hues all around me, vibrating, shimmering. I stand and listen. Sometimes, within the sounds of church bells, I feel strangely at home and secure.

Even as an atheist one is still a Christian.

Textbook: *Applied Kinesiology* (by Hans Garten).
Olli is studying something like this. He says (the theory says) that the fluid surrounding our nerves ascends and descends in a very slow, very specific rhythm within the spine, between the sanctum and cranium – that is, between the brain and the butt. Supposedly, the cranium and the pelvis make a kind of pumping movement: The pelvis contracts (ever so slightly), pressing the fluid upward, and, as a result, expands the skull (also ever so slightly). The skull then contracts to pump the fluid back down. According to Olli, you can train to actually feel this movement in your head. The fascinating thing, he says, is that this phenomenon corresponds to teachings within Chinese medicine, as well as t'ai chi exercises, meditation and so on.

Of course, I only partially understand what he is saying. But I am fascinated by this mysterious pulsating movement in our bodies, in which everything is rhythm, pulse, vibration and tremendously complex polyrhythms. There, within numerous intertwined layers and networks, lies a great, all-encompassing rhythm. And when one falls out of the rhythm, the whole system becomes discombobulated. The groove collapses, and that's when you get sick.

Bad Hofgastein

We were looking forward to snow, a real winter in the Alps. Not happening. Everything is a dirty green. We have to travel up the gondola, where then everything becomes stunning. We're sitting in the sun, blinded by the snow's glare, with alpine peaks stretching off far into every direction. Coffee, apple strudel with lots of whipped cream. I let my mind wander off into childhood memories, back when I would ski to school. On the way, if you were lucky, the big milk jugs on the side of the paths hadn't yet been picked up. I'd quickly pop the lids off, and with the spoon I always kept in my pocket I would skim some of the thick cream. If you got caught, it could be bad.

I'm here for radon therapy. Deep in the mountain, with 700 metres of rock looming above, I lie for an hour with at least thirty other sweaty men on bunks lining narrow mines. It's 40°C, the air is damp and you can smell the perspiration, but it's supposed to help my arthritis. Some people – even those with serious pain – swear by radon therapy and come back every year.

We hike around, occasionally it rains – even in January in the Alps! In Bad Gastein, which has long been a health resort for the wealthy and the gentry, some of the enormous hotels built at the beginning of the twentieth century have closed. In the middle of town is a powerful and glorious waterfall, whose constant roar makes the narrow valley seem even narrower. But maybe that's just the way I feel today, because I'm annoyed by this hideous 'modern' structure, which contains a parking garage, a health club and other stuff – a real blight on this strangely beautiful village.

We enter a small church. It's empty except for two children, a boy and a girl around five or six years old. They are playing Maria and Joseph in front of the altar. The girl squats in front of a small cradle with a doll, rocking him and humming quietly to herself. She gazes at her baby Jesus with a dreamy smile. Occasionally she turns to her Joseph, who, with a long stick in both hands, stands beside her, mute and donning a serious expression. Behind the cradle is a big stuffed lion. It's cold in the church. We pretend we don't see the kids, and they take no notice of us. Silently, we tiptoe out and carefully close the church door behind us.

While writing this, I remember the man in front of the hotel in Malta. With a happy smile he stares at an inexpressibly ugly Nativity scene featuring a dark plastic, life-size display of Mary and Joseph with the baby Jesus and a donkey. The man's hands and arms are in constant motion, his gestures full of the kind of grace found in baroque images. With his body slightly turned and his head tilted sideways, he looks at us through the hotel's glass door with an endearing smile and points ecstatically at the crib. Look, a miracle! Eventually, a stern-looking hotel manager approaches and accompanies the man to the exit of the hotel's front courtyard. He walks him out a bit further, with the man continuing to prance excitedly, almost floating alongside the ridiculously stiff hotel staff.

Then, as now, the memory called forth another: Merce Cunningham's performance in Avignon, 1988. Amidst his wildly swirling troupe, he stood as still as a statue, with only his arms and hands gesturing a magical dance, floating.

Excursion to Salzburg. The train makes its way past the town of Werfen. With images and shapes of memories, it's like Thales with the gods. For me, everything here is packed full of them. Sometimes the postman took me on a bicycle. He was a silent man. 'Hop on?' he asked. I nodded and climbed up on his bike frame.

Once, we rode from Eben to Werfen. At some point he turned off the road and travelled along a brook, through the forest and into a small, narrow valley. He got off the bike, sat on a rock and said, 'Listen.' The valley sang. It trilled, chirped, jubilated. 'The nightingales,' he said, and we sat there silently for a while and listened. If a fairy all in white would have waved to us while hovering over the brook, it wouldn't have surprised me one bit.

After that, I didn't hear nightingales for a very long time.

Then, one day, Mogli and I were picnicking under a large plane tree next to a dilapidated, overgrown water basin, when behind it, somewhere in the bushes, a nightingale sang. That's when we fell in love with the place. We then learned that it was listed in the land registry as 'Les Rossignols' (The Nightingales). This is where our house stands today.

In a large Meese exhibition in a museum in Salzburg. Mogli likes two pictures. I like none.

During our time in Eben, my mother sometimes rode with me to Salzburg. Vague memories of churches, organ concerts, cakes and cacao. Clearer memories of the trick fountains of Schloss Hellbrunn.

In the summer of 1964 I was in Salzburg for two months, taking a course in conducting at the Mozarteum taught by István Kertész. It was an exciting time that culminated in me being awarded first prize. For the final concert, I conducted Dvořák's Fourth Symphony. It garnered so much applause that I had the orchestra perform the third movement – this lovely waltz – as an encore.

After that, Mogli and I drove to Spain, and in the car we spent a good portion of the trip discussing my bright future as a conductor – without having even the vaguest idea that in only three years I would be doing something very, very different.

At the time, the town of Javea, near Valencia, was still untouched by tourism. There was only a single modest hotel. We also found a small, secluded cove that was difficult to access. On the beach there was a small wooden shanty with an awning covering a table and chairs. For days, the shanty belonged to us alone. Then, one day, four men were sitting at the table. Laughing, they motioned us over to join them. The table was filled with melon, sausage, ham, cheese and lots of wine. This was their shack. The oldest of the group spoke some German and he insisted that we sing with him 'Der Mond ist aufgegangen' (The Moon Has Risen). And from that point on, the singing didn't stop. We even had to sing every single Christmas song we knew. At some point, the man suddenly became quiet and said, 'We sang much with German friends.' From a few careful hints we deduced that the friends had fought with him against Franco during the civil war in 1936.

Roussillon, January 2014

Looking out of one window with a view of the village of Joucas, the sky is pale blue. The town is grey and without any real contour. Through the adjoining window the sky appears a soft pink. Shining bright, as if artificially lit, are the rooftops behind the dark cypress trees. Placed next to each other, both variations of the landscape appear strangely unreal.

Where I'm looking now I once sat on a stone thirty-five years ago on a summer afternoon. To my right was the castle of Joucas, the 'Commanderie', while to my left, a few kilometres away, was the cliff-side of Lioux, which appeared strangely close in the light, glowing like the walls of a mythical city. Somewhere in the hills across from me was the piece of land we had just purchased, with the large plane tree and a few oaks. I will spend part of the year there, mostly in the summer, restoring the old water basin with the well, listening to the nightingales, and allowing myself to be groovily entranced for hours by the cicadas. Suddenly I heard a dry creaking sound and then a deafening whip-like crack. The lightning must have struck extremely close. For a moment everything was quiet – no birds, no rustling in the pines, no cicadas. A hole in time. Then, after a heavy gust of wind, the pines rustled, the cicadas buzzed like an orchestra and a dog began barking like crazy. Only then did I see the small, extremely dark cloud, as compact as bedrock, above me in shining blue.

'This is how a god speaks when he speaks to you,' I thought. Perhaps Jupiter or Hermes, the god of secret messages. Or perhaps it's a god who is much older, as this region has been populated with gods and ghosts and men for thousands upon thousands of years. 'We're all around you,' I understood. 'If you don't bother us, you can stay.'

°

Votre chien pue, mademoiselle, lui dit un monsieur. – Non, monsieur: c'est moi [Mademoiselle, your dog stinks, says the gentleman. – No, monsieur: it's me] – Jules Renard, *Journal*, 1908.

Cannes
Midem.° Mogli and Sandra have lots of meetings. I accompany them and feign interest.

Lutz Ilgner and his daughter invite us to a restaurant to eat with them. On a sideboard next to our table are two Japanese swords displayed on stands. One is long, the other short. 'Just for decoration, of course,' says Lutz. 'Real ones wouldn't be allowed to be displayed here.' He is knowledgeable about Samurai swords – *katana* the long and *wakizashi* the short. These swords have the sharpest

---

° Music-industry trade fair.

blades in the world, and there are only a few master sword-makers in Japan that can make them. They stem from a centuries-old tradition of enormously skilled craftsmanship and mastery, as well as deep spirituality. They are artworks. 'Even if you have the money – 30,000 to 50,0000 euros – the master builder will only sell you a sword if he thinks you're worthy,' Lutz explains.

After the meal, Lutz is determined to take us to La Chunga bar. Dr Moser and Jürgen Thürnau join us. La Chunga, lots of hot Barbie dolls. The men that accompany them could easily play in some really trashy Mafia thriller. But there is one exception: a small, fragile, elegantly dressed man with grey hair. He is sitting up straight, almost on the edge of the chair, diagonally across from his date. He gazes at her steadfastly as if hypnotised. I can only see her beautiful shoulders and shimmering back. She is eating hungrily and downing champagne. The bottle is only for her; he doesn't have a glass. He is air to her. He is non-existent. Every now and again his hand makes its way to her thigh, until with a quick and casual movement she jerks her hand with the fork downward. He pulls it back and holds it to his mouth, never taking his eyes off her. Dr Moser, Jürgen Thürnau and Lutz Ilgner have all sunk deep into their chairs and are smoking thick Havanas. They exude total satisfaction. The DJ is playing Chet Baker, Horace Silver – stuff like that. Mogli and Sandra cough. We don't stay long.

Oslo, February 2014
26.2

René tells us about Oslo, how last year in February he worked on a production with Emil Nikolaisen and his band Serena Maneesh. 'It was great,' he says. Very cold but often sunny, and the snow was piled up a metre high. We arrive in Oslo at 5 p.m. It's dark and raining.

27.2

Rain. It's possible that Oslo is a beautiful city in the sun and snow, but right now it is ugly as sin.

We're driving out to the Astrup Fearnley Museet of modern art. The exhibit is Kitaj – *Diaspora*. It stops raining, we can see the ocean, the building is by Renzo Piano, the exhibit is enjoyable. Everything is going to be fine.

The museum café. These young ladies with long thin necks and elegant necklines. Behind their pale eyes and pleading looks something destructive glitters: they are descendants of elves. They have powerful hands with bony fingers that are slightly red. Perhaps it's from the cold. Or maybe it's from doing some kind of work we don't know about.

In the evening we're invited to eat with Rob in a private apartment: large comfortable kitchen, long table, cheerful people. Two professional chefs are making a delicious salmon dish. Sometime later more people arrive. One of them seems familiar to me. 'James Murphy,' Rob says. I look at him not knowing who that is. (My constantly embarrassing weakness: names. 'Artists aren't interested in fellow artists – only in their techniques,' Louise Bourgeois said.) 'James Murphy,' Rob repeats. 'LCD Soundsystem.' It sounds vaguely familiar; perhaps I've seen a video or something on TV . . . Right! That guy! He wore a *Future Days* T-shirt. Somebody says, 'He's a massive fan of yours.' I go to the other end of the table. 'Hi, I'm Irmin.' 'I know,' he says. We sit for a long while, until the wine is done.

28.2

Q&A with Rob.

James invites us for dinner tonight to the Maaemo. Someone tells us you have to book there months in advance, but James, his Danish friend Jonas Hartz and both of us are greeted like old friends of the owner, Pontus Dahlström. All of the tables in the restaurant are occupied, but we are led up some stairs and into a separate room with only one table, which is surrounded by glass. One wall of windows separates the room from the kitchen, where you can watch the chefs working. What they prepare is unique. Pontus stays with us the entire time and explains something about each of the fifteen courses. It's an adventurous trip through incredible landscapes of different flavours. It's art. Esben Holmboe is the artist and head chef.

Thank you, James.

1.3

9.30 a.m. Taxi to the airport. It's dark and rainy. Who cares. Oslo was beautiful.

Cologne, March 2014

2.3

Severinstrasse, 5 p.m. The carnival parade is over and the street is being cleaned and swept. A couple of old people with shopping trolleys collect bottles. A few stragglers are standing in front of the bars and singing along with whatever is coming out of the speakers. They're in costumes but it's as if they'd be in their everyday clothes. The voices, the different carnival songs coming from the bars, the hum of the street -cleaning machines, distant church bells: it's a web of sounds full of intimations and melancholy, a relaxed and dreamy atmosphere. That's how I like Cologne.

Berlin

7.3

2 p.m., Lido Club, Cuvrystrasse. An interview for a documentary about German rock music in the seventies or something. They're

not finished yet with setting up. Across the street – all of which is a comfortable, alternative scene – is a small restaurant. (Around the corner in Tritonus Studio I mixed *Impossible Holidays* together with Gareth Jones in 1989.) Behind the bar is a spindly cook and a wonderfully beautiful young woman. She switches back and forth between speaking English, Turkish and German with the patrons. The spinach–sheep cheese pastry tastes fantastic. Right now I'd actually like to stay here and enjoy an illusory hour of peace on earth.

For the interview I'm placed in an enormous, threadbare leather chair on top of a high podium. It's impossible to sit even halfway casually in this monstrosity. But that's how they planned it: a shabby atmosphere (during the day nightclubs appear so quaintly shabby), awful chair, and in it a small, older man who tells tales of his wild days. Great. While attempting to get the hell out of there at the very end, the fucking chair slips backwards off the pedestal and comes crashing down to the floor. It had been only a centimetre away from the edge, unfastened, without any stage hook, ready to slip off at any time. Ah, the crazy old days when you still had professionals!

In the evening I head over to Max Dax and Luci. She's pregnant, but you can't see it yet. Still, her movements already possess this beautiful, dreamy slowness. Max makes lamb chops with mushrooms. Tim (Robert Defcon) joins us. Relaxed evening.

9.3

Klaus and Birgitt head with Mogli to a park. I go to the Gemäldegalerie to visit some old friends:

Konrad Witz, *King Solomon and the Queen of Sheba*
There's a unique tension in his images between the almost constructivist level-headedness of the spaces depicted – his *Annunciation* is the best and soberest example – and the virtuosic colour frenzy

of the figures' clothes. He keeps the 'pathos formulas' of his day at a distance. Here, that sober quality is in Solomon's sceptical look, which is actually how I imagine the painter himself: mistrusting of exultations, except for those related to a passion for the glow of colours.

Hans Baldung Grien, *Lot*
Strange: observing this image I am reminded of Karl Kraus for some reason. God knows why.

Rubens, *The Holy Cecilia*
I imagine a heavy gust of wind blowing into a Veronese and exploding the colours. For a moment, everything is in a wild upheaval. Wonderful.

Hobbema, *Village Street under Trees*
. . . which leads directly to Constable.

Philips Koninck, *Dutch Plain Landscape*
A low-altitude flight above the wide, flat land. Koninck painted this image again and again, as if it evoked some unforgettable experience or dream – a weightless flight towards the horizon, where the deep sky and land come together to lock the world.

In Edinburgh I saw another painting like it. While standing in front of it dreaming of flying, the museum's alarm went off. Bomb warning. Turned out to be nothing.

Vermeer, *Woman with a Pearl Necklace*
She's painted in such a shimmering and blurry fashion, while the curtain, which is at the same distance, has well-defined contours. I see her dreaming herself into a sunlit, sun-yellow world, away from the grey that surrounds her. And threateningly, to her left, this chunk of blackish-blue looms like the clang of a deep bell. Together with the promise of sun-yellow and reality of everyday grey, they form a profoundly deep triad.

Anna Dorothea Therbusch, *Self-Portrait*

I love this painting. The sober irony of the painter's expression with that idiotic monocle – which, nevertheless, establishes a certain distance. A reflection on creating; the clever balance between perfect and unfinished.

Giovanni Battista Tiepolo, *The Martyrdom of St Agatha*

The entire brutality of this horrible story emanates from the blood-red-clad executioner dominating the image. All of the blood is drawn to him. The deed is done and he is already gesturing towards his next victim. Next to him, the snotty young page with the tablet, upon which lie both of St Agatha's appetising breasts, ready to be served. And, as so often in his paintings, the two peculiar men in turbans peer out from the right and left. It's a wild, evil and mysterious image.

Georges de la Tour, *St Sebastian Tended by St Irene*

When I stand in front of a painting by Georges de la Tour, Peter Przygodda reappears, discussing how much film owes to de la Tour's images – especially in 'how to use light'. There is a large, holy silence in this painting, something monumental. And still the figures possess a wonderful tenderness.

Velázquez, *Portrait of a Lady*

The lady, with her mocking and cautiously lascivious smile as if on the go, ready to flee at any moment, and with 'the look of being painted'. Yes, all of these expressions together.

Botticelli, *Venus*

. . . whose hair winds around her body and down between her thighs, like the snake in paradise.

10.3

Perhaps it was the Tiepolo. I thought about Max Beckmann when I stood in front of it. Then I thought about Peter Sorge and how much

I wished I could speak about the paintings with him. Maybe that's what caused the dream, which I can only remember the end of.

The room is dark. I'm lying on my back in bed. Peter wants to go out. At the door he turns around. I've closed my eyes, but I still see him. Am I sleeping? Very quietly, on his tiptoes, he comes back and kisses me gently on the mouth. Is he leaving again? Will he stay? I have a vague memory that he takes me in his arms, combined with an indistinct feeling of salvation. At the same time, he leaves on his tiptoes and gently closes the door. Images and feelings overlap.

I tell Klaus about the dream. He says, 'Peter freed you from feelings of guilt for not having helped him enough.' While Klaus is speaking, tears are streaming down my face.

Peter Sorge, later known as Ben Sorge. With him – and through him – I learned how to practise seeing. I discovered both the painted images and the ones that surrounded me every day. We tackled modernism and the modern art that was hated, destroyed and forced from Germany into exile. In approaching the reviled works of modern art, we often met with the resistance of our parents and teachers. We read the same books and listened to the same music. We sat for hours hovering over art books, stunned, confused and enrapt. Lovis Corinth, Wassily Kandinsky, Ernst Ludwig Kirchner, Karl Schmidt-Rottluff, Max Beckmann – these became the foundation of my world of images, especially Beckmann. It's a world of images that keeps changing and expanding, but one which began with Peter between 1952 and 1953, when we were fifteen or sixteen years old.

London, March 2014

24.3

Went with Max to the Serpentine Gallery. Conversation with Hans Ulrich Obrist. Unfortunately, it wasn't so fruitful. My fault. I say too many stupid things. At the end, everyone who has this kind of conversation with HUO is supposed to write a motto or an expression on a card. I write: 'Today I'm speechless.'

25.3

12.30. Interview at the BBC.

Then, 2 p.m., interview with Bobby Gillespie and Andrew Innes at Faber & Faber. Actually, I have no idea how to conduct interviews like this. But both guys make it easy for me. For Bobby, music history starts with the Sex Pistols. Andrew occasionally goes to the symphony. We talk for a long time.

26.3

Bristol. Meeting with Geoff Barrow. Mogli and Sandra are with us. Geoff wants to know a lot about Can – how the improvisation worked, how the pieces came about, etc. 'It took me ten years to understand, I didn't comprehend it.' With Geoff, too, music history starts with punk and PiL. Then, one day, he discovers *Ege Bamyası* – and is shocked that it was already twenty years old by then.

In contrast, I find it difficult to understand what was so incomprehensible about our music. Perhaps because pop and rock music in England had already become so formally standardised that the emotional immediacy in our music – which we expressed in very different and unconventional ways – only became understandable to most people years later, after they were freed by punk.

On the other hand, there were enthusiastic audiences at our concerts from the very beginning. One time in Glasgow, the crowd stormed the stage by the dozens and one guy hugged me so hard he broke my rib.

The first time we played in Bristol, a gang came into our dressing room: three enormous Hell's Angels-looking types and one small, frail guy with quick, darting eyes. With him was the delicate and spooky girl in black – that is, black around her eyes, black around her mouth and dressed in black clothes from head to toe. She must have invented Goth or something. No one even thought of stopping them from entering the room. One of the group said, 'You make the best music out there.' Another, the largest and most impressive of the bunch, kept repeating with a stutter, 'The best music.' When they were leaving, the girl pressed an impressive piece of hash into Michael's hand (Black Afghan, of course).

They came back again during the intermission. They looked at us as if we were from another planet. Then one said, 'You've cured him. He's stopped stuttering!' He had tears in his eyes. Then suddenly the large stutterer started speaking incredibly fast without a single stammer. He couldn't stop speaking, until somebody took him by the arm and led him out of the room. The others followed without saying a word.

After that, they followed us on our tours of England with their bikes, when they had time – even up to Edinburgh, if they had to. The stutterer eventually stuttered again, but that didn't matter. The girl (we affectionately called her 'the witch') provided us with dope.

Whenever we played Bristol we always tried to arrange one free day to hang with the witch and her boyfriend in the dark room in the back of their store, out of which they sold hippy stuff. She was very in love with her small, delicate boyfriend, whose darting eyes were always attentive. He also had a great hand and made excellent psychedelic ink drawings, which she sold in the store in the front. 'He's a genius,' his friends would say.

He was a trained lithographer and he was very talented indeed. So talented, in fact, that he managed to make counterfeit money by the time he was sixteen. Shortly before he turned eighteen, he and his gang got caught. He was able to get off lightly and swore to himself never again to do something so stupid. Instead, he simply counterfeited a single document, made sure it went to the right place and then regularly received £1,200 from the postman. This went on for three years. 'He's a genius,' his friends kept repeating. At the time, he hadn't been out of jail for very long. He actually still looked like a sixteen-year-old.

Geoff recommended we go to eat in Za Za Bazaar, a huge hall filled with food stands and all sorts of different restaurants – European, Asian, Moroccan, Mexican and every other kind of food imaginable. Good times. We return to the hotel satisfied.

Idiotic habit: furnishing hotel rooms in my mind. I always imagine that I am forced to remain here. I wonder where the grand piano would go, or maybe just a small piano. Where would the books go? What about the desk? What about the bed? Today, I'm doing this in the Bristol Hotel and there's enough space for a grand. The room is large.

27.3

We spent the night because we have a meeting today at 12 p.m. with Julian Cope. We're just on our way when his daughter calls us to cancel the appointment. No explanation given. (Well, never trust a hippy.)

We decide to go for a walk through the enormous housing-development wasteland on the other side of the river across from our hotel. Then to the beautiful cathedral, which boasts vaulted arches – even in the choir, with its enormous and unusually placed organ and gigantic bass pipes. It must make incredible noise. A friendly chaplain approaches us. We find out that his son is an actor and that the organ was completely restored in 1987. He doesn't know the original date of its construction.

Lunch on the river quay. There has to be a reason why so much good music comes from Bristol – Portishead, Massive Attack, Tricky, Smith & Mighty . . .

On the train to London we realise it's our fifty-first wedding anniversary.

29.3

London. Faber Social. In a club like this you understand what the British mean when they say 'civilised'.

Q&A with Andrew Weatherall. He does an excellent job, the crowd enjoys it. There are lots of laughs.

Behind the bar is a very young master of his trade. Among the excellent drinks he makes is one he calls 'Classic Rhum': laying a napkin over a glass filled with rhum, he places a sugar cube on top and bastes it with angostura. Both dissolve into the glass. Removing the napkin, he places ice cubes in the glass and stirs until it is all dissolved. Then comes a drop of concentrated orange juice, after which he squeezes out thin slices of orange peel and rubs them on the edge of the glass. The rest of the peel goes inside. Delicious, as is Mogli's margarita.

Amsterdam, April 2014

3.4

We arrive at 8 p.m. Mogli forgot her neck pillow in the plane. Lots of commotion and running back and forth, but we get it back.

Jozef picks us up. We drive to the theatre café, where he has arranged a meeting. ('Surprise guest,' he says.) First, gin and tonic. Then, enter the artist, his colourful scarf tossed jauntily over his shoulder, looking into the crowd at the café, searching. We're sitting directly beside the door, and next to Jozef and Hildegard is a free chair, but with coats and bags on it. He searches out a seat next to Hildegard, but Jozef asks him to sit next to me. He does so somewhat begrudgingly and immediately makes it clear who the head rooster is. Charming, funny, aggressive: Peter Greenaway. He finds my black leather jacket to be a German cliché, insists musicians to have 'no visual imagination'. 'I bet you have no visual imagination.' He believes operas based on novels – we're discussing *Gormenghast* – to be total nonsense. He thinks all music between the baroque and modern is awful. Bach apparently is OK, but after that it's all 'programme music'. Things only pick up again after Schönberg. I almost ask, 'What about rock music?' But then I realise how stupid that would be. The right to express opinions is sacrosanct, as long as they don't violate the ten commandments, human rights or the constitution, etc.

I would like to meet him again. Hildegard too.

And also the hotel that Jozef booked for us, Sweet Dreams, is fun. The restaurant, decked out in original seventies GDR design, is called Café Modern.

We'd easily be able to fit a grand piano in our room. The standalone king-size bed is located in the centre of the space. The silk sheets are a pinkish-salmon, and on the wall is an enormous, white angular elk head (art?). In the corner is a vacuum cleaner with a hat on it, while the jutty is adorned with high-quality seventies design objects: a small TV, a red typewriter with a scantily clad Monica Bellucci on top (a photo book with more of her inside), an elegant purple-clad mannequin and a shiny chrome tea cart containing everything a very modern kitchen in the sixties was supposed to have. Lots of art books. And on the back of the bed's backboard a sign with the word 'Hotel' in neon – just in case you forgot where you were. When we entered the room, we thought, 'This must be some kind of mistake – this is private, somebody lives here.'

I wake up in the middle of the night. In the room's half-light I see someone standing in front of the jutty's windows, a headless figure straight of childhood spook stories. Oh right, it's the mannequin.

4.4

On a walk with Mogli and Sandra through the quaint seventeenth century. And then smack in the middle: prostitutes in windows. In one window I see two very young, very attractive and very dark-skinned women dancing half naked. The white-tiled wall behind them suggests purity. In the next window a woman in street clothes stands motionless in front of the same tiles; her face tells the story of a harrowing life. She stares off into space. I don't want to stare at her. I want . . . well, what do I want? 'Come, let's escape.'

Excellent meal that evening with Jozef and Willemijn at Café Modern. After that, party in the film museum, where we all make silly pictures in the party photo booth.

5.4

With Mogli in the Rijksmuseum, then off to see Nora in the afternoon. A romantic house on the languet, directly next to the lake. Behind the house, on the other side of the dyke, the ocean.

An evening *en famille* chez Jozef and Willemijn, with their three beautiful daughters.

Roussillon

I dream I shave off a piece of my eyebrow, which changes the expression for that eye in an astonishing way. I spend a long time staring at my foreign-looking eye in the mirror.

❀

'Is that music for ghosts?' Lara asks when she enters the room and finds me listening to Luigi Nono's *Fragmente – Stille, an Diotima*. Back when she was eight, after a concert at the Ludwigsburg Castle Festival where I conducted some music I've composed for film, she drew me a picture of a white ghost, its arms spread out wide and with enormous three-fingered hands, cheerfully challenging, 'Go ahead, do something!' Something like a candle is growing out of his forehead. Lee Perry told me, 'This is your unicorn – you are free, you can use it for good or for bad.'

To the left of the ghost is a small, black, block-headed figure with two white eyes peering out of it: a violinist. A conductor and a violinist, surrounded by a dark-blueish green that resembles the bottom of the ocean. At the very top of the picture is a strip of golden sky. Today, Lara is twelve and has a diving certificate. She's interested in underwater archaeology. The ocean floor and the past: what could be more ghost-like? The picture she drew me is my good ghost. It hangs in my studio and is also the cover of *Villa Wunderbar*.

❀

'Goethe beautifully translates *"Habent sua fata libelli"* as *"Auch Bücher haben ihr Erlebtes"* – "Books have their own experiences too". Indeed, that which is experienced not only refers to the book, but also to its reading' (Uwe Timm). This is also true for music, composition, interpretation, reception and listening.

When did people start writing music down? That is, in such an accurate way that it could be perfectly reproduced at any moment? For millennia the forms and rules and methods of playing were passed down orally, from master to student, from parent to child. Perhaps there were symbols and rules that would help jog the memory – tips for melodies or rules, like only playing a certain piece on the river bank on a summer evening. Or perhaps there were instructions that related to the sequence of a ritual or a celebration of some kind. But what a piece of music actually consisted of – how it was to be played, how it should sound, the actual music and the practice of making it – was passed down from memory to memory. That's why what was preserved had to also be protected, for it was too easy for things to get lost if you carelessly mixed the new into the old. But preservation on the one hand and spontaneity or freedom in improvisation on the other hadn't yet come to contradict each other.

During the recording of my film music for *Flight to Berlin*, Reebop played a unique and truly fascinating rhythm – a groove that you can't break down into the regular component parts so necessary for European ears. Reebop called it 'Assagrai'. As he explained, when in his home country of Ghana a group of people were returning home at night from a celebration in a neighbouring village, they would have to march in single file through the jungle, with each person placing their hands on the shoulders of the person in front of them. Their steps would follow the rhythm that the leader would drum. It was a rhythm of a walk that carefully felt out the path ahead. Every irregularity or obstacle in their path would be signalled with rhythmic patterns. They literally were able to follow the drummer blind. The drummer was the only one who wasn't allowed to get drunk at the party. If he would drink or make even minute changes to the groove that had been trusted for generations to lead them through the jungle, the walk home could end in disaster.

Around the thirteenth century in Europe, a new kind of thinking emerged in France that showed an excitement for structure, a special desire for taking formal risks. Gothic cathedrals are the most visible evidence of this. Also, music became increasingly 'constructivist', it became polyphonic. The related problems that arose surrounding synchronicity gave rise to the development of 'musical notation'. Also, conversely, the more accurately you could notate music, the more complexly you could construct your compositions. In turn, this demanded the greatest possible precision in reproduction. Written music could no longer get lost and new music could be developed without the risk of losing the old. The Great European Game 'New!' could now be applied to music. What was the bet? Courage to break rules, courage to use unknown musical forms and create sounds no one had ever heard before, courage to be 'original'. (Often, composers, musicians and instrument-builders would play the game together.) What you could win when playing this game: creating 'timeless compositions' and a name to go along with it. Perotinus is the name of the composer who is associated with the very beginning, but the game doesn't really get going until the fourteenth century, with *ars nova*', 'new art'. This is what some composers in France called their music – 'new music' (sounds familiar?) – which featured a formal complexity and sonic beauty no one had ever heard before. And promptly occurred what had been a part of the 'New!' game for seven hundred years: they got into trouble with the preservers of old traditions, and even with the Pope. There is also something else that belongs to the game: every new form of music since then sheds light on what had come previously. This is because new music opens the ears to new ways of hearing, new modes of feeling and new kinds of understanding. It gives the old new meaning, a new mystery, a new beauty.

Ars nova: the name of the composer and poet Guillaume de Machaut is most closely connected with this new music. His *Messe de Nostre Dame* is among the most beautiful and moving compositions I know. This music has 'experienced' Bach, Mozart, Brahms, Stravinsky and spirituals. I hear Machaut charged with these 'experiences'. This is what makes it completely contemporary.

'Historical interpretation'. This sometimes really gets on my nerves, this screech of string instruments. It's as if vibrato had been an invention of the Romantics. If memories of your own life are inaccurate or more or less inventions, how incredibly fictive is a 'historical interpretation'? That could even become really dangerous. For example, not long ago while listening to a Mozart piano concert on the radio in my car: the strings were sawing away, resembling the dullest eighties synth-strings – a kind of mechanical dwarf baroque but with a giant modern piano in front of it. I got so angry that I wasn't paying attention and ran a red light, and only missed causing an accident by a hair.

'Is that music for ghosts?' Yup, you got it, Lara.

How would that work together in, say, a production of *The Magic Flute*? The stage design is twenty-first-century art, while the music emanating from the orchestra pit is a fictional representation of the past 'just like during the days of Mozart'. The strange thing is that it sounded so overcautious. Avoiding sounding like a modern orchestra at all costs. It didn't matter how preciously and delicately the idea of playing 'historically' was interpreted: the guys in the pit were in a different film than the ones onstage. (Apropos film: Miloš Forman's Mozart had clearly 'experienced' Sigmund Freud and Oliver Sacks. His take is both puzzling and incredibly lively.)

But the conductor somehow did appear historical to me, like he was built by Vaucanson* and wound up for the duration of the opera.

'. . . this dialectic of the present in the past, and the past in the present, with an essential implication of the future – this is the fundamental demand that should be satisfied by all interpreters' – Pierre Boulez.

'Give the operas of the classical repertory as if they were contemporary works . . . and vice versa' – Alban Berg.

* Jacques de Vaucanson (24 February 1709–21 November 1782), French inventor of automata.

Roussillon

Dream: I'm standing outside at the front door and ring the bell. I'm supposed to go and visit them in their house. It's urgent, and I'm happy to see them again. Nobody comes to open up, so I open the door myself. A tiny room, the door to the living room must be on the left. It's been turned into a wall. I walk around the house. An open entrance, some stairs. On the wall is a silver sign with an insignia and an eagle. It says 'Police Station' and it hangs crooked. Upstairs is an office, nobody answers. But I hear something like a voice that is trying to lead me.

There they sit, small and apparitional: my first piano teacher and his wife. I can't remember their last name any more. But that doesn't matter because the piano is there – also small, but *the* piano nonetheless. I'm ecstatic and deeply touched, and as I approach it I immediately wake up. Immediately I remember their last name: Schenuit. Mr and Mrs Schenuit.

Groove, Improvisation, Form, Non-Form

'I wanted to be lost in focused intensity.' Hans Ulrich Gumbrecht quotes this sentence in a speech. It's originally from Pablo Morales, a world champion and Olympic gold medallist in swimming. 'In the midst of such intensity, you don't control the gaze of your attention towards certain objects, but rather are completely open (lost) for everything the world presents and will present to you. This openness includes your own unexpected epiphanic reactions to feelings, images and ideas.' In other words: 'Lost in focused intensity.' When you can achieve that – in the studio or onstage – then coincidence is magically eradicated from the world. In order for it to work, you have to practise. (For musicians, this is a kind of platitude. Professional athletes like Pablo Morales call it 'training'.)

The vagrancy of the imagination is often inept and contradictory – especially contradictory ('Away with skill' – Louise Bourgeois). The playful, the unfinished – whatever you want to call jamming or improvisation – is practice if it has form as its goal. At least that's how it was with Can. Groove is form, and Jaki is its prophet. It's form that is 'open for any and all unexpected epiphanic reactions' of feelings and sounds. Groove is strict rules and total freedom. But the more freedom you have, the more mistakes you can make.

From my thoughts in the *Can Box: Book* (by Hildegard Schmidt and Wolf Kampmann):

It was the experience you have playing when you're truly happy – of the band becoming a single being, one powerfully pulsating organism. Our music is the constantly renewed attempt to produce this state of being. This doesn't just happen. Rather, it comes from incredible concentration and wakefulness, presence of mind, presence of ear. Your entire being is transformed into an ear and everything that surrounds you is music. The door to the garden is open and outside cars and the occasional starfighter jet are whizzing by. Jaki has been tuning his drums for the past hour, tapping out some secret rhythm with extreme concentration – a rhythm only his drums and the related deity understands. 'Music should only be made by machines or gods,' he once said. Holger is extremely far away in his mixing board space capsule, alternately producing incredibly shrill screams or earthquake-like thuds. Michael is staring at his guitar, which lies in front of him feeding back and picking up the 8 o'clock news. Damo is lying on a trash bag filled with Styrofoam, sliding around and giggling because it's sexy and squeaky. I'm sitting at my piano and playing a B until all of a sudden it combines with the starfighters, tapping sounds, Styrofoam squeaks, guitar hum and seismic tremors into a single groove. After an hour the whole room is pulsating, your body and everything else is in this groove, you're listening to everyone else and what your own hands are doing. It's blasting off, you're happy, and after two hours you suddenly have the stupid idea of ditching your riff on the B for another little melody. Everything starts teetering, you want to go back to playing your riff again, but it's gone. Everything collapses. Instead of beating you up, Jaki continues to beat on his drums for half an hour. Michael goes back to silently staring at his guitar. Damo is grumbling about something and Holger rewinds the tapes and announces that he's going to make a piece out of it that will become our retirement pension in 30 years. I know we'll take a listen to it shortly and although we'll find it pretty good, we'll say the opposite. We'll complain and fight and then eventually start playing again because we can do it better, more together rhythmically. And sometimes it worked.

Irmin Schmidt

'It is precisely the most demanding kind of freedom that needs the most severe discipline . . . Any rash surrender to the frenzy, or indeed the hysteria of the moment, will destroy the original motivation of the music by destroying its essential ambiguity' – Pierre Boulez.

Form, Non-Form: 'It's as deadly for the mind to have a system as it is to have none' – Paul Valéry.

'Living means defending a form' – Anton Webern.

Groove is 'focused intensity', groove is endless. Groove is mysterious.

Die Form ist
ja das, was sauer
macht; überhaupt

die Festlegung
auf eine Form
von was da ist.

[Form is
that which
makes sour;

The determination, above all,
of a single form
from what is there.]

Rolf Dieter Brinkmann,
'Ice Water on Guadalupe St.'

Ambient

From the very beginning we often spent hours or entire days turning the studio and the space into a sound installation. One microphone, two speakers and perhaps a little delay were enough to get the room vibrating. Every noise, every sound was meaningful. Footsteps, a chair, a few words, a chance sound made by touching an instrument. We explored the room playfully, alertly and without intention, homing in on the sounds of objects and movements, more as careful listeners than agents of sound. If we got lucky, a magical sound atmosphere arose. The space and everything that surrounded us, the 'ambience', became music. – The Can version of Ambient, School for Magicians.

(From my liner notes to 'Evening All Day',
No. 3, CD1, Can: *Lost Tapes*)

It's the whole body that listens and vibrates with sound, from the very beginning. The constant beating and groove of the mother's pulse, nine months long, always present. Our universe pulses, bathed in constant static, while our body develops. The noise remains with us in all forms – in the background, in the underground, in the foreground.

Tout grand art procède [. . .] de la musique, parce qu'elle transforme le bruit de fond en un préalable du sens' ['All great art proceeds [. . .] from music, because it transforms background noise into a precondition of meaning'] – Michel Serres.

The mother's voice – how does that sound from inside the womb? She sang a lot, and she laughed a lot. Her laugh was bright like her soprano, replete with small, glittering coloratura.

First Ambient.

And still it's the entire body. Sound wants to be smelled, touched, tasted and seen in order to be both heard and revealed. It's the entire body that bestows the unexpected messages of objects with space and time; a stage where the individual moments of the outside collide and melt in a transient and fragile internal sound, destined to splinter and reassemble and break again and again and again; every time a different way, always mysteriously, always a different puzzle.

Ambient is transformation.

'. . . *la participation des pulsions, tributaires des zones érogènes (orales, anales, urétrales), dans la formation des consonnes et des voyelles. Le corps érotique s'imprime dans les phonèmes, la chair parle . . .'* ['. . . the participation of human drives are dependent on the erogenous zones (oral, anal, urethral), manifested in the formation of consonants and vowels. The erotic body is imprinted in the phonemes, the flesh speaks . . .'] – Julia Kristeva, in *Du mariage considéré comme un des beaux-arts*.

Can tour in England. Taunton, Saturday afternoon. Uli comes onstage to fix something and tells us most people aren't listening.

'They're getting drunk, blabbing, yelling and having sex in every dark corner.' Michael is excited. 'Wonderful! Music for shagging! Best possible ambience.' After that he only plays rhythm guitar, grooving like the devil, and Jaki, who usually looks incredibly strict while playing, has a huge smile on his face.

Afterwards, Hildegard says, 'That was really great.' She spent the whole time at the bar with a retired colonel from the Royal Navy drinking cider, lots and lots of cider. She is in an incredibly good mood.

'Joy not entertainment' (says Brecht).

Bubble baths, being covered in mud, hammams, massages – I love that stuff. That is, if it wasn't always for . . .

The masseur is actually great. After fifteen minutes he asks, 'Am I doing something wrong? You're still so tense, nervous somehow.' I reply, 'Can you please just turn off this shitty new-age wellness music?' He's not happy about it, but he complies. After a few minutes: 'Well, what do you know! Suddenly you're completely relaxed.'

Silence.

I'm listening to his breathing. Outside a seagull whines.

I love Marseille. Even the airport. Airports are spaces of transfer: you're not really gone and haven't yet really arrived. The French sociologist Marc Augé calls these 'non-places'.

Brian Eno had the beautiful idea of making *Music for Airports*. Ambient. Turning non-places into places through sound; places which are no longer impossible to linger in; places without the dreary atmosphere created by bothersome muzak.

Departure lounge Marseille. The loops are comfortably boring, sometimes cautiously jazzy, but the sound doesn't want anything from me. It absorbs all of the sounds and voices. I am waiting to be called for boarding, my departing melancholy floats around and makes acquaintances.

Ambient. Marseille Airport.

Noise

There was music on the radio, both of my parents played piano, but not so much in my earliest childhood memories; the very vague feeling that I occasionally feared music. I also have a vague memory of my mother's singing around the same time – perhaps because it was such an integral part of her daily life.

But the noises!

Gravel crunching under the yellow tyres of the black car across the street whenever it drove into the driveway. I played on the balcony, often just waiting by the railing for the car and the crunching sound. I couldn't have been more than four years old, because in 1941 we moved to the Sensburger Allee. There, between the pavement and front lawn, was a small strip filled with gravel. Over and over again I drove my pedal car onto the gravel – but it just wasn't the right crunch.

One time, as punishment, I was forced to sit under the table. It was wonderful – a cave beneath a mysterious imbroglio of sound, the clatter of plates and strange-sounding voices that expressed no meaning. I entered a kind of trance.

While eating a few days later, I asked my mother if I could sit under the table again.

Sometimes in restaurants, suddenly and without warning, everything becomes a hallucinatory blur of sound, and I'm back in the cave under the table.

Near our house, on the periphery of a bright, sandy little forest, I discovered a small, cave-like hole between the roots of a pine tree. I used to sit there for hours and listen to the sounds around me. In the tree above me there was crackling and creaking, sand fell quietly through the tree's roots, and from the nearby houses came indistinct voices and sounds, birds flapped their wings and tweeted from the surrounding treetops, and everything was embedded in the swelling and receding sounds of the pines. Occasionally the nearby train would shoot past. The booming sound seemed to come directly from the earth.

One key childhood experience occurred during an overnight train ride from Berlin to Innsbruck in the summer of 1942.

The monotonous rhythm of the wheels, interspersed by wild clatter and constantly changing driving sounds, into which I hallucinated choruses and swooshing orchestras; the mysterious voices at the train stations, suddenly interrupted by booming sounds that disappeared as fast as they appeared – all that put me in an alert state of euphoria, until early in the morning, completely exhausted, I started bawling, and I could only respond to my concerned mother in between sobs with 'No, nothing's wrong – it was just so beautiful.'

(From my liner notes to *Flies, Guys and Choirs*)

Marseille Airport, Again.

It was a Dornier with propellers – suddenly it reappeared, the dark, polyphonic drone of 'enemy bombing brigades' (*'Feindliche Bomberverbände'*, as they called them during the war). These were clusters of many, many airplanes flying in an extremely dense formation at high altitude, and passing overhead for minutes at a time. It was as if the sound, which wasn't exceptionally loud, became an overarching clamour into which I dived, like an enormous ringing bell.

Luigi Russolo, Futurista, *L'arte dei rumori* (Milano, 1916).

Chapter 1 is the Futurist Manifesto from 1913. This is the year Igor Stravinsky premiered *Le Sacre du printemps* in Paris and Arnold Schönberg conducted Anton Webern's *Six Pieces for Orchestra*, as well as the *Five Orchestral Songs* by Alban Berg, in Vienna. In both cities there were protests and riots among the crowd at the performances. In Vienna the event became known as the most significant 'scandalous concert', with fist fights breaking out and the concert being forced to shut down.

Compared to Stravinsky, Schönberg, Webern and Berg – at the time the most avant-garde and today classics – Russolo is punk.

He wanted to 'create a new musical reality' by using the 'endless variety of tones in noise'. He offered 'generous sonic slaps in the face' and to 'completely reform music through sound art'. In order to compose with sounds from the environment, he had to make them reproducible. So he categorised them and constructed bizarre mechanical instruments with which to simulate these sounds, as well as change them – albeit within a small-ish framework. For example, transposing by an octave. (Unfortunately, none of these instruments exist today, though some have been partially recreated.)

He studies intensely the acoustic properties, sonic hues and rhythms of sound in an attempt to create a theory of composition. He also invents a graphical notation for his instruments. He is actually a painter – as a musician he is an amateur. Punk. With the invention of the tape machine, recording equipment and electronic sound production, his visions became reality.

Because of my 'classical' musical training and the established musical approaches, I only later began to understand my fascination with 'noise' being a part of my musical world. I was nineteen years old when I heard Karlheinz Stockhausen's *Song of the Youths* (*Gesang der Jünglinge*) one night on the radio. It opened up an entirely new universe of sound. I was fascinated, confused, perplexed.

Shortly afterwards I began my studies at the Dortmund Conservatory, initially pursuing a diploma as a piano teacher. That was necessary because having not completed my A levels (I had been kicked out of school), I wouldn't be allowed to go on to study conducting and composition at university. Getting my degree to teach piano made that possible. It was also part of my pedagogical training to work for a time with a group of children. I was assigned a group of six- to ten-year-olds who, until then, had been more or less joylessly playing on xylophones, glockenspiels, recorders and other cutesy kid instruments, following Orff's curriculum. I then started to include the objects in our practice space – chairs, note stands, clothes hooks. It was somewhat chaotic, but more fun. Finally, I suggested they explore the sounds of various objects at home and to bring into school whatever Mum allowed. It was a huge success! They came with pots, bowls, glasses – one kid secretly schlepped a frying pan to school. It became even more chaotic in class, but it was a lot of fun. After a while we had developed a zany, joyful, percussive sound. But it didn't take long until I was called in to speak with the principal. In his office were a bunch of parents all looking extremely serious and concerned. 'Mr Schmidt, this won't work! This has nothing to do with music.' 'My kid broke a crystal vase.' 'Every day this incredible racket.'

No more fun. The kids were extremely pissed off. Forty years later: recording the kitchen scene for my opera *Gormenghast*. Jaki drums on pots, plates and glasses, while rhythmically shaking an entire drawer full of cutlery and dragging a knife to the groove. I drop large chunks of porcelain from the mezzanine of my studio onto the stone floor. Using samples of these sounds, Kumo and I also then created the track 'Fledermenschen' on our album *Masters of Confusion*.

Concert: John Cage and David Tudor, 1960.
Cage has a contact microphone attached to his throat. He is gurgling and swallowing water. Again, this mix of fascination and

bewilderment. Occasionally I laugh loudly out of helplessness. I am sitting very close to the stage in the second row. After the concert, I go backstage to apologise for laughing – which I am sure he must have noticed. I try to explain that it's not like . . . uh . . . well, I wasn't, um . . . Cage looks at me for a moment searchingly but affectionately and says, somewhat amused, 'What's wrong with laughing?'

My self-consciousness instantly disappears. We continue to speak a bit. I didn't know it then, but something new had begun in my musical thinking.

A couple of years later, around 1963 or '64: a performance by the Merce Cunningham Dance Company, featuring John Cage and David Tudor, at the Folkwang Akademie in Essen, where I'm still a student. I meet Cage that afternoon and help him a bit with staging – I knew my way around the performance hall. Afterwards we went to a restaurant around the corner, and he told me about his adventures collecting mushrooms in the swamps of Alaska. Only later, directly before the beginning of the performance, did he ask if I would be interested in performing a warm-up – a kind of overture – with him.

Above the parquet in the hall was a U-shaped balcony, narrow on either side and larger at the back. That's where the professors sat. When the lights dimmed, Cage and I, on opposite sides of the balcony, took chairs and pushed them firmly down into the wooden floor and slid them forward. It created a dull rumble and then screeching, then suddenly a very quiet, evil scratching sound, before suddenly going back to piercing squeaks. This is how we worked our way from the back towards the professors. A few of them stood up and stared speechlessly in my direction. Others were gesticulating wildly. 'Have you completely lost your mind, Schmidt?' 'Stop this nonsense immediately!' I heard. Of course, they all knew me, and hardly anyone paid attention to Cage. 'Definitely keep pushing,'

Cage had said, 'until we meet in the middle of the back – even if they try to stop you.' We managed to do just that, despite the tumult. 'Thank you, Irmin,' Cage said, utterly unaffected by the uproar, and went downstairs and got onstage.

'Noise' is mimesis.

Perhaps something totally primal appears in our music: mimesis. The noises of the world, the music of things.

Collage

'Individuum im spezifischen, nicht bloss generischen Sinn, ist, wer im eigenen Dasein einen Kulturwandel austrägt' ['An individual in the specific – not just generic – sense of the word is someone who can carry out cultural change within his very being'] – Sloterdijk.

'Inspiration ist das Resultat des Zusammenstosses widersprüchlicher Codes in einer Psyche' ['Inspiration is the result of the collision of contradictory codes within a single psyche'] – Sloterdijk.

Alexander Kluge: 'And the friction, the errors and the mistakes are very important. Our shared taskmaster would be the philosopher Gottfried Leibniz, because he said that where two supposedly or actually incompatible elements collide, the result is never a boundary, but an enclave on either side. That's to say, there are always innovations.'
Kerstin Brätsch: 'Collage.'
Alexander Kluge: 'Collage, yes. And the reason I emphasise these contrasting elements is because an invisible image appears in the small gap between two images, and an epiphany pops out.'

(From the catalogue *Das Institut*, Serpentine Sackler Gallery, London; Alexander Kluge, Hans Ulrich Obrist, Kerstin Brätsch)

'*Si ce sont les plumes qui font le plumage, ce n'est pas la colle qui fait le collage*' ['If it's the feathers that make the plumage, it's not the glue that makes the collage'] – Max Ernst.

'*Et l'anarchie, au point ou Heliogabale la pousse, c'est la poésie realisée. La poésie, c'est la multiplicité broyée et qui rend des flammes*' ['And anarchy, to the point where Heliogabalus pushes it, is poetry realised. Poetry is crushed multiplicity and makes flames.] – Antonin Artaud.

Representing the complexity of insanity – what Foucault had suggested and Susan Sontag considered in the form of a novel – what would that look like in music? Might Karlheinz Stockhausen's *Gruppen* for three orchestras come close?

'It's essentially considered proven that insanity is an immanent element in every profound artistic expression. Schopenhauer defined the lunatic as someone who has lost his memory. A subtle definition' – Giorgio de Chirico, 1919.

Through the keyhole, the landlady sees him, Nietzsche, dancing alone in his room, naked.

Mani Löhe constantly reminded us that it was important to be beautifully and imaginatively dressed while playing music in the studio.

'Whoever fears tastelessness will eventually be consumed by frost' – Pablo Neruda.

Do we need an aesthetic? Especially for pop or rock music?
Adorno had to exclude lots of things in order to formulate an aesthetics of music. The words 'denounce' and 'liquidate' often appear in his texts.

There should always be dialects that are foreign and difficult to understand within the so-called 'global language' of pop music.

Variety in languages, styles, techniques, traditions, high and low (Bakhtin sends his regards) – collage – has existed in painting since the twentieth century, while in music it only really started in the fifties (however, from further back, regards from Gustav Mahler and Charles Ives). Recording technology and electronics can be used wildly and with glee to force a collision of the most disparate and distant things; and now, with computers, software allows for unbridled and disarming arbitrariness; or, perhaps, it's the tension of crackling contradictions and the coolness of multiple interpretations created in the mind of the listener and a mysteriousness caused by always combining sonic elements anew with every listen.

Alan mentions he listens to Stockhausen's *Klavierstück X* when writing. It relaxes him.

'Suivre sa pente au lieu de chercher son chemin' ['Following one's slope instead of looking for one's path'] – Talleyrand.

'Suivre le dieu' ['Follow the god'] – Casanova.

'Let things happen' – Cage.

Sometimes Michael and I – both with Can and later on with my own work – would record entire sound cascades on their own, without any relationship to a track, and then copy the whole thing onto a piece.

Sampling is collage, Can is collage.

And then there's the collage that my *'Möglichkeitssinn'* – my sense of possibility – lived?, not lived?, dreamt?, and then still . . .

'Somehow order is transformed into the need for manslaughter' – Robert Musil.

Silence

Not even the slightest breeze. A few vague noises hang in the warm air. High above are clouds moving at high speed. Strange that these don't make any sound.

The poplar tree shakes in front of the window. No sound, just Mogli breathing. Tonight she appeared in my dream. I was wandering around lost but then found my way again. Then I was back to being lost. Suddenly she appeared in some kind of hair salon. I wasn't allowed in. There were half-naked women with incredibly large, vertically styled hairdos. Then her face was in my hands, so close and incredibly beautiful that I melt from love. I continued to wander around, getting lost and then finding my way.

   Now. Protected by the silence. Secure. Perhaps it's already memory. The poplar shakes excitedly, but I can't hear it. Only Mogli's breath. It's completely silent.

Silence is a metaphor.

Dream
On a large lake. I paddle out far in my small rowboat. I'm alone. The lake is calm and empty and sparkling silver under a white cotton sky. The horizon is a shiny, lit streak. I turn around. A dark ridge sits between the brightness of the lake and the sky. On top of a hill, black and sliced razor-flat, is a horse reared up on its hind legs. In front of the horse, a man throws a spear in mid-run. The spear hangs in the air like the images on a Greek vase. For whom? There, in the direction it points, the lake becomes a wide river, which narrows into a distant perspective. On both sides of the river and partially submerged in water are large, leafless trees with black trunks and powerful branches. Glowing fog floats above the water. Endless calm and supernatural light.

I tell Mogli the dream, but it's impossible to communicate its over-powering beauty, the immediate emotional and physical beauty of these dream images in words. And while I'm speaking, suddenly comes the thought that these were images of death.

❀

Roussillon
Outside it's spring, inside Silvia and Lara chirp and giggle small ascending and descending melodies.

Under a pine tree there's a dark, roaring buzz. On a branch hanging above me I see a large brown clump the size of a shoebox surrounded by bees. I take to my heels.

Patrick knows a beekeeper, who comes immediately. He looks like Treidel after he moved to the countryside: older, still with round metal-rimmed glasses and a belly that has become solid with age. He's gone grey but somehow looks younger.

He and Kevin are dressed like astronauts. Kevin bends the branch down, and Treidel shakes the clump into a box and quickly puts into it two honeycombs, puts the lid on and is done. The remaining bees buzzing around the branch immediately start building a clump, this time in the form of a long cone. He puts this one in the box too. The point is to capture the queen bee. If she escapes, it's all for nothing. (That he looks like Treidel is, of course, not a coincidence.)

❀

'Historical interpretation', again: these are *'lectures littéralistes'* – literal readings – which is to say, a fundamentalist interpretation that denies historical evolution.

The rise of fundamentalisms.

'Je conclus que l'indifférence en matière politique est une partie de la sagesse. Il faut ajouter un peu de fanatisme par explosions' ['I conclude that indifference towards matters of politics is a part of wisdom. We must add a little fanaticism through explosions'] – Alain, *Correspondance avec Elie et Florence Halévy*.

Incredible that a butterfly can fly through such a heavy mistral. This one here happily made its way through the heavy gusts of wind – such an exhilarating image in the middle of the wildly swaying trees.

In the TGV experiencing a light somnambulist's euphoria, speeding past a changing landscape with the feeling of driving to encounter a life unknown. Occasionally a train in the opposite direction whizzes by with a dampened explosion, concealing the slices in the time warp. Perhaps I and the rest of the passengers are driving into an irreversible forgetting.

Revisiting my dream of the lake: 'Images of death?' No – death isn't beautiful. What's this nonsense about?

Paris-Gare de Lyon
Standing in front of the display panel, waiting to see from which track my train is departing. In front of me is a woman. I stare disengaged at her feet in sandals. Suddenly she turns around and gives me a strange look, then glances at her feet, confused.

It's nothing out of the ordinary for people to sense a gaze from behind, but on your feet? How odd.

Roussillon
A wonderfully beautiful dark-brown moth with bright stripes; a brocade as if it were painted by Veronese, with a small, bright-red, shiny slit between its wings, sitting atop the black varnish of my piano lid.

From My Notebook

Dream

A large hall with a complex beam construction, old virgin stone walls, a large church door and a few small windows with ogee arches. Not much light. I discover the outlines of similar church windows, which have been walled over. I tell Mogli I want the walls covering the windows smashed open. She starkly objects – it's the darkness that she likes about the space. Lots of people, lots of chaos. A blonde woman explains something to me before turning around mid-sentence and hobbling off; her leg looks sick and red and inflamed. She's wearing two completely different shoes: a flat shoe on her sick leg and a stiletto on the other. Suddenly she trips – she has three legs. While they become increasingly entangled, flashes of lightning shoot around her like luminous snakes. Then she continues to walk away normally.

A dragonfly sits on my book. Above the pond there's also small light-red and metallic-blue ones and large green-blue iridescent ones. The dragonfly on my book is grey.

In front it has a small, round, furry body, which is attached to a thin, straight, stick-like form five to six times longer. It floats away as silently and ghostly as it appeared.

Bandol

At sundown, seagulls begin gathering above the small island. They glide quietly around one another, ascending and falling, a floating ballet, an incantation. The beauty of this movement possesses something heartbreaking. It nevertheless becomes dark.

Dream

A dark blanket of clouds closes the sky and races low across the flat landscape. On the periphery you can see trees and bushes growing on it. Soon the last patch of blue sky will have disappeared, but it won't rain or become cold – only darker, for ever.

I wake up with an angsty feeling that I can't get rid of all day.

The people around me continue to grow larger.

Vico attributes the 'gigantic size' of the Barbarians and Germanic tribes to the 'animalistic rearing of their children'. There's something to that.

Geological menu: a gabbro nest embedded in basalt with feldspar and green granite.

Bandol

The sea is grey and calm, the sky is soft and full of dark and clear-coloured shades in cloud grey.

Occasionally a seagull sails by our window. Mogli is typing, there's a buzzing in my ear and ants are marching across the table. When they encounter each other, they kiss briefly and then continue on, each in their own direction.

It's getting darker. The island of Bendor and the Bay of Bandol look as if they've been deserted a long time ago. How peaceful.

Roussillon

Cage wanted 'sounds to emerge from their own centre', to let them simply occur without forming them or instilling them with emotion. No intentions. The musician is 'within his own centre' when creating sounds without intention, letting them happen unimpededly.

In 1967, within the context of a new-music concert series, I staged Cage's *Atlas Eclipticalis* with his *Winter Music*, performing them together with the Bochum Symphony Orchestra. Cage suggests that the conductor signal the passing of each minute with slow, circular arm movements, but I passed on the idea. Instead, we practised the very long pauses which all of the musicians are supposed to observe. During the performance I played *Winter Music* on piano, and I recall the orchestra displaying an impressive readiness and highly professional approach to the piece – which was somewhat uncommon for the time. Still, it proved difficult to maintain concentration and focus for more than thirty minutes.

Unbeknownst to the rest of us, the orchestra's two clarinettists were involved in playing a secret game – one which would prove surprisingly helpful despite being impermissible on account of its intentions. While the first clarinettist was a passionate supporter of new music, the second detested it. Whenever the first clarinettist played a note, the second clarinettist would attempt to harmonise with it by playing a third or a sixth. In response, the first clarinettist would immediately change the original note to create dissonance. They played this game doggedly the whole way through and without making a mockery of the performance. And both went along with the rest of the rules for the piece, which included playing extremely quietly for almost the entire duration, as well as observing the long pauses.

Somehow, the extreme level of concentration it took to play their game had a positive effect on the orchestra and helped establish the performance's uniquely beautiful atmosphere. It was a game within a game. The clarinettists took Cage's rules, which cater to separating the musicians, and inserted into them their own subversive system. While the result certainly influenced the performance, it strangely managed to do so in accordance with Cage's original concept for the piece.

Cage.
Stockhausen.
The conceptual haikus of Fluxus.
Game theory.
Artaud: 'Why shouldn't it be possible to imagine a piece born and developed directly onstage?'

John Coltrane.

Max Roach.

Two months in New York, beginning of 1966. I met La Monte Young and Terry Riley. Steve Reich gave me a copy of *It's Gonna Rain*.

The first LPs by the Mothers of Invention, the Velvet Underground and especially Jimi Hendrix.

Things were brewing and rumbling.

In 1966 I began working on *Album für Mogli*, which is composed of nine pieces or 'games', with different rules for actions and reactions – essentially processes for developing sound structures. Some had defined compositional structure, others included freely interpretable material that could be used to develop musical games. The number of players for most pieces was specified.

Although the premiere of No. 6, 'Hexapussy', in Frankfurt had been a success, the joy of inventing these kinds of games was eventually exhausted. Ultimately it seemed to be a pretty abstract affair. *Album für Mogli* remained unfinished. Can got in the way.

One of the final catalysts for Can's formation was meeting the group Musica Elettronica Viva, which included Frederic Rzewski, Richard Teitelbaum and Alvin Curran. Not only did they make exciting, lively, spontaneous and physical music, but they were a group. This is when the idea of forming one myself began to take shape; a group that, when working together, would be able to absorb all that was rumbling and brewing in order to invent a new kind of music.

Later, around the spring of 1971, Richard Teitelbaum visited us in our apartment in Cologne. At the time he was enamoured by *Tago Mago*, particularly 'Aumgn' and 'Peking O'. The album had just been released, and Richard and I seized the moment to celebrate his contribution to Can's formation.

III: Nerves Strung Across Landscapes

Kai Althoff. He was seven years old the first time he came into the Can Studio. He listened quietly and seriously. At some point, he slowly and respectfully approached the drum set and watched Jaki play. When we took a break, Jaki put the sticks in his hand without saying a word. Shy but determined, he took a seat at the kit. After feeling it out with a few hits, a pattern soon emerged – one which he then repeated with increasing precision.

Michael was the first to notice: 'Listen, he's playing in 5/4 and it's got a melody.'

Perhaps only very few drummers truly understand what I'm saying, but melody is also what made Jaki one of the greatest. He sang on drums.

At seven, Kai had already understood. And it was Michael who heard it immediately. Kai continued to come to the Can Studio often. There was an immediate, intuitive understanding between Kai and Michael.

Even later on, when Michael and his wife Shirley moved into the old oil mill on the bank of the Vésubie, in the mountains behind Nice, Kai was often there to visit and worked with Michael in his studio.

I thought their deep connection, their friendship, should be told in this book. And who better to do so than Kai himself.

I thank him from the bottom of my heart for doing so.

By Kai Althoff

You, my nerves.

If I am to dedicate my youth to a single person, it's you. I'll gladly give it to you as a present. (I know – what are you supposed to do with it?) Since I always want to produce everything in the soul and in the attitude and the coils of thoughts – everything that appeared later to me as an addition, but never again as an origin – it's quite clear that I try to conjure up this most beautiful time, with all its secrets, when all things good seek to escape my grasp. As a means against the horror of time advancing. No, we did not deserve that.

The time is when I was twelve until when I was about sixteen, at the oldest. That's when things were best. And I wanted to be made of the stuff that you – all of you – had made: of what you did, how you spoke and thought, what you laughed at, how you moved and dressed. How life felt in your souls and formed itself for you was always my greatest aspiration. Within there, everything appeared to occur magically. It really was like that for me; everything was marked by magic. All light, from morning to night, all smell, all sounds, from the air of the weather, insects, cats and dogs, river, stones and soil, all the murmurs and groans of the vegetation and living creatures. Finally, above all, the words, the laughter and the whispers. Even a quarrel and anger seemed to me to be a part of a great structure that could never have really been in danger, ultimately because it was created by a manifestation of the highest-ranking spirits, under divine direction. One was allowed to do and try everything. I did not question anything that you were, because I assumed (well, I know) that you really had access to a possibility of experiencing given to very few by God – or only to you alone. The gift is that they are made familiar with even His most secret things; because He is so gently disposed to them, they can use these gifts; they can rearrange all creation, and everything in its foundation, into the boldest new arrangements for themselves without the structure collapsing. One can trespass, enter something unauthorised, and emerge without significant wounds. One can see into the most beautiful construct of the most brutal-looking truths without groundlessly falling victim to the thing in madness. The gifted can see this, and because he sees that he is truly an inseparable part of the divinity, he can calmly learn everything, examine, smile, marvel, reject or even completely participate in creation. To condemn something in non-acceptance or to combat it in silly aggression is not necessary because it will surrender itself to him.

That's why he is not afraid. What are You doing today? nothing. What are you doing today? Music. what are You doing today _ no answer.

The slightly reproachful demand, against my mother's sense of honour, to wash the salad because the vinaigrette wasn't right was fulfilled by the other girlfriend.

Whether or not someone wanted me to or not, all that has become the reason for me, just the same as my parents' reason upon which one later builds something in life; often in really feeling your way through, on rickety stalks, or in the misunderstood application of the experienced. In unspoken hope that something of you all sticks in me, something which will slightly direct my form of expression in that direction and which seemed to be in all of your sound. Later, for example, one also compared those perceptions one had with others made as a young adult, one who now also, let us say, looks at five other people as higher beings. This comes with age, this lame smarty-pants relativisation. There is always an argument that sneaks in from alleged accumulated knowledge claiming to be able to now say where it came from – where the notes, thoughts and attitudes are headed. But therein lies the mistake: the application of everything I later experienced, this only sustained me here and there, but I was only truly held by the ineffability of you. Whether I'm aware of it or not doesn't matter. And I'd so like to say it more precisely, what it is; but when I'm supposed to describe it, then it's not the description of a human being with character and soul and stuff like that. It's MUCH MORE: a vibration of strands of nerves strung across landscapes. These never touch the ground like a jump rope, they only almost do. In their years-long, intangibly long units, hills irregularly aligned against each other and the resulting valleys describing the curves, with each nerve turning into itself, and within such a turn the strands offering endless possibilities of rhythms together, emerging from the control of the strands' ends. That's what the hands do that hold them, not stopping, but rather carefully creating the most beautiful intervals, through manipulation, lightly whipping against one another, or: letting them hang. Or pulling them taut and spinning them fast, so that the first, the late-day and the final sun rays are fragmented when, following their movement, one peers into the burning light. Or panting, fragmenting the air like rods, in the night that always follows. And so on, continuously.

Occasionally the landscape above which they are strung, which leaves no space for a sky (the aforementioned sun shines through a slit in a curving, tube-like earth that spans the horizon from east to west), is strewn with immortelles, or stones or dust. Occasionally it's strewn with the oldest pine trees on sandy ground, occasionally ferns brimming with dew. Occasionally it forms itself like basins or unfinished basements, excavated and with a formwork of concrete walls, but without a superstructure. With braiding in the grout or scrubbed so that nothing more will grow. The nerves above adapt or work together, or work in numb sagacity against it.

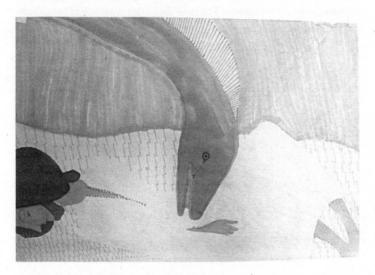

That shows itself in the sounds and colours and consistencies and degrees of forcefulness created by You, which could also be us (yes, created). In our many variations. Isolated from the nerves, they are hurled away, some a distance from destructive disinterest, others in the near realm of friendship. Some, nevertheless, are tolerated and left alone, never sent off, by you later like a wind flattened, a parasitic attack of love, there is a life together.

In the South and North, they spring up from nowhere, wherever one suspects the hands to be.

Where they're from, haste or struggle had no meaning. There, intelligence is a crippledness. One forgot them, just like their chic sister, intellectuality. This is only one of many suspicions. I would like to see their origin. But one must wait. One must wait to say something right, to truly understand something, to no longer be sad; because the reason for being so can no longer humiliatingly force you down; because the power was taken from him through your elucidation and direction. I have less and less patience, which is why I'm seized by irascibility, and now you say nothing. Therefore, I assume, I can only wait. You also said one is smartest at around thirteen. And at thirteen my most complete and most loving heart in recollection was with you and her.

IV: Film Music

Wolf-Dietrich Brücker: The special thing about your music is that it's sparse and dramaturgically considered. Over the past twenty years, it's become increasingly fashionable to fill up entire films with music from beginning to end. The whole time there's music, which narrates absolutely nothing.

Irmin Schmidt: Perhaps that's also because it makes post-production easier. Previously, one would put in endless amounts of effort with sounds and noises: someone's walking down the street at night, you can hear things from the houses and bars, cars honking, a dog barking . . .

WB: Exactly. The noises established an atmosphere, a space, a depth . . .

IS: Today you can barely hear the footsteps for all the music.

WB: It drives me totally mad when, even in documentaries or on the news, the music is playing constantly. You see refugees, shot-up buildings, a car accident, and the whole time there's music. The news anchor has barely paused when it bubbles back up, entirely, I mean entirely unrelated to the content.

IS: *Au contraire!* The music is actually supposed to relativise the images, make them more consumable.

WB: In a good film everything is relational: the edit, the light, how the actors move – this is what music should be reacting to and connected with, as well as the psychology of the characters, their emotions. Your music does exactly that – for example, in *Rote Erde* (Red Earth), when the Russian, who had been hiding for a year deep down in the mines, in the tunnels, finally comes out and blinks into the light. There, the music has such an emotional quality that the tears start flowing. This heartbreaking guitar – was that Michael Karoli?

IS: Yes, Michael. The interplay between this insanely distorted feedback guitar with the dark, vocal-like cello. For me, this was the key scene – the emotional core of the entire second season – from which I developed all the music. I didn't question it at all. It was simply an extremely immediate and powerful feeling.

A couple of years later, during a reception at the Munich Film Festival, I was standing with a couple of writers and directors, all around my age, talking about our recollections of the war, the first few years after and the childhood memories that shaped us – all of which we still have a lot to say about in both film and literature. An experience surfaced that I had completely forgotten about. It was Austria in the summer of 1945. The Americans were in our village, Eben, occupying the large guesthouse and operating an army field kitchen in the courtyard. The cook was an enormous Russian who always had a deadly serious look on his face. Not even the hint of a smile. But us kids sometimes received pancakes from him. One day he wanted to give me a piece of chocolate, when he suddenly froze, stood completely still and looked at me, squinting strangely, before pulling me with both arms to his chest and bursting into tears, really heaving from the sobs. A couple of soldiers ran over, but I had wrapped my arms around his head and held him tenderly in total silence. I had no fear.

In Munich I could only tell the story to the end through sobs of my own, barely suppressing an increasingly intensifying weeping. Something had embedded itself into my childhood – only to be released forty years later as music. But only at that moment in Munich did I become aware of the connection.

✹

Klaus Emmerich: I could pretend as if you weren't there right now. The special thing about working with you – both in theatre music and, first and foremost, in film music – is your ability not to take a patronisingly assertive stance towards the material, but rather to let it first make an impression on you. This ability to observe and listen betrays a kind of respect for the senses. I know how enjoyable it can be to go with you to exhibitions and discuss our thoughts on them. You always see something special, it's always your gaze. I have that experience with very few people. With you it's a pleasure to experience how you process what's being seen. On top of that comes your ability to listen. It's a great pleasure to go for walks with you and learn the language of the trees. You differentiate between the trees with an enormous accuracy, which is also how you approach sound. And therefore it's no wonder that you found these techniques to use your studio like an instrument. Because only with this instrument is everything possible: letting the trees speak, the rattle of trains on tracks – whatever it may be, it's material that was heard, which is then subsequently transformed into the unheard. It's this special sound created when an intelligent, well-read human being merges things that don't belong together. But after they're combined, they give the impression of having always belonged together. There's nothing boastful in the music, but rather it emerges from patience – and, yeah, from an unheard-of freedom, one possessed by a person who takes his own feelings and narrative desires seriously.

✹

Irmin Schmidt: So you mean that because romantic music developed together with photography that . . .

Wim Wenders: . . . and conversely, with photography coming into its own first with this music, I think both are woven together and have managed to become so wonderfully wed to one another. Because the musical ideas that followed in the twentieth century were all considerably cooler, more cerebral and less emotional than those that were brewing in the nineteenth century, I think photography and film have a much greater affinity to Beethoven, Schumann and especially Mahler than to what came after in the twentieth century.

IS: I think that could have something to do with opera. Film and opera are somehow related, don't you think?

WW: Hmm. You could see it like that, but you don't have to. Especially when it comes to the domain of 'dramatic performance', I think opera unfortunately has remained within the theatrical and learned nothing from new art. But musically, I'm sure you're right.

Back when music was still played live for silent films – and especially during the transition from silent film to sound – an insane amount happened in film music. Pure silent-film music was much more naive, still fully stuck in the nineteenth century. The music that mixed with language and sounds for the first time – and that became wed to this new kind of cinema emerging around 1930 – was much more complex, and could now also emotionally generate much more than before. Previously, music had only been possible by being played live – from piano accompaniment to the film organ – and the possibilities of live music were limited. That is, with the exception of some fantastic explosions, like those of Abel Gance, who had set an entire orchestra in front of the movie screen. But essentially, the first proper 'film music' emerged with sound film. And because there was a kind of competition between sound and language, there developed a need to have music which had 'air' in order for dialogue to remain comprehensible. That's when musical swells and fades were invented in the first place and used for dramaturgy! The insight that music needs to remain 'airy' so that the other elements of film can have their space – atmospheres, sounds and especially language – this, in my eyes, is the true beginning of film music that truly wanted to belong to the film and not just be overlaid. From Beethoven to Wagner, romantic music simply didn't have much 'air'. Perhaps at most with Mahler, who was the most copied and plundered from.

IS: Yes, I think that's an especially exciting thing, because in early film – actually, up until the seventies – the music truly had 'air'. These days, the music I hear in films starts at the beginning and continues right through to the end.

WW: It's a sad new phenomenon, this 'wall-to-wall music'. I'm really getting clobbered by it, because for the new film I am listening to composers and watching all sorts of films that I probably would otherwise never have watched. Already with the third one I was wondering, 'Which film is this? And which composer?' The music sounded the same everywhere and was loud, above all. And long. Essentially back to silent film, where the music was also laid on top of the film like a plank.

IS: Yes.

WW: You can go to America or Europe or wherever else – film music everywhere is essentially levelled out. And the sheer amount that 'sound design' has taken over from composition is frightening. Often a 'film score' is now just 'sound design'. Even if an orchestra is playing, they don't play 'music' any more but rather whatever notes that supposedly serve the purpose of whatever is today obviously considered to be score – which has nothing to do with exhausting the possibilities of film music, but serves instead only elaborate speaker technology and simulating a certain amount of bass or movement or 'grandness' or bombast. It's actually all pure pretending – it's not music that produces anything but rather the surround-sound technology and the volume. Currently, I think film music is in a rut. If you listen to what's coming out of the 'score factories', you'd think you don't need composers any more, but rather only computers that play whatever is required of them. On top of that comes a huge thick layer of sauce, which usually goes on for ever.

IS: Yes, that's the strange thing! When I turn the TV on, I get the feeling that there is actually only one single film composer – maybe two – responsible for all the film music, appearing each time under a different pseudonym. Because it all sounds the same. Always piano with an extra helping of custard!

But the question of sound design also leads to something else. Because the environment in these films becomes the music, and the music becomes the environment. This means that what we used to carefully create with noises – providing space and atmosphere – is now done with complicated sound design. So at best you can still hear the car drive by, but no longer any noises or atmosphere from the noises. Do you think that creates completely new ideas of listening? Do people have these ways of listening by now . . .

WW: Absolutely! People have internalised it. If you observe how kids play today [*makes booming, hissing and crackling noises*], then they mostly imitate sound design. [*Irmin agrees.*] They play with their plastic figurines, and what are they doing the whole time?

IS: Brrrroooooom!

WW: These kinds of 'whooshes', as they're known in technical terms, a 'whoosh!' here and a 'WHOOSH!' there are what destroy every film because half of the sound design is essentially made up of whooshes or hissing sounds; sounds that only serve the purpose of forcing the eye to follow 'movement', making it more physically experienceable. Here, too, the great surround-sound technology is more important than the content of the film. The whooshes completely enter the music, which is essentially made up of sounds one sees above Mickey Mouse: Crash! Boom! Hiss! Bang! And those are there so that the eye is specifically drawn somewhere. Whooshes are there to draw your glance towards something or away from something. It's a real sickness at the moment, one aimed at illiterates. Basically, music for people who don't want to understand music any more. Or even better: for those incapable of understanding music, people who need to be shown and explained what they should be understanding, musically as well as narratively.

The whooshes are an infantilisation of music because they take the beautiful function that music once had – namely, of gently guiding the gaze – and simplify it in a doltish fashion. Or better: they make a cacophony out of it. These effects are now such a regular fixture of musical performance that people think it's actually music. And if I now watch children playing with their plastic figures from films, either alone or together, then they are constantly 'whooshing'. The whooshes only accompany all their games because the kids find it more emotionally engaging. They cannot have gotten it anywhere else than from the films they've seen. They certainly didn't have that in puppet theatre.

IS: Sure, from TV.

WW: Exactly, from TV. And from movies.

IS: And then in their games.

WW: Absolutely! There is nothing left but whooshing nowadays! Because it's become a convention for what music should do. It's supposed to help you to understand the story, or the game, in as reduced a fashion as possible – and that's it. Reactions at the push of a button. I sometimes wish I had another button in the cinema to turn off all the whoosh effects! Then you could finally hear and see both dialogue and music and image again, and feel freer again. All this added stuff makes you so unfree! This is my main problem with the whole sound-effect-ification of music.

Irmin laughs.

WW: You laugh, but this stuff makes you stupid!

IS: Let me make a slight detour. There has been an accumulation of environmental noise into contemporary music – since Cage, at least, but it started already before with the futurists. That is, noises are developed in a highly artificial fashion and then made into music, and music takes over this artificially created world of noises. Could that not actually be something quite beautiful for film?

WW: Hmm.

IS: So I mean, it could be . . . a kind of, how can I say . . . This is the mimetic which prevails in all art. It's the repeated reformulation of the world. Film does the same. And that could also be the case for music. Sometimes it happens. But I think that this tendency towards noise isn't the worst. It's – as you say – the fact that it makes you stupid.

WW: Because this simplification of noise is no longer specific. The worst thing about the whooshes is their non-specificity. Every kind of noise – a wind in the trees, footsteps, any of the sounds that happen in reality – is specific and therefore beautiful because it enriches the image. But whoosh effects go in the opposite direction. They're unspecific, made on a computer, and ultimately they separate us from any notion of reality. This, of course, is also connected with certain kinds of films, which, in large part, aren't even shot in 'reality' but in front of green screens. No sound is recorded while filming; everything is added afterwards. And because everything is generated afterwards, the whole relation to reality of the sounds is gone. And then you may as well reach for the whooshes, which are just as unreal as anything happening on the screen. I think what happens in the music at the moment is an echo of what's happening in the image – namely, a general alienation from reality; or that every form of reality of the image is only second- or third-hand. The noises are also only present second- or third-hand, with whooshes ultimately appearing fourth-hand. There is then no reference to reality whatsoever. That's what the children simulate these days when playing. This divergence between something real on the one hand and something non-specific and computer-generated on the other can be observed in images as well as in music.

V: The Luberon

'They came by on vacation on their way to the Côte d'Azur – and twenty years later, they're still here.'

Anne Gallois in her book about Lacoste,
Du côté de chez Sade

Romain Urhausen. 1952. On the way to the Côte d'Azur, Romain went to visit a friend, the painter Tchernotka, who had settled here, near Gordes. Tchernotka showed him the area and the beautiful old villages – Lacoste, Bonnieux, Menerbes . . . Romain is captivated. In Roussillon he makes the acquaintance of an architect who owns the most beautiful house on the idyllic Place du Village, which he immediately tries to sell to Romain. The architect travels to Roussillon regularly from his home in Lyon in order to play boules as well as belote, a card game which, as he explains, has some gambling away house and farm. He explains that he recently won his house in Roussillon playing belote and wants to give Romain a good price. Romain is twenty-two years old and has just finished art school. While he has already won a prize for his avant-garde photography, he has no money. So what's he doing in this remote area anyway? Regardless, the region's magic has already captured him: Roussillon, the idyllic village square, the bell tower, the house with the beautiful baroque facade. A year later he returns. The architect is sitting in the sun in front of the bistro, as if he had been waiting for him. He invites Romain to dinner. The bistro is named Maman Jeanne after the *patronne*. She's famous in the region for her cuisine, particularly the *Lapineau aux herbes*, which is being served today. During the *digestif* – an excellent Marc de Châteauneuf – and after Romain marvels at the *patronne's* magically naive paintings, the architect goes down again with the price and the two strike a deal. Romain will borrow the money from his father. He buys the house – and a painting by Maman Jeanne.

Eighteen years later.

We had arrived at night, and in the morning, standing on the rooftop terrace of Romain's house, I almost began to cry. It simply blew me away – the view in every direction, the colours, the light, the expanse. But that wasn't all. It was this oddly overpowering feeling – here! Like a profound recognition. Then, downstairs in front of the bistro while drinking a *café au lait*, I explained to Mogli that I truly belonged here, and that at some point we must have a house here. She found the idea adventurous, but ultimately correct. (Mogli always tends first and foremost to find adventure to be the right thing.)

At some point I asked Romain whether he by chance knows a painter named Herbert Wolfertz. 'Yes, of course,' he says. 'He lives quite close by, in Auribeau.'

Herbert and I attended the same high school, but didn't especially like each other. Herbert painted, and at seventeen already lived on his own in a kind of obscure, ramshackle apartment, wheeling and dealing with cigarettes and whisky, getting the girls, and bragging about the latter. I had my school orchestra, which I conducted. I also read Thomas Mann and Arno Schmidt and bragged about it: a smartass vs a lecher.

After school we didn't see each other for years. But after a Can concert at the University of Frankfurt, he suddenly stood directly in front of me, enthusiastic about the music and my transformation. He told me he lived in Provence, and named the location, which I soon forgot the name of.

So that would be Auribeau, high up in the Luberon, with a couple of ancient houses, lots of ruins and a great, millennia-old tranquillity. Jean Giono country. The entrance to Herbert's house is almost impossible to find amid the dark ruins. He had rebuilt the house – a former ruin – on his own, learning to mason with virgin stone like people had done for centuries, as well as trimming, plastering, timbering the roof. This time, Mogli and I are the ones who are impressed: the stunning fireplace, glowing tiles, old beams, and the tangible love put into the materials. Then there are the walls, with two large and fascinating still lifes, which is what he paints today: tables with empty plates, empty glasses, carafes.

Herbert had actually wanted to go to Marseille back in 1959, but shortly before Apt a pedal broke, he crashed the bike and the front wheel broke. In Apt he found an auto shop and made a friend for life: Gitou *le garagiste*, a Gargantua of Herbert's heart. Herbert stayed.

He became our Cicerone, our guide: degustation in Châteauneuf-du-Pape, where to find the best olive oil, how to cook Daube Provençale, building us a fireplace – and all the rest.

✻

Klaus Emmerich: I believe I'm here for the same reason that most people are here: because I visited somebody who lived here – in this case, you – and then it happened to me just like it had happened to all the others. After a long trip and a serious morning hangover attributable to the fact that at your place it's almost unthinkable to go to bed without drinking lots of wine beforehand, I looked out for the first time into the landscape and couldn't believe how beautiful it was. Then, as it goes, one takes one's first walk and realises how multifaceted the landscape is and how quickly it changes. It's this moment – like falling in love, in this case with the countryside, so that you don't want to give it back. So it usually ends up that someone says, offhand, 'Maybe there's some land or an old house available. Would you be interested? Wouldn't it be funny?' And you indeed think it's a fun idea. In my case, the funniest idea was that I can't build a house without having a French neighbour. This I achieved by essentially barging down Bernard's door, who at the time I didn't know very well, and asking if he could imagine buying a piece of land together and us each building a house on it. And that's how it happened.

*

Werner Richter: What kind of crock is that – what I'm saying? This crock?

Irmin Schmidt: Yes.

WR: And your crock?

IS: Of course.

WR: Then it's fine.

IS: Herbert stayed because his bicycle broke.

WR: Good reason!

IS: And you?

WR: Well, it wasn't because of the Côte d'Azur. I always thought that place was bullshit, pompous and totally overrun, but Luberon was a fantastic discovery. It happened during a photo gig I had in 1975, when I was supposed to shoot a calendar. Foam mattresses. So I travelled down with a delivery truck with thirteen mattresses, two girls and a pile of nightgowns.

IS: Why nightgowns?

WR: Because they were supposed to wear something while frolicking around the mattresses. It wasn't yet the time when you could let them do as they pleased. I drove through every street searching for locations to shoot where the sun rose and set. Two photos every day: sunrise, sunset. The girls were extremely pissed off because they had to spend all day sitting on mattresses in the delivery truck. But I was doing fine. I thought everything was beautiful and then happened upon Lacoste. Right in the middle of the afternoon you go into a café and two women are dancing, some utterly drunk person is playing the piano and two dogs are darting about. That atmosphere made a powerful impact on me. In the evening a horseman with a long cape would ride his black horse through the village, scaring tourists. Men with de Sade fantasies [*laughing*] and the like. In the café one farmer stood at the bar cradling his little piglet. The barman, Maurice, was anyway really crazy . . .

IS: Maurice was wonderful. The greatest storyteller, and he cooked incredibly well.

WR: Exactly. And so I thought, 'A village like this, with all sorts of nut-jobs and great people and strange birds – that's not so easy to find. A village totally off the rails, with people who are true individuals.' There is nothing to change or bend about people like that; they were who they were. That's something very, very beautiful. Because in cities you mostly encounter the assimilated – people who don't want to look stupid or stand out and are always following the rules.

Then Erika and I and four friends who came to visit went on vacation, staying in the Hotel de France. Two weeks of total chaos. Every day was a party. Discovering red wine was also a very important story. Before that all we drank was beer. It was just a way of life here.

IS: And when did you buy this house?

WR: Ah, right. That was also something else. 1979. There was an old asthmatic standing around in the café with a dog in his arms, who was also asthmatic, and the man was very agitated, his head beet-red because his tenant had disappeared and had turned on the faucet, which kept running for two months. The tenant already hadn't paid rent for three months. Now the asthmatic had had enough and wanted to sell the place. So we asked if we could check it out. He was sceptical and found us all pretty suspicious. But he agreed to show it to us, and what a beautiful piece of land it was! All pure nature, nothing damaged or destroyed, incredible trees, with small fields in between, like in paradise. We immediately seized the opportunity, and then we had the house too: two hundred years old, small but already liveable, with a fireplace and plenty of wood. An open fire – what a wonderful thing. And then there are the neighbouring villages. Everywhere you went, history, from the ancient Romans on. This creates an entirely new attitude towards life.

*

Hans Silvester: Very early on, in 1957, I was riding my bike through the Alpilles, a wonderfully beautiful landscape. At the time I had absolutely no money and simply slept in the ruins. That was exactly when farmers were switching from horses and donkeys to tractors, with many simply giving up and the young people especially losing interest. Some of the ruins were for sale, going for between 2,000– 5,000 francs. The surrounding fields simply belonged to the property – that's how it was. Nobody wanted it back then, but when I saw it, I just started to dream and fantasise, because where I'm from in Lörrach, near Switzerland, as soon as there was anything good available, anything of interest, the Swiss bought it up. So yeah, I started to dream and went back there once, and then again to the Alpilles. I read Jean Giono, and of course, Provence is a land of culture . . .

In 1960 both Dora and I came here with the idea of buying something, but by then it was already over; everything was too expensive because the Algerians – the *Pieds-Noirs* – had returned. They often bought in the Alpilles, which made prices shoot up. In Les Beaux we met a Czech man, Tchernotka, who had a house in Gordes, and he told us that on the other side of the Durance there were still some good buys. He said he knew of a ruin for 2,500 francs – half the price of a Citroën Deux Chevaux – that would be a perfect fit for us. We met in Gordes, he showed us around and that was it. Parmentier: we saw it on Friday, then on Saturday Kurt, the neighbour and seller, gave us the OK. After that it all happened very quickly. On Sunday we drove, dead broke, to the Camargue, to a friend who lent us some money, and that was that.

IS: That was actually Kaminski, Stefan and Anita! Anita told me you arrived and said to her, 'I've found my place . . .'

HS: Yes, but Stefan, a banker, said he would of course lend us the money, but he had to see the house first. He didn't want it to be a stupid buy. So he came and checked it out and said, 'You're crazy, but it is very beautiful.' Then we went to the notary.

✧

Jozef Hey says the house in Lacoste is his 'healing place', his real home – even if he lives most of the time in Amsterdam, where he runs his company, Beam Systems; or if he is in Moscow, Shanghai or London displaying his enchanting light works and projections in a theatre, exhibit or onto the surrounding facades of a city square.

In the garden of Jozef's house stand several of the large, two-metre-tall sculptures that his mother, the sculptor Ans Hey, made from stone carved here in Luberon and sourced from quarries that the Romans used over two thousand years ago.

In 1958, while returning from Italy to Amsterdam, Ans discovered Lacoste and instantly fell in love with the place, the magic of the landscape, the Luberon. From then on, she returned every year and lived in an abandoned ruin without water or electricity. Jozef was six months old when she took him with her for the first time.

Years later she purchased the property. By then she taught at the

Rietveld Academy in Amsterdam and took her students with her during the holidays so they could help her with building the house. Little Jozef laid the foundation.

Now, under the oak trees behind the house, they still celebrate Ans' birthday every year on 10 August, just like when she was alive. They do so with Jozef's family and many friends – and with the large sculptures, which, like witnesses of an unknown civilisation, guard the house, though one of them now sails the oceans of the world on the *Queen Elizabeth*.

✦

Irmin Schmidt: It drives me crazy, these kinds of designers: they need to invent everything new, like in hotel bathrooms . . .

John Malkovich: Trying to figure out the shower? Can't be done. Nicole generally now just calls me, and only because I'm slightly, kind of, autistic – mentally handicapped – so I'll very slowly go through all possible options, you know? But most times it's impossible.

Laughter.

IS: So, actually, one part of the book – a very small part actually – is meant to be a few interviews with friends about what was the reason they came here. Why Lacoste?

JM: Well, I'll give you the briefest version of a kind of several-tiered story. My ex-wife found out – when she was twenty-nine or twenty-eight, I can't remember – the night before we were to get married that in fact her father was not dead, and her father was in fact not her father at all, but that he was a Frenchman who, as far as her mother knew, was very much still alive. So a couple of years passed, and she got more and more . . . not obsessed, but a bit tortured and very eager to . . . well, you know, you want to meet your father. So eventually I tracked him down through a French photographer friend, and he called me when I was making a movie in Spain and my then wife was with me, and he said his name and he asked if we could come to Paris as soon as possible. He wanted to meet his daughter.

So we came, and that was more or less my introduction to France. I'd been there once before, but that was a huge impression because he was actually a marquis as well, as was de Sade, and he had a cha-teau – has, he's still alive – in the Loire valley where Louis Quatorze played boules . . . I visited there many times and I was very fond of them, and that was a very kind of strange, odd, not normal introduc-tion to France.

Then we split up, my ex-wife and I, nine years later, and later I met Nicole. We had children. She lived in Rome, I lived in America. I briefly had a house in Hollywood, I had already lived in Chicago and New York, and I wanted to get away. I wanted to live in another world, in another place, and probably not in a city. I think a huge part of it was bringing our children up not in a city environment, and not in New York or Los Angeles or Chicago, all of which I'd already done. So we travelled all around. We happened upon this place in Lacoste, and it was owned by a South African woman. I went, and actually I only went through the house for about . . . certainly less than two minutes. I mean, I just kind of walked, like this, and came back and I sat with her in her little kitchen. But what really sealed it was I looked up on the hill right outside of what was Betty's terrace and I said, 'What's that?' And she said, 'Oh, that's the chateau of the Marquis de Sade.'

I had read the book about de Sade by Maurice Lever, which was called *Sade*, which was just hilarious: stories of his *notaire*, who he hated and who cheated him, etc., etc. And it's one of the funniest books, really funny. In it, de Sade becomes not quite such a mon-ster. He receives a very human scale, and is very – as a writer of invective, in my opinion – unmatched and hilarious. And sad too.

Anyway, I thought, 'How fantastic!' So we made an offer on the house. I thought it was another world. Peaceful, quiet. I really never have had a bad day here, despite the irritation that any country can bring, especially if you're native and sometimes even when you're not a native. But here it seemed to me to be a different world. A kind of *How Green Was My Valley*, and to me it was a kind of paradise, really.

We raised our children here, and I had my tax war with the French, and this and that and blah, blah, blah.

There was something. We went all over France, and some of France I knew fairly well, but we went to Normandy, Brittany, the Atlantic coast, Bordeaux, you know. It was far away from everything, meaning we were in the valley and we'd look up at the cliff villages, at Lacoste, which we went through and was a kind of village until Cardin bought it. It was, sort of, medieval, unchanged from . . . it's medieval, was medieval. Now, not so much, but that won't last either! And it will go back to being medieval. Bonnieux, which had also made some ugly mistakes, is also pretty medieval. It's really unchanged. It's a kind of lost world, and modernity, per se, was very far away. Here there was just a lot of blue skies, a lot of mistral too, but a lot of blue skies, physical beauty, some culture and all these beautiful little places around, like Oppède or . . .

IS: The last time you spoke to me, a fascination with the personality of de Sade played a certain role in your story.

JM: Oh, huge, yes!

IS: Looking at his castle had some kind of . . .

JM: I always thought it had a kind of mystical power, de Sade's place, and I was told that there were a lot of hippy-type *événements* in the sixties there. And, of course, because from our house we look up at it, when you sit on our terrace that's really kind of all you see. So it's an incredible view of it, and because I knew a decent amount about de Sade and had read his writing and had read about him, that had a big influence on why not Goult or why not L'Isle-sur-la-Sorgue. It had a kind of romance and a sort of history, of course, going back to de Sade and then later Man Ray doing photos of it. And kind of throughout French history – even modern history – it had quite a draw, the chateau of the Marquis de Sade.

And so, to me, that was just a huge, huge factor, to walk out your kitchen door and look up and see that. It's . . . you're not going to find it many other places. This is the only valley in the world that has a view of the chateau of the Marquis de Sade. Also, of course, our house itself was a property of de Sade, because he owned everything.

IS: Yes. Actually, wasn't it his aunt who owned the castle, and he returned and sort of . . .

JM: Well, he grew up, if I remember correctly, with the Curé – or Abbé? – de Sade, who had his chateau in Saumane, kind of above Fontaine-de-Vaucluse, which we also looked at to buy, weirdly enough! And he is the one who kind of tutored de Sade in the Sadian arts, let's say. But, you know, it's an ancient family that goes all the way back centuries and centuries and centuries.

And there's always something a little bit romantic about it, but I think you have to be a little bit . . . well, the people I know who came here all had a kind of dream of it, which maybe doesn't quite turn out the way it should, but it keeps you here. You know, we have our friend Nicky, who I'm sure you guys have met at our house, an English girl. She lived about a kilometre from us for years and years and years. Then she sold and left, and moved back to London. She came back here and bought a house a mile from her old house [*laughing*]. It's crazy! But it has a kind of hold on you.

IS: And it's not only the beauty; it's also demanding in a way.

JM: Yes. They say, '*Provence, belle Provence*,' but it's quite brutal in a way.

IS: Yes, exactly. It has a brutal side and it has something demanding, and also you feel in every stone, every field, that people have been here – living – for thirty thousand years. And there has been culture here for thousands and thousands of years.

JM: Yes, there has, which I think de Sade and the ruins of his castle exemplify. It has a very, very powerful pull.

IS: At least for us!

JM: Not for everybody. But, you know, my friends come here and they never forget it. They will talk about it ten years later, twenty years later.

Index

The following initials denote Can members: DS (Damo Suzuki); HC (Holger Czukay); IS (Irmin Schmidt); JL (Jaki Liebezeit); MK (Michael Karoli); MM (Malcolm Mooney); RG (Rosko Gee)

Index

Index

and MCI JH-16 multitrack recorder, 243, 274; and MK's unassertiveness, 278; and MM's mental state, 112–14; RG and Reebop's issue with Can collective, 287–8, 303–4; in Rossacher documentary, 317–18; and silence, 110; 'spiritual communication', 87; telepathy, 9–10, 196, 204, 211–12, 259, 275, 303, 319, 337

HISTORY OF: band name, 77–8; birth of rhythm, 69, 71; *The Can Project*, 328–9; 'Can Solo Projects' concerts, 324–5, 326; DS joins, 107, 126; DS leaves, 217–18; DS's first concert, 126–8; EMI/Virgin deals, 247–8; Fallowell invited to join, 238; first album, 90–2; Gilmour, Hickmott and Tinner join entourage, 240–2; HC leaves, 291, 302; HC stops bass-playing, 274–5; Hildegard becomes manager, 159; Johnson leaves, 75–6; last performances, 290–1; last UK performances, 284; Liberty Records/ United Artists deal, 93, 117; lifecycle as machine, 8; MM leaves, 110–15; Nakao audition, 254; no US tours, 5, 260–1, 318, 334; Reebop joins, 279–80; refusal to re-form, 9; remastered back catalogue, 327; resurrections, 9, 110, 115, 307, 310–19; RG joins, 257, 273–5; split, 303–6; Weilerswist departure, 300

IMPROVISATION: Alessandrini on, 239; and AMM, 29; discipline in, 236; Freynik on, 86; increase in, 237; IS on 'instant composition', 55; IS on 'shapes', 273; JL's opposition to, 273; *Melody Maker* on, 226; MM on, 88; and opposition to HC's 'puzzling', 88; on 'Soup', 185–6; on *Tago Mago* sessions, 80, 157

INFLUENCE: ambient music, 235; Bowie, 293; Buzzcocks, 299; Cabaret Voltaire, 228, 334; Cologne–Berlin electronica/techno, 336–7; The Fall, 317–18, 334; Happy Mondays, 334; Hawkwind, 227; industrial music, 268; Jesus and Mary Chain, the, 318; Joy Division, 334; LCD Soundsystem, 335; Loop, 318; My Bloody Valentine, 318; Needs on, 321; Pavement, 318; Primal Scream, 334–5; Radiohead,

335–6; *Sacrilege* remixes, 320–2; Spacemen 3, 318; Stereolab, 335; Talk Talk, 335; Talking Heads, 334; techno, 252; 23 Skidoo, 334

INFLUENCES: Beiderbecke, 145; Brown, 148–9; Hendrix, 83, 84; Moroder, 264; Morricone, 134–5; Neu!, 236; New York avant garde, 25–6; Reich, 268; Schönberg, 145; Stockhausen, 151, 281; Velvet Underground, 25, 83, 93, 94, 263

INSTRUMENTS AND MACHINES: African thumb piano, 314; availability at Weilerswist, 166, 332–3; bağlama, 267; banjo, 164; bottles and saucepans, 61; bouzouki, 79; clarinet reed in flute, 79; congas, 280, 292; cowbells, 145; dictaphone, 281; drum machine/rhythm box, 157, 168, 169–70; finger cymbals, 79; French horn, 312, 314; glockenspiel, 61; gong, 79, 145, 157; harmonica, 295; Hawaiian slide guitar, 198, 232, 266; Jew's harp, 61, 129; kithera, 150; mandolin, 154, 157; marimba, 80; Middle Eastern horns, 85; Morse code tapper, 284, 285; Neumann microphones, 182; oboe, 183; pan pipes, 79, 297; radiator, 61; radio, 58, 281, 284, 285, 314; saxophone, 60, 246; scraped catgut, 150; Selmer organ, 246–7; shakers, 79; shaver and piano, 59; telephone, 281, 284; tin whistle, 154; violin, 183, 231, 232, 246, 266; xylophone, 80, 222; *see also* Alpha 77

LYRICS AND VOCALS: ads for MM replacement, 116; and appeal to rock audience, 61, 69, 219, 237–8, 254; below the instruments, 88, 94, 263; Cousins trials, 261–3; DS on *Future Days*, 209; DS whispers nothing, 141; DS's pseudo-language, 141–2, 145, 146–7, 169, 186–7; effect of MM's arrival, 74–5; Gilmour as writer, 242, 252, 266–7, 282, 287; Hardin performance, 257–8; IS as singer, 267; IS's sole lyrics, 232–4; Johnny Rotten offer, 300; Löhe, 58, 59; MK on MM and DS, 232; MK as singer, 232, 234, 239, 243–4, 246, 266, 268, 281, 282, 296; MM and DS as impossible precedents, 263; MM's lyrical sources,

555

Index

Index

Index

Hitler, Adolf, 120
Hödicke, Karl-Horst, 15
Höfer, Werner, 143–4
Hogg, Hermi, 240
Holiday, Billie, 129
Hopf, Thomas, 326
Hot Butter: 'Popcorn', 169
Humboldt, Alexander von, 194
Hunters and Collectors (band), 336
Hütter, Ralf, 195

I Ching, 214, 268
Ilgner, Günther, 247
India, 66, 68–9, 73
Indian music, 25, 48, 73
industrial music, 268
Inherent Vice (film), 335
Inner Space/Inner Space Productions
    (Can precursor): at Schloss Nörvenich,
    52–6; too hippy as name, 77; *Agilok
    & Blubbo* soundtrack, 50–2, 59,
    73; 'Apokalypse', 51–2; 'I'm Hiding
    My Nightingale', 73; 'Im Tempel',
    73; 'In Kalkutta I', 73; *Kamasutra
    – Vollendung der Liebe* soundtrack,
    72–3, 74; 'Memographie', 51; *Das
    Millionenspiel* soundtrack, 60, 168;
    'Mundharmonika Beat', 73; 'There
    Was a Man', 73; *see also* Can
Inner Space (recording space), *see*
    Nörvenich, Schloss; Weilerswist
Invaders of the Heart, 323
Iran, 65–6, 80, 301, 302
Istanbul, 65

Jagger, Mick, 186
Jah Wobble, 228, 323; *Full Circle* (with
    HC/JL), 307; on Needs's 'Oh Yeah',
    321; *Snake Charmer* (with The Edge/
    HC), 308; 'Voodoo' (with Eltes/
    Marland), 310
James, Jesse, 314
jazz: HC's teenage band, 20;
    improvisation in, 55; IS expelled from
    college, 198; JL's free-jazz background,
    43, 44–7, 338; JL's playing vs editing,
    216; MK's teenage bands, 38–9; MM's
    clarinet and sax, 62–3
Jazz Cookers, the, 44
Jehovah's Witnesses, 217
Jesus and Mary Chain, the: 'Mushroom',
    318

Jews, 13, 33
Jimi Hendrix Experience, the, 77, 79, 83;
    'Spanish Castle Magic', 84; 'Voodoo
    Chile (Slight Return)', 84
Johansson, Sven-Åke, 45
Johnson, David: advises on *Can
    Free Concert*, 176, 177; and
    Agilok & Blubbo, 50, 51; *Hymnen*
    (Stockhausen) role, 29; IS wants to
    form group, 26; and *Kamasutra –
    Vollendung der Liebe*, 73; LSD trips,
    24; mixing, 81; Paris 1968 recording,
    57, 58; at Rheinische Musikschule, 17;
    steals WDR tapes, 30; tension over
    MM role, 74, 75
Johnson, James, 160, 179
Jones, Elvin, 48, 145
Jones, Gareth: 'Oh Yeah' (with Miller),
    321
Joy Division, 334
Juvan, Margarete, 73

Kagel, Mauricio: *Exotica*, 80–1
Kaiser, Rolf-Ulrich, 229–30
Kamasutra – Vollendung der Liebe (film),
    72–3, 74
Kappen, Norbert, 102, 103
Karaca, Muhtar Cem, 188
Karajan, Herbert von, 21
Kardaşlar, 188
Karlstad, Sweden, 124
Karoli, Constanze, 38, 72, 201, 228
Karoli, Hermann, 37–8, 76–7
Karoli, Michael: Africa trip, 269, 271,
    277–9; *Alice in the Cities* session, 221,
    222; as Andreas Baader lookalike, 173;
    appearance, 3, 256; Argwings-Kodhek
    relationship and marriage, 277,
    278, 310; on audience as anemone,
    253–4; on Can as apolitical, 56; on
    Can as applied mathematics, 9; and
    Can band name, 77; Can formation,
    37, 40, 42; as Can mediator, 290;
    on Can's fighting, 184; on Can's
    geometry, 291; commands buzzing
    organ, 224–5; commits to Can, 76;
    death, 326; drug use, 257, 258, 286;
    on DS's singing, 129; Fallowell on,
    298; family supports, 90; on *Future
    Days*, 204, 208–9, 212–13; Gilmour
    as friend, 241; Grunwald split, 277–8;
    guitar feedback, 42, 127; hammer-ons,

563

Index

potential, 7; on Can's transport, 286; changes a rhythm, 98; clock prediction, 224; with Club Off Chaos trio, 323, 325; commits to Can, 76; death, 329; on *Deep End*, 133; dislikes *Future Days* 'movements', 215–16; double-tracked hi-hat, 60; with Drums Off Chaos, 323; drums as tuned instrument, 211; and DS recruitment, 126, 127; early years, 43; on 'E.F.S. No. 99' ('Cancan'), 297; Eno collaboration, 270; Fallowell on, 299; finances, 90; flatshare and relationship with MM, 70, 72, 89; flute-playing, 164, 315; at Groucho Club, 4; on 'Halleluwah', 147, 148–8; HC on 'infrasound', 89, 211–12; HC on *Tago Mago*, 139; on Hickmott, 240; 'infrasound' on *Plight and Premonition*, 315; IS on criticism of, 305; IS requests drummer recommendation, 43, 47; Jah Wobble collaboration, 307, 323; jazz background, 43, 44–7, 216; Johnny Rotten on, 300; on medieval music, 58; *Musk at Dusk* (IS) collaboration, 309; new 'E-T' drumming method, 3, 323; and new microphones, 182; on 1968, 57; opposes improvisation, 273; as orchestral director, 212; on 'Paperhouse'/'Mushroom', 144–5; perfectionism, 47; in Phantomband, 309; plays on HC solo albums/ collaborations, 301, 307, 315; Reebop admires, 280; on Reebop, 280; relationship to HC's bass, 84, 286, 287; reticence, 87; RG on, 287; rhythmic regularity, 46–7, 210, 212; rhythmic urgency, 71; on *Rite Time* recording, 312; Rother collaboration, 269–70, 309; on 'Spoon' rhythm box, 169; stage outfits, 249; suggests Can band name, 77; on *Tago Mago*, 151; trumpet playing, 43–4, 236; on Weilerswist, 166; and Wiska recordings at Weilerswist, 188, 226–7; and word 'Babaluma', 233; *Full Circle* (with HC/ Jah Wobble), 307
Ligeti, György, 12, 16
Limburg an der Lahn, Germany, 20
Lindenberg, Udo, 331
Lippegaus, Karl, 273, 315
Liquid Sky, 322

Lisbon, 290, 334
Liszt, Franz, 206
Loch, Siegfried 'Siggi', 93, 117, 118, 183, 247, 272
Löhe, Manni, 58, 59, 284
London: Barbican, 326, 328–9; *Deep End* filming, 129, 130; Drury Lane Theatre, 257, 258; DS in, 125; Grunwald in, 278; HC seeks record company, 305; *Das Messer* scenes, 168; Lyceum, 225–6; New Victoria Theatre, 276; Paris Theatre, 196–7; Rainbow Theatre, 181; Rock photo session, 254–6; Sound Circus, 284; UCL, 179; *see also* BBC
London Symphony Orchestra, 328
Loop: 'Mother Sky', 334
LSD: DS's 'Oh Yeah' lyrics, 147; IS tries, 23–4; at Rheinische Musikschule, 17
Lübke, Heinrich, 33, 34
Lüpertz, Markus, 15
Lydon, John, 142, 228, 300
Lynyrd Skynyrd, 245

MacDonald, Ian: on 'Bel Air', 206; on *Ege Bamyasi*, 191; on 'Father Cannot Yell', 69; on *Future Days*, 215; on 'Oh Yeah', 147; post-*Babaluma* article, 236
Macero, Teo, 149
Machaut, Guillaume de, 58
MacLise, Angus, 26
Mädchen . . . nur mit Gewalt (film), 110–11
Maderna, Bruno, 16
Magaletti, Valentina, 329
Mahavishnu Orchestra, the, 210
Mahler, Gustav: Fourth Symphony, 24
Malkmus, Stephen, 318
Mann, Egon, 176
Mann, Thomas, 31
Manzanera, Phil, 251
marijuana, *see* cannabis
Marland, Ollie, 310
Marley, Bob, 280
Marshall, John, 309
Martin, Hearlon 'Cheese', 148
Mauser (industrial manufacturer), 100
Mayer, Hans, 15, 48, 52, 68, 90
Mediterranean Sea, 138, 194, 195, 214
Meid, Lothar, 44
Mein schönes kurzes Leben (TV series), 115–16

565

Index

Index

Niven, David, 127, 128

NME: on Can at Free Trade Hall, 275–6;
on Can at UCL, 179; on *Delay 1968*,
310; HC interview, 305–6; Kent's
Can article, 235–6; Krautrock survey,
191; on *Monster Movie*, 93–4; on
Out of Reach, 293–4; on *Soon Over
Babaluma*, 235; on *Tago Mago*, 160

Norddeutscher Rundfunk Orchestra, 23

Nörvenich, Schloss: ballroom recording,
151; Can leave for Weilerswist,
165; Can performances, 70–1,
98–9; daily routine, 82–3; *Delay
1968* material, 310; Fallowell as
observer, 156; firecracker recording,
146; flashing amber lamp, 161,
333; Freynik on, 86–7; hall as
'Inner Space', 53; HC on spirit of,
151–2; microphone placements, 82;
MM's first visit, 67, 68; Przygodda's
footage, 86; Rückriem at, 54, 85,
99, 136; as sound installation, 60–1;
soundproofing, 55; *Soundtrack* sleeve
shot, 136; studio footage on WDR,
164; in 'Turtles' promo film, 161;
Vohwinkel offers to Can, 52; WDR
interview, 163

Norwegian Wood (film), 335

Nunes, Emmanuel, 18, 64

Obermaier, Uschi, 32

Ofarim, Abi: Can replace as manager,
159; disputes with Can, 117–19,
159–60, 190–1, 196, 247, 248; music
career, 117–18; Niven at first DS Can
concert, 127, 128; non-involvement
in Can, 159; signs Can–United Artists
contract, 117; Stuyvesant 'ad', 178; *see
also* PROM

Offenbach, Jacques: 'Infernal Galop'
('Cancan'), 297

Oldfield, Mike, 249

Olympic Games, *see* Munich

Orb, the, 321

Organisation, the, 195

ORTF (French TV station): *Pop 2* show,
198–9

Osaka World's Fair, 76

Palm, Siegfried, 16

Paris: Bataclan, 199, 239; Grand Studio
RTL, 220; MM at Tcherepnin flat, 64,

66–7; Olympia, 199–200, 221; Salle
Wagram, 262

Paris, 1968 *événements*: German
precursors, 35; Johnson's recordings
and Can, 57, 58; MM and Zim, 62;
and Sanders-Brahms's films, 220

Parliament, 210

Pavement, 318

Peake, Mervyn: *Gormenghast* trilogy,
324

Peel, John, 197, 213, 225, 228, 317

Penman, Ian, 293–4

Perry, Lee 'Scratch', 6, 154, 267

Phantomband: *Freedom of Speech*, 309;
Nowhere, 309

Philips Records, 118

Pink Floyd, 162; *Meddle*, 160

Plank, Conrad 'Conny', 18, 254, 270, 293,
301, 309

Plantamura, Carol, 30

Platz, David, 147

Podmore, Jono, 4, 324, 326, 328

Polonski, Boris, 323

pop art, 25, 48, 71

Popol Vuh, 73, 338

P-Orridge, Genesis, 334

Pousseur, Henri, 16, 17, 164

Pretty Things, 162

Primal Scream, 334; 'Kowalski', 335;
XTRMNTR, 335

progressive rock, 146, 196, 201–2, 210,
228, 253; *see also* cosmic rock

PROM (publishing/production
company), 118, 141, 159

Przygodda, Peter: directs *Can Free
Concert*, 175, 176, 178; at *Deadlock*
session, 135; early footage of Can,
86; edits *Messer im Kopf*, 308; *Ein
grosser graublauer Vogel* work, 108;
recommends Can for *Deadlock*, 133;
recommends Can to Wenders, 221

Public Image Limited, 300

punk: and early Can, 70, 81, 116;
Johnny Rotten on Can, 300; Shelley's
Cannibalism liner notes, 299; ugliness
in, 256; Virgin signs Sex Pistols, 283;
von Biel's proto-punk, 41

Pustelnik, Ken, 197

Puxley, Simon, 278, 311

Radio Caroline, 118

Radiohead, 335–6; 'The Thief', 335

Index

Dedicated to:
Peter Pryzgodda (1941–2011)